FINISH

AN ORAL HISTORY OF
OREGON STATE UNIVERSITY'S
2017 & 2018 BASEBALL TEAMS

BOB LUNDEBERG

Copyright © 2021 by Bob Lundeberg

All rights reserved. No part of this publication may be reproduced, distributed or transmitted in any form or by any means, including but not limited to information storage and retrieval systems, electronic, mechanical, photocopy, recording, etc. without prior written permission from the copyright holder.

Cover image by Oregon State University and Karl Maasdam

Roster headshots by Oregon State University and Karl Maasdam

Back images by Bob Lundeberg

Book design by Anna Burrous

ISBN 978-0-578-99002-6

First Edition: November 2021

TABLE OF CONTENTS

INTRODUCTION — 1

CHAPTER I — 7
Building a champion

CHAPTER II — 43
The redemption tour

CHAPTER III — 94
Highs and lows

CHAPTER IV — 124
Welcome to Omaha

CHAPTER V — 161
Running it back

CHAPTER VI — 212
Clearing the mind

CHAPTER VII — 237
Playoff Goss

CHAPTER VIII — 267
Return to Omaha

CHAPTER IX — 306
Finishing the job

CHAPTER X — 362
The aftermath

ACKNOWLEDGMENTS — 396

ROSTER

Below is a list of players and full-time coaches from the 2017-18 seasons who appear in the book.

PLAYERS

Kevin Abel
Position: RHP
Hometown: San Diego, California
Years active: 2018-19, 2021

Jack Anderson
Position: OF
Hometown: Lake Oswego, Oregon
Years active: 2015-18

Andy Armstrong
Position: INF
Hometown: Salem, Oregon
Years active: 2017-21

Andy Atwood
Position: INF
Hometown: Everett, Washington
Years active: 2016-17

Jordan Britton
Position: LHP
Hometown: Caldwell, Idaho
Years active: 2016-18

Nathan Burns
Position: RHP
Hometown: West Bend, Wisconsin
Years active: 2018-21

Elliott Cary
Position: OF
Hometown: Niceville, Florida
Years active: 2015, 2017

Joe Casey
Position: OF
Hometown: Corvallis, Oregon
Years active: 2017-21

Christian Chamberlain
Position: LHP
Hometown: Reno, Nevada
Years active: 2018-20

Troy Claunch
Position: C
Hometown: Vacaville, California
Years active: 2018-21

Zach Clayton
Position: INF/OF
Hometown: Oconomowoc, Wisconsin
Years active: 2018-19

Christian Donahue
Position: INF/OF
Hometown: Mililani, Hawaii
Years active: 2015-17

Brandon Eisert
Position: LHP
Hometown: Beaverton, Oregon
Years active: 2017-19

Max Engelbrekt
Position: LHP
Hometown: Seattle, Washington
Years active: 2013-14, 2016-17

Bryce Fehmel
Position: RHP
Hometown: Agoura Hills, California
Years active: 2016-19

Grant Gambrell
Position: RHP
Hometown: Clovis, California
Years active: 2017-19

Cadyn Grenier
Position: INF
Hometown: Henderson, Nevada
Years active: 2016-18

Michael Gretler
Position: INF
Hometown: Bonney Lake, Washington
Years active: 2015-18

KJ Harrison
Position: INF/C
Hometown: Kailua, Hawaii
Years active: 2015-17

Luke Heimlich
Position: LHP
Hometown: Puyallup, Washington
Years active: 2015-18

Mitch Hickey
Position: RHP
Hometown: Morgan Hill, California
Years active: 2015-17

Preston Jones
Position: OF
Hometown: Vancouver, Washington
Years active: 2017-21

Steven Kwan
Position: OF
Hometown: Fremont, California
Years active: 2016-18

Trevor Larnach
Position: OF
Hometown: Pleasant Hill, California
Years active: 2016-18

Nick Madrigal
Position: INF
Hometown: Elk Grove, California
Years active: 2016-18

Tyler Malone
Position: INF/OF
Hometown: Roseville, California
Years active: 2017-19

Kyler McMahan
Position: INF/OF
Hometown: Seattle, Washington
Years active: 2018-21

George Mendazona
Position: INF
Hometown: Redmond, Oregon
Years active: 2017, 2019

Jake Mulholland
Position: LHP
Hometown: Snohomish, Washington
Years active: 2017-21

Kyle Nobach
Position: OF
Hometown: Marysville, Washington
Years active: 2015-16, 2018

Dylan Pearce
Position: RHP
Hometown: Central Point, Oregon
Years active: 2018-19

Drew Rasmussen
Position: RHP
Hometown: Spokane, Washington
Years active: 2015-17

Adley Rutschman
Position: C
Hometown: Sherwood, Oregon
Years active: 2017-19

Zak Taylor
Position: INF/C
Hometown: Sherwood, Oregon
Years active: 2016-19

Jake Thompson
Position: RHP
Hometown: Florence, Oregon
Years active: 2014-17

Sam Tweedt
Position: RHP
Hometown: Salem, Oregon
Years active: 2015, 2017-19

Mitchell Verburg
Position: RHP
Hometown: Lake Oswego, Oregon
Years active: 2017, 2019-Present

COACHES

Pat Casey
Head coach

Pat Bailey
Associate head coach/recruiting coordinator

Nate Yeskie
Pitching coach

Andy Jenkins
Assistant coach

BOB LUNDEBERG

INTRODUCTION

The odds of becoming a Division I college baseball superpower were always stacked against Oregon State University. In fact, when Oregon native Pat Casey was hired to replace retiring head coach Jack Riley in the summer of 1994, the system in place was set up to prevent that exact thing from happening. The ultra-competitive Casey, who came to Corvallis after seven successful seasons at nearby NAIA George Fox University, walked into a Pac-10 Conference that was separated into the sunny South Division haves (Arizona, Arizona State, California, Stanford, UCLA and USC) and the gloomy North Division have-nots (Gonzaga, OSU, Portland, Portland State, Washington and Washington State). Unlike the modern Pac-12 football setup, the divisions did not play each other — they essentially functioned as separate conferences. While the southern powers piled up NCAA Tournament appearances and national titles, the northern schools were mostly spinning their wheels in the mud, going nowhere.

Riley had done his best in 22 years at the helm. He led the Beavers to five North championships, and NCAA Tournament appearances in 1983, 1985 and 1986. Arguably his biggest achievement was keeping the program afloat during a time when many schools, including in-state rival Oregon, dropped baseball. "The program, I always felt, was a really strong program," said Casey, a Newberg High School graduate and former all-conference outfielder for Portland, who reached AAA during his eight-year minor-league career. "The issue was the fact that they were pretty much restricted to playing in the North, so it was a regional-type program. That's not something they may have wanted, but nobody in the South wanted to come play teams in the North. I just thought it was an unfair situation that they were never granted that opportunity. And when I got there, that's the way it was."

In Riley's final season, Oregon State won the 1994 Pac-10 North title with a 22-8 conference record (35-16 overall). As champion of the South, Stanford received the Pac-10's automatic bid to the NCAA Tournament. No divisional playoff, no anything. That was the system. Fellow Pac-10 South schools Arizona State and USC got at-large bids to the 48-team tournament. Washington, which finished two games back of OSU in the standings but won both head-to-head series between the teams, was also selected. The Beavers were left home. The following year saw the introduction of a best-of-three championship series featuring the division winners — hosted by the South representative, of course — to give the North a shot at an automatic post-season bid. But OSU didn't have the same horses in 1995 and dipped to a 25-24-1 overall record. The team rebounded to 32 wins in Casey's second year, and compiled a strong NCAA Tournament resume in 1997 with a 38-12-1 overall record and a runner-up North finish at 18-6. Again, it wasn't enough for the selection committee. "So, I became a huge advocate of 'let's play the South teams or we're never going to get out of being looked at as regional clubs up here,'" Casey said.

To appease their northern brethren, the South finally agreed to play three inter-conference series during the 1998 season. Though the games would not count in the Pac-10 standings, the cold-weather schools now had the opportunity to boost their Rating Percentage Index (RPI) — a critical metric used by the NCAA Tournament selection committee — by playing some of college baseball's top teams. "We were pushing for (Pac-10 unification) and I was the lead coach," Casey said. "There were some coaches that thought this was a good idea, some maybe not. So, the South actually gave us nine games in '98 to keep us from getting into the league." The North teams proved to be no pushover as Oregon State swept homes series with UCLA and Arizona while taking one of three games at USC, the eventual national champion. Washington lost a competitive series at South champion Stanford, and defeated California and Arizona State at home. The Huskies later swept Stanford in the Pac-10 championship series to claim the conference's automatic NCAA Tournament bid. Arizona State, Stanford and USC all received at-large berths. OSU, boasting strong overall (35-14-1) and conference (15-9) records, was once again left out. "(USC head coach) Mike Gillespie, who I have the utmost respect for (Gillespie passed away in 2020), told me that year when we got done playing them: 'Case, with that pitching staff, if you guys get to a regional, you've got a chance to go to the World Series,'" Casey said. "But we didn't get invited. Our RPI didn't meet what the NCAA wanted and at the time we didn't have any street cred, we hadn't been there."

Everything changed prior to the 1999 season. For the first time since the 1960s, the Pac-10 abandoned its division structure and unified as one conference. Gonzaga and Portland had bolted for the West Coast Conference following the 1995 season, and Portland State cut its program in 1998. That left nine schools — Arizona, Arizona State, California, Oregon State, Stanford, UCLA, USC, Washington and Washington State — to compete in the newly consolidated Pac-10. Each team would play eight three-game series to determine a true conference champion. At last, a fair system for the Pacific Northwest schools. The program also entered the 1999 season with a sparkling facility, renamed Goss Stadium at Coleman Field. Many alterations have occurred over the decades, but home plate has remained in the same location on campus since 1907, making Goss the oldest continuous college ballpark in the country. "We had to change (the stadium) to play in that conference and get kids to come here," Casey said. "We had to build something they were willing to play in."

Casey's dream of Pac-10 unification and a new stadium had finally come to fruition through tireless work and dedication. Next up: recruiting the right players to compete against college baseball's elite. "When you're building something, most of your opponents don't pay any attention to you at all," Casey said. "We knew we had to expand our ability to recruit, not only expand the area but get a better player every year. So, that piece was a difficult task." The Beavers were not an immediate success in the unified Pac-10, finishing 19-35 overall with a 7-17 conference mark in 1999. The following year was better (28-27, 9-15), and the 2001 team closed out a strong regular season with a three-game home series against USC. Sitting at 30-22 overall and 10-11 in Pac-10 play, a series win would have likely secured an invitation to the recently-expanded 64-team field. The Beavers went toe-to-toe with eventual MLB All-Star Mark Prior in the opener before succumbing in extra innings. Undeterred, Casey's troops came back with a 6-0 win to even the series as Scott Nicholson tossed a complete-game shutout. Tad Johnson also went the distance in the finale, but Oregon State left nine on base in a 1-0 loss. USC won the Pac-10 title by a game and the Beavers, well … "We lose to Mark Prior in extra innings on Friday night, we give up one run in the next 18 innings of the season and didn't go to a regional," Casey said. "Those things were difficult and it was difficult on me to continue to say 'we can do this, we can do this, we can do this.'"

But Casey did, and the right players started showing up. They came one at a time, mostly from the Pacific Northwest. Most importantly, they believed Casey's message that championships could be won at Oregon State. A Jacoby Ellsbury here, a Darwin Barney there. Talented pitchers Dallas Buck, Kevin Gunderson and Jonah Nickerson were all part of the 2003 signing class. "The whole thing was really built with people, it was the guys," Casey said. "It was the guys' willingness to believe in something that nobody else believed in." The Beavers once again found themselves on the wrong side of the postseason bubble in 2004 before breaking through the next spring, winning the Pac-10 behind strong pitching and defense with a 19-5 conference record. Hosting a regional for the first time since 1963, OSU won all three games to set up a home super regional with conference rival USC. In a dramatic three-game series, the Beavers survived for the school's first College World Series berth since 1952. The little program that could had made its way to college baseball's grandest stage: Johnny Rosenblatt Stadium in Omaha, Nebraska. It wound up being a quick trip to the Midwest for the inexperienced Beavers, who went two-and-out with consecutive losses, one to top-seeded Tulane and the other to Baylor. OSU had its chances in both games, but couldn't find a way to win. "As time goes on, the unfortunate thing is … the '05 team might be a little overlooked as far as what they accomplished," Casey said. "They're the ones that got us there, and a lot of those guys were on the '06 team."

The Beavers lost some key pieces to the Major League Baseball Draft, including Ellsbury, first baseman Andy Jenkins and pitcher Nathan Fogle. But plenty of talent was back on campus for another shot at glory. Oregon State repeated as Pac-10 champion in 2006, swept its way through home postseason play and returned to Omaha with valuable experience and motivation. "Like (Gunderson) had said, 'we'll be back,'" Casey said. "We haven't been to the World Series in 50 years, Gundy stands up on the podium (in 2005) and tells everyone 'don't worry, we'll be back.' Well, that puts a target on your back. I still think there were a lot of people in the country questioning it, saying 'hey, it's a great story. They go in '05, and everybody gets to go every once in a while. Good for OSU, you won't see them again.' I can't tell you how cool it was that that team said 'no no, we're one of the best teams in the country, we're going to be one of the best programs in the country, and nobody is going to deny us.'"

The 2006 College World Series could not have started more poorly for Oregon State. Miami cruised to an 11-1 opening-round victory. With the Beavers sitting at 0-5 all-time in CWS games, the team rallied back two days later to defeat Georgia and earn a rematch with the Hurricanes. OSU won the second meeting 8-1, and then shut out Rice in consecutive games to set up a best-of-three championship series matchup with North Carolina. "The perseverance and the toughness and the fight and the never-say-die attitude on that team was amazing," Casey said. The Tar Heels came from behind to steal Game 1 of the finals, but the Beavers rode the arms of Gunderson and Nickerson to back-to-back victories and the program's first national title. OSU set a CWS record with six elimination-game wins and became the first champion to lose twice in Omaha. The Beavers were also the first northern school to win it all since Ohio State in 1966. Just a few years prior, Oregon State couldn't even schedule games with West Coast powers like Arizona State and Stanford. Unification gave the Beavers a chance to compete with the big boys, and history was made.

Despite losing eight players to the 2006 draft, including Nickerson (CWS Most Outstanding Player) and future Major League outfielder Cole Gillespie (2006 Pac-10 Player of the Year), the Beavers got off to a 23-3 start in 2007 before falling back to earth in conference play. Oregon State took two of three at UCLA to close the regular season, finishing 38-17 overall and 10-14 in conference, firmly on the postseason bubble. Left out with better resumes in past years, the Beavers finally had street cred. OSU was given one of the last at-large NCAA Tournament bids, and the team knew what to do with it. Shipped off to Charlottesville, Virginia, as a regional No. 3 seed, OSU went 2-1 in three matchups with host Virginia to advance to the super regionals.

Michigan did the Beavers a favor by upsetting No. 1 overall national seed Vanderbilt, allowing the defending champions to host another super regional at Goss Stadium. OSU capitalized on the fortunate break, winning both games for a third straight trip to Omaha. "The confidence and the looseness that they played with after we won two out of three at UCLA (to close the regular season) was unbelievable," Casey said. "I said to my wife 'this team may not lose another game' after we lost to Virginia and came back and beat (Rutgers) to get back to Virginia," Casey said. "We had Michigan at home in the supers, which was a good draw for us, and when we got to the World Series, they did it so easy. It was amazing." One year after scratching and clawing for everything in Omaha, OSU won all five of its CWS games — a record four of them by six or more runs — to become the first repeat champion since LSU in 1996-97. North Carolina was once again the Beavers' final victim as Barney, Mitch Canham, CWS Most Outstanding Player Jorge Reyes and others dogpiled on the field. "That team just got into a rhythm," Casey said. "They played with such confidence and such rhythm and such continuity, it was really impressive."

Draft departures caught up with Oregon State in 2008 as the team again found itself on the postseason bubble at 28-24 overall and 11-13 in Pac-10 play. This time, the resume had too many warts for the selection committee and the Beavers were not invited back to go for a three-peat. By that point, high-profile players from outside the Pacific Northwest were willing to listen to the Beavers' recruiting pitch. OSU signed one of the nation's top classes in 2007 and continued to go after big-name recruits in following seasons. "Part of that was really, really good and part of that wasn't quite so good," Casey said. "We had an unbelievable (incoming) class in 2008 and part of that was difficult, because we had a bunch of high-profile guys and maybe not every guy was in it for what we do, and that's winning at the college level. It was a good learning curve for me as far as handling players like that and handling a group like that and how to go about that. ... It ultimately helped us redefine what we were about, who we were, how we wanted to recruit and who we wanted to recruit."

Oregon State went a combined 69-43 (27-27 in the Pac-10) with two regional appearances in 2009-10. Casey blamed himself for the highly-talented group's inability to put it all together. Things picked back up in 2011 as the Beavers surged to a top-five ranking before losing out on the Pac-10 title with a 1-6 conference finish. The team still won a home regional but was no match for SEC power Vanderbilt in the supers. OSU was right back in the postseason the next year and finally returned to the College World Series in 2013, going 2-2 with future MLBers Michael Conforto and Matt Boyd leading the way. The team kept up its winning ways in 2014, repeating as Pac-12 champion — the conference expanded from 10 to 12 teams after the 2011 baseball season — and earning the No. 1 national seed for the first time in program history. Expected by many to cruise back to Omaha, OSU fell victim to the unpredictability of college baseball as regional No. 3 seed UC Irvine slayed Goliath at Goss Stadium. It was an abrupt end to one of the best regular seasons in program history, and potentially Casey's last real chance at a third national championship.

Many stories would end there, but a prodigious wave of talent was about to enter the program. A few months after bowing out of the NCAA Tournament early, the Beavers signed one of their best recruiting classes since 2007. While that group finished up its senior year of high school, Oregon State challenged for the 2015 Pac-12 title and notched a seventh straight regional appearance. The class of 2015 was about to arrive, and that is where this journey begins. The following 10 chapters attempt to paint the picture of OSU baseball in 2017 and 2018, one of the most memorable two-year runs in college baseball history. More than 40 people graciously agreed to be interviewed for this book, and every single person played a role in what the program accomplished. This is their story, told in their words.

All the way back in the mid-90s, Casey inherited a program stuck in the Pac-10 North and turned it into a two-time national champion. Would the venerable coach get an opportunity to chase another before the time came to hang up his jersey? It always felt like the answer would be "yes."

CHAPTER I

BUILDING A CHAMPION

To assemble a championship roster, you have to find the right players. And to find the right players in modern college baseball, you need to start early.

Nick Madrigal, infielder: Oregon State was the first college that offered me, and it was in the eighth grade. I came up to an infield camp just for fun with a couple friends. Marty Lees was still a coach there, and by the end of the camp we were talking more serious.

Pat Casey, head coach: Nick must've been 13 years old or something like that and the guy was just different. I mean he had hands ... I had the good fortune of playing with Ozzie Guillen when I was in AA and Ozzie at the time was probably 20 years old. Well, this kid's 13 or 14 years old and I thought "man, this guy reminds me of Ozzie Guillen!" And that's saying a lot because that guy could do things I'd never seen people do before when I saw him field it. Nick was amazing, he was absolutely amazing. But I think the thing that's most impressive is he was an absolute baseball junkie. I mean this kid, all he wanted to do was play baseball and talk. You can be standing around there at the camp and most guys would be BSing, eating a sandwich, doing this and that. Nick, all he wanted was for someone to hit him more ground balls. He was an amazing kid to watch, unbelievable hands, and that never changed. Sometimes you see some high-profile kids be real good real early and then all of a sudden you go back and see them a couple years later and they don't have the same passion or the same work ethic or the same drive now that they've been to a lot of high-profile tournaments and showcases and things like that. Maybe they're a little less aggressive and less hungry. Nick wasn't. I mean every time I saw that guy it was like "man, this guy is different. This guy is a game-changer." There are so few game-changers, really, if you look at people in sports in general. Tiger Woods, he's a game-changer. Michael Jordan, he's a game-changer. And you look at guys at our level in college baseball, you talk about getting a game-changer on your club and what they do to the program and how they influence other kids, he certainly fit that bill.

Pat Bailey, associate head coach: Coach Casey and I ran all over the country watching Nick play. If Case wasn't watching him, I was. I went down to San Diego one time. I went out to North Carolina another time to specifically watch Nick and Cadyn (Grenier) play when they were trying out for Team USA. The recruiting part, it's fun going out and watching talent.

Nick Madrigal: Oregon State was the first college that recruited me. I didn't commit right there. A year went by and I traveled to other colleges and checked them out, but once I saw a game in Corvallis I knew that was the spot for me. I did have opportunities to play other places in the Pac-12, and a couple schools in the WAC and things like that, but Oregon State was the right spot for me.

A four-year varsity standout from Elk Grove High School near Sacramento, California, Nick Madrigal was generously listed at 5-foot-8 and 155 pounds on his Perfect Game *recruiting profile. Madrigal's offensive and shortstop skills were so developed that he was still rated the nation's No. 101 overall prep recruit by the publication despite his diminutive stature.*

Pat Bailey: Baseball is an interesting sport. If he was a guy that ran a 7.2 60- (yard dash) and was a corner outfielder, (his size) would've been a concern. But because he can fly and is a middle infielder ... I just loved the way he played the game. I knew that he was going to be a really key factor in us doing well if we got him and he didn't sign (professionally). He's just a special player and really smart as well.

Ron Northcutt, director of baseball operations: I remember the first time I saw him at one of our camps, and our coaches were gaga over him. I made a comment to one of the coaches, "why are we foaming at the mouth at some little (person)?" That turned around very quickly, just watching his actions at the camp. He was an amazing player along with being an amazing kid.

Pat Casey: Guys were trying to backdoor us all the time with Nick after he committed to us. We had schools that were trying to call him and tell him this, that and the other trying to get him to decommit. We just thought that was pretty funny, it was also frustrating to us that someone would do that. But Nick stayed true to his word.

Nick Madrigal: A big person in my recruiting process was Jake Rodriguez. He played at Oregon State (and Elk Grove High School) and is someone I got real close to, and still to this day I talk to him almost every day. He told me it's one of the best places to be, along with a great coaching staff. He loved it there and he was someone I looked up to when I was younger because he played at the same high school I did. He was one of the best players around, and once he told me that was the spot I would probably want to play at, I listened to him and I eventually took his advice.

Jake Rodriguez, undergraduate assistant coach: I met the Madrigal family before I was in high school, right when I moved to the Elk Grove area. I played sports against his brother all the way through high school, so I knew Zack. I started to see Nick and his twin brother (Ty) at the ballpark all the time watching games when we'd play Franklin High School. Obviously, I knew Mike, the dad, so that relationship started then. I wouldn't say we were really close back then just because our high schools were kind of rival high schools, so his brother and I battled quite a bit on the football field and baseball field. Nick ended up going to Elk Grove High instead of Franklin like (Zack) did, so I'd get updates on Nick all the time and talk to him quite often when I would go back for Christmas break or whatever. I'd hit with him and started growing that relationship.

Nick's kind of an old soul, he's not big into things like living in Los Angeles or living in a big city, he's really low key. He likes to hang out at home, he likes to go to the golf course, he likes to just do nothing, really. He's just low-key and he's all about baseball, and I told him that if you want to be at a place where all they care about is baseball, then Corvallis is the right place. Because Beaver Nation, their focal point in Corvallis is baseball and this is the greatest place I've played. In my career at Oregon State, we traveled to a lot of great places to play and the consistency at Goss Stadium with the fans is unbelievable. I think that was a huge part of it, knowing we would have sold-out games, but I also told him about the lifestyle. It doesn't take very long to get to the grocery store or even if you want to head out of town and get to Portland, it doesn't take very long. I think he enjoyed that, and his mom and dad could buzz up here for the weekend, watch a three-game series and drive home on Sunday after the game. I just think once you sit down in a room with coach Casey and he gets real with you and tells you how it's going to be — the thing with him is there's no BS. He's as straightforward as it gets and I think with the Madrigal family, all they wanted was somebody to talk to them straight up. The recruiting process, for me it was easy. I got to tell him about my experiences and that trust built up with him and his family.

FINISH

Madrigal wasn't the only elite class of 2015 shortstop that liked what he saw from Oregon State. Down in Las Vegas, Bishop Gorman High School's Cadyn Grenier also had a lengthy list of suitors.

Nate Yeskie, pitching coach: I got a phone call in regards to Grenier when he was a freshman from a guy that had played for me. So, I went down to see him.

Cadyn Grenier, infielder: Coach Yeskie first saw me play during one of our legion summer ball games at UNLV. The only reason he was there was one of the high school coaches (Chris Huseman) was friends with him.

Nate Yeskie: Chris had played for me when I started coaching at UNLV. His last year as a player was my first year as a coach, so we got to experience that together. We ended up winning the Mountain West Conference that year, both the regular-season and tournament titles. There were some growing moments in there for him as a person and as a player, and we still maintain that relationship to this day, years later. It was just good, it was really good for both of us. So, he called me one day, he was coaching for a scout ball team in Las Vegas and he just said "hey, I've got a guy down here who I think is going to be pretty good." So, I said "well, we're going to be in Phoenix in a couple of weeks. We'll go check it out and see what you've got." What's funny about it was that it didn't unfold the way we anticipated, only because I was supposed to go watch another young man throw on a different field, and he was supposed to throw the first half of his game, which would get me to Cadyn's game in time to be able to watch it. Well, the first game that I went to, the guy didn't throw until the back end and he threw maybe one inning at the very end. So, I was like "shoot!" We head back to the other field and the game is getting ready to wrap up, there's one inning left. So, I get there ... and I see Cadyn at the plate, he hits a ground ball to short and grounds out, then he goes out in the field and plays shortstop. I get to see him field one ground ball in the game and I get to see him ground out to short, and I remember looking at Chris after the game and saying "I need to get to know this guy A LOT better and fast." He just did some things that were explosive and unique for a kid his age. He did some things that could've played at our level at that time, and knowing some of the other members of that coaching staff and what they had to say, they were people that you could trust.

Pat Casey: Cadyn's a guy we saw at high-profile showcases, I think the junior national team. Just unbelievable tools. You talk about run, throw, power, hands, everything. Unbelievable tools.

Cadyn Grenier: When I got into fall ball, scout ball, (Huseman) was one of my coaches on the team. So, it just went along that I started to see Yeskie at my games here and there, over the summer and all that.

Nate Yeskie: It was funny because I'd met Cadyn's dad years before, unbeknownst to me. His dad used to work for the Las Vegas 51s. They were the Las Vegas Stars at the time, which was the AAA team for the Padres. We had mutual friends and there's a lot of overlapping in this baseball world. Once that whole thing kind of played itself out … we talked on the phone for about a year and a half, most of it wasn't about baseball. Cadyn was really into culinary arts, he liked cooking, music. We talked about all kinds of things and then, I don't know, he may be able to explain it better than I because it was from his perspective, but I think we just developed a good relationship and one that he could trust. It worked out well for him. He was up at our place for the super regionals in 2013. He happened to be in the area and he watched it and just said "yeah, I think this works." He felt comfortable with those things.

Cadyn Grenier: I think it was right before my first year of Area Code games during my junior year of high school when I realized that I didn't want to go to any of these other places that I'd been talking to. I called Yeskie up and was like "hey man, I want to come to Oregon State." Obviously, everyone was pretty juiced. I hadn't even told my parents I was doing it. I just walked in and was like "well, I'm going to Oregon State." And they were like "no way!"

Perfect Game *rated Grenier, the top recruit out of Nevada, No. 41 overall in its national rankings. Oregon State was also in pursuit of Bay Area product Trevor Larnach, the country's No. 381 recruit according to the publication. An imposing figure at 6-foot-4, Larnach was a tremendous all-around athlete.*

Trevor Larnach, outfielder: I went to College Park High School, a public high school in Pleasant Hill, California, which is right behind Berkeley next to Walnut Creek. When it came down to it our senior year, we had seven Division I baseball commits on our team from UC Davis to Stanford to Cal-Berkeley to Washington, Oregon State and UC Santa Barbara. We had a big class and that was pretty much thanks to (future Washington ace) Joe DeMers, who was one of my best friends growing up. We grew up together playing all different sports and all that stuff, and he hit the ground running when he was really young playing USA Baseball three or four times in a row, being a huge national pitching prospect. So, we didn't really have to go far when it came to getting seen, *Perfect Game* tournaments and showcases because all these scouts were already coming to see Joe when he was in eighth grade. He kind of gave us the spotlight when the spotlight was on him, we were in the background doing our own thing. I believe that's what helped us hitch a ride to these DI schools.

Nate Yeskie: Larnach had a little different trajectory, just in the sense that we'd seen him play a couple of times and how that unfolded. I liked him and I remember I had asked coach Bailey to come with me to a game because we were at Stanford. I told him that I'd seen a guy I liked, and I always thought it was a value to have someone else see him when they can — another coach to formulate another opinion. He came and saw him and goes "yeah, I see what you're saying. I like him. Let's go here."

Pat Bailey: It's funny, I do remember that, and I remember that the place we went to was out in the middle of nowhere. That specific team ended up having (five) guys on it who were Pac-12 baseball players, so it was one of the top high school teams in the country. For me, what stood out about Trevor was just how athletic he was for how big he was. A really athletic guy, good circular motions. What I mean by that is sometimes you see big guys and they're stiff and they don't run very well, but Trevor was just a really good athlete. When I watched him, I remember saying "this guy is going to be special when it's over with."

Trevor Larnach: Oregon State was the first school to really approach me, and I can't thank them enough for that. They were my first offer and once my parents and I visited the campus and believed in Yeskie when he said "it really doesn't rain THAT much here," we loved it, man. It was a beautiful thing. We all had this same type of feeling where it was just "where else would we rather go?" And it was nowhere, so it all settled in on its own.

Nate Yeskie: Larnach, everybody thought he was a pitcher. When he committed to us he was labeled as a right-handed pitcher and I thought "all right, well this is nice. Maybe people will forget about him and not pay attention to him." He kept grounding out to second base one of the first times I saw him, groundout, groundout, groundout. But I remember talking to him on the phone and it was just like "this kid is different. He thinks different, he thinks the way we like our players to think." He was just great. Through that whole process, you could hear it on the phone and go "this is a guy, man. He thinks like we do and this is going to work fine, we've just got to be patient." We knew it would take a little more time with him, but we knew the pieces were there.

Also residing in the Bay Area was Steven Kwan, an undersized outfielder from Fremont's Washington High School who impressed the coaching staff with his motor.

Steven Kwan, outfielder: I knew the Gastellums really well. Peyton Gastellum was a bullpen (manager at Oregon State), his dad was my coach and his brother, Landon — me and him are like best friends. I played on their travel ball team and they were always I would kind of say in Yeskie and Bails' ears about me, and I don't know if they took me super seriously or not. But I remember there was a tournament down in San Diego and I played my balls off in front of Yeskie, so that was pretty cool. Then I went to Arizona and Bails saw me there. They gave me an unofficial visit after my sophomore year in the summer and Case offered me there. It all happened really quickly, actually.

Pat Bailey: Steven plays the game with his hair on fire. He loves the game and is just really enthusiastic about the way he plays the game. Probably the main concern back then when he was younger was that he wasn't real big, and he's not a burner. I mean he has good speed, but he's not a burner.

Nate Yeskie: Kwan was a fun one. We divvied it up into areas to recruit from, and Kwany was one of those guys in my area. I'd seen him pretty good and I asked coach Bailey at some point "hey, have you ever seen this guy?" And he goes "yeah, I saw him. I kind of liked him. Have you seen him recently?" And I say "yeah, I just saw him today. He was pretty good." And he says "OK. Well, if you like him, let's get moving on him then. Let's get him coming." So, he comes up on a visit and coach Bailey is gone and we're at the point where we're pretty much ready to make him an offer. I remember we got to the point where we put the offer to him and he says "can I go in the hall and talk to my parents?" So, coach Casey and I are sitting there, and coach Casey looks at me. Because at the time, Steven is probably 5-6 and 145 pounds. He's not really looking the part ... and he says "you sure about this one?" You go through this process and you want to make sure you're getting the right guys and this and that. So, I go "are you sure about Nick?" And Case kind of looked at me and said "OK, yep. Sure."

Pat Casey: I don't recall ever saying that, but what I do remember is verifying from more than one source, including our recruiting guys, Nate and Bails, what kind of energy this guy played with. That was something I felt like you always need. You need a guy to come out and play with his pants on fire, can defend and is willing to do all the little things.

Nate Yeskie: So, Steven commits to us. I think the next day or two after he goes home, and word gets out that he's committed to us, I'm at an event back in an area I was covering and there were a couple coaches sitting around talking. Somehow his name came up and a guy turns to me and says "hey, is that guy committed to you guys?" I said, "he is," and they start kind of chuckling and saying "you really think he can play at your guys' level?" And I said "well, yeah. We committed the guy so I guess we're going to find out. It doesn't really matter what you think or I think, it's what he thinks. So, we're going to give him that chance."

I always remember that one because here's Steven Kwan, who doesn't really pass the looks test in a lot of guys' minds, but all I could keep thinking in my mind was "this guy could be (former MLB outfielder and current Los Angeles Dodgers manager) Dave Roberts." My first college start was against UCLA, and my college coach showed me the stat sheet from the year before and showed me the lineup, it was a pretty crude format of scouting reports if you will. He said "now if this guy gets on first, he's the leadoff guy, he can really run, so this is maybe how you're going to want to try and pitch him." I come to find out years down the road when Dave cracked into the league, I'm like "holy shoot, that's Dave Roberts." It's something our industry does. You compare guys, more often than not probably unfairly than fairly. But looking at Steven, I saw a guy who could really run, really defend in center field. What sealed the thing for me, when I said "hey, we probably need to make a move on this guy," was when he was actually playing in a tournament in San Diego against Luke (Heimlich). He had gotten two hits off Luke and he got at least one if not two hits against a guy named Michael Kopech, who is a big prospect for the White Sox. He was playing with Nick and I was like "man, this guy can just play, he can really play. If we thought Luke was good enough to play here, which he was already committed to us, then this guy should be able to play here, too." He just did some things stylistically that worked well … and gave us some different options in how we could build an offense, but at the same time have a defense with what we believed to be a strong component out in center field. I'll never forget those two coaches who said "hey, you think that guy can play there?" And I'm like "yeah, yeah we do. That's why we offered him." When I see those two coaches every now and then, I try to make sure that I somehow work his name into the story so they are able to see what he accomplished later on. He's a good one, man.

Another out-of-region player to come aboard was Bryce Fehmel, an infielder/pitcher from Agoura Hills in Southern California. Fehmel was Perfect Game's *No. 370 national recruit for the class of 2015. He caught the attention of Pat Bailey with his work on the mound.*

Bryce Fehmel, pitcher: During travel ball, I played for an awesome coach in John Paino at (California Baseball Academy). He said "you never really know who's watching, you never know what school is going to call you. So, make every at-bat and every game count because your dream school is watching you."

Pat Bailey: When I go out and recruit — and I think every guy who recruits would say this — you go out to watch a specific guy and sometimes you see somebody else and you go "I like him more than the other guy." It's funny, and that's kind of what happened with Bryce. I honestly went to go watch another guy play for Mike Garciaparra, who is Nomar's brother, who runs Garciaparra Baseball (Group). And I saw Bryce pitch and I went "oh my goodness, he reminds me a lot of an Andrew Moore," a guy that's just a strike-throwing machine that can add and subtract and do things to help you win baseball games. So, that's how I saw Bryce.

Bryce Fehmel: I never really had Oregon State on my radar as one of the schools I wanted to go to, but as soon as I started getting in contact with Bails and going through the recruiting process with him, I almost fell in love right away just because of the way we interacted. It was far enough away from home but also close enough to home, because I did have some interest from schools in Southern California, but it was too close for me. Oregon and Oregon State were both far enough but also close enough, and the coaches made the biggest difference and made the transition easy for me.

Pat Casey: For me, having the opportunity to recruit guys is so much different than for a lot of people. Because I think a lot of guys go out and look at the physical attributes, and that's what we need. Bails did a very good job of that. I mean everybody in the country knew that Nick Madrigal and Cadyn Grenier could play, everybody in the country knew that Trevor Larnach could hit, it was a matter of why do they want to come to Oregon State and not go to Texas? What are we going to do to make them believe that Oregon State is a better place than Vanderbilt? That's my key in recruiting, really trying to get to know the kid and have the kid believe in what we're doing. Then there are some kids on the other side of the coin, too. When you look at a guy like Steven Kwan, there were a lot of people that wouldn't go on him because they felt like he was too small. For us, we felt like that energy fit into what we're doing. We felt like that was exactly what we were looking for in that particular spot.

Most guys that are recruiting at this level can go out and come back and tell you the tools a guy has. And those are important, but they're not as important to me as the makeup that he has. If you took Michael Gretler, that guy was unbelievably important to our program for four years, and he hit under .200 his freshman year. But his makeup, his desire to be Beaver, his desire to be the ultimate teammate was as important as it was to have more tools. If you look at Michael, he was a very, very good baseball player and he had talent, there's no question he was a Division I player, but he wasn't a guy that was going to wow you with anything special. He was just going to come out and play every day, every day. And then when you get a guy like

FINISH

Adley Rutschman, who has every tool in the world and also has that makeup, I mean that's why he was the (number-one pick).

The foundation of the Beavers' back-to-back national championship teams were players from Oregon and Washington, but the class of 2015 was different at the top. Of the Beavers' seven highest-rated signees, four were Californians (Madrigal, Fehmel, Larnach, Kwan), with lone representatives from Nevada (Grenier), Oregon (Zak Taylor) and Washington (Ian Oxnevad). Lined with star power, the incoming class was ranked as high as ninth nationally by D1baseball.com.

But unlike football and basketball, where high school players are barred from the draft, baseball recruiting classes are regularly pillaged by Major League Baseball. If a high school player opts to attend a four-year college instead of heading directly to pro ball, they must stay at least three years in most cases. Oxnevad, a pitcher from the Seattle area, was drafted in the eighth round by the St. Louis Cardinals and never made it to college. Grenier and Madrigal, Oregon State's top pro prospects for the class of 2015, were both projected to be early-round picks.

Nate Yeskie: When you're recruiting some of those kids, initially when that process starts, (the draft) doesn't really enter into your mind a whole lot. You're looking at the dynamic of how they fit into your team, what they identify with, with regards to your university and some of the other elements that you think are important in recruiting. … We knew they had a chance to be very good baseball players. With the draft looming, we knew that each one of them possessed some interest from the professional ranks. To what degree, we weren't quite sure.

Pat Bailey: There were two guys specifically (I was worried about), Cadyn and Nick.

Pat Casey: Getting one of them to show up was something we were thinking we'd be excited about.

Morgan Pearson, assistant to Pat Casey: I remember in the spring of 2015, Pat (Casey) handed me two cards. The cover was a picture of Omaha and inside the cards it said "we hope to see you in Omaha." They were addressed to Cadyn Grenier and Nick Madrigal. Because at the time, we were really unsure if Nick and Cadyn would even end up on campus.

Cadyn Grenier: We had a pretty good game plan going into the draft. I had heard where guys were looking to draft me and what they were putting my value at, so I crafted a number for me to sign. I really wanted to go to Oregon State, and I'd been telling everyone forever that my Plan A was to go to college. Plan A was always to go to college and play college baseball. Plan B started to develop in high school as I started to get more draft attention and it was kind of like "well, OK, I can get drafted now." But my ultimate goal was always to get a scholarship and go play college baseball. So, I planned and got a number in my head where it was like "hey, if a team meets this number on a signing bonus, I'll sign and go to pro ball. If not, no problem, I'll go to Oregon State." So, the day of the draft comes and I get a call, (the St. Louis Cardinals) call and offer a number that's just a tad under what I wanted. So, I was still like "no. I set this number, no thanks. You knew what it was." After that I called coach Casey and told him that I had good news and bad news. He wanted the good news first so I told him I wasn't signing and was going to Oregon State. He was confused about what the bad news was so I told him that he had to deal with me every day for three years, that was the bad news. He got a kick out of that.

Pat Casey: I just laughed. I mean, how many guys do that? That's never happened to me in my whole career, a guy called and told me that he'd just turned down first-round money and a first-round slot.

Cadyn Grenier: After Day 1 of the draft, my mind was already set that I wasn't signing and I was going to Oregon State. ... (My number to sign) was $1.5 million, and the slot they wanted me at was like $2.1. Their offer came within a couple hundred thousand but they didn't want to give me any more, so I was just like "no." Because there were still other chances in the draft later on where people get more money, so I was just like "no, I'm not doing it." And it ended up being the right choice.

Pat Casey: Those things are what makes those guys really, really good, what makes them great. There's that edge to them, that stubbornness to them, that ego to them that makes them go "you know what, you're not going to short-change me." And to think that he did turn down first-round money and he wasn't scared when he came to college, he had no fear whether or not he was going to see that again. He just wanted to play.

The St. Louis Cardinals inquired about taking Grenier with the No. 23 overall pick. Instead, the 11-time World Series champions went with high school outfielder Nick Plummer. The Cardinals ended up grabbing Grenier in the 21st round, but the shortstop's decision had already been made: he was going to Oregon State.

FINISH

Madrigal found himself in a similar position. Would he take the life-changing money or attempt to improve his stock in college and get drafted even higher three years down the road?

Nick Madrigal: I had a couple opportunities. I wasn't regarded in the first round, so my best option was right around third-round money.

Pat Casey: Nick told me "hey coach, I feel like I'm a first-rounder," and I said "so do I." I don't know if this is verbatim, but then I said something to the effect of "if you don't go in the first round, come here and show them you're a first-rounder."

Nick Madrigal: It was one of those things where I thought about it, my family thought about it as well. I think they were shocked when I turned down that kind of money and that opportunity, but there was something in my heart where I truly believed I was a first-round player. I saw some of my friends going in the first round and I knew I was just as good as them or better than them. That was one of the biggest reasons why I went to college, to prove those scouts and GMs and all of them wrong.

Pat Casey: There are very few guys that are Nick's size who have the courage to turn down the money he turned down out of high school and say "hey, you're wrong. I'm too good for you not to take me in the first round." And I loved that about the guy, I absolutely loved that about him.

The Cleveland Indians selected Madrigal in the 17th round. But just like Grenier, his mind was already made up. Two of the best prep shortstops in the nation were headed to Corvallis, putting an already talented incoming class over the top.

Nick Madrigal: Now that time has gone on, I've heard the coaching staff was pretty surprised that they landed both of us. I think they were kind of in a panic once it happened, having two shortstops and everything like that. But it ended up working out perfectly. It's kind of one of those weird scenarios because it's pretty rare that both of us made it. I was thinking about going in the draft and I know Cadyn was as well. He had a tough decision. But yeah, it ended up working out and thank God we both made it there.

Pat Bailey: When we got both of them, I was just elated. I thought "oh my goodness, it's going to be so much fun to have both those guys in our infield," because they were both so athletic and great players and fun to watch.

Pat Casey: It was really, I think, a testament to our program and guys wanting to be in our program and guys we really believed in. I'll tell you what, it isn't always getting the most talented guys, it's getting the right guys. And when you get guys that are talented and the right guys, then you're lethal.

If we were told all those guys would show up, we would've said "you've got to be kidding me," because Madrigal and Grenier could've signed easily and had tremendous offers, but they both showed up. Larnach, if he wouldn't have been injured his senior year, would've had an opportunity. So yeah, we knew that class was going to be special.

Trevor Larnach: When it came down to the draft, I had surgery my senior year and it was almost like I didn't have a choice to go out of high school in the draft. It was like the decision was already made for me. … The surgery was an (ulnar) nerve transposition. I took a basketball class my senior year because I didn't play basketball that year. My high school (baseball) team was going to the National High School Invitational in North Carolina, which is like the top 16 national high school teams competing in a big tournament at the USA Baseball Complex. We ended up coming in second, but before that me and a couple of my buddies were doing a bunch of different dunks in class and I was doing quite a few windmills. I did one and it really messed up my arm, and it wasn't the same. I had multiple MRIs and multiple opinions on it, and nothing came up other than the fact there was an extra muscle in my elbow that was compressing the nerve. That's ultimately what was hurting me throughout my whole senior baseball season, so we had to get it done when it was finished.

Nate Yeskie: When you go through this process and you get them through the draft and eventually get them on campus, it's like a sigh of relief. There's a tiered stairway if you will. You move up a step, and then you move up the next step and the next step. So, getting them to commit, great. Getting them signed, great. Getting them on campus, massive step. Now, you start putting those pieces together.

After the draft, Grenier and Madrigal spent the next two months competing in the West Coast League — a collegiate wood-bat summer league — before officially joining the program. Grenier played for the Bend Elks while Madrigal suited up for the Corvallis Knights, a team managed by former Oregon State player Brooke Knight. The 2015 MLB Draft concluded June 10 and Madrigal caught a flight to Portland the next day, expecting to play in the Knights' June 11 home game against the Bellingham Bells at Goss Stadium. Knight planned to have Madrigal start the game at shortstop, but his star roster addition got stuck in traffic and was in danger of missing the first pitch.

FINISH

Brooke Knight, Corvallis Knights manager: He was rushing to get to the park, text messaging us, and I was like "well, what do I do with this lineup card?" Based on the timing, it was going to be pretty close and you don't want to hold the game up with your starting arm.

Christian Donahue, infielder/outfielder: I think at the time, me and Jackson Soto were the only Oregon State players on the (Knights). So, we knew about Nick, and we knew he was coming that day. We went out to warm up, he wasn't there and we were all wondering like "when is he coming? Is he going to just come straight to the game?" We went back into the locker room after warmups. We had like an hour until the game and the whole time I'm kind of just waiting and waiting, and he wasn't showing up. So, the coaches came in and said "someone else might have to play shortstop," because they had Nick penciled in to start.

Nick Madrigal: One of my friends picked me up from the airport. He lived in town. The game was at (6:40 p.m.) and I think I landed around four. We were racing to the game, and when we got to the stadium from the airport, there was like five minutes until first pitch.

Brooke Knight: He got there with maybe, oh my gosh, maybe three or four minutes before first pitch, right before that anthem starts and I'm just scrambling. I said to him "hey, I had you in there and we'll get you in there later. I'll make a change and they'll probably forgive me for the scratch." And he's like "no, no, I'm good, I'm good!" I'm like "well you've got to play catch, you've got to warm up," and he's just like "no, no, I'm good, I'm good." We had his uniform ready for him and he threw it on. The pants were three sizes too big, the jersey was a little big. We were wearing our creams that day which is a loose uniform anyway.

Christian Donahue: His uniform was too big; it was way too big. Especially back then because Nick was a little bit smaller than he is now. He kind of looked like a little toddler out there.

Nick Madrigal: It was one of the worst-fitting uniforms ever. The jersey was over my elbows, the pants were huge. Yeah, it was pretty funny. I had never even played on that field. I had never done anything. I ran into the clubhouse, they pulled everyone into the clubhouse, I had never met any of the coaches, I had never met Brooke Knight, any of those people. They threw a jersey on me real quick, I jumped into clothes and I actually went up to shake Brooke Knight's hand and he said something like "we don't have time for this, get ready!" So, I threw on my gear and just ran straight out to shortstop, I didn't warm up or stretch or anything like that.

Brooke Knight: Boom, boom, boom, the anthem is over and I'm trying to slow things down a little bit. The other infielders are getting their ground balls and we're missing a shortstop. It was literally (the catcher) throwing the ball down to second, and not long after that, there he goes. I was like "hey, I'm going to walk out there and let you play catch a little bit," and he's again like "no, no, I'm fine, I'm fine." So that was a little comical in itself.

Nick Madrigal: Yeah, it's really funny now that I think about it. It was probably a little dangerous to go out there and not stretch or throw or anything. I remember running onto the field and looking at the Oregon State stadium and thinking it was the coolest thing ever because I had never been on that field before and was taking it all in.

Brooke Knight: And then the guy that started (Ryan Walker), he went 3-0 to the first hitter. I looked over at (pitching coach Connor Lambert), kind of gave him a look and went "oh boy, what's going on? Did you not get this guy ready or what?" Then Nick just called time with the field ump and jogged on over to the mound. I was looking at Lambo like it was probably time to make a little visit and develop this guy, and we didn't need to because Nick had already run up to the mound to this guy he didn't know and whatever he said, it was probably something to the effect of "calm down, it's going to be all right. We've got your back, we're back here to do the job for you and make the play, so just can it and throw it over the plate." It saved us a visit, and I couldn't tell you the result of the inning, but I'm pretty confident we got out of it. It was a really unusual, unique moment for a young guy that was scrambling that just wanted to get out there and was hungry to play, and amidst all that had the wherewithal to be the calming voice because he's super confident in his own abilities and is thinking about how we're going to get out of this jam and win the game. Not that we didn't know he was a special player coming in, but just being such a smaller stature guy too ... he doesn't know he's only 5-foot-7. He thinks he's 6-foot-8.

Christian Donahue: After coming off the plane, driving down and being late, he still had a good game. I want to say he had like two or three hits. I think that just exemplifies Nick. No matter the situation, whether he's late or if he feels rushed or anything, he's still the same guy all the time. It's pretty cool and something I admire about him. That was my first time meeting Nick as well, so that was pretty crazy.

FINISH

Nick Madrigal: By the end of the day, I was just laughing about it all because it was a crazy game and I think I had a good game, too. That was one of the craziest things I've done I would say.

Brooke Knight: It was a Superman-type effort.

Playing on a team full of strangers, and with no warmup, Madrigal went 3 for 5 at the plate in his Corvallis Knights debut with two doubles, two runs scored and a stolen base in a 5-4 win. Madrigal became an instant star for the Knights, winning team MVP honors while stealing a West Coast League-record 40 bases. It was a sign of things to come.

Nick Madrigal: It was nice just to play in the stadium and get familiar with some of the fans. They get pretty close to selling out some of the Corvallis Knights games, especially the big ones, and I thought it was cool that I got to play in the stadium and get familiar with the field. One of the things I remember that I enjoyed was every time I got announced, they would say "Oregon State commit Nick Madrigal" and the crowd would get a little bit more excited hearing Beaver players playing at the home stadium. That's something I really enjoyed, and it was nice to play in that league. Cadyn was in that league as well, so playing against him and all that was a lot of fun.

Brooke Knight: It's really tough to say just one thing about the type of young player Nick was when he came our way. Competency, off the charts. You can call it baseball savvy or that baseball IQ type of thing. Confidence, big-time confidence. You could put him at first base or out there to catch and he probably would've just done it. Those are the two big things for me, confidence and competency. It wasn't that first day, but within the first week or so you're like "man, we've got a field general in this young guy," who was not overly outspoken. In fact, he was pretty quiet, especially at that time, but all of the things he did and being in the right spot at the right time and those little moments where he's doing more than you're even aware of as a manager to make sure other guys are in the right spot … the look on a double cut where you're looking to backdoor the guy at second, or a long single and he's looking to backdoor the guy at first, those little things were special. His ability to compete in the box, obviously he advanced like everybody does on his plate approach. He was super aggressive early, which is great. There was no tentative approach to what he was doing, but he was still a tough guy to strike out, especially when he engaged early in the count. The wood bat is an adjustment for guys. He broke a few wood bats early and he just made an adjustment. He had the ability to go "hey, you might've beat me in there before, but now I know there's a pretty good chance you're going to come back in there, and I'm going to cheat to it and hurt you."

Jake Thompson, pitcher: Nick, he literally didn't change in a good way from Day 1 until the last day I was there. He came in as that leader of the team. Usually as a freshman you have to earn that, but he almost demanded it and got it right away. It's interesting for a guy who is 5-foot-6, you look at him and he's different from everyone, but he comes in and you realize that he's not just different in size, he's different in talent, leadership and everything like that. Madrigal just took over that leadership role. I don't want to say when he wasn't supposed to, but he demanded it, we gave it to him and he took off with it.

Kavin Keyes, undergraduate assistant coach: You didn't really know what Madrigal was going to do because you take your first glance at him and it wasn't "hey, this is going to be the guy that leads the entire team." But once you got to know him a little bit, hear him talk and see the way he went about his business, it wasn't too long before you went "OK, maybe he is."

Christian Donahue: Me and Nick became real close that summer and when everybody else came in, gosh, we knew we had a very, very talented class with that group. All those guys were one-of-a-kind players and we had a feeling that they were going to be what they are now back then. It was cool to see them come in and do their thing. They meshed well with everybody, and they were just awesome to be around.

Once summer ball concluded, players headed to campus for the beginning of official team activities. Introductions were made and it quickly became apparent that there was no shortage of talent.

Trevor Larnach: Because I was coming off surgery, I didn't play any summer ball going into freshman year while everyone else was hitting the ground running. Social media was somewhat new to me at that point, I'd just got on it sophomore year of high school or something like that. You saw guys like Cadyn and Nick already tearing it up and turning heads, meanwhile I was fresh off of surgery. So, I come into the Bridge Program. I can remember it just like it was yesterday, it was probably one of the most exciting times of my life because it's something new, a change of scenery, you're growing up a little bit and getting older. I remember the first day I got there, my dad drove me up and the first person I met was Cadyn. I met his family right off the bat, he comes driving in with his Camaro and I didn't even have a car yet! We started talking, and I congratulated him on a hell of a summer and whatnot.

Nick Madrigal: I already knew a couple of the guys going in. Steven Kwan and Trevor Larnach, I'd played with them before stepping foot on campus. So, I knew them, I knew they were good players and I was excited to play with them again. Other than that, I didn't know a whole lot of the other guys. I knew Cadyn was a big prospect and was also a shortstop, and I honestly thought it was going to be a great competition. It's kind of funny going into Oregon State, being recruited by coach Casey along with the staff. I knew that Cadyn was coming in and he was a great player. I wasn't afraid of the competition or anything like that. Coach Casey told me that one of the things you want on a team is to have all the best players you can, and he believed Cadyn and I were some of the best players in the country and it was going to make for a great team. And he was exactly right.

Cadyn Grenier: The only guy I really knew about beforehand was Nick just because I'd played against him in USA tournaments and stuff like that. But I didn't really know any of the other guys. I wasn't religiously following who was signing with my class. I had talked to Trevor a little bit through text because that's who I was living with my freshman year. We had been hooked up through I think coach Bailey. So, we'd talked a little bit, and he was the only one I'd talked to beforehand. I didn't know any of the other guys, so when we first showed up for Bridge it was just new guys, and we were obviously all staying together in the dorms during that time and we got to know each other pretty quickly. Everyone seemed to get along really well and we were immediately doing things together and all that stuff outside of class. It was a good, easy transition into a new group of guys.

Trevor Larnach: It was a fresh start almost, but you're also getting to know the guys, who they are. Especially your class because — I didn't know this at the time — but those are the guys you're going to be with for the most consecutive years when you're there. Everyone got along great, man. Everyone was really cool. You could see some guys sizing each other up a bit, not in a super aggressive way but more in a competitive way just to see who's who and who's got what. I remember they took us on the field not too long after we got there for batting practice, and of course they're throwing us these Jugs balls that go a hundred feet further. I was thinking "oh this is going to be cake," because I was hitting them off the batters' eye, hitting them off the scoreboard, and so was everyone else. Then it was like "oh, everyone's really good here." As Case would say, it's who's got the most willpower?

Zak Taylor, first baseman: I started to meet all the guys in the Bridge Program, because that was the first time I got to meet everyone in person, especially the guys like Nick, Cadyn, Trev and Kwan, the guys from out of state. I knew some of these guys had some national recognition and were really good players, had played for Team USA, things like that. When we got on the field for some of those first practices, it blew me away the talent pool we had in our class. I mean we were at the field taking BP and I'll never forget — you've got Trev hitting balls over the scoreboard and we're just coming out of high school. I'm trying to get a ball like into the outfield, and you've got things like that taking place. So, I wasn't aware of things until those first couple of practices on the field, then you start to realize "holy cow, this class can really do something special."

Steven Kwan: I knew we had an above-average class for sure. I'd played with Nick before on travel teams and I told everybody at that point that he was the best baseball player I'd ever seen in my life. I had played against Trev so I knew he was good and I knew we had some solid dudes, but it really set in when I was on Twitter over the summer and we were rated the (ninth)-best recruiting class in the nation. And I remember being like "oh wow, that's pretty crazy." I really had no idea the extent of how good we'd be, but I knew we'd be solid.

We had a little BP session with all the freshmen and I remember Trevor hitting balls over the scoreboard in right-center and I was like "holy cow, that's crazy!" The one that really stuck out to me was Ras, Drew Rasmussen. He was taking BP and was hitting nukes. I was like "this guy freaking rakes, we're going to have some big hitters on our team." And this was before I knew that he was a pitcher! I just remember it being a full-out slugfest in practice.

Andy Jenkins, assistant coach: There was a lot of hype around Grenier and Madrigal. I remember throwing BP to those guys and Larnach when they showed up and were getting situated with the Bridge Program, and thinking to myself, "these guys can hit." Every group that comes in at a program like Oregon State, you see talent right away. But there was a baseball mindset and background of where those guys played before they got to Oregon State. Whether it be the high school they came from or playing Team USA ball, that was definitely appealing and exciting to the staff.

Jack Anderson, outfielder: I remember those first couple times when we were hitting all together, and they pretty much seamlessly came into the program and were ready to play. A lot of us, like myself and Kyle (Nobach), the transition to college baseball was just like getting thrown into a hurricane and getting blown off your feet. But those guys never really had that moment. They'd played high-level baseball before so they brought that next level of confidence, even when they were freshmen. They were ready to play, and it was super impressive. I remember seeing Nick and Cadyn and being like "these guys, it just doesn't seem like they're having a hard time out here." They were ready to rock, and I was still trying to figure stuff out and it was like my third fall.

FINISH

Josh Therrien, trainer: Cadyn, Nick, Trevor, Steven. Obviously in terms of position players, you look at that and are like "these guys are going to be really good for a few years here." And the big thing, and this is where I think coach Casey and the rest of the coaching staff really shined, is that those guys are big personalities, different personalities. How do you mix Nick Madrigal and Cadyn Grenier at the same position? How do you make sure that there's enough ABs for everybody? And the year before that, too, you've got guys like Christian Donahue and KJ Harrison, a bunch of really talented position players there. You're just sort of wondering "is this all going to fit, or is there going to be an issue there?" The fact that those guys could come in and respect, honor and listen to guys like Jack Anderson, Kyle Nobach, Michael Gretler — some of those guys that had put in the work. They respected how they went about their business and how they were supposed to do things. They weren't afraid of the work.

KJ Harrison, first baseman: The thing that stood out to me as soon as they showed up on campus was the kind of people they were. We got to know them when we took them around on their visits, so we grew a bond there. We all knew they were talented players, but the main thing was they all worked hard as well. They were talented and good players, but I think we really bonded well as a team because we all worked hard together as a whole. That was something I always appreciated with those guys. They were ready to go when they came in. They weren't nervous, they weren't scared, they wanted to play and get after it.

Morgan Pearson: I knew right away we had something special and Pat (Casey) saw it, too. These were guys that wanted to win, wanted to play together. They had similar goals, a similar mission and if they didn't have that mission of getting to Omaha and making a run, they would've never come to school. They would've never headed to Oregon State.

Kyle Nobach, outfielder: When those guys rolled up, you could instantly just tell. It doesn't take much to tell being around certain types of people. That's why they were unique and that's why that program was successful, because of the unique individuals that go there and the mindsets they have. Mindsets are contagious, and that's exactly what Oregon State baseball was with Nick Madrigal, Cadyn Grenier, Trevor Larnach, all these high-profile guys who are crushing it in professional baseball now. They set the tone for everything we did. They led us. There were a lot of leaders, and they created that environment and that's why it was so special. They grinded in the weight room, they pushed each other and trained like a bunch of warriors in there, and it translated to the field and how we practiced.

Bryce Fehmel: We had a bunch of guys from all over and we all knew that we were good as a class. And when we put our class together with some of the other classes, it was just a bunch of great players and a bunch of great teammates coming together. I think the combination of good players and being a good guy and a good teammate made the perfect recipe for success in our eyes.

Luke Heimlich, pitcher: My class was a large freshman class as well, so in pairing that together we knew we'd have a good team going forward. And then you add all the other guys that became very vital pieces that maybe weren't necessarily the biggest prospects — the Fehmels and other people who didn't have as many accolades coming in, but still ended up having incredible college careers.

Kavin Keyes: When I finished playing in '14, that was another good class that was finishing their junior years and getting drafted, and then there were the seniors like (Ben) Wetzler and (Scott) Schultz. It was cool when I got there in '16 and all these guys were coming in that had that same kind of stature. … It was just a good group of personalities that really meshed together and they were always pushing each other to get better. There wasn't a moment in the nighttime where they weren't in the cage. They wanted to be the best, and it was fun to watch.

Nate Yeskie: One thing that always jumps out in my mind is we were scrimmaging one day and it was a high, high-level scrimmage their freshman year. Max Engelbrekt was sitting behind me during the scrimmage and Nick was making some great plays, Cadyn was making some great plays, Larnach put some good swings on the ball. He's just talking out loud and at one point I turn around and go "Max, can you keep it down? What do you need to be so talkative for today?" And he's just shaking his head going "how did all of these guys end up here? This guy, this guy, this guy … these are some of the best players I've ever seen!" And Max had a very advanced baseball mind, still does, having grown up at the Kingdome and spending his later adolescent years there at Safeco with his dad working for the Mariners. Max was very keen to paying attention to those types of things, and he was watching this unfold with these guys and he's saying the same things we are as coaches. He goes "when they figure out what to do and how to do it and then do it together, this has a chance to be just spooky." And this was a time when guys like Rasmussen and Luke were coming into their own a little bit, so the pieces were there.

Jake Thompson: I wasn't there for their junior years, I mean I watched on TV and everything, but seeing how those guys became incredible, elite baseball players and how they were able to set the tone early from their freshman years, it was just amazing.

I got a chance to play with (Michael) Conforto during his last year at Oregon State, and they set that Conforto-like tone.

Picked to win the Pac-12 in the preseason coaches poll, Oregon State entered the 2016 season with College World Series aspirations. The Beavers had three freshman All-Americans coming back in ace Drew Rasmussen, reliever Mitch Hickey and first baseman KJ Harrison to go along with top junior prospects Logan Ice (catcher) and Trever Morrison (shortstop). Morrison, a returning two-year starter, was talented enough to hang onto the starting shortstop job. Madrigal found a home at second base while Grenier primarily played third.

Despite several key injuries, OSU got off to a sparkling 16-2 start and was ranked as high as second in the country heading into its first Pac-12 road series at California. Rasmussen, who threw the first perfect game in OSU history as a freshman, went down with an elbow injury in the opener, leaving an already depleted pitching staff in even worse shape. The Beavers were swept in Berkeley and played inconsistent baseball over the next two months, going 15-17 overall.

Steven Kwan: That was just a huge learning year, for me and the team. I remember I was really, honestly, not very confident in my abilities at the time, and I think we all went through some growing pains as a team.

Zak Taylor: That was a good year for me because I got to learn a ton. Jumping from the high school game to the college game at that level, everything was sped up a bit but I was lucky because I had guys that I could really talk to and just pick their brains, especially with not playing a ton and being on the bench. I felt like that was a big growth year for me.

Jack Anderson: That was the first year I really played and had some big moments in my career. I think it was just an up-and-down year. We were super young. I mean we did have a little bit of experience, but we were largely freshmen and sophomores all the way around. I just don't think we had the confidence every day, I think we were on a roller coaster a little bit. Nick was still our leader, but he was just a freshman so he was trying to figure it all out, too.

Luke Heimlich: That season had a lot of ups and downs. I remember I started the first two weeks of the season down in Arizona and then I got pushed back into the bullpen. So, I was just going along in the bullpen until Drew went down, and that was obviously a big deal. He had started all freshman year and was our Friday guy, filling that role left by Andrew Moore and was doing a really good job. So, to lose him was a big piece of it, he was the base of our pitching staff and the leader in everything we did. Him going down definitely had an impact, but that was the season where we started to see the offense really step up. When people think of Oregon State baseball, it always goes straight toward the pitching staff and the success Yeskie has had there, and for good reason. But that year was when things started to shift and we began to grow as an offense.

Jake Rodriguez: We had a bunch of young guys. I just remember how young Trevor Larnach was, Steven Kwan and Nick and Gretler, guys like that. It was a lot of young guys and I remember coach Casey kept telling us "just wait, just wait another year. These guys are going to be unbelievable. This is one of the best teams we're going to have at Oregon State." He kept reiterating that to us.

Max Engelbrekt, pitcher: We started (16-2) and then we were terrible. We must've gone well under .500 on the road that year. Really, we were just a young team. I was easily the oldest guy on the team at that point, which was interesting because I hadn't played in so long. The year before, I mean I went to some of the games but I was pretty separated from the team because I wasn't even on the roster. I was just trying to get back into the swing of things (recovering from a torn ACL), but I remember that we could field like two teams' worth of guys that were really good players.

Jack Anderson: I don't know what our away record was that year but I know it wasn't very good, in the Pac for sure (9-11 overall, 5-10 Pac-12). I think we were just trying to do a little too much on the road. Goss was Goss, we got our wins there, but our road record was what hurt us really bad. We played at Arizona and got swept, and that was our first "oh shit" kind of moment. That series was brutal. Case got thrown out of that third game, Logan almost got thrown out and Max Engelbrekt almost got thrown out, all on the same play. I forget what happened … but that's kind of when the wheels fell off at the end of that series. And then I just remember losing to Portland because that was the first time we did that (since 2006) and we were like "you've got to be kidding me." That was brutal because Case always took pride in beating them because he played for them, I feel like. He never let us take our foot off the pedal, but for Portland he was always trying to put a little extra into them, I think.

Max Engelbrekt: I don't remember who said this, but at one point it was brought up that we'd lost fewer times to Portland in 10 or 12 years (once) than we had national championships (two). We were sitting there just like "man, what happened this year?" Because previously, I'd only been on two teams before that. I missed my junior year (in 2015), and we didn't lose very much. We were a national seed when I was a freshman, we were the number one seed when I was a sophomore, so I really hadn't lost much. That was crazy. We really didn't have an answer. I remember I had an interview with (radio play-by-play announcer) Mike Parker before one of the games and he basically asked "well, what are you guys going to do to fix this?" And I was like "well if we knew, we'd do it." We were giving up too many runs and we weren't scoring enough. It was pretty strange. The pitching depth on that team was definitely less than any other year, but we certainly were talented enough to be better than that.

Kavin Keyes: I think everyone was earning their stripes and getting used to what this was all about. Once they figured out that they belonged there … I mean obviously they knew they belonged, but I didn't know if they'd totally convinced themselves yet.

Trevor Larnach: Well individually, it was a really weird year for me because I was working my ass off to be a part of the team, join the program and help win. Then I got hurt, and that stemmed down my development. (Strength and Conditioning coach Chris Anderson) and I joke around about it because when I got there I was 190 pounds. Obviously, I was super stoked to be there, having all the nutrition in the world available, having all the strength equipment in the world available. When I got there, I knew I was down in weight because I was 205 pounds my senior year (of high school), which I'd worked to get towards. And then when I got hurt (in high school), I couldn't really do much upper-body stuff. So, when I got there, I was 190 pounds and two or three months later I hit my goal weight of 216, which was the weight they wanted me to leave at. I gained that much weight in a really short amount of time, and I ended up getting a stress fracture in my foot. Me and coach A would joke about how I got hurt because I got too jacked too quickly for my body. We were doing double-days at the time mixed with 6 a.m. weights and scrimmages and all that stuff. For whatever reason, it started to hurt more and more. I tried to play through it but they eventually told me to get off the field.

Jack Anderson: If you're either injured or redshirting it's definitely a scary time in your career, and coach A is really the only guy you see because you're lifting like four days a week and the coaches are working on the season, so you become really good friends with coach A. He puts so many hours a day into the redshirts, the injured guys and then puts just as much effort into the players that are playing and playing every day. I think everyone's had those moments that are tough during seasons, and coach A is always there to lift you up and kick you in the butt and say "keep working." He doesn't let you sulk over it too much, and I think that's why we were successful. He was able to develop players when they were injured or redshirting. I think he's part of that puzzle that gets overlooked and that's what a strength coach is. They are behind the scenes truly, and I think they are one of the more important parts of a program and easily one of the most under-compensated as well. They just keep working hard and don't let it get to their heads too much.

Trevor Larnach: So, I ended up joining the team like a quarter of the way through the season. And we were good, we had a young team and a lot of us were starting. I witnessed some struggling, I witnessed … if I could compare it to the 2017 and 2018 teams, it wasn't that tight-knit of a group. It's hard to compare those groups because I don't think it could get any tighter than those '17 and '18 teams, but I just think maybe that was something that led to a lack of success. And ultimately when I got back, I put a ton of pressure on myself about producing when I'd come into games, and obviously that doesn't help. When you try to make all these individual adjustments from the standpoint of hitting, it doesn't work out. The game needs to be simplified because there are so many aspects going on at once and there's a lot of pressure that you can be putting on yourself, and that's what it did. And it didn't help.

Cadyn Grenier: It was a tough year for the team. We were still fairly successful, but during the year we had some issues and a lot of guys were getting frustrated and the coaches were getting frustrated. We had a lot of player-only team meetings and things like that. Honestly, I don't remember a ton from it because I don't feel like a lot of great stuff happened for us. But I do remember a lot of times I was sitting on the bus after a road trip, the coaches would get off and we'd stay on the bus. A couple guys would talk and we'd kind of just be like "hey, it's baseball. We're going to figure it out, blah, blah blah."

Nate Yeskie: Nick played second his freshman year, Cadyn played third. Larnach had some struggles, Cadyn had some struggles. The league can be unforgiving in that sense, so how they respond to adversity is a key element.

Christian Donahue: There were some people who were a little upset about playing time and things like that. If you have that on a team, even just one person sulking can ruin the whole morale of the team. Over the course of a full season, I think it takes a toll on the team. I mean we still had a great group of guys, we still had awesome teammates and … people were trying to find their place and everything.

Bryce Fehmel: We had a lot of guys from different classes. We had seniors, we had juniors, we had sophomores and freshmen all playing. I don't want to say it was tough to mesh with everyone, but there were guys in different headspaces trying to do what they needed to do to move on. Once we were able to move past that at the end of the year, we were able to kick it into gear.

The Beavers did turn it around late in the season, and Fehmel was a big reason why. Primarily recruited as an infielder, Fehmel quickly noticed in fall ball that playing time would be hard to come by with Madrigal and Grenier on the team. Fehmel was committed to doing whatever it took to see the field and approached the coaching staff about trying something different.

Bryce Fehmel: In high school, I only came in to close. I played shortstop all game and if we had the lead, I'd come in for the seventh inning and try to shut the door. I think my senior year, I threw about 20 innings in high school. I was pretty much just recruited for the infield. I want to say I was the backup plan for Madrigal and Grenier not showing up on campus, but both of them ended up coming to campus so I had to find something else to do. Early on in the fall there were position meetings. The infielders met and we got a packet, then (Pat Bailey) called the outfielders together and I was like "Bails, is there any chance I could try to work out with the outfielders as well? I'm just trying to find a place to play." He goes "yeah" and let me sit in on the outfielders' meeting with a packet, and I took some reps in the outfield at one point just because I wanted to be on the field. I'm a competitor, so I was trying to find a spot as early as I could. Bails let me try everything, and pitching was my home.

Pat Bailey: I recruited Bryce. When he came in that fall as a shortstop/pitcher, just based on what he was doing defensively, he wasn't where our other guys were. But I also saw him pitch a few times. In fact the first time I saw him play he pitched. He was what I call a target practice pitcher. And what I mean by that is he was like Andrew Moore, Sam Gaviglio. Those kind of guys, wherever you put the target, they're going to hit it. I just really felt that for him, his best chance of helping us out in our program was to be a pitcher, not a position player.

Nate Yeskie: Fehmel was great. We felt like we were a little short on the mound his freshman year, and we entertained the idea of maybe giving him a chance out there. He'd pitched a little bit in high school, was signed to come in as an infielder. Finally, we just said "well, let's sit down and talk with him and see." You're always a little bit cautious because sometimes kids aren't readily available to so much as even "hey, you played shortstop, we want you to play third." That can be a tough conversation, or "we want you to move from second to the outfield." I think it was coach Bailey or coach Casey who said "why don't you bring Bryce into your office and feel him out and see how open and receptive he might be to this." He comes in and I say "hey, we're a little short in some areas and think you could help us out here, would you be open to this?" And his response was "yeah. These other guys are really good and I don't know how much time I'm going to get in the infield." And then he was very serious and said "any way I can help the team, coach, you just point me that direction."

Bryce Fehmel: I always loved pitching, I just never did it a ton. But it didn't take long to get used to it. In the fall I threw a couple innings, and I want to say winter break is when I really sat down with the coaches and they wanted me to just focus on pitching. So, winter break I went home solely focused on pitching and what I could do to help the team going forward in the spring.

It was frustrating (being a two-way player in the fall), but also fun at the same time because I was competing to try and play in the infield with a bunch of first-rounders. I probably had no shot to ever play if I stuck with infield, so to have that backup plan and the trust from the coaching staff to give me the opportunity on the mound, I had no other option but to take it and run with it and just compete every time I had the chance. I can't thank them enough for giving me the opportunity to pitch for them.

Fehmel wound up being one of Oregon State's top pitchers in 2016, making 26 appearances (six starts) and going 10-1 overall with a 2.31 earned run average. In his first Pac-12 start at USC, the Southern California native went 7 1/3 innings and gave up just one unearned run in a critical series-clinching victory. Fehmel, a strike-throwing right-hander, stayed in the weekend starting rotation and was recognized as a freshman All-American by several publications.

Bryce Fehmel: They kept throwing me out there, and I kept competing and getting outs. I wasn't overpowering guys with my velocity as most people know, I was just trying to do my best to switch sides of the plate and change speeds on the hitters. It worked out my freshman year, and I stuck with that process throughout.

Nate Yeskie: The guy was just the consummate professional. He's a guy who's made the most of his talents and his parents really helped shape his toughness and his overall mental approach and vision to how things should be done. He's a lot like Andrew Moore and a lot like Jack Anderson where if you ever hear their names, you never hear anyone say a bad thing about them. The first thing that generally happens when their names are brought up is somebody smiles and they're excited to talk about those individuals.

Pat Bailey: I knew that when we got Cadyn and Nick, Bryce's best chance at playing would be at third base. We looked at him at third in the fall and just based on what he was doing on the mound ... I mean he ended up being a freshman All-American. It was one of those things where do you want to be average or above average at both, or do you want to be great at one?

Nate Yeskie: As we watched '16 unfold and watched these freshmen play and do things, you're kind of seeing kids grow up, some faster than others. But the lasting memory from that season for me is really UCLA.

Things were looking dire for the Beavers by mid-May. Madrigal injured his shoulder during a five-game losing streak, the program's first since 2011. Oregon State entered the USC series at 30-18 overall and 11-13 in Pac-12 play, likely on the wrong side of the postseason bubble. After splitting the first two games in Los Angeles, Fehmel led the Beavers to a victory in Game 3 to keep their postseason aspirations alive. Most projections had OSU in the NCAA Tournament field of 64 with a series win over the Bruins. The Beavers went a step further, sweeping UCLA with three consecutive shutouts. It was a combined effort from Travis Eckert and Max Engelbrekt in the opener, while Luke Heimlich and Fehmel did it all by themselves to close the regular season. Sitting at 35-19 overall and 16-14 in the Pac-12, tied with Arizona and Arizona State for third, OSU appeared to be a near-lock for the playoffs.

Jack Anderson: When we won that Sunday game against UCLA, I remember hugging Max Engelbrekt and saying "we did it, man! We did it. We're going to the postseason!" It was like for sure, we're a shoo-in, we got one of those last spots. Even the coaches, Bails was all fired up. Everyone was in such a good mood.

Andy Peterson, undergraduate assistant coach: We had that incredible finish against UCLA and the team finally found its identity. Things were good, it didn't feel like anybody could beat us.

Bryce Fehmel: We thought that would give us a really good chance to hear our names called on selection Monday.

Nate Yeskie: We finished tied for third in the Pac and we had the tiebreaker over Arizona State, and they were a team that was being talked about as hosting. So, we're thinking "well if they're hosting and there's that much buzz around them, then we're good, we're in." You shut out UCLA, who is a perennial power, three times, you beat USC the weekend before two times out of three, which was Fehmel's first (Pac-12) start and he goes (7 1/3 innings) in place of Jake Thompson that weekend. It just looked like some things were coming together.

Josh Therrien: It almost felt reminiscent of that 2007 team that barely snuck in but was really firing on all cylinders.

Steven Kwan: As a team we all went out the night before because we had just swept UCLA. I remember Case telling us if we took that series, did what we needed to do, then we would have a really good chance of keeping the season going. So, we were all fired up, really happy.

The NCAA Tournament selection show began at 9 a.m. Pacific time Monday, May 30, the day after Oregon State completed its UCLA sweep. The program often holds a public gathering for the ESPN broadcast in which fans are invited to attend, but the coaching staff chose to have a private team-only viewing party inside the Reser Stadium club level instead. The Beavers were playing arguably their best baseball of the season but still had an imperfect resume that included a few unsightly losses and a mediocre RPI of 44. OSU's fate was in the hands of the selection committee, and Pat Casey was all too familiar with what could happen in that situation.

Jack Anderson: I don't think Case wanted to have a selection show (gathering) because him and Yeskie probably knew more than we did, but they'd already booked the room and everything. I was blind to the fact that we might not get in. Like when I was walking in there, I thought we were going to the Miami Regional and I had *Welcome to Miami* by Will Smith ready to play on my phone.

Luke Heimlich: We all showed up, the selection show was at 9 a.m. and we scheduled a team lift for 10:30. So we all knew we were going to watch the selection show, things were going to go according to plan and we were going to have a team lift right after. Obviously, we were all dressing up for the selection show, but we brought our workout clothes with us so we could go right to the weight room afterward, just assuming the season was going to continue and we'd go on with our business.

Max Engelbrekt: I remember thinking it was a bad idea to do a selection show (gathering). As a product, it's not a very good atmosphere. Two out of the four times I did it we were the number one overall seed, so that was OK. But I just remember sitting there and thinking "what if we don't get in?"

Nate Yeskie: We had gotten some ideas the night before and felt pretty good about it. The next morning, we wake up and some of the people who told us we were in were now saying "man, I think you're out." And I thought "no way, there's just no way."

FINISH

Drew Rasmussen, pitcher: The vibe was kind of weird. I mean in 2015, we already knew we were in so it was more about where we were going and if there was a possibility of us hosting. The feeling was completely different. In 2016 I had gotten hurt, maybe I wasn't as emotionally invested. I obviously wanted all the success we could've possibly had, but I was able to also take a step away and see the bigger picture and understand "hey, we had some speed bumps throughout the year." But we'd played really good down the home stretch, and we all thought that was going to get us over the hump and in. But walking into Reser (for the selection show), coach Yeskie stopped me and said "hey man, there's a chance this thing isn't going to happen. Just be willing to share support with guys and try to help motivate them going into 2017." It caught me off guard, but I didn't really think anything of it at the time because heck, we're Oregon State, man. We're one of the perennial powerhouses in the country and we had a pretty good final record on the year. Not great, but I thought it would be enough for our guys to get in and allow our guys to experience the postseason and all that.

Andy Jenkins: I remember Nate having a relationship with some guys, some writers. As a coaching staff, we knew that morning that Nebraska and Arizona State and maybe some other teams were getting in, so as we were sitting there watching with our kids and support staff in collared shirts, we all sat there and knew exactly what was coming. We did get tipped off a little bit. I think we understood what was coming and that made it even harder to watch, personally.

Luke Heimlich: We knew we would be one of the last teams in. I hadn't really looked at projections beforehand, so I didn't know where we were supposed to go … and I was just sitting there until the end.

Max Engelbrekt: They did a commercial break after 32 teams were announced, and you could see our coaches kind of pacing around.

Jack Anderson: Every regional was getting shown, and I was just like "oh, it doesn't matter. Miami is the last one and we're going there, at least that's what I heard where we were projected." But I think Yeskie knew more than we did because there was one team that got in and I forget what he said, but it brought the air out of the room. I was like "oh, was that not good?" Because I thought we were for sure in, being third in the Pac.

Nate Yeskie: You're on pins and needles and we're watching some things unfold. The board keeps going, teams keep coming off and you're going "man, is this really happening?" It's kind of like watching a car crash or two trains colliding in slow motion. There's nothing you can do about it but it's happening in front of you, it's taking forever and it's just dragging out and the agony of it all.

Steven Kwan: What hurt the most was ... obviously we haven't heard our name the entire time, teams keep popping up and it's not us, and the last regional was the Miami Regional. We were all like "oh crap, here we are!" We'd been hearing all about how this is the one we're going to be in. So, it had us all the way up until the end, and for us to not be on there, we were in complete disbelief. It was a sucker-punch.

For the first time since 2008, Oregon State did not make the NCAA Tournament field of 64. The Beavers' season was over.

Luke Heimlich: It was just silence. Nobody knew what to say, nobody knew what to do, we were just sitting there in shock.

Jack Anderson: Once our name didn't show up, they went right to analysis, and before they could turn the TVs off they were talking about why Oregon State didn't get in. We were watching it and just going "this is not OK, why are we here right now?"

Steven Kwan: I remember the videos were playing and Case was like "shut this off, we don't need this." Case gave us a short speech and that was the end of the year.

Jack Anderson: Case, the leader he is, just said "some things aren't fair in life. Don't let this define who you are as a baseball player. Seniors, we love you, juniors getting drafted, we love you, but next year starts now."

Jake Thompson: To go up to Reser, expecting our name to be called and feeling like "yeah, we didn't have a great season but we've easily made it in," and then not to get called ... I just remember Casey shutting off the TV right away and he had this tone and was like "yes, we were absolutely ripped off." He was furious, but we all knew we were in charge of our destiny and we made too many mistakes along the way. It was the smallest little mistakes, maybe not covering first, maybe missing a ground ball, not making a pitch, that could've been the reason we didn't win that extra game to get in there.

Nick Madrigal: Watching the selection show with the older guys and the whole team and hearing the news we didn't get in; I was in shock to be honest with you. I remember right after the selection show just really thinking about everything that went wrong and knowing ... I was truly embarrassed to go back home to all the people I knew. It's funny, my twin brother was playing for St. Mary's and his team got into the playoffs and we didn't. I remember thinking "this isn't right. I didn't come to Oregon state for this."

KJ Harrison: I'll never forget how bitter we were sitting there and waiting during the selection show. We thought our name was going to be called because we finished the season strong, and as soon as that ended it was an empty feeling because we all expected to play and go to a regional somewhere. It was heartbreaking. You're so close to these guys and you don't want it to end.

Cadyn Grenier: We had taken into account everything that everyone was saying. They were like "they need to do this, they need to do that, they need to do this and then they'll be in," and we did all of it and then some. And to be in the last three out or whatever, it sucked.

Michael Gretler, infielder: As a player at Oregon State, you have a lot of respect for the guys that came before you and paved the way. You want to continue that incredible legacy, and when things don't go your way and you are one of the couple teams in that 10, 15, 20-year period that doesn't make the playoffs, it's obviously not a good feeling. You feel like you not only let your teammates and coaches down, but all the players that came before you. That's definitely a tough pill to swallow.

Max Engelbrekt: That was weird when we didn't get in. It was so awkward. We had an optional lift right afterward, and I remember Drew was upset that we didn't go. I was like "are you kidding? We're not going to be playing for nine more months," or whatever. Man, that sucked. I remember thinking about things like that was the last time I was going to play with Logan Ice, and at that point I didn't know if I was going to get drafted and leave. So yeah, that was pretty unbelievable. Not a great day.

Andy Jenkins: That was one of the saddest days I've had coaching, watching a team deserving of going to the playoffs not get an opportunity to do that. I remember thinking about Logan Ice who was a catcher I worked with pretty closely that was a great college baseball player who had an awesome year in 2016. I just remember thinking that he didn't get that opportunity to do some of the things that I got to experience as a player going to Omaha, and the things I've watched all the guys experience going to Omaha throughout the years. He didn't get that opportunity.

Jack Anderson: You felt for the guys that weren't going to play again. We all assumed we'd have another game together and it got taken away from us, so that really hurt. We all went to breakfast after and sat there and were like "wow, that's it." We were just starting to play good baseball again.

Pat Bailey: Let's be honest, the number one reason we had some of the issues we did is we ended up having so many crazy injuries that year that inhibited us from winning more games than we did.

Josh Therrien: It was weird things. There were some times early on where we had a bunch of shoulders, and if you remember a few years before that Andrew Susac and Jake Rodriguez both broke their hamate like a week apart. (Injuries) are definitely a part of it and that's adversity, you're always going to have that. It's tough and it can take a toll on a team.

Pat Casey: We had a ton of injuries, but there was nobody on that team that felt like injuries kept us (down). We won five of our last six games, we played UCLA at home, Madrigal plays with a dislocated shoulder and says "I'll play now, why not? I've got to have surgery anyway." We didn't give a run up in three games, I think it was the first time in the history of UCLA that they didn't score in a three-game series. We win five of our last six which is supposed to be a big part of it, how you finish, and we don't get in. So, I'm not going to use injuries (as an excuse). That team fought through every injury, that team was well deserving of being in a regional. Would I have liked to have had everybody healthy for the year? Absolutely. Do I think we would've won more games if we had everybody healthy for the year? Absolutely. But we didn't do it, it didn't happen.

Nate Yeskie: That was a pretty somber moment for a lot of us when we walked out of there because we knew that those kids deserved a chance to play in the postseason. The people who were involved with taking that opportunity away from them, it was borderline criminal going through that process in the way that they did because those kids had earned it and they deserved it.

Oregon State was undoubtedly hurt by the outside perception of the Pac-12. Utah, picked to finish last in the preseason coaches poll, implausibly won the conference with an overall losing record. The top five teams in the preseason coaches poll — OSU, UCLA, California, Oregon and USC — all missed the NCAA Tournament.

Regardless, the selection committee's decision was hard to comprehend when comparing resumes. For example, OSU and Arizona State finished with identical 16-14 conference records and analogous RPIs (ASU 43, OSU 44). Not only did the Sun Devils make the field of 64, they received a regional No. 2 seed. The Beavers swept the season series between the teams but were left out. Washington, which finished below OSU in the Pac-12 standings and lost two of three in Corvallis, received an at-large bid with an RPI of 55. According to the selection committee, the last two teams to make the field were Nebraska (RPI 48) and South Alabama (50).

During a media teleconference call after the field was announced, chairman of the selection committee Joel Erdmann, who was also South Alabama's athletic director, said that RPI was just a starting point and "not the end-all, be-all." He also said the West Region Advisory Committee (RAC) had OSU "beneath a few other teams in the west region." The five RACs — East, Midwest, South, Southeast and West — are comprised of member institution coaches and are supposed to rank teams primarily on the eye-ball test. The Pac-12's representative on the seven-man West RAC was Washington head coach Lindsay Meggs. Pat Casey said he's never spoken with Meggs about the final RAC rankings.

Pat Casey: The kids were robbed of an opportunity to play in a regional. They finished with (almost) the exact RPI as Arizona State, we swept Arizona State, we had the same amount of (conference) wins, they were a No. 2 seed and we didn't even get in. That was an injustice, and that was unfair. We're supposed to have people that are advocates to get teams in our conference in, we just didn't have that representing our conference that year. What's sad for me is that it's sad for the collegiate student-athlete that was denied the opportunity. I don't need to go any further than that.

Trevor Larnach: We all felt like we got screwed. Even though we didn't have as good of a year as we knew we could've had, we got screwed and there's no reason we shouldn't have made the playoffs. But it was a blessing in disguise because it really fueled the fire.

Nate Yeskie: Unfortunately for them, and I say unfortunately for the people involved, they ignited one of the biggest fires in the history of college baseball. Because if you look at what we know happened in '17 and '18, those things were very fresh. Those wounds were still not healed in a sense in the back of our guys' minds. 2016 was used heavily to motivate us.

Jake Thompson: It was one of those things where by the end of the season we just looked at each other and said "that's never going to happen again." It was that kind of tone. We knew we underperformed and we weren't going to let that happen again next year.

Nick Madrigal: I really just focused all my attention on thinking "next year, I'm going to do whatever I can to lead this team and say whatever I need to say, but we're not going to have this happen again." I remember that was a lot of peoples' thinking and focus, that we're not ever going to feel this again. Everyone was really focused, and it was a special thing.

Nate Yeskie: I heard a story that Madrigal reached out to everybody at the end of the selection show when we didn't get in. I don't know the exact timing, but at some point Nick basically had taken charge of grabbing the reins and texted everybody saying "if you're going to play summer ball, get yourself ready. If you're staying here this summer, get yourself ready. Because next year, it ain't going down like this." That really started our charge for the 2017 season when guys were walking out of there in '16 going "what just happened here? How come we didn't get into this thing?"

Andy Jenkins: For me, 2016 was the reason 2017 and 2018 happened. Obviously, you have to have talent, but talent really doesn't do a lot when you don't gel, you don't know why you're playing together, you don't really have a purpose.

One thing I remember about 2016, after that day where we all sat up there and watched other people get their names called, I remember coach Casey talking about how life isn't always fair and this is a tough situation, but it's something that should hunger you and motivate you and inspire you. We all left that day and Nick Madrigal came into the office the next day and I saw some clarity on his face, seeing the disappointment and knowing that he certainly knew what it took and why he was at Oregon State now. It wasn't to feel out your freshman year now, it was to go to Omaha and win. I think Nick had a look in his eyes that day that we've talked about as coaches. Basically, he said "I've got this, I've got this figured out. We're going to be good." And that's the same time he chose to not go play for Team USA because he wanted to get his (torn left labrum) taken care of so he could practice with his team in the fall.

Nick Madrigal: That was one of the toughest decisions I had to make because one of the best feelings for me was wearing the Team USA jersey. Gosh, I remember talking to my family for weeks and trying to figure out what I should do. At the end of that offseason, I felt like the Oregon State season was way more important than going to play for Team USA, just because I was there for my team and I didn't want to let my teammates down the next year. If I were to have played for Team USA and then go get the surgery, I maybe would've been cutting it close for the college regular season, so I decided to forgo the USA team and get the surgery. By the time fall came around, I was ready to go and I'm glad I did that because of how big of a year the next year was for me.

Drew Rasmussen: It was shocking quite frankly to not make the postseason. At the time, it was heartbreaking and gut-wrenching, whatever adjectives you want to use to describe it. But I honestly think motivation-wise it was great. We had a young team so we had a lot of guys returning. I mean the amount of talent they had assembled on those rosters was incredible, so to light a fire under us really just pushed us over the edge going into the summer of 2016, the fall of 2016 and then the spring of 2017.

Jack Anderson: It took us a day or two to get back up from the ground, but from that point on it was personal that we didn't make it. Because we knew we were a good team, we just didn't play to our potential that year.

Jake Mulholland, pitcher: I was watching their last series against UCLA on TV. They had won and I was fully expecting them to make it. I remember waking up that next morning and my dad told me that they didn't get in, and I was pretty upset because I knew I was going to be playing for them next year and I wanted to see my future teammates do well. Looking back at it, I felt terrible for the ones where that was their last year, but in the end, I think it motivated the guys that were on that team and the incoming guys like myself. They talked a ton about how they were so motivated and this wasn't going to happen again, so we were all immediately on board with that and we made it a goal that we were never going to put our fate in someone else's hands. We weren't going to let it be decided by a committee, and if we win enough and do well enough there's nothing they can do to keep us out of anything.

Pat Bailey: There are two things from 2016. The negative part was that we didn't make the NCAA Tournament, which I personally thought was ridiculous. I just thought we should've made it, I mean the last weekend we swept UCLA and didn't give up a run, which is crazy in and of itself. But I can remember sitting there at our group get together to see if we were going to make it, and when we didn't make it the next day I came straight into the office, I called some people to find out where a tournament was, and there was a tournament in Denver, Colorado. I called up our travel agent and I left the next morning at seven o'clock. I was so mad I had to get out of town. But what it did was make us hungry, it springboarded us into the next season. We were bound and determined to not let that happen again.

CHAPTER II

THE REDEMPTION TOUR

While 64 teams geared up to compete in the 2016 NCAA Tournament, Oregon State's players got an early start to their summers. KJ Harrison headed off to play for the USA Baseball Collegiate National Team. Nick Madrigal would've joined Harrison, but opted to undergo shoulder surgery instead. Others played in various summer leagues. Several pitchers spent the offseason in Corvallis, eager to get back to work after the selection-day snub.

Luke Heimlich, pitcher: There was a group of us that stuck around Corvallis that summer, mostly pitchers. Rather than going to play summer ball or going home, we decided to stay in Corvallis, lift, take a couple classes but really just focus on our workouts and try to make progress going into the next year. That summer was big for me in changing how I went about my business. There was a big group of us and we really had a lot of focus that summer staying there as a group. I can't say that when I was in the weight room I was thinking "oh man, we got screwed over" and that was my motivation, because that's not how it was. But something like that definitely leaves a mark moving forward and you never want to feel something like that again.

Bryce Fehmel, pitcher: We got a week or two off so we could go home real quick, and then it was right back to work in Corvallis. We were lifting four to five times a week; we took a month or two off from throwing so it was strictly lifting. And there were more than just pitchers there working out with us, I want to say about half the guys that weren't out playing summer ball were there with us lifting and trying to get ready for the next year. So right away, we all had our heads on straight and were ready to go.

FINISH

Steven Kwan, outfielder: It was definitely a very motivated summer. I ended up playing with the (Corvallis) Knights that summer, so I got to be around a lot of great people like Max Gordon, (Kevin Gunderson) and all of them. Our class knew that we had to put our heads down and start getting to work. Like whatever we had done last year, something obviously didn't click there. It went unspoken, but I think we all knew we had some work that needed to be done.

Zak Taylor, infielder: I played with the Knights that summer and that was an unbelievable experience for me. I learned a lot from Brooke Knight and that entire coaching staff, Connor Lambert was there at the time and now he's at (University of Portland). Those guys really took me under their wing and helped me grow as a leader and develop my skills, especially as a leader on the field. They helped me with those little nuances of the game that I feel are so important and really instilled confidence in me and helped build me up.

Trevor Larnach, outfielder: I think the first thing coach Casey said after (the selection show) was "remember what this feels like." That alone was like "OK, now it's time to rebuild, come back even stronger and prove a point." Because the last thing I think the teams in this country would want is for a team like Oregon State to feel like they're an underdog and have that chip on their shoulder. When it came to that offseason, everyone got to work. Everyone headed their own separate ways. KJ went on to Team USA, a few of us went to the Cape (Cod League) and we just developed and learned from it. You could tell there was a different attitude when we showed up for our sophomore year. I didn't feel like there was a real, real big team captain on that '16 team, whereas in '17 and '18 Nick (Madrigal) was hands down our team captain. Him and coach Casey did a really, really good job of setting that bar and showing what it was going to take to win and dominate at that level.

Cadyn Grenier, infielder: It was my freshman year and I wasn't entirely sure how bad it was (to miss the NCAA Tournament). I got over it pretty quick, I knew I still had at least two more years there and I was going to Cape Cod, the best summer league on the planet. So, I was super excited about that and Trevor and I were together still. We had the same host family, we were on the same team (Falmouth Commodores), so it was cool. I still got to be with Trevor, some of the other guys were playing on the Cape as well … so we were all doing our own thing. It was a good offseason and the summer season was a lot of fun. We had a lot of good times playing some good baseball.

By the time fall practice began in September, the team was ready to rock. Starting pitcher

Travis Eckert, catcher Logan Ice, shortstop Trever Morrison, seldom-used reliever John Pomeroy and utility man Caleb Hamilton were the Beavers' only draft losses. The talented 2015 class had a year of experience under its belt and several more impact freshmen were entering the program.

Pat Bailey, associate head coach: How we went about our practices and just how focused our guys were from the time we started fall ball, I mean we were on a mission. I knew we had a chance to be really, really, really good.

Christian Donahue, infielder/outfielder: We all went up and were there like a week before the fall practices started. Us as players, we went down and took batting practice on our own and we did our own workouts. I remember there was one day during that where everyone was kind of like "this year is going to be our year. I don't know if you guys feel that, but it's different this year." People kept saying that and especially at the beginning, you could feel that.

Jack Anderson, outfielder: We heard every day that we didn't deserve anything because we didn't make the tournament last year. Even if we saw glimpses of greatness, we didn't let that get to our heads. Not getting in was the main reason why we had that redemption tour feel to each day.

Jake Mulholland, pitcher: Day 1 coming out in the fall, you were watching everyone work and seeing just how talented they all were. You saw Nick, Cadyn, KJ, Trevor, all these guys working and being so good. I was just like "wow, I don't know anyone who's got guys like this all over their team."

Bryce Fehmel: We had guys at every spot. There was a competitive atmosphere because people were fighting to play. It didn't really matter who was playing because even the backups were legit.

Max Engelbrekt, pitcher: You start to fill out a diamond ... even my dad would always ask "who's going to start?" And I'd be like, "I don't know, we've got like 15 guys who are really good."

Nate Yeskie, pitching coach: When you get those guys together and you get that collection of talent, everybody responds a little bit differently. Some kids start peeking over their shoulder like "oof, I've got some competition now." And for some of the guys, I thought it brought out the best in them. I thought it really made Michael Gretler even better, and that was hard because the guy did a lot of things really, really well. But just being surrounded by someone who's going to push you and go … and some of those other guys, they didn't even care if there was more talent. They were oblivious to it, and they just knew that they needed to do their job, and that's what was going to get them on the field. It was fun watching them come together as a group of what were individuals looking to make their mark on a program, and realizing that if they did that together it would lead to the ultimate accomplishment, which is finding a way to get to the pinnacle of our sport.

Preston Jones, outfielder: Joining the Beavers in the fall of my freshman year, the thing that stuck out to me with all my teammates was just the hunger and the desire to get to Omaha after being left out of the postseason the previous year. I think the older guys made sure every single practice, scrimmage, everything, they made it all count and made sure we grew as a unit and as a family.

Andy Armstrong, infielder: I knew we had some great players. We obviously had a great middle infield, we had KJ Harrison, we just had a lot of studs on that team of course. But in the fall, I wasn't really sure how we would compare to other teams because I had never played at the Division I level, so I didn't know how good we were going to do at all. I knew we'd be good, but I didn't know how good.

Brandon Eisert, pitcher: Coming in as a late recruit I was nervous to see how things were going to go, but I was definitely excited to play for the Beavs. It was always a dream of mine. Coming in, I lived in a house with a bunch of the older guys like Luke Heimlich, Max Engelbrekt and Drew Rasmussen. They kind of helped me get used to what Oregon State baseball was going to be like.

Tyler Malone, infielder/outfielder: You learn the culture and what we were about right from the beginning. The coaches definitely made that clear, and just how the guys acted and practiced were in line with that, too.

Mitchell Verburg, pitcher: I had a little bit of a bicep thing in the fall where it was tight, so I really had time to sit down and just watch guys throw. I was watching Ras come off an injury, I was watching Luke Heimlich throw, I was watching Sam Tweedt throw, I was watching Bryce Fehmel throw, I was watching all these guys. When I look back, I was so lucky to come into a team with so many hard-working guys first off, high-character guys second off, and just some really, really talented guys. I remember guys like Nick Madrigal and Luke Heimlich were so nice to me. The way I treat freshmen, I really try to embody the way they treated me because they were so nice to me. That's what you look at with somebody who is a legacy guy, somebody who leaves a large impact on the people below them.

Christian Donahue: Nick and a few of the other guys stepped up and became our leaders, and that's when it took off.

Nick Madrigal, infielder: I remember intersquads in the fall, going against each other and seeing how competitive it was and how focused it was. That was the biggest thing that really stuck out, everyone was on a mission. There wasn't any question about what anyone was thinking about other than getting to Omaha and doing big things that year. For me, trying to be the leader on the team, it made my job really easy because there were so many leaders on that team. Gosh, there had to be five, six, seven leaders on that team, all in their own ways.

Pat Casey, head coach: When you have what we had coming back and guys were driven by the fact that they were slighted, it was the perfect storm. Now, could I predict what was going to happen over the next two years and 125 games or whatever it was? No … but I felt like we were a team that was going to be in the hunt. What we didn't know was how good (Adley) Rutschman was going to be, because he played football. We knew his talent. What we didn't know until he really got into the heat of things was the impact that he would have on our pitching staff from a defensive standpoint.

Before setting foot on Oregon State's campus, Adley Rutschman was already a known name to many sports fans in the state. Grandson of legendary Linfield College coach Ad Rutschman — the only coach to win national titles in football and baseball at any level — Adley booted an Oregon all-time record 63-yard field goal during his senior football season at Sherwood High School. He earned all-state honors in football and baseball — where he was a standout switch-hitting catcher and pitcher — and was Oregon's 2015 Gatorade Player of the Year on the diamond.

Pat Bailey: First of all, Randy (Adley's dad) coached with me at George Fox University, and the first year he coached with me was in 2004 when we won a national championship. His grandpa, Ad Rutschman, won three national championships in football at Linfield and a national championship in baseball. And his mom, Carol, she's a great lady and she's very competitive, too. So Adley grew up in a competitive environment where losing was probably not ever even talked about in their household. Maybe when Carol and Adley played each other in ping pong, Carol might've made some smart comment about beating him.

FINISH

Zak Taylor: I moved to the Sherwood area in sixth grade. Adley and I played on the same baseball team growing up, I think from seventh grade, on. Growing up I would go to the George Fox games, that's one of the few camps I actually went to, just because I knew Randy Rutschman was there and still, even back then, he was the catching guru. He was the guy you wanted to see.

Adley Rutschman, catcher: Basically, I wasn't getting recruited at all by anyone up until I went to the Oregon State prospect camp and Baseball Northwest my sophomore summer going into junior year. I went down to the prospect camp and got on the mound and was throwing like 92, 93, and they basically offered me there. Then I went to the Baseball Northwest event, and that's when I started to get on the map for pitching. Then my senior year of high school, I was playing a lot of catcher and they asked me if I wanted to be a two-way guy in college. That's how it went for me as far as the recruiting process for Oregon State.

Pat Bailey: When Randy started coaching with me, Adley was I believe 5 years old. He'd come to our camps. My wife, Susan, and I got to know Randy and Carol really well because we both have very similar philosophies on life, both families are committed Christians. And then when I started recruiting Adley, that just made it really easy.

I'm going to say about six months after we offered Adley a scholarship, I called him up and said "hey Adley, go grab your mom, dad and Josie (Adley's sister) and put me on speakerphone." So, he went and got them, put me on speakerphone and I said "hey Randy and Carol, we're good friends. I know ... " because Carol, she wanted Adley to go to a Christian school. And I said, "Carol, I promise you I'm going to take care of your son. I've known him for a long time and I'm a committed Christian, so I'm going to take care of him from a spiritual viewpoint as well and make sure he's taken care of." So, then I said "here's the deal, you guys have a week to make a decision because we've been working on this for a while." And Adley was starting to become a national recruit by that point. So, I said "here's the deal, either Adley commits to us within a week, or I'm coming up and burning your house down!" I was joking because I'm really good friends with them and Randy started laughing, and I go "hey Randy, I'm not joking." I think Adley called me the next night and committed to us.

Adley Rutschman: I've always been a big Beaver fan growing up and that was my dream school. I did look at other schools, but I was always pretty set on Oregon State.

Rutschman played in 10 games for the Corvallis Knights in the summer of 2016 and was invited by then–head coach Gary Andersen to try out for the Oregon State football team. He went on to become the team's kickoff specialist, tallying 20 touchbacks with a pair of successful onside kicks. Most notably, Rutschman tackled Stanford star and eventual NFL All-Pro Christian McCaffrey in the open field on a kick return.

Playing football left the 6-foot-2 Rutschman with little time to practice baseball in the fall. His talents on the diamond were still apparent to everyone.

Brooke Knight, Corvallis Knights manager: He had a little wrist deal early on with us and it was prudent for him to just rest it. I'd known Adley since he was young, Ad was my football coach at Linfield for a year before I came to Oregon State. So Adley, the vintage he comes from is unbelievable with Ad and Randy. Just tremendous attitude, amazing makeup, great human being, so all of that was there. The arm really worked. He had pitched in high school and ran it up there pretty good, but it was kind of like "is that where he's best suited?" And that was a decision for him and Randy and Pat Casey to make. Obviously, he can do a number of things, he was just a really good player.

Adley Rutschman: When we were in Arizona (for opening weekend of the 2017 college season), I remember I caught the first three games and then I had a bullpen scheduled the next day. The coaches just said, "this is not going to work out," basically. Just catching that much, with that many throws as a catcher and strain on the arm, it wouldn't be smart to be a pitcher. And I was very OK with that. Obviously, I want to hit. It would've been cool to close or throw a couple innings in relief, but it just didn't work out.

Brooke Knight: His first game for us was up in Bellingham. He was catching and his flexibility has always been really, really advanced. We played a night game, and the guy who was throwing for us (Ryley Widell), it was firm and it was erratic. Adley had clanked a couple balls, which I already knew was not his style. He had one get by him, clanked a couple balls and I knew he had to be nervous as heck. I remember (pitching coach Connor Lambert) going "gosh, I know he's a damn good player but come on." And I said, "first off, our guy is all over the map and he's going to be fine." And the lighting was just OK, I think they've improved it since then, and Lambo goes "all right, all right, all right." Adley came out after the inning and he was a little frustrated with himself for a bit and I said, "hey, you're going to be OK." So, he runs back out there, he's doing better and he settles in. I look at Lambo and I said, "hey, I think he's got a chance to go one-one in a few years." And he goes "what? You've lost your mind. I'd give him first round, but one-one?" And I said "you don't see guys that are that flexible. You don't see guys that can hit like that from both sides." That night, and I think it's an accurate time, I had him at a 1.87 (seconds) twice (the

2019 Major League average pop time — the time it takes a catcher to catch a pitch and complete a throw to second base — was 2.01 seconds). One was a pre-inning throw-down, and the other was a game throw, and it was on the money. The release is just ridiculous and it's still coming out pretty hot. As soon as I saw that I go, "this is really, really good."

Cadyn Grenier: It doesn't take too much to see that Adley is a special athlete, for sure. The fact that he was able to walk on and become the starting kicker for the football team, you're just like "oh, this dude's a freak athlete." But I really didn't get to see him a ton his freshman fall because he was at practice for football a lot. So I didn't immediately see like "oh, this dude is unbelievable." It was more like, "yeah, this kid's good," but I hadn't seen enough of him to know he was really legit.

Bryce Fehmel: It was unbelievable to watch him transfer over from football immediately into baseball and compete right away. He's a gifted athlete and for him to step in as a freshman catcher from football and handle the staff the way he did was very impressive.

Nate Yeskie: The guy is a winner, man. You could just see it; you could feel it. We knew what kind of worker he was; we knew what kind of family he came from. The way a man looks you in the eye when he's a 17, 18-year-old freshman, he's looking you in the eye like he's a 28-year-old man. He handled things differently and then just seeing the things he did in practice … Jake Thompson was 95 to 98 miles per hour on scout day (Rutschman's) freshman year. Adley comes over from football and practices with us maybe once a week, twice a week. On scout day, Thompson's up to 98, with an 87, 88 mile per hour slider, and Rutschman is putting together at-bats where it looks like two big leaguers going at it. Adley singles off him and it's like, "what can't this kid do?" He had some of those special qualities that the special ones have. You see those things and you know it's only a matter of time.

Jake Thompson, pitcher: I remember coach Yeskie talking about Adley before he was even there, saying "this dude's going to be a first-round pick." And when you have someone say that, you kind of think "oh yeah?, well I'm going to go strike him out in the fall!" I remember specifically I faced him during the fall, and I was commanding my curveball real well that day and things were going good. I was throwing hard. He gets up to the plate and I was like, "all right, I'm going to flip in this nice, hard curveball." I'm not saying my curveball is great, but it's first pitch and when people see spin, they take it. Nope. He decided to swing first pitch on this good curveball and he smacks it to right field like it's no problem. Afterward I asked him "dude, how'd you know a curveball is coming? Did I tip something, did someone tell you something?" And he was like "no, I just sat back, saw it come down and had a normal swing." And I was like, "oh my God, are you kidding me?"

Nick Madrigal: I'd heard about how much hype there was to him coming out of high school and playing two sports, seeing him on the football field and seeing how big of a kid he was. When he was coming out for fall ball here and there, and playing in some intersquads, you could see little glimpses of his power and his arm and some of the tools, but it just seemed like he wasn't in sync yet. I thought there was a chance he could be pretty good, but I wasn't sure how good he was going to be. Everyone got real close to him. He was a cool guy to be around so that wasn't an issue at all, even if he was only at practice a couple days a week. But honestly, the first time I saw him … you could see how great of a player he could be, but like I said he just wasn't polished yet. He would swing outside the zone, swing at anything. He had big power, he had the swing, but it wasn't as fine-tuned yet.

Andy Peterson, undergraduate assistant coach: He'd come out to practice a couple times a week. He'd usually come out, take some BP, he'd hit in a couple of the scrimmages and one of the days he struck out twice or something like that, I want to say they were both looking. I remember coach Casey was talking about how well he takes, and how he was in such a good position when he takes. We were all thinking, "well, he needs to swing the bat!" And I remember that day Case said, "that's the best player in the country right there." He said that and a couple of us were right there looking at him like "uh-huh, that's crazy." But the year before, he'd said that about Nick Madrigal, too. We were at a practice and obviously Nick's hands and defensively, he's unbelievable. But I remember Nick was taking BP, he hit a couple dinker line-drives off the L-screen over and over and over and Case goes "that's the best player in the country." And all of us, it was the same thing, like "all right, Case." Lo and behold, those guys end up being two of the best baseball players I ever got to watch. I think it's pretty funny how Case just knows some stuff we don't.

Trevor Larnach: Adley was playing football while our team was working out. We had no idea who this kid was because he was a freshman and a dual-sport athlete, so we were waiting to see what he was all about. Us not really knowing who Adley was and how he is as a person, we didn't know what to expect. So, when he first got there, we didn't realize he was Adley, and how he is as a person is a little different than most people think. He's a little spacey sometimes, and it's not a bad thing at all. But when we're first meeting someone who's going to be our starting catcher and we don't even know who he is, we're kind of like "who's this guy?" We obviously knew he's this huge prospect out of high school, and we got rubbed the wrong way a little bit. It wasn't like a thing to where we'd make a big deal out of it, but we were like "who is this kid?!" He's coming from football practice, getting two or three hits in scrimmages. Then he goes back, we never see him again, he barely talks to us. So, we were just like "all right, this is going to be an issue," and it ended up not being an issue because he's a great person with a great family. When he got to the end of football season, he started working out with us more and we became closer and closer. But you could tell he was special, that's for damn sure. And that's how he carried himself. That type of person really goes a long way, obviously, and it comes back to how his family raised him and that's why everybody loves them because they're just great people.

KJ Harrison, first baseman: Ever since the first time I met him and saw him play, it was obvious he was a freak athlete. But Adley is such a great guy, he's such a hard-working kid and he's so humble. It was really cool being able to play with him and see his development.

Drew Rasmussen, pitcher: The talent was off the charts and he could hit from both sides of the plate. But most people don't get to know him as a person, they just read about him. Especially as a freshman, he was kind of a puppy dog. Fun-loving all the time, always happy, always in a great mood, always in high spirits, always positive. The confidence he had gives confidence to a pitching staff when he's behind the plate. The kid was incredible as an 18-year-old and you only knew he was going to grow from there, but who he is as a person is better than what he is as a baseball player, which is incredible.

Jake Thompson: He is seriously probably the nicest person I've ever met in my life. And then to have that guy as a catcher, who can make any pitch look good … that guy stole a lot of strikes for us made us look a lot better than we probably were. He is by far the best guy I've ever thrown to just because you know he's going to throw guys out. You know he's going to make every pitch look good. You can spike five in a row or throw it to the backstop and he'll come out and be all nice about it and say, "hey, just relax. I've got you, let's do this," everything like that.

Max Engelbrekt: He was amazing. I remember he wasn't there very much. I felt extremely old on that team, so me relating to freshmen … I mean I was 23, I was in grad school, so I had a bit of a different relationship with the freshmen and honestly the sophomores and juniors. So, I wasn't like hanging out with those guys all the time, we were just different ages, but I remember I was really impressed with him. An extremely nice guy, really hard-working, he's built, has the perfect body for baseball. It's just one of those guys where he shows up and it's like "well, this is clearly going to work."

Pat Casey: From Day 1, that guy handled the pitching staff like nobody else, and we've had some great catchers. He was different.

As a catcher, Rutschman was the complete package. He entered the program with a cannon of an arm, and elite flexibility that helped him block balls in the dirt. Rutschman was also adept at pitch framing, stealing countless strikes for Oregon State's pitchers. After every inning-ending out, he would jog out to meet the pitcher and say a few words of encouragement as they headed to the dugout.

Adley Rutschman: A lot of the receiving at the high level, a lot of that came when I got to Oregon State. The staff there really did a good job of breaking down what I did from a receiving standpoint and taking my natural technique that I had catching-wise. They were able to formulate a better receiving method based on how I already received, which was very cool to see that process unfold over basically the sixth months I was there from September to the start of that first season. Just simplifying the movement, trying to adjust from catching guys in high school who were 80 to guys who throw 95, you have to make adjustments. They did a really good job as far as receiving goes. Obviously, I had a really good base with my dad coaching me growing up, and my dad always stressed the importance of the presence on the field when you're a catcher, the leadership aspect and verbal communication, keeping guys engaged, that kind of stuff.

Nate Yeskie: It was funny, at one point he was running over like he typically does and puts his arm around the guy coming off the mound. I look at him and said, "hey, maybe let that guy breathe a little bit. Let him get in the dugout and get a drink of water or Gatorade and let him calm down before you come talk to him." He says "OK, I'll do that," and the next inning he runs right back over with his arm around the guy. We were almost just like "Adley, there's a time to push and a time to pull" and we kind of thought, me in particular, "hey, let that guy breathe! Because he might handle things a little bit different, and he might not want you there right now, catch him back in the dugout." But it's just funny, he stayed true to who he was and kept doing things that I think were innately built in him.

Adley Rutschman: I think it was one of those things that started in high school, and it just carried over into college. I remember watching a video, and I think I saw my dad do it on video. He had some old tapes that we'd watch. I don't know what it is, it's one of those instinctual things after innings, you're excited to get out of the inning, excited for what your pitcher just did or excited basically about an event that happened that inning, anything that relates to that, or maybe something they can work on. Whatever it is, it's kind of that affirmation from me that "hey, we got through it, let's go get 'em the next inning" type of deal. I think it started in high school and carried over, and I remember one of the coaches coming up to me in the fall when I was catching and saying "you know you don't have to greet your pitcher every single time after the inning." And I was like "oh, OK." But it was just one of those instinctual things that carried over.

Nate Yeskie: I think his dad, his grandfather and his mother had a lot of influence on him and taught him the right way for so many things, that I think it was just ingrained in him to want to be right there, right beside the guy he's trying to help. So, if he's 60 feet, six inches away being expected to help that guy get the most out of himself, when he got a chance to put his arm around him, he was going to do that. Now, I'm telling you, when you watch baseball at all levels, you'll see it a lot where catchers are coming up to that guy coming off the mound pretty frequently, and I think a lot of it has to do with Adley's influence. I had a coach just the other day tell me that. It's interesting to see the influence of why guys do certain things. Well, everybody wants to be like the best. Just like *The Last Dance* with Michael Jordan, how many kids started hanging in the air and wearing a knee brace on one leg when they were younger, wearing Jordan shoes? They still wear them to this day. The kid was just special in so many ways. Strong, a worker, great in the classroom. He checked off all the boxes you hoped he would, there was never any baggage with him and you knew that when he came to the park, he was coming to work.

Brandon Eisert: I played with Adley a few times in high school, didn't know him super well. But coming in, he was just a normal piece to the puzzle. As a freshman he was confident, even at times when he was struggling at the plate he put the extra work in behind the plate. His defensive skills as a catcher were phenomenal even as a freshman, and being able to pitch to him and go through each game with him was just a lot of fun.

Adley Rutschman, to Baseball America in 2018: They needed someone to lead behind the dish and be a wall back there and command the field. Case told me the hitting will come, but you need to be able to handle the staff.

Pat Casey: He didn't set the world on fire offensively (as a freshman). I think I put him in the four-hole in Game 1. I wanted Adley Rutschman to know that coach Casey says "you're going to be a superstar. And you may not hit in the four-hole tomorrow and you may not hit there in Game 5, but you're hitting there today because I want you to know that you're going to be a superstar," because that's the way I felt about it.

Dating back to the 1990s, Pat Casey's best Oregon State teams always featured dominant pitching. The trend continued under the tutelage of Nate Yeskie, who came aboard in 2009 as the Beavers' third pitching coach in three seasons.

An all-Big West pitcher at UNLV, Yeskie struck out a single-season school-record 147 in 1995 and was drafted in the ninth round by the Minnesota Twins the following year. Yeskie played six seasons of pro ball and began his coaching career in 2005 at UNLV. He was let go after the 2007 season, and spent a year out of baseball before landing at OSU, where he inherited a strong pitching staff that included future MLBers Sam Gaviglio and Josh Osich. The Beavers found immediate success under Yeskie, finishing the 2009 season with the eighth-best team earned run average nationally at 3.93. After solid seasons in 2010-12, the staff ascended to new heights in 2013. That year they had the country's second-lowest ERA (2.28, a school record) en route to a College World Series appearance.

Yeskie changed things up a bit that offseason, implementing pieces of a new throwing program: Driveline. Based in Seattle, Driveline was the first data-driven baseball training facility in the world. Its programs have since become widespread across baseball at all levels, but Driveline was still an unknown to many when Yeskie brought it to the Beavers. Much like 2009, the results were expeditious. OSU finished with an ERA of 2.29, as the starting rotation of Ben Wetzler (12-1, 0.78 ERA), Jace Fry (11-2, 1.80) and Andrew Moore (6-5, 2.77) gobbled up 60% of the team's innings. In a conference known for high-end arms and defense, OSU had become the standard-bearer for Pac-12 pitching.

The Beavers continued to pitch well in 2015 and 2016 despite key injuries, and entered the 2017 season with the program's deepest group of hurlers since 2009. Settling on three starters for the weekend rotation was going to be a challenge, but Luke Heimlich locked down one of the spots with his performance in preseason camp. Heimlich graduated a year early from Puyallup High School — he was Washington's Gatorade Player of the year as a junior — to join the Beavers for the 2015 college season. Used primarily in relief as a freshman, Heimlich made 11 starts the following year and went 7-4 overall with a 3.53 ERA. He was an effective Pac-12 pitcher, but the left-hander wanted much more as a junior.

Luke Heimlich: The last week of the (2016) season we played UCLA at home. We went 27 innings with them and our pitching staff didn't give up a run, so we felt really good that weekend. I started the Sunday game and that was my first complete game, my first shutout, basically my first start where I felt like a legitimate pitcher. Having that to finish the year, having any sort of success helps motivate you and show you what the possibilities are, how you can improve moving forward. Going into that offseason, I met with Yeskie right before summer started to talk about what we wanted to focus on, what are my weaknesses, what are my strengths. I sat down in the room with him and said, "I want to throw harder." So, going into that offseason, I was very one-track minded. I threw 88 (miles per hour) and maybe touched a 90 on a good day my freshman and sophomore years. For me, throwing harder didn't just mean I needed to throw harder in-game, it was more of an all-encompassing mindset. I fixed my diet; I fixed my mentality in the weight room. I had that focus of 95, that was the number I wanted. And all offseason, that's what I was focused on. I was still trying to develop a changeup and a slider, but I knew if I threw harder those pitches would come with it. So that was really my one thing: throw harder. Keep it simple.

Nate Yeskie: Heimlich was just OK his first two years and going into '17 is when he made his big jump. With him, we felt like it was always there. He was a kid that graduated high school a year early, so he gets into the college ranks and he's doing his deal, figuring out how to get guys out. He would drop down and I'd tell him guys who do that, they do that because their other stuff maybe isn't good enough and they've got to find some ways to be creative and maybe even try and trick somebody. And at some point by the end of his sophomore year I said "something's going to have to change here. Otherwise, you're staring down the gun barrel of playing this game a couple more years, and that might be it." He took that to heart. It's funny, his junior year we were having a discussion and he was throwing the ball really well. I said, "what would you today say to you as a freshman?" He said, "that's funny, we were just talking about that at our house with my roommates the last couple of days." And then he said, "I would really shift my efforts and focus onto doing things in the classroom, the weight room, my nutrition, my sleep," whatever it may be, and he explained how he would go about those things. So, I said, "well, is that where you're at now? Because it's kind of what it sounds like, but I want you to explain that more to me." And you could just see it. He knew what he needed to do, he held himself to a higher standard and really what that meant. It wasn't just "do we have weights in the morning?," but it's how you go in and lift weights, lifting weights with a purpose. It's about how you play catch. Are you playing catch to get loose or are you playing catch with a purpose? His focus just changed.

Andrew Moore's influence on helping Heimlich and Rasmussen and those guys get better, they'll tell you that he had as much to do with their development phase as anybody in terms of how to look at things from the top of that mound out there. I remember telling Andrew (in 2015) "I know this is unfair of me to ask, but it's something I'm going to ask you to do anyway." He said, "what are we talking about here?" And I said, "we've got to get to a point where you're starting to lead some of these guys and show these guys what to do." Andrew had done it at a high level for so many years and it was really a lot to ask from him, but the reason we asked is because we knew he could do it. He helped Luke along. Ras pushed him, too. If you watch Ras in the weight room, you better not get too close or you might get picked up and thrown around that place. I think Luke saw how guys were starting to advance their game and he just made a conscious decision that "I've got to do some things in a different fashion for how I get myself better." And by doing so, we saw the end results.

Drew Rasmussen: First off, I think physically he just matured a little bit more. But on top of that, people don't see … everyone that understands college baseball just assumes pitchers go out and play summer ball, and that wasn't the case for us. Coach Yeskie wanted to keep pitchers on campus, he wanted guys to lift, to become more mobile, eat right, sleep right and basically just prepare for fall and the following season, especially if your workload the prior spring had been pretty significant, because it gives your arm a chance to rest and you can strengthen the rest of your body. The dedication he had the summer going into 2017 was incredible. The guy crushed it in the weight room, he ate right, he slept right, he did everything he possibly could to make sure 2017 was going to be his best year. And I think by the time spring had come, he had been in enough big moments in 2015 and 2016 that the moment was never going to be too big. And then on top of it he'd put in the hours, put in the time. The man earned everything.

Bryce Fehmel: Luke's one of the hardest workers I've ever been around. He just put his head down, went to work and knew what he wanted to do on every given day. It was pretty impressive to watch from that aspect of it. He did his job day in and day out, and I definitely learned a lot from him.

Heimlich's fastball touched 94 miles per hour on opening day in Surprise, Arizona, as Oregon State eked out a 1-0 victory over Indiana. Heimlich struck out a career-high 11 in 5 2/3 innings and was named Pac-12 pitcher of the week. It was clear the Beavers had a true ace atop their rotation.

Heimlich went on to make 16 starts in 2017, going 11-1 while leading the nation with a school-record ERA of 0.76, surpassing Wetzler's 2014 mark. He was the Pac-12 pitcher of the year, a Golden Spikes Award semifinalist and a first-team All-American.

Luke Heimlich: When I look at those numbers, I just thank God I had Nick and Cadyn playing behind me and Kwan out in center field. I was confident in my defense,

I was confident in what I was throwing, I didn't have any worries. Our offense was good, so I didn't feel like I had to throw a shutout. If I gave up a run or two, I knew it wasn't going to be the end of the world. I'm glad obviously that didn't happen much, but it wasn't going to come down to if I gave up a hit, we might lose. I trusted our offense, I trusted our defense, and I was able to go out there and have fun every week.

Michael Gretler, infielder: The guy was the best pitcher in the country. It's pretty fun to be able to play defense behind him and watch how special he was that year. He's on the long list of guys that Yeskie did an incredible job with.

Joe Casey, outfielder: Every time he took the mound, it was like he was never going to give up a run. I swear he went seven, eight or nine innings like every game that year. There were times in the dugout where we'd be like "all right, Luke's pitching, let's go hang out and get a snack. We'll be back, and I'm sure we'll be hitting in no time." That was something special, that was probably the best pitching season I've ever witnessed at Oregon State. Facing him in practice wasn't fun either, that's for sure.

Bryce Fehmel: I had the best view in the house sitting next to Yeskie every Friday night. A couple of times, we made comments about how it was just like a video game for him. He could throw whatever he wanted to whatever spot he wanted to. It was almost too easy for him to go out there and do what he did.

Pat Casey: His numbers were video-game numbers. It was crazy for a starter. You can see that with a reliever because they come in and maybe see a guy once, you only pitch once or twice on a weekend. But for a starter to go seven, eight, nine innings and have those kinds of numbers, it was unbelievable. His secondary stuff just got so much better. He was more than a fastball guy. He could locate his breaking ball. His competitiveness had always been off the charts, he always had deception.

Brandon Eisert: It was just incredible, all the situations that he got himself out of when he was in a tough spot by making pitches and having that confidence. I mean the whole team was confident that we were going to pull out the win each and every time he was on the mound. It was just remarkable what he was able to do and how he improved from that previous season. The confidence that he had was fun to watch, and I definitely learned a lot from him.

Jake Mulholland: He is such a good guy, such a great leader on the team. I think he saw a lot of himself in me early on. He was a freshman who came in and pitched, contributed a lot early on. He talked to me all the time about the mental side of the game, telling me I was here for a reason. He was big into trying to pour himself out into the younger guys and give them confidence, letting them know they should be here, you shouldn't be doubting yourself, you should have all the confidence in the world. We all trust you to go out and do great, so you should, too.

Heimlich wasn't the only veteran pitcher to have a breakout year under Yeskie. Jake Thompson, a hard-throwing junior righty from Florence, Oregon, regularly struggled with consistency and confidence prior to the 2017 season. By focusing on the mental side of baseball, Thompson blossomed into one of the country's top starters.

Jake Thompson: My freshman year at Oregon State I had an OK year, and the next year I got hurt. Then I just had an off year (in 2016) and it was like I could either keep doing what I was doing, which apparently was not working well for me, or I could change something. But what did I have to change? We always had a mental skills coach, Greg Warburton, who would come in and talk and invite us to come talk to him however often we wanted. I had always ignored that; I didn't want to be the guy to go work on the mental game or anything like that. And that's something a lot of guys ignore. Obviously you have guys like Madrigal who are born that way, but a lot of us aren't and we fail to accept that. It's not a sign of weakness, but it's more about "hey, the mental game is huge in the sport of baseball, why are we not training that more?" So, I worked with Greg Warburton, I worked with (renowned baseball trainer) Alan Jaeger, and (Oregon State director of player development) Tyler Graham was that third guy who put it all together for me. He added pieces here and there from his playing career, and he kind of said the same thing about how he wished he had picked up on this earlier. Just by talking to them, getting a piece of their minds, I felt more at peace going into the 2017 season, and I think that was a huge factor for me. Because I went in, I made those changes … and obviously during the offseason and the fall, our weight coach (Chris) Anderson did a phenomenal job at getting us ready, so I knew physically I'd be ready. Coach Yeskie had our arms ready and now I had my mentality ready. I'd say I caught up to a lot of guys on that team, the Madrigals, the Larnachs, the Greniers, KJ Harrison, I caught up to them. I wouldn't say competition felt easier, but I just felt more at peace while competing, and that built on through the year.

Nate Yeskie: Who ever knows specifically what it is for guys. I think he finally made it up in his mind that he was ready to go compete, it was now his time. He'd gone through some ups and downs and some things he was trying to work at, and it all just started to come together. He got out of the gates pretty good and it picked up some steam, picked up some more steam and things started to roll for him. By the end of it,

FINISH

he was going pretty well and he had a good time. And that's the thing about baseball and for a lot of kids in sports, they just develop at different times. I think we want them all to be world-beaters as fast as possible, but you've got to exercise patience because these kids, from a mental and emotional standpoint, they are dealing with things sometimes that we just discount as adults because we deal with it every day not realizing they are things they're trying to deal with while trying to accomplish their goals as well. Jake wanted to go on and continue and play professionally and he wanted to help the team in his time there. He didn't feel like he was holding up his end of the bargain and he was putting pressure on himself at times. Once he started to go out there and just play and do some of the other things that he was capable of doing, it was pretty good.

Max Engelbrekt: I think we were expecting him to be a reliever because he kept pitching in short bursts in the fall. I remember him pitching to KJ on pro day and he touched like 98 or 99. He was just great, and another guy that kept getting into better shape. I actually lived with Jake for three straight years, so seeing him grow up and seeing him develop into an All-American, it was amazing. Seeing his stuff continue to improve and his confidence ... he was always kind of a reserved and shy guy, so he was another guy who just continued to get more and more confident. He even got more confident when we were just doing normal stuff around the house.

Nate Yeskie: He lived with Max, and I would ask him "hey, how much baseball do you guys talk?" And he'd go, "nah, we don't really talk. We just kind of watch TV." And I'm like "the two of you are living together and you guys don't talk?!" And he says, "no, he lives upstairs and I live down. When I see him I see him, I see him at weights." I just chuckle about those dynamics. It was fun to watch Jake do some things I thought were better for him, and as much as he learned from me or the other coaches and things like that, we learned from the players. They help provide some guidance for how we can help them get better, and I think as he matured he was able to give us more clarity on some of the things he was trying to accomplish and how he was looking at them and processing those things to shrink that curve at the time.

Thompson came out of the bullpen to face one batter in the season opener and started the fourth game of opening weekend. He struck out eight in 5 1/3 innings and never left the rotation, typically throwing the final game of Pac-12 series after Heimlich and Bryce Fehmel. Thompson embraced the role of "Sunday starter," going 14-1 overall with a 1.96 ERA en route to first-team All-America honors.

Jake Thompson: Usually you see teams who have their dude on Friday, a dude who throws Saturday and then Sunday is a tossup. Going into that year I thought I was going to be a reliever, and we needed four starters down in Arizona so I was that fourth starter. I remember I came out and I walked the first guy on a full count, a lot of close pitches. The second guy got a bloop hit, and I remember Casey sprinting out to me and basically telling me to figure it out, calm down. The message was "hey, your leash is short." I remember striking out the next three guys and it took off from there.

Max Engelbrekt: At a program like Oregon State, this would be the same at any high-quality program for a long stretch of time, I don't think the talent level between those who play and those that don't is that high. You could probably make comps to this at a big football school. If you start out poorly, you still might be one of the better guys on the team. But if you start off with two bad outings and another guy starts off with two good outings, you might not be pitching for a long time, even if you're skilled. With Jake, his first outing … he's probably too talented to have gotten buried, but he's a couple balls from getting pulled there and you're in the doghouse. To have those two divergent paths where he ended up striking the next guys out, he threw extremely hard that day, and then he had the season that he has.

Those first couple weeks, there's so much nervous energy because you haven't played yet. Nobody wants to start off the year with an 18 ERA. If you give up a couple runs in your first couple outings it might take you a month to feel OK about yourself. So yeah, I was really, really happy for him because he did it. He proved he could pitch at the highest level in college baseball.

Jake Thompson: After it was kind of settled that I could really do this and be the Sunday guy, I made a promise that I was going to go out on Sundays, throw strikes, do what I need to do for the team and anchor that. The biggest thing for me once I found out I was going to be the third starter was that I didn't want to be that guy who goes out on Sunday, walks a bunch of people and we have a bullpen day. And it just went from there.

Pat Casey: (Thompson's) a guy that would probably tell you himself that for three or four years "I wasn't mentally the guy that was tough enough to get out of myself what I should've." And whatever turned and changed that summer, he grew up, man. And that stuff that year was unbelievable. But the demeanor, the makeup, the guy he became was phenomenal. Part of that had to do with his own desire to find himself, part of that had to do with confidence I think other guys on the staff gave him, and part of that came from the guy receiving it, Rutschman. You can throw the ball anywhere you want if you're a pitcher and Rutschman is catching. You'd have to throw the damn thing over the backstop, he'd kill himself to try and stop it. Here again, it goes back to what our players do for one another that make them the players they are.

Luke Heimlich: I think for everyone that season … we knew we were good and it was a process of getting to that point. The year before, we still had the same thought that we were a really good team, it just hadn't come to fruition yet. You've got to go through struggles to get to where you want to go, and on that team the results started showing for the work we had done. Jake was just tremendous that year, I think in Pac-12 play he might've had a lower ERA than me (Thompson did, 0.88 to 1.08). He was amazing all year and once you get a couple good games under your belt, you're not overthinking, you're not nervous. You trust your stuff, you trust your approach, you trust the guys behind you and it's easy from there.

Jake Thompson: With me and Heimlich, it was almost like a competition that we had between each other. He'd throw a shutout; I'd go out there and try to challenge him with another shutout. And even Fehmel, I know that he had a little bit of a struggle at times that year, but he had some great and very important pitching performances as well. The three of us on the weekends always seemed to want to compete with each other, see who could have the better performance, and the bullpen would follow. I felt like the friendly competition between Heimlich, Fehmel and myself, we didn't want to be the one that got that loss. Heimlich would go out, pitch excellent and shut them out. Then Fehmel would go out and do his thing, work his way through seven innings super quick, throwing strikes and everything, and he'd come out with the win. Then it was me on Sunday, and I couldn't be the one doesn't get a win.

Pat Casey: When you take (Heimlich's) numbers and Jake's numbers and combine them (25-2, 1.38 ERA), those are just numbers that you never see from two starters. With the aluminum bat and playing in a league like ours, those are statistics that you may never see again.

The Beavers' pitching prowess extended far beyond Heimlich, Thompson and Fehmel. Drew Rasmussen, the team's ace in 2016 before requiring Tommy John surgery, was on the mend and figuring to join the team by the middle of the season. Max Engelbrekt, a fifth-year senior who earned Pac-12 baseball scholar-athlete of the year honors, was a proven option at the back end of the bullpen while freshmen left-handers Jake Mulholland and Brandon Eisert — a pair of under-the-radar Pacific Northwest recruits — went on to become the team's most-used relievers. Mulholland, from Snohomish, Washington, impressed the coaching staff early with his willingness to ask questions and learn. Eisert, an Aloha High School graduate with an unusual delivery that hid the ball from batters, was headed to the Northwest Athletic Conference before Oregon State came calling with a late offer.

Jake Mulholland: Going into high school, you don't have the kind of coaching that you're going to have (at Oregon State), obviously. I had good coaches in high school, people who really helped me out, but at a higher level I wanted to really heighten my sense of awareness. I wanted to be able to figure out what I should be doing with runners on versus not runners on, how to approach hitters, scouting reports, some things you don't really learn as much about in high school. I wanted to be able to read a swing and know what to throw off of that, not be robotic. I wanted to have an understanding of how we were going to approach certain things. I always wanted to make sure my mechanics were OK, I didn't really have a ton of help with that in high school, so having Yeskie there to help me out was great. I basically just wanted to learn as much as I possibly could and see what I could absorb and take into my own experiences and how I could adjust it on my own after that. So, my first year, I was trying to absorb as much information as possible so I could use it for myself in the future.

Nate Yeskie: I think a lot of freshmen have these moments when they throw the ball 85, 87, 90, whatever it is, and all of a sudden somebody else goes out there and takes the mound and it's 95 miles per hour. Then they start having this aha moment where it's like "boy, I've got to find a way to get myself on the field." Not that they all go through that, but a majority of freshmen do. They're just trying to find out how they can play, so the types of questions that Jake and other freshmen would have with regards to "how do I get better?" were all in direct correlation to "what can I do to get on the field?" So, you have their attention when they're coming in and sometimes it's by nothing more than the players that you have dictating the temperature of the environment, the level of intensity and some of those things.

For Jake, he threw a lot of strikes. He threw a lot of quality strikes. I think there was an advantage for him at the time because nobody had seen him before, he was an unknown to our league. When you haven't seen a guy, you can look at a scouting report and take all the notes you want and you can watch all the film you want, but it's just different when you see it. I can remember going up to Yakima when he was playing summer ball before we committed him and he threw a game and I think he was 81 miles an hour, maybe 84 on the high end, and he threw seven innings and chopped up a decent team he was facing. We just thought that if this kid could get stronger and get himself going a little bit, there were enough pieces in there that he'd have success.

What was funny about his freshman year was he was untouched all fall, untouched all spring. I mean he didn't give up a run, and it was just like clockwork watching him work. And then his last outing before the season started in '17, he got his brains rearranged. He got absolutely smoked in a scrimmage, and we're sitting there going "well, this is interesting." Because, believe it or not, you want them all to fail at some point so you see how they respond to that failure and be able to understand that everything is going to be OK, and then they can move along. Well for him, he hadn't failed up until that point and now we're done with the scrimmages and ready to start Game 1 of the season, so you're wondering how he was going to handle this now that he's had a taste of failure. We were going to find that out in games that counted, and he obviously did a great job. We used him in some spots that I think really benefitted him and benefitted the team.

Jake Mulholland: I remember in Arizona I was the first freshman to come out. I was so nervous warming up, but the batter gets in the box and it all goes away. It's kind of crazy. From then on, there's no looking back. It's only the present, that's the only thing that matters, and when you have that perspective I think it can help you regardless of the situation you're in. If you can focus on making a pitch, doing what you can right now, it can kind of help get rid of being a freshman or not playing or having expectations or worries.

Nate Yeskie: How they make their way to campus is funny with regards to each one. Brandon Eisert was a guy that wasn't recruited by a whole lot of people, and the ones he was recruited by obviously weren't really excited about maybe what they thought he could become or could offer at that particular time. There was a scout in the area that kept saying "hey man, he just misses bats. There are some things about him." I saw him twice and he was OK, the third time I left the radar gun at home and went and watched him. He lost 2-1, but he struck out 15, and at that point I just said to myself that he's done this three times now, I've got to trust this guy who's been around the game longer than I have that is providing some perspective and insight. That was I believe in late July or early August, and Brandon was getting ready to head to (Linn-Benton) if I'm not mistaken. The timing of him coming in, he was the last person in from that particular class.

Brandon Eisert: I mean I've always been confident in my abilities, but coming in as a freshman, you don't know what to expect, there were a lot of returning guys. You just try to do your best and help the team out any way that you could, and fortunately for me I was being able to pitch quite a bit as a freshman and I'm very thankful for that opportunity.

Nate Yeskie: Eisert threw in a midweek against Portland and kids were in the dugout just bewildered because we brought him into the game and he gives up a double on his first pitch. He throws a first-pitch slider to a guy who hooks the ball into the corner at Portland, and then (two batters later) he throws a fastball, a slider, a couple more fastballs and walks the guy. So back to the mound, I go, "Brandon, we're going to have to do this a little different, or else I'm going to have to go get somebody else out of that bullpen and I don't think that's what you, me or anyone else wants us to do. So, can we change that?" And Brandon, he's a man of so few words, he says "OK." Just OK, like I asked him if he wanted to go eat lunch and get a sandwich. His heartbeat never got going in a bad way. He then proceeds to throw (47) straight fastballs, strikes out (eight) in a row and the last guy he's got (3-2) and he hits a (fly ball to center). We record the out, our dugout is going nuts and everyone's giving him a hard time when he comes back in saying "how could you not strike that guy out?!" Brandon's probably oblivious at the moment being like "what do you mean, I got him out?" And it was just fastballs, one after another after another.

Max Engelbrekt: I'd be interested to see him throw on a Rapsodo or see some of his pitch data. He was very deceptive. I mean he had good stuff; he maybe gets short-changed for how hard he threw. He did kind of only throw a fastball, but he was just unhittable. His strikeout numbers were great.

We actually lived in like a 10-person house and I lived on the same floor as Eisert, who was 18. So, me and Eisert would actually drive to campus on most days. He was always really quiet, but I really liked Eisert so we had a pretty good relationship. It was really cool to see him do well and he was another guy who picked up confidence as the year went on.

Brandon Eisert: (The older guys) helped me get used to the Oregon State program and made me feel more comfortable being around the program, talking about the coaches and past experiences that they had. I felt like I wasn't the only one going through it. They had all gone through it before, so they'd share the past experiences they had and helped me that way.

Power. Finesse. Left-handed. Right-handed. Experience. Youthful exuberance. The Oregon State pitching staff had it all in 2017, and the results were extraordinary. The Beavers led Division I with a school-record team ERA of 1.93 and also topped the country in several other statistics including hits allowed per nine innings (6.27), shutouts (14) and WHIP (walks and hits per innings pitched, 0.98).

Nate Yeskie: We felt like we had a good batch of arms coming back. We knew that that freshman class of kids (from 2016) had now cut their teeth in the Pac-12 environment, playing on the road and doing some things. We felt like we had the right guys … and looking at those pieces and how they were able to do what they needed to do was pretty unique. We had balance. There's never been a coach in the history of the game that looked down the dugout and went "you know, we just have too much pitching."

Andy Peterson: It all starts with Yeskie, I think that guy is one of the best to ever do it on the pitching side of things. They just bought in. It's easy to see the success the guys the year before had, so when guys show up they are in it right away. The work ethic, the hours they put in, all that kind of stuff on top of having the right guys … I mean, gosh. Heimlich, Jake Thompson, Fehmel, Ras, Engelbrekt, they just never stopped showing up. They were so locked-in all year long. You could count on one hand how many spots each guy missed throughout the year. It makes it a lot easier on the offensive side of things, I can tell you that much.

Mitchell Verburg: The great thing about that team was that I wasn't really worried about my playing time, and I think that's why the team was so successful. I was just trying to help in any way I could because I had the utmost respect for any guy that was going in. There was never a point where I thought I should be going in instead of someone else, and that was what was so great about that team. Everybody had their role, obviously some people had a bigger portion than others. My role was a righty out of the pen, coming in to get righties out. And I had 17 or so appearances and I had less innings than I had appearances, which showed that I was going to come in, get my guy out and then somebody else was going to get the ball.

Brandon Eisert: It was definitely a lot of fun being a part of that staff. It was a joy to watch all the other pitchers go out and compete, and then being able to do your job, you didn't feel extra pressure but you wanted to live up to how everyone else was doing and just continue the trend of being successful on the mound. Being able to watch the seasons that Luke, Jake, all our starters and bullpen guys had and being able to experience that was amazing.

Max Engelbrekt: It really is hard to put into words because the worst pitchers on our team had an ERA of like two. Nobody gave up any runs.

Cadyn Grenier: It was dumb. We had the best pitching staff in the nation, and when you have the defense that we had with me, Nick, Gretler, KJ … we were the best infield in that nation. So, you combine that with how good our pitching was, we felt like we could win every game 2-1 because we weren't going to give up any runs. We weren't going to make mistakes that cost us the game, and we didn't. I don't know how many games we won by one run, but I can tell you right now that in none of those did we feel like we were going to lose.

KJ Harrison: To be honest, sometimes I wouldn't really even pay attention to what was going on because you get that feeling when you're in the infield like "wow, this guy is getting nasty today." It was just great. Whenever the pitchers are dealing, it obviously takes a lot of the pressure off the offense and I think that was another huge thing for that year. When the pitching did well we'd hit enough to win, and when the pitching struggled we'd hit more and we'd put more guys across to back those guys up. The team camaraderie was very important, but when you've got a pitching staff like that, I mean it's unbelievable. And then you've got good defense behind it, so that was just the recipe for the really good team we had that year.

Max Engelbrekt: The starters were just incredible. Luke had one of the better seasons probably in the history of college baseball. Jake on Sundays was just about as good, and Eisert and Mulholland put up pretty insane numbers. I think Yeskie deserves a lot of credit for the way he would use relievers in leverage. Less so now, but I think previously you'd put a lot of stock into the closer being the guy who gets a lot of saves. Mulholland ended up with a lot of saves, but really he was like an extra starter with pretty unbelievable rate stats. He didn't give up many runs, neither did Eisert, and if you add those two together ... and add Fehmel, who was still pretty good that year, it's really hard to lose games when you give up two runs or less in almost all of them, especially if you have four first-round picks in the lineup. Just do the math, it's pretty hard to lose. That team was just loaded.

Nate Yeskie: Having Engelbrekt back gave us another guy who had some history and had some success, had pitched in the postseason. It was going to be the last run for him, and sometimes that can be a great motivator, it can be a great fuel source to get guys going and experience things, and Max went through a lot. Max had torn his ACL prior to getting to us, he'd done it a second time when he was on campus. I remember talking to his dad saying, "let's give this a run. We've got him back for his fifth year." We stuck our neck out there a little bit because I remember telling his dad "my goal is to get him to Omaha; I want to get him there and get him a chance to pitch there." Because when Max was a freshman in '13, he didn't pitch there. So, he was a big piece of that connective tissue from the '13 group that had (Michael) Conforto and Tyler Smith and Danny Hayes and Matt Boyd, guys like that.

What I had told Engelbrekt going into the season was "if I have to use you in the seventh, I'm going to use you in the seventh. If it's a big spot in the game and the three-hole hitter is up and we think it's going to be the difference in the game, we don't care about saves, we care about wins." And Max, to his credit, was like "I'm on board, let's go, let's do it." It was funny because that (previous) year the Indians had gone to the playoffs and (manager Terry) Francona was using Andrew Miller in the fifth against David Ortiz. Max texted me like "are you talking to Francona?!" And I just go "no, the game's changing." You have to find ways to play the way you need to play. And I thought with that type of team in '17, if we could always play from ahead … I mean everybody says that, but that team in particular was always doing a tremendous job of giving ourselves a chance to do things offensively, having the lead just changes that. We chose to take a different look at it. We felt like if we could win through seven we could definitely win through nine, so we used (Engelbrekt) in that role and Mulholland ended up finishing games for us. We found what we believed to be a pretty decent formula. Watching those pieces start to unfold, you could see the potential for something special coming out of '16 and going into '17. And just knowing how motivated those guys were …

Oregon State opened the 2017 campaign with eight neutral-site games spread across two weeks in Surprise, Arizona — a typical early-season schedule for many northern teams. The Beavers started 5-0 before dropping a 6-1 decision to Ohio State, a seemingly unremarkable result during a regular season with 56 scheduled contests. At the time, it wasn't known that every Beavers loss in 2017 would be a notable event.

Drew Rasmussen: We lost a game the (second) weekend down in Surprise and I remember Case … I mean you know how Case is, he never enjoyed losing. But we were in Game 6 or 7 and we lost, and he came into the locker room and was definitely fired up and not happy about the way we played.

Jake Mulholland: I remember getting back in the locker room and it was just the worst feeling. Because being a freshman, you are (5-1) in your first (six) games you're going to be pretty happy about that, but everyone was just so upset. I saw that this team, we're not happy being (5-1) right now, and that's a good sign for what's coming. I think we did a great job of showing that we didn't care what outside people thought. We had expectations for ourselves and if we weren't meeting them, it wasn't OK.

Max Engelbrekt: Yeskie kept us on the bus afterward. We'd lost a bunch the year before, and I remember he gave us a little bit of a talk. I remember just sitting there, we were kind of talking, people were like "I think we'll be fine" and I'm like "I don't know guys, I think we're screwed!" Obviously kidding, but then we didn't meet again for like two months because we didn't lose.

Nate Yeskie: We were in Surprise and I couldn't sleep. It was probably three in the morning and I just happened to look over and my laptop screen was still blue. I had been doing scouting reports until midnight or one o'clock just trying to go back through some notes and make sure I had it all right because you usually have a pretty quick turnaround that morning and there wasn't going to be time to do it. I was just so soured because I thought these were those moments as a team where if you want to be elite, you can't relapse, you can't fall back into old habits that are bad habits. So, I started typing some things up that came to my mind and I remember asking Pat (Casey) "hey, can I read this to the team?" And he says "yeah, sure." So, I read it to them and shared some perspective with those guys about it. They are kids and sometimes they think "it's just one game. No big deal, it's just one game." We reflected on '16. That there was maybe one game or one inning or one pitch that could've gone the other way — had we really willed ourselves to getting it done — that would've put us into the postseason.

We went out and took BP and when we came back in I hung it in their lockers. I come to find out a year or two later that Mulholland or Fehmel, maybe both of them, still had it taped up in their lockers. I thought "OK, this is great."

Drew Rasmussen: Right after that we won 23 games in a row, but it's just funny looking back on it. (Pat Casey) freaks out after Game 6 or 7 and then all of a sudden you're looking back at it and we're 24, 25, 26-1, and you just kind of laugh. That was the perfect way to describe Pat Casey. He's going to harp on the little things, it doesn't matter what your record was. And that was just the perfect scenario to describe who he is.

Andy Jenkins, assistant coach: Obviously we were rolling. We got off to a good start and we didn't lose a lot of games … but there weren't a lot of blowouts. I mean, there were a lot of games where we came back and showed our will to win at the end of the game. I'm a big believer in the end of the game and the end of the season being a reflection of your head coach. Case was a warrior, he was a competitor, every pitch mattered. And when you have a team that's relentless, I feel like he inspired us and kept us in it every pitch. We never gave up. And we did have the ability to put a game away or have a blowout every now and then, but as great as the record was, there were a lot of late-inning stretches where we needed to do something or we needed to walk off. As coaches know, those are the most important innings of a game and we had those on lockdown.

Michael Gretler: From the very first day we just rolled, and that's what it felt like. I don't think anyone looked back and said "oh, we're 15-1" or whatever it was. We were just playing and were going to go out and take care of business.

Nate Yeskie: Not to sound like too much coach talk, but they legitimately looked at every game like "guys, we're 0-0, so let's win today and get this thing done." They really maintained that perspective. They didn't care who was pitching, they didn't care where they were hitting in the lineup, they didn't care whether we were playing at home or on the road. They just knew that when their name was called, what's the task at hand that needed to be accomplished? Then they went out and did their best to accomplish that. They were professionals to the extreme.

Jack Anderson: We didn't really play anyone in our non-conference schedule. Who knows if people were scared to play us or not. But I think in non-conference we did what we needed to do, and at ASU we took it to them. They were a young team and we were ready to go then, so I didn't really think too much of that series either, but obviously sweeping on the road is huge. I think we were all marking our calendars for that series against Arizona because they'd swept us the previous year and they had a lot of the same guys.

Sitting at 14-1 overall entering Pac-12 play, Oregon State outscored Arizona State 16-1 en route to a three-game series sweep in Tempe. OSU rose to No. 1 in D1baseball's top 25. At the same time, Arizona, ranked ninth in the poll, was off to a 16-4 start and featured one of the deadliest batting orders in college baseball.

Game 1 between the two teams was an instant classic under the lights at Goss Stadium as Heimlich and Arizona ace J.C. Cloney faced off in a pitchers' duel. Both teams scored once in the second inning and twice in the eighth, and Mulholland worked out of a jam in the ninth to give OSU an opportunity for a walk-off win. Harrison delivered, ripping a two-out single up the middle that plated Rutschman for a 4-3 victory. Game 2 was even wilder. The teams entered the bottom of the ninth locked in a 4-4 tie. Zak Taylor reached on a throwing error to lead off the inning and was pinch run for by Preston Jones. The freshman speedster wound up stealing second and later scored on a wild pitch from second base when Arizona catcher Cory Voss couldn't locate the ball. It was the Beavers' second walk-off win in as many nights.

Preston Jones: It all started with Rutsch at the plate, and I think he missed a hit-and-run. So, I was able to steal second base, thank God. (The final play) was a dropped third strike, he swung through the third strike and it got past the catcher. Obviously it was a passed ball, I ran to third and I saw that he didn't know where the baseball was. As I was rounding third base I realized that and decided that I was going to try and score this run, and I guess I did. I don't know if Jenkins was trying to hold me or not, but I had my instincts take over and I knew I could get to the plate before he could find the baseball and make a throw home.

Andy Jenkins: I didn't do anything. I honestly didn't do anything. That's the best time to be a third-base coach, when your baserunners are trained to be confident in their decisions. You can help them think, but you can't think for them. What Preston did was he got a great jump and when he got to third base, he didn't coast in. He kept his eyes up to where the ball was as he approached third and he gave it a chance. I didn't tell him to go, I didn't tell him to stop, I just knew that he was for sure going to get to third base and he just kind of kept going. That was all on Preston and it was great instincts from a great baserunner and speed guy.

Pat Bailey: That was just crazy. Most guys on a wild pitch will kind of go three-quarters speed and check in at third base, and he went full-speed from the get-go. To score from second base in that situation, that part was really amazing to me.

Steven Kwan: I remember that exact sequence of him taking off for third, and that kid just did not stop. And that kid flies. Like right when he rounded third, our whole dugout evacuated and we started sprinting toward home plate. I feel like we were racing him to home plate, like we knew he was going to be safe.

Adley Rutschman: I didn't even know what was going on. I just remember striking out on a ball in the dirt, first instinct was to run to first base. All of a sudden I get to first and I look back and I see Preston coming around to score. The crowd was going nuts and I had no idea what was going on for those five or six seconds I was running to first base. Just, just unbelievable. You get caught up in that moment for a second, and then you realize we won.

Preston Jones: I'd never done that before (scoring from second on a wild pitch). And for it to be a walk-off, that's pretty crazy. It was bizarre, especially on the field. I just remember all my teammates running towards me and I got put into a headlock by Elliot Cary. I couldn't really move and I lost my footing, I fell and he was right on top of me and goes "thatta boy, way to win it for us!" It was special, and then back in the locker room … I thought it was funny because it didn't seem like that big of a deal, but to everyone else it was.

Andy Jenkins: I think that was the first time I'd seen that, especially to walk off a game. And I don't remember the exact things that transpired up until that moment, but it was a rainy game and they were kind of throwing the game away a little bit, giving it to us more than we deserved it. Obviously when you're in a game like that, their team was probably going "that was all completely avoidable."

KJ Harrison: You get this feeling like "wow, we're not going to lose!" We would always find ways to win. That's how we knew it was a special year and a special time for us, because of all these crazy things we were doing. We would always come together at the right times, and I'm a firm believer that things like that don't just happen. We worked really hard during the fall and bonded as a team, and all these magical moments all happened because we all played for each other and all worked hard for each other.

Brandon Eisert: Every single person had their role on that team. (Preston) came in to run and I don't know if anyone else on the team would've scored on that play. All the pieces that we had, it was a different hero each time.

Preston Jones: It was special. I didn't really think about how special it was until the season went along. You don't really think much of going in to pinch run or having to play defense late in the game or whatever it is until it's all said and done. After you think "wow, I was in some special moments and a part of some great things." It was a great feeling, but I think in order to be a special role player or whatever it is, you've got to prepare and get ready to play that day, even though it didn't happen all the time.

Pat Casey: That was pretty crazy. I don't know how many it was, 14 or 15 one-run games we won that year. Obviously a very high-intensity series at home with Arizona, and to win back-to-back walk-offs I think always gives you a little momentum.

Jack Anderson: I didn't play the first two games that series because KJ hurt his hand and was DHing. Zak Taylor had to play first and they put Larnach in right field. Before that the third game, I was just putting my shoes on. Case never told us who was playing until like 30 minutes beforehand, so I was just going through my stuff and assuming "all right, I'll probably be on the bench again today. Just be ready to pinch hit." So, I'm putting my shoes on and I see Case's shoes stop where I'm at. I look up and he goes "you're in left field and you're hitting second," and then he just walks away from me. I hadn't played left field all year and I hadn't hit second all year, so I was like "all right, I guess it's go-time now. Time to get the game face on!" I ended up having a really good game and God knows what was going through Case's mind to put me in that situation, but I think he always went with his gut. And with that team, he could put a whole different nine guys on the field and we were just loaded and ready to compete. I think he had some fun with his lineups that year because he could mix and match them any way he wanted. I think I hit at every spot that year, one through nine. I was just filling any role Case threw at me, didn't change anything and tried to have fun with it.

Jake Thompson: Those were some good wins. Arizona has always been a great hitting team, and I know I gave up a few runs that game. Heimlich even gave up a (run), which was rare that year, but that was a big series. You get two walk-off wins and you realize you just swept the series. It's crazy how all that adds up, one-run wins like those change how we were from the year before. You win those games, that's what gets you into the playoffs, and that's something we realized later in the year. We could've gone 1-2 against Arizona and had a battle in the Pac-12 late in the year, needing to win two of our last three to clinch. But instead, we took care of business early.

Jack Anderson: When we swept Arizona, I think that's where our belief in ourselves was really taken to the next level. That series was our liftoff point.

The Beavers went on to win the finale 11-7, completing the three-game sweep. The following day, college baseball had a new consensus No. 1 team in the major national polls: Oregon State. That didn't change for the remainder of the regular season. The Beavers kept winning and winning, eventually reaching a high-water mark of 28-1 overall and 12-0 in Pac-12 play. The 23-game winning streak included seven one-run victories — four by walk-off.

Pat Casey: I never really thought "hey, we've won 20 in a row." I just never felt that way. I felt like we had to go to the yard and stay on line because we wanted to make sure there was no doubt, we wanted to leave no doubt who was the best team, and we wanted to do that every weekend. And that's a tribute to those guys, man.

Christian Donahue: When we showed up to the stadium on game day, everyone on our team knew we were going to win, it was just a matter of what was going to happen that day. Like how we were going to win, or by how much, that type of thing. And especially with our lineup and our pitching and our defense, it was pretty tough for us to look at matchups and be like "oh, this is going to be hard." We always had the mindset that we're playing against the top team going into every game, and it didn't matter who we were playing against. ... There were so many things that went on through that season where you were just like "wow, that actually happened."

Andy Peterson: They expected to win, but it wasn't an expect to win like they would just show up and kick somebody's butt. I think the maturity they had to keep it rolling and to not let the pressure get there, it was just day in and day out. Guys showed up every single day. And if one of the guys didn't show up that day, somebody else did. If Rutschman didn't hit that game, Gretler probably had four hits. It just didn't stop.

Luke Heimlich: Our attitude didn't change at all, how we viewed our team didn't change at all. My sophomore year we obviously had some struggles and lows like losing to Portland, but then the next year when we're winning 23 games in a row or whatever it is, our attitude wasn't any different. We still looked at our team the same way, maybe the coaches were freaking out a little bit more in one of those situations. But as far as our team and our internal group of guys, how we viewed ourselves and how we went about our business, nothing really changed.

Nick Madrigal: It was a really close knit-group, especially as the season went on. It felt like every time we stepped foot on the field, we were going to win every single inning, every single game. I've never felt that feeling on any other team. It was something really, really special.

Andy Armstrong: You look to win every single game, but in the game of baseball that's pretty unlikely because of all the different possibilities that can happen. We were just on an absolute, unbelievable roll and it was so fun to be a part of something special like that.

In my past in all sports, football, basketball and of course baseball growing up, I was on good teams, but never really any teams that were absolutely dominant. I mean, if this counts for anything, in youth football from like third grade to fifth or something we never lost a game.

Brandon Eisert: It was a little weird because it was my first college season so I didn't know anything else, like how it actually was a struggle to win so many games. There were a lot of close games that we fought through and got out of, and now looking back at the record that we had is actually amazing. Just going through the winning streaks and knowing that we're a part of history, Oregon State history, was remarkable. Looking back at it, it's kind of unbelievable what we were able to do that year.

Jake Rodriguez, assistant coordinator of camps: People always talk about the '18 team, but the '17 team, I mean it was just crazy. It was the most incredible thing I've ever seen. We clicked on every cylinder and Adley wasn't even Adley at that point. He was good, but he wasn't a freak of nature like he was in '18 and '19. He was getting his freshman feet underneath him coming over from football and things like that. It was just an amazing year, easy for the coaches because we had so many leaders on the team. We were winning, we could throw, we could hit, we could play defense and we literally did everything.

Max Engelbrekt: Man, that was just a ride. It really, really flew by because we won just about every game. I remember as the closer to start the year, we'd have weekends where we'd win by like 10 every time and it didn't matter. We'd have other times where Luke and Jake would pitch like the whole game, the whole weekend. We'd use like four pitchers, maybe Mulholland throws twice and nobody else even pitches.

Steven Kwan: It actually took a little bit into the season for us to realize that we had something special. Surprise went how we expected, we always expected to do real well down there. The win streak, it didn't even really hit me there. I think it started when we had all these walk-off wins that were ridiculous. We had Arizona twice, there was a Utah one. There were games where we were behind and the mood in the dugout was super calm, super relaxed, and then we'd pull out on top. It wasn't even like "oh my God, I can't believe we won that!" It was "let's go, we knew we could do that."

Joe Casey: It was crazy being in the dugout. It was like we couldn't lose, even if we were losing in the ninth inning. We play Utah for 16 innings, Mully has gone (six-plus) as a reliever and gives up a solo shot. Most teams would be like "ah, top of the 16th, give up a solo shot, it's probably over, we fought." Then Jack Anderson comes up, hits a game-tying triple, (Rutschman) drives him in, and I think that is when we knew that this was all just crazy.

Every day we came to the yard, we knew we were going to win. I think the other teams knew, that was part of it. It just happened every time. Especially since I wasn't playing that year, I was just watching it. If there was one year I didn't get to play, I'm glad it was that one because it was fun to watch.

Jack Anderson: I'll always remember the Stanford series because we didn't lose to them or Cal in like four or five years down there. Case would always tell us the story of him trying to get (Pac-10 unification). Case was one of the main guys trying to get this to happen, make it like a real conference feel. I remember that Stanford's coach (Mark Marquess) flat-out told Case "why would we come up and play you guys?" That was like in the late 90s. I mean at that point, he was probably right. The Northwest schools weren't as good as they are now, but I think Case would always remember that when we played them and made sure we knew that these guys didn't respect the program when it was in its infancy. And we kind of always took it to them because of that, and took great pride in doing so. I think Sunken Diamond was always fun to play at. Case just let us loose and let his boys play a little bit.

Cadyn Grenier: The team, we never had any panic at all. There was an unbelievable chemistry throughout the team and whenever something was going on, nobody ever freaked out, nobody started to get frustrated. We all knew how good we were just from the previous year and who we still had. From the beginning of the season, we were like "hey, we've really gotten after it this year, we have a lot of talent and nobody is going to stop us." I think the whole team had that mentality, and when we got on that winning streak, it was like "hey, we might never lose again!" Everybody felt that good about the team. When we finally did lose at Washington, it sucked. But it was one of those moments where we knew it was just one loss, and we were going to get right back at it.

After opening Pac-12 play with sweeps of Arizona State, Arizona, Stanford and Utah, Oregon State's school-record 23-game winning streak finally ended April 13 at Washington. A motivated Huskies team scored all three of their runs in the sixth inning — two coming on a rare Madrigal throwing error — in a 3-2 upset win.

Michael Gretler: That was a rough game. I think there was a little bit of a delay with the rain, and we just didn't play good. We had a couple situations where we didn't get guys in when we had opportunities to early in the game, and obviously Washington is super competitive. I feel like they are kind of our rival, so in those games when you don't put a team away early and you give them hope, hope's a dangerous thing. They played well that night and they beat us, and it was tough. Because at that point we'd won (23) in a row … and were maybe looking ahead a little bit, and sure enough we lost.

Jake Rodriguez: This wasn't the reason we lost, but I just remember Nick throwing the ball into the stands, which never happens. You remember those single plays because we only lost four games in the regular season. I only bring that up because I use that against him on the golf course sometimes.

Jack Anderson: I remember when we lost that game to Washington, that's when Nick took the next level in his leadership. He made an error (late) in the game that by no means lost the game for us, but it was a big moment. After the game, Nick just walked on the bus and said "hey, this game's on me. That's my fault, that won't happen again. It won't ever happen again; I promise you guys. This one's on me and we're going to come back tomorrow and be ready to go." And we were all like "dude, it ain't your fault," but I think that's the kind of leader he was. If he made a mistake, he was going to own up to it. I think that showed me at least that he's really just an outstanding leader that you want on your team. He took everything seriously and I think that error ate at him that whole night. You could see how much it meant to him and that's tough for a really good player to do, own up to his mistakes, because he does so much for us every game. Even that one little mistake he had, he definitely took to heart. That's just the kind of kid he is.

Nick Madrigal: I was in the moment and I felt like something needed to be said. After my freshman year, I remember thinking to myself that I was going to say whatever I needed to, whatever was on my mind to the team because I was going to be one of the leaders this next year. So that sophomore year, after that Washington game, I felt like it could've been a turning point one way or another. We could've lost a couple more games after that, or maybe it could spark us and we could do something great. I can't remember exactly what I said, but I was just trying to tell the team "this one game is not going to define us. We're going to do something great this year and we're going to keep doing it." It was just in the moment and I'm glad I said it. I hope it stuck with some of those guys, but there were so many leaders on that team that I probably didn't have to say much.

Madrigal and Cadyn Grenier alternated between second base and shortstop for the first half of the 2017 season. Madrigal notched 24 starts at short and six at second through the first 30 games; Grenier had 20 starts at second, six at short and four at third base. About halfway through Pac-12 play, Grenier settled in as the regular shortstop while Madrigal became a full-time second baseman. Both players wanted to be the starting shortstop, but the position battle never resulted in friction between the two.

Pat Casey: Either of them could've played shortstop for anybody in the country, either of them could've played second base for anybody in the country. Nick just happened to be more of a natural at second base and it made us a better team, so Nick said "let's go." I don't think Grenier ever complained when he moved over to short, and he said the same thing. The competition was outstanding.

Cadyn Grenier: I think it was good for both of us. Obviously we always took ground balls together. Like if I was at short, he was at short. If I was at second, he was at second or vice versa, and we were always learning from each other. I learned a lot about how to play second base from him, so I still to this day will teach people when I'm moving around things that Nick might've taught me at second. I think it was good for both of us, and now looking back I'm glad it happened because now I could get called up to the big leagues but they might go "hey, you're not playing short, you're playing second, can you do that?" And I'd go "yeah, you want me to play third? Because I can do that, too." Being able to play for an extended period of time at all three of those positions in college was just huge.

Nick Madrigal: I'll be honest, it was tough. I wanted to be the guy at shortstop and I felt like that was my position, and I know he felt the same as well. But you know, you could see that Cadyn was a great player and great defensively, so I knew I had my work cut out for me. At the end of the day, once I put the team in front of my own feelings and my own thoughts of wanting to play shortstop when I knew what was best for the team, I felt a lot better and I had a lot more fun. And you could see how much it helped the team. So yeah, it was a lot of fun in practice having us both out there, competing with one another. He'd make a great play, then I would want to go out there and make a great play. I would truly say that we both made each other better, along with a number of guys on the team. When you have competition all around the field, I really think iron sharpens iron. Coach Casey would always say that and yeah, it was a lot of fun looking back on it. I don't think you ever have that much talent at one position on any college team out there. It was a lot of fun and we turned some great double plays, it was pretty special.

Trevor Larnach: I don't think there really ever was a huge issue between those two. Obviously in practice when we'd watch those two work together at second and short. I think it was evident that we were watching the two best middle infielders in the country because there were no mistakes. I don't think I ever saw them once in three years make a mistake in the infield during practice. Being that I'm an outfielder it's different, but every time I'd look in they'd always be smoother than hell and they'd always be getting their technique right or their footwork down or their transitions, whatever it was.

Andy Jenkins: There were a lot of scouts and coaches who were like "how is Oregon State going to do it with two high-profile guys that turned down pro contracts?" I had some scouting buddies who were actually taking bets with each other on who was going to play short. I will say that was a conversation that we had a lot. I think we let them both compete in the fall, Case started moving them in and out, and I remember it got to the point where we knew we were a better team with Nick at second and Cadyn at short. I think Case worried about keeping Nick happy and keeping the guys not just playing hard, but happy with their roles and happy with their decisions to come to Oregon State. It got to the point where we had to keep telling him "Case, Nick doesn't care. Like, he just doesn't care."

Pat Casey: There was never a moment where I didn't think either one of those guys could be the best shortstop in the country. I always felt like Nick would be a second baseman in the big leagues, and because he is so determined to be the best defender, to play 162 games in the big leagues at shortstop at his size would be difficult to do. Could he do it? Absolutely. But I always felt like it would take away some of the offensive ability he had because it's such a difficult position to play.

But my decision there had nothing to do with either one of them. It came down to the fact that we were a better team because Nick could do some things at second base that Cadyn wasn't really equipped to do. They are just different athletes. Both guys — elite, elite defenders. I always felt Nick was more of a natural turning the double play at second base. He was more of a natural in that position and therefore it made us a better team. I guarantee you right now if you ask Cadyn Grenier if Nick Madrigal helped him became a better player, he'd tell you "absolutely." And I remember talking to Nick about that one time. I said "it's guys like you, because you're great, who can make players around you better."

I don't think either one of them ever worried too much about it. I think that they both wanted to play short because they're supposed to want to do that, that's what they did in high school. That's where you're supposed to play, that's what your manhood tells you you should do. And to think, as high-profile as those guys were, that they were both willing to say, "wherever you want me to play coach, I'll play." Unbelievable. And to think that their freshmen year, here's two guys that could've started for anybody in the county at shortstop as freshmen, anywhere, and neither one of them played short! That's how much those guys cared about the team. They both sacrificed their ego to play a position their freshmen year that neither one of them thought they'd be playing.

Andy Jenkins: I remember sitting in Arizona and I said to Case, "you know we're going to be in the national championship in the next year or two, and Nick's going to come up and ask where he is playing." And that actually happened, but I told Nick to do it. The night before we played Arkansas in Game 1 (of the College World Series finals), I said "hey dude, you've got to go in there and ask Case. Everybody is going to be watching, so you've got to do a good job." So, he was like "hey coach, am I playing short or second? I just want to know where to take my pregame." And Case totally had a blank stare and everybody started laughing.

Nick Madrigal: He always joked around about that, and it was one of those things in the locker room where we ran into each other and he told me to go up to Case, and Case laughed immediately. But that was just our style. We kept it light no matter how big the game was, and in the locker room it was always fun and games. It wasn't ever too serious. We could lock it in when we had to, but we kept it light in the locker room for the most part.

Pat Casey: You know I don't remember that, but he probably did that because he'd always ask me about that because he wanted to play short! That would make me laugh to think about it, and I'm sure he did do that. If I really had time to think about all the things that go on during a season, all the things that happened and all the things that I don't know that happened, it's an amazing journey.

Pat Bailey: It was just so much fun watching those two play the game. Nick Madrigal for me is probably the best all-around player I've been around, just in terms of the stuff he did on the field. He did things that you never see, whether it was taking an extra base that nobody else would or acting like he's throwing to first and back-picking a guy at third base on a relay. Whatever it was, he just had an acute awareness of the game and it was fun to watch and be a part of. And with Cadyn, he was such a great fielder and such a great athlete. Defensively, watching those two guys was a lot of fun.

Andy Jenkins: They are the same type of players, but they are completely different at the same time. Nick is always moving at a rapid pace; Cadyn is a calm, cool player who kind of sits in the pocket a little bit.

Pat Casey: Nick and Cadyn, completely different guys as far as how you handled them and how you coached them and what their backgrounds were and how they went about their business. I cannot tell you how much credit I give them for what they became together and how they became the best middle infielders in the country. That combination was the best in the country without question.

Andy Peterson: My goodness, they were the Team USA shortstop and second baseman. It's pretty special to get to work with a couple guys like that. They were both freaks of nature in their own way. Cadyn obviously is one of the best shortstops I've ever seen play the game. He could just do things other guys couldn't. And Nick Madrigal of course is arguably one of the best players ever in college baseball. It was really fun watching those two because they had a competition every single day in practice with each other from the day they showed up. They both wanted to play shortstop, and it was really fun to watch them almost go at it every single day. You see them push each other, they didn't have to say anything, they didn't talk to each other that much. It was really about sizing each other up and measuring each other. It was a lot of fun watching those two compete for those two middle infield spots. They worked more at their infield craft than anyone I've ever seen.

Andy Armstrong: Coming in, I obviously knew we had a few studs up the middle and it was probably unlikely that I would get to play much. For me, my priority was becoming the best baseball player I could be and I think an important step in doing that is being around guys that are the best at what they do, and that is exactly what Nick and Cadyn are. So, I learned so much and I progressed on my infield play a thousand times over just in the first two weeks I was on campus taking ground balls next to them, seeing what they do. I learn usually by observing what other people do and that helped me tremendously. It was pretty special to have that opportunity.

Joe Casey: Cadyn was one of the most skilled guys I've ever played with. He had all the tools — he could run, throw, hit. He was so physical. I was locker buddies next to Cadyn, so we were pretty tight. We had some fun times back there, but I really love Cadyn. He's a great guy and he's one of the nicest guys, and I think on the field he can show his skills. That man can field anything. … Best defender I've probably ever seen or played with, him and Nick are probably the top two.

Jake Thompson: Grenier had some of the best hands I've ever seen. He was someone where you gave him one year to get his feet under him, and from there he just took off.

Grenier had his struggles at the plate as a freshman, hitting just .240 with a .311 slugging percentage. He did draw 22 walks — tied for third on the team — but was still one of Oregon State's weaker links in the lineup. With a year of Division I experience under his belt, Grenier was much more dangerous at the plate in 2017. He put together a slash line of .275/.393/.435 (batting average, on-base percentage and slugging percentage), with five home runs and 37 RBIs.

Cadyn Grenier: Every year it got a little bit better in terms of being comfortable. I think it was just getting used to the competition at that level. My freshman year, it didn't go great and my sophomore year was a little bit better and junior year was better than that. I think it was just a slowly progressing thing of me getting a little bit better and getting a little bit more used to the competition and figuring out what teams were doing in terms of pitch sequence and stuff like that in the Pac-12. You get a better feel for it and, I can't remember like one moment or anything, but it was just a slow progression over my three years.

Nate Yeskie: He was challenged in his time with us. We've always had a pretty good relationship with things. I can give him a hard time and he knew it was coming from a good place.

I think this was his freshman year, he used to walk by and go "hey, when can I throw a bullpen?" And I'd say, "you keep swinging the bat the way you're swinging it and you're going to be down here pitching in no time." I would have moments with him where it would be back-and-forth and taking a couple jabs at each other and having some fun. That's just part of how I think those relationships work. When you trust people and you know they've got your best interest in mind, it might hurt a little bit but it's a pill you can swallow and you just move on. He and I always had that good relationship, and still do to this day.

Max Engelbrekt: His struggles offensively were probably overblown. Maybe from a scouting standpoint they would've been real, but Cadyn walked so much that he was probably still a positive offensive player his freshman year. He's just extremely talented, and you knew he would figure it out. It's hard to hit as a freshman sometimes, look at Larnach or Kwan, and even Adley ... but what you get defensively and what he would do for our pitching staff was extremely, extremely valuable. He's an incredible defender.

Andy Peterson: I remember there was a game, I'm pretty sure it was in '17. Cadyn had an error. It was a routine ground ball and he booted it. That was one of the first ground balls I saw Cadyn boot, and everyone was kind of like "oh wow, I can't believe that actually happened." Later that night, I was leaving the locker room and Cadyn was out on the field by himself taking imaginary ground balls. Nobody's hitting it to him, nobody else is out there. I don't know, he probably got 100 reps or so. He's out there all by himself pretending he's fielding ground balls, and I thought that was one of the most amazing things I've ever seen. Especially for a young kid who was 18 or 19 years old.

While Grenier had an up-and-down freshman season, Madrigal slashed .333/.380/.456 in 2016 en route to Pac-12 freshman of the year honors. He did a little bit of everything as a sophomore, leading the team among regulars in batting (.380), slugging (.532), OBP (.449), hits (90), doubles (20), runs scored (53) and stolen bases (16). Along with playing standout defense, Madrigal also had four home runs and 40 RBIs. The conference's coaches voted the 5-foot-7 standout Pac-12 player and defensive player of the year.

Max Engelbrekt: Nick would just make you laugh. I think Nick was probably the most respected player by everybody that I've ever played with. His stats are unbelievably impressive, but if you think of it from like a home runs standpoint, size or even position value, it's maybe a little bit less impressive than a Conforto or Adley. But Nick was easily the most fun player I've ever seen play. He was really a joy to be around. He had fun doing everything and especially as his profile grew, he was still really fun to be around. He was just amazing. Between him and Cadyn playing defense, they saved so many runs and helped us get so many leads. I couldn't think of anybody I hold in higher regard than Nick. He's an incredible player.

Joe Casey: Nick was just a leader. He got after it every day, and you could tell by the way he played. He was a goofball off the field, great guy to be around, and then on the field you could tell by the way he attacked. Attacked at the plate, attacked baserunning, you could tell on the bases just how hard he played the game. He was the guy where every time he went to the plate, you thought he was going to get a hit or at least do his job if someone was on base. That guy grinded, he worked extremely hard, took tons of ground balls. On offense and defense, he was great, but I think the best part about him was how good of a leader he was. He was the one who would talk to the coaches too, he was that guy for us.

Pat Bailey: I call Nick "Mr. One More" because I'd throw batting practice to him and he'd go "one more, one more, one more, one more." Adley was a bit that way too, but Nick was the worst with that.

Andy Peterson: With Nick, every rep, every ground ball, every swing he takes has a purpose. I'd be shocked if he missed more than three balls in practice during his entire time at Oregon State. He just had that laser, locked-in focus every single play.

Christian Donahue: One of the craziest things to me was when we played St. Mary's and Nick faced his brother when we were down. And of course, Nick comes through, and I was just like "wow, that's pretty cool."

Prior to their Pac-12 series at Stanford, the Beavers played a single non-conference game at St. Mary's in Moraga, California, a homecoming for Oregon State's Northern California products. The Gaels led 3-1 entering the top of the sixth when Ty Madrigal, Nick's twin brother, came on to pitch in relief. Ty threw a 1-2-3 sixth, worked around a Michael Gretler leadoff single in the seventh and gave up just one hit in the eighth — a one-out single to his brother. St. Mary's made a pitching change after Ty walked Trevor Larnach to lead off the ninth, and the Beavers went on to score three runs to grab the lead. Nick was the hero, singling up the middle to plate the tying and go-ahead runs with two outs.

Nick Madrigal: That was a lot of fun. I had a lot of friends and family there. It was something (Ty and I) had joked about for a long time, and for it to actually happen was pretty cool. That whole year leading up to that game, we'd text back and forth and call each other. He was joking around that he had our game circled on his calendar on his fridge and he was waiting for us and their team was ready for us. It's funny because that game, they should've won. They had it coming down to the last couple of innings, but we ended up coming back and it was another great game for us.

    Me being able to face my twin brother, that was really cool. He still jokes about it and just mentioned the other day that he thinks his third baseman should've had the ball that I hit. He thinks he got me and all this stuff. It's a lot of fun that we got the chance to do that. That was the only time we've ever faced each other in a real game because we'd always been on the same team or playing at different places. That was the only time other than practice games and things like that. So yeah, that was pretty cool.

Jake Rodriguez: We were down 3-1 going into the ninth, and the at-bat (Andy Atwood) had where he walked, it was an unbelievable at-bat. Then Nick got the go-ahead single. The dugouts are pretty close to the field there, and I've never heard chirping back and forth at each other like that. I mean, we were rolling at that point, we'd only lost one game and we're here at St. Mary's on a Tuesday. The atmosphere, there were so many Elk Grove people. My high school coach was there, tons of the players who were in high school at the time were at the game, all of Nick's family was there. I remember the atmosphere was so cool and we could not get anything going offensively. Nick's brother came in in relief and shut us down for (three) innings, it was crazy. I went down to the bullpen because I couldn't believe what was happening. I had to go to the bullpen and walk it out for a little bit.

Mitchell Verburg: I think the moment I realized how special that season was, was at St. Mary's. First off, I realized how special Nick Madrigal was because he was going up against his brother. That was really cool to see and his brother is a great player, too. I remember we were down two or three in the top of the ninth and we were like "shoot, we're going to lose our first midweek game." The thing about that team is I didn't ever think we were going to lose. And that's what was so cool, we were in the top of the ninth in that game and I was still going "we've got a chance, we're not out of this." And all of a sudden … the bases were loaded and shoot, we're about to win this game. We ended up winning it and it was amazing because we had played terribly the entire game and then boom, snap of the fingers in the top of the inning we turned it on.

Jake Rodriguez: That was one of the games I definitely remember, and the way we came out on top, that was such a 2017 win. It took everybody's at-bat in that last inning, and there were some really, really close calls. Adley hit a ground ball that could've been a double play to end the game, and he busted it down the line and beat the throw out to give us another opportunity. And we ended up scoring the winning run.

After taking two of three at Washington and UCLA, the Beavers sat at 32-3 overall and 16-2 in Pac-12 play, five games clear of second-place California in the standings. Oregon State was leading the country in team ERA. And Drew Rasmussen — arguably the program's top arm — had yet to throw a pitch. Rasmussen, voted a team captain along with Madrigal, had continued to make steady progress in his recovery from Tommy John surgery. He was cleared for action by the time OSU headed to UCLA. He didn't pitch in Los Angeles, making his 2017 debut the following weekend at home against USC — 13 months after surgery. Rasmussen retired both batters he faced for his first career save and was mobbed by teammates coming off the mound.

Drew Rasmussen: I think maybe my first outing in Arizona as a freshman in Surprise I had a similar feeling. You take the mound, it was an electric atmosphere, and you get chills. I could feel it in my legs, it was incredible the amount of excitement and anticipation. Coming out to an ovation from the crowd just amplified all those feelings and emotions because most people don't see the work put in behind the scenes for a regular healthy player. And when you're hurt you're working twice as hard because you have more to focus on. The electricity in that stadium alone can feed the team. But then on top of it to be overcoming some emotions and that kind of stuff of finally getting back on the mound, it was surreal, man. It was incredible.

Luke Heimlich: That was an awesome moment. I thankfully have never had to do it but people who go through surgeries, it's a really rough situation because they're not on the active roster, so they're not always at practice. They kind of feel secluded at times, get in their own little bubble, and they can't do a lot of the stuff that the rest of the team is doing. But that whole recovery period, Ras was there with us every day in the weight room, he was with us every day at practice. He still had a large influence on the team even though he didn't play the first three months of the season. Being able to get him back on the field was amazing.

Pat Casey: Ras is such a competitive human being. His work ethic to get back and do the things that he wanted to help us do ... he's just a crazy competitor. I mean that guy, there's nothing he wasn't willing to do to become the best he could become. I just really have a lot of respect for his desire to get back on the mound, but more than that his desire to help everybody on the staff when he got back. You talk about a special guy, he had as much impact on the club when he wasn't playing as he did when he was. That's how special he was, that's what kind of leader he was.

Nate Yeskie: He's easy to root for all the time. Ras, he's a guy's guy in the sense of he just shows up to work every day, he pulls for everybody. You know what you're going to get out of him and generally that's his best, and he's going to try to get the best out of you. He doesn't care if that comes at the cost of him maybe not getting an extra couple of innings or maybe not getting the win or whatever it was. He was never consumed or motivated by those things. He just wanted to be better than he was yesterday. So, seeing him come out was exciting at that point, and coming off an injury you're always looking and seeing how guys are going to respond to those kinds of things. It was nice to have him get ready to help for the rest of that run.

Christian Donahue: Drew was the ultimate competitor that you want on the mound. He's not going to give in, he's not going to back down from anybody. An awesome leader, a great guy, just having him back was huge. That guy has been through so much and is one of the hardest workers, so for him to come back and be able to be there for that year was pretty cool and pretty special to see. ... It was crazy, we had three (projected) top-three round picks in Heimlich, Ras and Jake.

Rasmussen's return meant there would be fewer innings to go around on an already stacked pitching staff. But everything fell into place when one of the team's most reliable arms needed a break. Fehmel, who pitched sparingly prior to college, threw 70 innings as a freshman. Twelve consecutive weekend starts to open the 2017 season left Fehmel with a sore arm. After sub-par outings against UCLA and California, a weary Fehmel took some time off and was replaced in the rotation by Rasmussen.

Bryce Fehmel: After I came out from a start, I couldn't bend or straighten my arm. There was something going on in there, from what I remember it was an inflamed nerve in my elbow. Right away we got it checked out and I had to take a month or so off, which was tough because I wanted to be in there with the guys. I wanted to fight, but I did whatever I could to help them from the outside looking in. I was all-in supporting whoever was pitching, whoever was playing. It was kind of fun in one aspect to step back and take it all in because we couldn't be beat either way. Being able to be on both sides of it, watching and playing, was a cool perspective.

Jake Thompson: I mean nobody wants to lose their innings and everyone was performing really well, so it was almost like "where does Drew fit it?" And Drew is this incredible pitcher, so when you have a problem like that, you know you're doing pretty well.

Max Engelbrekt: It was pretty funny because it was like "we don't even know what to do with Drew." He needed to be worked back in. I remember we did it, we worked a long time to get him back into it and then he gave up a grand slam against Cal. But yeah, he was if not the most talented guy on the staff, he was right there in the top three, so it was great to see him back. I remember seeing him throw live before coming back and he was throwing like 97, 98, and this is just a minimum-effort type deal. By the time he pitched in Omaha, he looked like a Major League-type closer.

It was great to see him back, although it's funny because we already had a staff where nobody gave up any runs, and now we were going to add someone. It was a bit like "well, there's only 27 innings (on a weekend) and the starters already throw 21 of them. So, I don't know when you're going to pitch, but you're certainly good enough."

Bryce Fehmel: It worked out perfectly because who else would you want to step in and take your innings other than Drew Rasmussen? I wouldn't want it any other way looking back on it. It worked out perfectly and I'm glad it happened the way it did.

By mid-May, Oregon State had piled up enough conference wins to put an early end to the Pac-12 title race. The Beavers' magic number to clinch was two entering the Civil War conference series with in-state rival Oregon in Eugene. The Ducks dropped baseball in 1981 but reinstated the program for the 2009 season, a move that was announced right after OSU captured the second of its back-to-back College World Series titles. Oregon poached decorated coach George Horton from Cal State Fullerton and spent nearly $20 million to build PK Park, a sparkling facility next to Autzen Stadium. At his introductory press conference, Horton quipped, "we're going to try to make everyone forget where Corvallis is, by the way. … Our mission will be to dominate the Northwest in recruiting, and that will be no easy challenge."

Horton didn't succeed in making everyone forget about Corvallis, but the Ducks were an immediate contender under his leadership. Oregon won 40 games in Horton's second season and received an at-large NCAA Tournament berth. From 2012 to 2015, the Ducks went a combined 176-80 with four postseason appearances. They came close to reaching the CWS in 2012, falling to Kent State at home in the super regionals. But by 2017, Horton's program was in decline. Oregon had missed the 2016 NCAA Tournament and was 26-18 overall (9-12 Pac-12) heading into the Civil War conference series. OSU fans packed PK Park as the Beavers cruised to a 6-1 win in the opener. A Game 2 victory would clinch the Pac-12 title.

In his first start of the year, Rasmussen went three innings before turning it over to the bullpen. The game wound up being a classic, with the Beavers clinging to a 5-4 lead entering the bottom of the ninth inning. Oregon loaded the bases with two outs for Ryne Nelson, who'd thrown the last three innings in relief for the Ducks. OSU freshman right-hander Mitchell Verburg, a Lake Oswego High School graduate, was on the mound with the game on the line.

Mitchell Verburg: That is one of my favorite memories playing baseball for Oregon State. I don't think you can write it up any better than it was set up. 3-2 count, bases loaded, two outs, up by one. I had hit the batter before, which adds a little doubt in your mind I guess. I would be lying if I said I wasn't nervous at all, but I think the nervousness was more butterflies about being excited. I had put the work in and I had built a routine to where I could do this. I had confidence instilled in me by my teammates, by Yeskie, by Case, and it really meant a lot to me that they went to me in that situation. If they trusted me to pitch in that situation, then I really had trust in myself. It was exhilarating, there's no high like that and that's why you play baseball.

Andy Armstrong: The place was full of Beaver fans, more Beaver fans than Duck fans. There was an Oregon State "O-S-U" chant going on at PK Park, that was pretty incredible to see. We also went up to UW that year in 2017 and they had record-breaking attendance at Washington's field, and of course it was majority Oregon State fans, so a similar thing happened there. Our fan base traveled and supported us unbelievably well.

Mitchell Verburg: I got them to pop up a bunt (with runners on) first and third, that was huge and got me to two outs. The next guy was a lefty and my ball has a little bit of a natural cut, I plunked him right in the back, it cut a little too much. That got me to a righty, which honestly was a little bit better of a matchup. I would've liked to have gotten the first guy out, but it doesn't always work like that. I went to a (2-0) count on (Nelson) and at that point, it's just "I'm going to challenge you with my fastball. If you hit it, you hit it." I got myself into the situation, but I'm not walking that guy, I can't walk that guy. When it got to a 3-2 count, the crowd stands up, starts clapping. It's a 3-2 count off a foul ball, and at that point I'm just locating the heater away. He swung through it, I threw a little bit extra on, and then it's just an exhilarating moment with all my teammates out there. And that's what I wanted, I wanted my teammates out there and I wanted to get that Pac-12 championship right there.

Pat Casey: It was really special. I think Verburg did what he did a lot of times that year, he'd walk a guy, strike a guy out, get ahead. So, he took it right to the limit, made it tough on us. 3-2 pitch, and it's special. Nobody's going to deny the fact that you want to win championships and you want to win them at home, but if you can win them on the road against your rival, that's pretty good. We were really in a pretty good groove and we were playing good baseball, and it was one hell of a game. Oregon played us pretty tough and to have a freshman on the mound in that situation and to win it all right there, it was a good night.

Andy Armstrong: I remember Verburg talking about it after. He said that if you would've told him at the beginning of the year as a freshman that he was going to throw the final pitch to win a Pac-12 championship at Oregon, he would've never thought that was going to happen. But you never know what situation you're going to be in, and you've got to perform just like he did. Winning the Pac-12 is pretty special, and winning it at Oregon made it even sweeter.

Ron Northcutt, director of baseball operations: Every year that we beat Oregon, that's always the best.

Zak Taylor: It's always fun when you can play Oregon, especially at their place. You want to win anytime it's an in-state rivalry, but that moment for Mitch striking out that last guy, especially with the things he's been through in his college career, that was important. To see that, and then you've got that Case reaction at the end on video with the fist-pump, things like that just fire you up and are things you'll never forget.

Andy Jenkins: It was definitely a fun way to clinch it, and an exciting game against a rival. When you grow up in the Northwest, what you play for is moments like that. Oregon was always competitive and we got the better of them most of the time, but what I will tell you is there weren't a lot of easy games when we played them. And certainly, there was no sweeter victory than to claim a championship against your rival.

Trevor Larnach: I remember being like "yeah, it's great to win the Pac." That last game with Verburg closing was really intense, and when we won it, it was amazing and everyone was happy and stuff. But it still felt like we didn't really do anything. I think that was because of the expectation that we'd put on the team, and the final goal we set for ourselves to win the national championship. When we won that, we celebrated and coach Casey was happy because he loves winning. But we still had our sights set on the big goal. That's what I remember. It came, it went, it was there, we won, it was great, we took some pictures and held up our banner, but it was more about that we were closer to our goal.

Verburg's heroics captured more than the Civil War series and conference title: it was also Pat Casey's 1,000th career victory as a collegiate head coach.

Steven Kwan: That situation (Verburg) was in, that's the stuff you dream about in the backyard. Bases loaded, two outs, 3-2 count, bottom of the ninth, up one for Case's thousandth win and the Pac-12 championship. You literally couldn't have written that up more dramatic. And the fact that he just did his thing, threw it down the middle and threw it right by him, that was awesome. It was a special time.

Andy Armstrong: I think we heard some things about him having 999 wins. I mean during the game, at least for me, I wasn't necessarily thinking about it like "oh, this

FINISH

is going to be his 1,000th win." But to do it that way, that was obviously special for him and special to be a part of.

Mitchell Verburg: I learned that right after, so that was just icing on the cake at that point. A win first off for the Pac-12 championship, and second off for Case, who is an absolute legend. It's fun that I had the opportunity to play for somebody like that. He's the reason I am the way that I am now.

Ron Northcutt: One of the great things about that is when Case and I first started coaching together at George Fox ... Case wasn't even there when he got his first win! He was going to school at George Fox and playing basketball. We had a doubleheader at Pacific University in Forest Grove. Case was there for the first game and I think we lost like 9-0. And the second game he left because had to go to his basketball game.

Pat Casey: When I was at George Fox, they talked me into playing basketball as well. The very first game I ever coached, we had a playoff basketball game (that night). So, I coached the first game and lost and drove home, got in my basketball uniform and played a basketball game against Eastern Oregon in the first round of the playoffs. And I heard at halftime that I'd won my first game. So yeah, pretty easy coaching, man. If it was that easy I would've just played basketball all along and won 'em all. ... I might be the only coach in history that wasn't there for my first career win but was there for my thousandth.

Ron Northcutt: Getting back to the point, Case's first recruit at George Fox was a guy named Frank Wakayama, and he was at his 1,000th win. Frank came down from Portland and was at the game when we won that 1,000th one. It was awesome.

Pat Casey: There's a lot of things in coaching that get huge accolades, coach of the year or whatever. And then there are the little things like that, that are really big things to you. Frank being there was huge for me not only because he was there at my first win, but because he was the first player I ever recruited in baseball. When I got the George Fox job, I had been released from the Minnesota Twins on Father's Day in '87, and Frank was the first player I ever contacted about coming to George Fox and playing baseball. So that relationship has been long and good, and he's been there from the beginning. We have a great relationship, and I was very grateful that he was able to come down to Eugene and be there. I have a special place in my heart for Frank Wakayama.

With the Pac-12 title locked up, Oregon State had the opportunity to ease off the gas pedal and cruise into the postseason. But that wasn't how the 2017 Beavers were wired. Instead,

OSU continued to treat every game with the utmost importance, beginning with its finale against Oregon. The Beavers completed the Civil War sweep and finished off their Pac-12 slate in style the following weekend — with three more wins against Washington State, including a dramatic Jack Anderson walk-off walk in Game 1. A sweep of the Cougars left OSU with a 27-3 Pac-12 record, the best mark in conference history. The Beavers then closed the regular season with four non-conference wins over Abilene Christian, an unusual series that featured an Anderson walk-off single in extra innings and a surprise Engelbrekt pinch-hit at-bat. OSU finished the regular season 49-4 overall, setting school records for wins and winning percentage (.925).

Jack Anderson: I don't think we ever had a game that was really out of reach. We always knew whether we were down one run or two runs that we were the better team and we'd won all those games, so there was never a reason we couldn't win this one. We'd always be like "never say die!" I think that was from *The Goonies*, and we'd always believe in ourselves. We knew we had the edge over the other team because we were better than them and we could just find a way to win. We had some wild walk-offs that year, I had the walk-off walk against Washington State. I'm pretty sure every kind of walk-off you could have, we pretty much had. It was just hilarious.

Nick Madrigal: It was one of the coolest things I've ever been a part of. I remember one of the games (against Washington State), we ended up winning because their pitcher walked in a couple of runs for a walk-off. I remember after the game we were all laughing and jumping around the dugout and the clubhouse and people were saying "we're never going to lose! We're the best team ever," stuff like that. It was just funny because we would come back in every single game. We were never out of it, no matter if we were down to our last out or last inning, we would always find a way to come back. The special part was it wasn't just one person doing it every single time, it seemed like no matter who came up or who was on the mound, everyone came through. It was so much fun. I think everyone would agree that year was the most fun for the regular season.

Nate Yeskie: We won a game darn near about every way you could imagine winning a game … and it was a different guy, seemingly, each week. Nick would have a game-winning hit, Cadyn would have a game-winning hit. If you go back and look at those one-run games, I bet half of them had to have been walk-offs. It was uncanny, just the volume of wins and the way they were being won. Max and I would always have a laugh because he'd been with me so long and we looked at things different. He'd shake his head and I'd look at him and say "how are we going to do it tomorrow?" Because it was like we were running out of ways to get these things done. It was really enjoyable to watch kids experience that because when teams play at their highest level and there's no hint of selfishness in a bad way, it's very pure and just very exciting to watch.

Jake Thompson: Since our season got cut short the year before, we didn't take any game for granted. So, we clinched the Pac-12 and we were like "we're not stopping. We're going to keep our foot down and win out." I mean that's not what we were saying, but that's how we felt. That was the mindset that everyone had. They kept us out over one game, so we're not going to take any game for granted.

KJ Harrison: I think for us, we didn't even look at our record at all, we just kept playing. Every day was another game to win, and we wanted to win and we wanted to be in Omaha at the end of the season as one of the teams competing in the World Series. We took that mindset into every game. I mean we obviously knew there was this pressure on us, we were the number one team and everyone was talking about this crazy win streak, but we weren't really thinking about it. We just wanted to win every game, and I think that was really helpful for us.

Pat Casey: I never had the capacity to think about how well we were doing during the '17 season other than thinking about the next game and the next inning. I think some of the guys felt the same way and I think that's what really made us good, because there were times we'd win a game or a series and we weren't satisfied with our performance. They were so easy to coach because you'd go to practice and practice was like a fist-fight — it was every guy going crazy. Our practice times … I remember one time we had a two-hour-and-40-minute practice scheduled and I think after about an hour and 55 minutes I looked over at Bails and I said "shoot, we're done." Those guys were just so efficient in what they were doing.

Andy Jenkins: When you get a good class that comes in, leadership is something that teams live and die on. Ultimately we knew we had a great leader in Case and he had done it before, but the players have to believe it and they have to run the farm a little bit. I think a lot of coaches don't like to say that because they want to dictate the pace of the team, but in 2017 Nick and some of the guys started calling shots and saying "hey coach, why don't we do this? Hey coach, can we stretch here?" They were wiggling around some of the things that we did on a daily basis. For me, I take that as players taking ownership of their team and holding their teammates accountable and understanding what the goal was. I think the players — not just talent-wise — but the personalities of Nick and Gretler and others, and having some freshmen that come in with big talent and have big roles, certainly helped solidify a championship-caliber team. Not just a great team that was talented.

Drew Rasmussen: I mean in 2017 and 2018, that locker room ran itself, essentially. We were all driving in the same direction and all wanted the same success and the same goal. … We had such big personalities and great leadership, not just from the team captains, it was from everyone.

Pat Casey: The leadership was phenomenal. Usually you look and you say "this guy is our captain" or "that's our captain." And certainly, you have captains, but there were so many guys that led in their own way. That made it even easier.

Kyle Nobach, outfielder: Obviously Pat (Casey) was a great leader as well. If we weren't performing well as a team, he would step in in certain situations. If he felt he wasn't getting the most out of us, he would talk to us in a certain way. You could be feeling down or doubting yourself and struggling as a player, he would come in and say one or two things that would stick with you that night and amplify your play.

FINISH

CHAPTER III

HIGHS AND LOWS

One year after a selection Monday to forget, Oregon State found itself in a much different position heading into the 2017 NCAA Tournament. The Beavers, who won their final 16 regular-season games, were a near shoo-in to be the bracket's No. 1 overall national seed. The selection committee agreed, giving OSU the top seed for the second time in four seasons.

Since 1999, the basic structure of the NCAA Tournament has remained largely unchanged. Sixty-four teams are divvied up into 16 four-team regionals, hosted almost exclusively by the selection committee's top 16 teams (eight of which are awarded national seeds, guaranteeing home-field advantage until the College World Series). Each double-elimination regional is paired with another, and the 16 winners advance to the super regionals with the higher seed again hosting in nearly all circumstances. The super regionals are a simple best-of-three series with the eight winners moving on to the CWS.

In each regional, the teams are seeded one through four. As the top national seed, OSU was the Corvallis Regional's No. 1 seed. The Beavers would be joined by No. 2 seed Nebraska, No. 3 Yale and fourth-seeded Holy Cross. Unsurprisingly, OSU was considered a heavy favorite to advance by the national media.

Luke Heimlich, pitcher: That selection show was a lot more light-hearted. I think we got a little bit nicer of a breakfast up there that day since things were more solidified. Obviously, we were all in a good mood. We knew how things were going to come out. And they release the host sites the night before, so we already knew we were hosting. There wasn't much thought going into it. It was "all right, let's go figure out who's coming to play us."

Kavin Keyes, undergraduate assistant coach: My first year (as a player) was in 2011, and I was so young and naive to what was going on. I was a kid who was a good baseball player that just wanted to go play some baseball. I got there and I don't think we were supposed to be that good. We lost (catcher Andrew Susac to injury) and were ranked forever and at the very end you kind of realize it and are like "holy cow!" That's the thing, you go through the season and you're not really worried about being the number one seed or whatever until it actually happens. And when it does, you're like "holy shit!" It's just one of those things that doesn't really dawn on you until it happens.

Andy Peterson, undergraduate assistant coach: In junior college, I remember one of the things I obviously wanted when I was leaving for (Oregon State) was to be on the best team in the country and to play against the best teams in the country. I think in 2014, it was a cool deal where it was like "wow, I can't believe we did this!" In 2017, it was more expected and it was like "all right, we did it. Can we get to the playoffs now?" Nobody was surprised, nobody's head got bigger, I don't think any of that happened. It was just something that they all expected.

Christian Donahue, infielder/outfielder: I think it was a small stepping stone for us. With the team we had and the mindset we had, I don't think we were really thinking about regionals or super regionals. Our eyes were pretty much set on the World Series and winning that. I don't know if that's the right mindset to have, but the way our team was and how confident we were, it was just a small goal that we reached. We kept our heads up and kept moving forward.

Max Engelbrekt, pitcher: I remember things were coming out that we were like the best number one seed in a long time. I remember even the bracket we got was supposedly weak for a normal bracket.

Michael Gretler, infielder: You've got a target on your back because everyone wants to upset the number one national seed, and we viewed that as a challenge. We were grateful for being named the number one seed and having set ourselves up well, but once that calendar turns to the postseason everyone's record is 0-0. Anything can happen. There was a time before I was there, it was my senior year (of high school) in 2014, when the Beavers were the number one national seed at home for the Corvallis Regional — and ended up losing. We were not going to let that happen again.

Andy Peterson: In 2014 we showed up expecting to win it, and I think that was our problem. And that was something that the 2017 team never had. They never had that "we're going to walk in and kick somebody's butt" kind of thought. They locked in with their lunch boxes and played ball. In 2014, I think we were almost expected to get back to Omaha, it was more of an expectation than a "let's go get it" type of thing.

In 2017, it was pretty special how those guys handled it. I'd like to say me and Kavin and (Andy Jenkins) and whoever else that was still there from 2014 had something to do with it, but we really didn't. They were just more mature than we were.

Kavin Keyes: We talked to them about it, and that was the idea of what the grad assistants were supposed to do. We tried to be that bridge between coach and player where we could be a coach at times and a player at times, which was really cool. That opened us up for conversation, and they always asked us questions. That's what made them so good. There wasn't anything they didn't want to learn, and they were smart. They took in the good, and left the bad. Obviously everyone's situation is different. Our situation was different than the '06 and '07 teams, their situation was different than our situation. Obviously that was explained, but it doesn't hurt to hear the experience. It was just a good group of people.

Oregon State (49-4) kicked off regional play against Holy Cross (23-27) and defeated the Patriot League champion 8-2 behind a strong outing from Jake Thompson. Seven different Beavers recorded an RBI in front of an electric capacity crowd at Goss Stadium. It was a perfect start to the postseason for OSU.

Max Engelbrekt: Opening day and then the opening regional game are probably my two favorite days of the baseball season, just the energy that leads up into both of those. I haven't experienced that in a few years but I certainly miss that. At the regional, everybody has a set practice time and you have to go onto the field at a certain time. Teams come to your park and you can tell scouting reports are a little bit more intense. Those first two games are such high stakes. And on my end, we lost that second game to Irvine when I was a sophomore (in 2014). If you lose one of those first two games, you're pretty much screwed.

Tyler Malone, infielder/outfielder: I get chills just thinking about it. Postseason Goss is a whole different animal. You've got the extension of seating out in left field, and the games are absolutely packed and loud. Whatever good thing we did, Goss would light up.

Michael Gretler: That was the first time I saw them put the bleachers above the wall out in left field. It looked like we were playing at Fenway Park. You went up there and it was like, "I'm scared standing up here and there's nothing going on. I can't imagine people jumping up and down up here."

Trevor Larnach, outfielder: It was crazy, it was nuts. I didn't play the field, I was DHing most of the time that year, but playing there was always really loud during the season. And then when they brought in the new seats and every game was packed, it's hard to compare anything to it because that's how special it was. And it's different when you have guys by your side that you truly love and have worked with since the end of August for one goal. All of that combined truly just gives you a warm and fuzzy feeling inside that you can't really explain because you're going to battle with these guys that you've trained with, worked your ass off with, gone through it all with. To have that kind of spotlight at our home field for such a big regional or super regional, it was really, really crazy and really exciting to say the least. Those are probably some of the times I miss the most. Yeah, the World Series was absolutely amazing and that's in a tier of its own, but regionals and super regionals at Goss Stadium in front of the crowd on Friday nights and Saturday nights is something else.

Jake Thompson, pitcher: We were doing a lot of matchup things, so I got the Friday start going into the regional. It was huge to know that my hard work paid off. That was the first Friday I'd ever started, and once you get to the playoffs every game is the most important game. So, it was like "all right, I'm pitching the most important game and this is going to set the tone for whether we go to the winners' or losers' bracket." I'd worked really hard talking to the mental skills guys, finding that inner peace. I felt so confident going in, knew what I needed to do and everything like that. I remember how the sky was, I have a picture of that, it was kind of that purple Oregon sky. It was perfect. I remember they had more bleachers out, and knowing that you're (49-4), everyone is watching you. Everyone on TV is like "this team can't be for real, there has to be a weak point." So, you know everyone on TV is watching, and non-Oregon State fans are probably rooting for us to lose, and a big upset. But you've got our crowd there, all these fans, all these signs up and the fans are going crazy.

I remember my last inning out there; I struck a guy out with runners on. I freaked out and that moment was one of the greatest moments, just realizing I went from where I was the year before to that moment on a Friday night — big pitch late in the game and I was able to execute that big pitch. I remember my dad told me to take it all in and everything like that, and it was huge, it was a lot of fun. I like to think I set the tone going into the next game, I mean we had Heimlich going who struck out basically everyone he faced.

FINISH

Luke Heimlich was close to perfect the following night against Yale (33-16), striking out eight in seven innings, while giving up only two hits. He exited after just 88 pitches, as Oregon State was well on its way to an 11-0 victory. Yale head coach John Stuper, who tossed a complete game for the St. Louis Cardinals in the 1982 World Series, praised Heimlich during his postgame press conference. "I've been here 25 years. I pitched in the big leagues. He's the best pitcher I've seen in college baseball. He's legit. I think he's the kind of kid who's going to be a first-round pick without question, I think he's the kind of kid that can get drafted right now and maybe help a team in a pennant race in the big leagues later on this year. I think he's that good."

When he took the mound in the bottom of the first, Heimlich was already pitching with a lead. OSU, the designated visiting team, plated two runs to open the game. The first came on a Jack Anderson solo home run to right-center. In a year full of surprising moments, Anderson's long ball may have topped the list.

Jack Anderson, outfielder: I still watch that video, to be honest. It was one of those random games where Case had me batting third, because a couple games before that we played Abilene Christian and I batted first and played center. I think Case was just having fun putting me wherever. So, I'm batting third and I've never tried to hit a home run in my entire life. The last time I'd hit a home run was junior year of high school, so it had been more than half a decade. I didn't hit one in fall ball, didn't hit one in scrimmages, I'd never hit a ball out of Goss during an at-bat. But for whatever reason, that ball kept going and I pretty much blacked out after that. Those pictures I have of all the guys meeting me at home, that just goes to show how big of a family it really is. Everyone is so fired up for you.

Zak Taylor, first baseman: I've never heard a dugout freak out more for a guy that hit a home run. I think it might've been his only home run, and it was a nuke, too. First off, we didn't know Jack had juice like that. And second off, he hits it and I mean coming around first base, you've never seen someone so excited. It was the best thing I've ever seen. When he got to home plate, we were all out of the dugout, hitting him on the helmet, just yelling and screaming. We were all like little kids.

Michael Gretler: I remember a picture of me and (Elliott Cary) in the dugout when I turned and grabbed him. It was just so cool for a guy like Jack to be a walk-on from Oregon, it couldn't happen to a better guy and obviously he was a huge, huge, huge piece of our team. I don't know if he ever hit a home run during BP, so for him to hit that home run in the regional was pretty cool. I don't know how many home runs he hit during BP, but I can tell you that it wasn't many.

Kyle Nobach, outfielder: Jack had never really hit a home run, and all of a sudden he hits one out of Goss in one of the deepest parts of the stadium. You're like "what the hell just happened?!" It was a colder night with that purplish sky and Jack smoked that ball out to Trevor Larnach territory in right-center field. I don't think he'd ever hit a ball that far in his life. I remember him running the bases and it looked like he was flying around like he was on an airplane, wings out. It was just a pure joy moment because Jack had been a Beaver fan his whole life.

Jack Anderson: I hit it and I thought "OK, I hit that pretty well." And I thought it was going to be a flyout because usually balls that go that high for me don't get out, but it went past the scoreboard. I didn't know I had that juice, I sure wasn't hitting it that far, ever. That was the furthest ball I've ever hit, and it came at the right moment against Yale. I was just happy I hit all the bases because I sure don't remember doing any of it.

I didn't get a hit again until Omaha, so it was kind of a curse that I got that home run. I got the home run and didn't get another hit until like a week-and-a-half later. But if I could go back, I'd still hit the home run.

Pat Casey, head coach: I told him that I had to take all the credit because I put him in the three-hole where you're supposed to hit home runs. We had a good time laughing about that, but Jack didn't need to hit home runs. Rutsch didn't need to steal bases. John Wallace didn't need to have a great arm. Like I've said many, many times, this thing has a lot of elements to it and you just have to figure out who fits in where and what and how they can influence your club, and that's the thing about Jack. Jack was a guy who did everything A-plus. Everything that Jack touched with his personality — who he was, what he believed in, how he would work — was A-plus. Now, to have drop-dead Division-I talent, there's not a lot of guys like that. So, he was in a pool of guys just like a lot of people who had to earn their position, and he was willing to do that. I think he probably never dreamed that he'd come to Oregon State and be a leader. I think he probably thought he'd come to Oregon State and really wanted to make the team, really wanted to contribute and really wanted to be part of the program that he'd seen growing up, but he may never have thought "hey, I'm going to be one of those guys that people are going to look up to." So, for me, it was really rewarding that that's the guy he is, and still is.

Oregon State had six first-team all-Pac-12 selections in 2017. Five were obvious choices — Cadyn Grenier, KJ Harrison, Heimlich, Nick Madrigal and Thompson. The sixth was Anderson, who walked on at OSU after graduating from Lake Oswego High School. Anderson considered playing football and baseball at Linfield College, but chose the Beavers instead, redshirting as a true freshman in 2014. Unsure about his future with the program, Anderson wrote an email to Pat Casey and Pat Bailey that summer about his status moving forward. Anderson thought about transferring to a smaller school but opted to stick with the Beavers, who had a lengthy history of turning under-recruited walk-ons from the Pacific Northwest into stars. The scrappy outfielder made the team in 2015, became a starter the following year, received all-conference honors as a junior and closed his career in 2018 by winning Pac-12 baseball scholar-athlete of the year.

Jack Anderson: When I redshirted I couldn't practice with the team. I was just lifting with the other redshirts. I went back to Portland that summer to play in what was pretty much the minor league of the West Coast League, and Case and Bails told me that it kind of depended on the draft whether or not I'd be able to come back, just a numbers game thing. They wanted me, but if certain guys didn't get drafted where they thought they would and they came to Oregon State, there was pretty much nothing they could do. So, I was watching the draft those couple days and just hoping, because I knew all these guys' names. So, I was like "oh man, I hope they get drafted early!" I was very much following the draft and hoping guys got drafted where they should to give myself another chance to make the team. I was back in Portland — this is after the draft — and I was hoping to get some clarity on where I was going to end up. I'd been talking to Ryan Gipson because he was (head coach) at Linn-Benton at that time, and I knew if I didn't make Oregon State I was going to go play for Gippy. I remember talking to him and he was like "hey, I hope everything works out. But if it doesn't, we'd be more than glad to have you." I pretty much told him, "I hope I never hear from you. But if I do, I'll come and play for you and play hard." That's where I was at, I was just in the middle of if I was going to be at Oregon State anymore, or where I was going.

I had a mentor of mine who told me to put everything out there, don't leave anything behind you and have no regrets about what you want to be and what you want to become. So, I penned that email and said I would do anything I could, and the rest is history. I went back to Oregon State, Case said, "hey, let's meet." The draft went the way they thought it would, so there was another walk-on spot on the team. That next fall was pretty much my second try-out, and the 2015 season was my first year on the team. But yeah, it's just wild thinking back to that. I held onto that email forever. I would look at it before seasons, whenever I was in ruts and stuff, to remember my purpose and why I wanted to be on the team so bad.

Pat Casey: First of all, I think those conversations are always difficult when you get a kid who's a real good athlete like Jack and could play more than one sport. If he was at a smaller school, there's a real good opportunity for him to play football and baseball. And then, being a great student and trying to make a Division I team is a challenge. There had to be that decision and that belief in himself along with us that he could do this and he could do it at a high level. Sometimes kids are looking for a coach to say, "oh yeah, we're going to make sure you make the team" or "there's no doubt you can do this." We wanted Jack to buy into what we were doing as far as believing he could do this, and part of that is just an unknown. There are guys who come to school like the Nick Madrigals and the Adley Rutschmans who are just drop-dead starters right away. Then a lot of kids, the majority of the kids, have to come in and earn their spot. Jack was one of those guys, and I think that was the big thing. He was obviously very athletic. He was able to play the outfield we felt very good. We felt he was going to be a guy that could be an offensive threat. Not anybody that was going to really harm you with the long ball, but he would do all the little things. Play the short game, get on base. But most of all, the number one thing, was the influence he had on so many other players with his attitude — his work ethic, his character and his commitment, and those things are what we build our program on. He epitomized that, and was therefore rewarded by having a very, very successful career. He maybe even got more out of himself than he ever dreamed he might.

Pat Bailey, associate head coach: Jack was one of those guys where we were just a better team when he played, throw the stats out. The guy was a below-average outfield runner, he wasn't a burner, he had a below-average arm. But when he played in our system the way Case coached, we were a better team when he played. It was kind of like when Max Gordon played for us (in 2012-13), we were just a better team when Max Gordon played. And honestly, 90% of Division I programs probably wouldn't have played Max Gordon or Jack Anderson. They probably wouldn't have even made the teams. But we saw things in those guys that have nothing to do with baseball and have everything to do with bringing energy to the team. How they went about their business and how hard they played. Those guys ended up being great Beavers.

Jack Anderson: Bails and Case both came from George Fox, a Division III school, so I think that kind of perspective let them know that there are a lot of guys in the area that if given a shot would make the most of it. I think they always had that soft place in their hearts for the local kid who wanted to do everything they could to be part of the team. I think that's what I'm seeing now (as a coach) at Regis too, there are a lot of kids that didn't get recruited but they're giving everything they've got every day, and those are usually the kids that play. I think Bails and Case always tried to seek those kids out instead of only going for the big-name kids because if you get too many big names I think egos can get in the way. Bails and Case sought out a good balance between players who were going to get drafted high and kids that just wanted to work their tails off. That's what I always thought, those guys had that local vibe and understood that giving a kid a chance is always worth it.

Pat Bailey: Even though Jack didn't play professional baseball, I can tell you right now from a college viewpoint, he was a true professional. He took care of everything in the classroom, he came to practice every day, he showed up and he worked hard. He did all the little things. If we needed to get a bunt down, he'd get a bunt down. If we needed a hit and run, he'd get the hit and run done. He was just one of those guys who was a really good college baseball player. And he was a great teammate and a great human being.

Kyle Nobach: Oh, Jackie Moon baby. Jack's a stud and an incredible person. He's hilarious to be around. He's creative, he loves bringing people together, he has great spirit. Everything about Jackie is why he's incredible. Jack is the All-American kid in terms of that. He did a lot of community service, he's smart — everybody loves Jack. Nobody doesn't like Jack Anderson. We're in D.C. and he knows somebody down here. This guy sets us up and takes us to all these awesome dinner places and we had a great time. That's what makes Jackie special, he always finds a way to make things fun around you.

Following its 2-0 start to postseason play, Oregon State met Ivy League champion Yale again in the regional finals. The game was a relatively mundane 8-1 Beavers victory, but Madrigal showcased his all-around skill to close the Corvallis Regional. Way back in the Civil War conference series, Madrigal took a Kenyon Yovan fastball off his left hand that resulted in a deep bone bruise. Madrigal missed just two games down the stretch but was still feeling the effects of the injury in the playoffs. On a day when his hand was particularly sore, Madrigal went 4 for 4 at the plate, with four bunt singles, as OSU punched its ticket to the super-regional round.

Nick Madrigal, infielder: At first I was thinking it would maybe take a couple days to go away because it was just a bruise, but it lingered on for the rest of the year. It was one of the most painful things I've ever played with. I thought it was broken. I went and got a bunch of X-rays and all this stuff, and it was just a really bad bone bruise. It was something that I played with all through the playoffs. I would wrap tape on my hand. That was supposed to help it heal.

I showed up (for the regional final) and didn't take one practice swing the whole day or do anything live. I did not swing one time that whole day. It was similar to my freshman year. I remember being out there hoping the ball wouldn't get hit to me because my hand hurt so bad on defense. If there was a strikeout, I told Cadyn to not throw me the ball because I couldn't catch it. So, when I got up to bat, I bunted four times and that was the only thing I could do. I only had a couple things in my arsenal that day, but it ended up working out all right.

Pat Bailey: Madrigal had just come off that hand injury and he puts down two pushes, two drags — four hits. And the guy hardly ever dragged or pushed. That tells you how good of an athlete he is. And they knew it was coming, and he still beat them out. That was impressive.

Max Engelbrekt: It seems like some sort of legend that's a hundred years old that you'd hear about Babe Ruth. Because he was hurt during that and it's also ironic that it was Yale who was the team that can't figure out that this guy can't swing, and he still goes 4 for 4.

Andy Peterson: Nick couldn't swing a bat and he played anyway, which was amazing. We were all kind of shocked he played. He couldn't swing the bat, and he got four bunt hits. That's one of the most amazing things I've ever seen. They knew he couldn't swing. He hadn't taken an on-deck swing the entire day. And he comes up for that fourth at-bat, gets a bunt down, gets over to first and I'm just staring at him and shaking my head going "you've got to be kidding me. You're unbelievable."

Nick Madrigal: I played with Kenyon Yovan on Team USA, and I remember telling him "yeah, my hand STILL hurts from when you hit me in the middle of the season!" And he laughed about it, but I was serious. It was hurting. I was still taking Ibuprofen after the year. It was a weird injury.

It's funny looking back on it now since it worked out that well, but yeah I remember thinking "I'm going to give everything I can to this team. I've put so much work into this that I can't just sit on the bench. I'm playing for 20, 30 other guys on this team, so I'm going to go out there and give it everything I have." And everything I had was just a couple bunts that day, three or four bunts. That was everything I had and I'm glad I played and I'm glad it all worked out. It's one of those things, I could never look coach Casey in the eye and tell him "I can't play today." There was something about it, I was never going to do that unless I was seriously injured. It did not sit well with me. He could motivate pretty much anyone. He has a special way of talking to people and he's someone I look up to, so I just couldn't do it. I was going to go out there no matter what.

To go along with their six first-team all-Pac-12 selections, the Beavers also had six players receive honorable mention: Brandon Eisert, Michael Gretler, Steven Kwan, Trevor Larnach,

FINISH

Jake Mulholland and Adley Rutschman. Kwan, a part-time player in 2016, spent the first third of his sophomore season platooning in the outfield. After strong offensive performances at St. Mary's and Stanford, Kwan stuck in the starting lineup and became a menace atop Oregon State's batting order, hitting second behind Madrigal. Kwan, who quickly became a fan favorite with his disco walk-up song selections and electric play, went on to bat .331 in 2017 with a .440 on-base percentage and one home run — a grand slam against California. He won Corvallis Regional Most Outstanding Player honors by going a combined 8 for 11 with two RBIs and four runs scored in three games.

Steven Kwan, outfielder: I was actually really surprised at the end of that. I had some good at-bats, some balls were falling through and I was named MVP. I was really surprised because guys were hitting home runs, guys were hitting bombs. So, I was really grateful and it was nice that I was able to perform there. But honestly, it was just another couple of games that went by and I had a lucky couple of good streaks. So that was definitely real neat, but that regional was flying by. We felt pretty good at that point, we knew something special was brewing.

Trevor Larnach: When I was watching him, it felt like he was everywhere. On the field defensively, offensively, on the bases, he was all over the place. It felt like he was on base setting the tone every single at-bat, and it was just non-stop. I don't know how to explain it from our end, but I'm sure from the other teams' perspective he was a bastard to deal with. Obviously, you can't take away from what he did because he won that award, but it was a group effort that whole regional. It was more like he was all over the place, you couldn't stop him and it set the tone for our team.

Pat Casey: Kwany brought such a spirit of enthusiasm to what we did, an injection of what it means to be a college baseball player. And being very good defensively up the middle, which is something we've always felt is huge. We've always had good center fielders, we've always had good catchers, we've always had good middle infielders. We just believe we have to defend up the middle, and that was really a big part of our success.

Christian Donahue: Kwany is my guy. We became really close throughout college, and he's another super hard worker. Shoot, every guy on that team was really hard-working and a great guy. We just had a bunch of great guys on that team. But yeah, to see Kwan put it all together after he was a guy who did struggle at the beginning, to see him learn from those mistakes and get better every day ... I mean we all knew he had talent, the guy flies and is a great outfielder. And then when he put the hitting together, it was something fun to watch.

Kwan hit just .215 in 65 at-bats as a freshman, but he demonstrated a knack for bunting as the season progressed. The bunt wound up becoming one of the speedster's biggest weapons.

Steven Kwan: The bunting came my freshman year because Case always talked about how there was one guy on the team who will get playing time because he can bunt. I wasn't really very confident in my abilities swinging-wise or my all-around game, but I knew I could control my bunting. Literally just to find a way on the field, I made sure bunting was my biggest thing. And Andy Peterson was a huge part of that. He made sure I stuck with that, kept me accountable.

Andy Peterson: God I love that kid. He's just a big sponge and he wanted to get better in every single way. I actually had him on his recruiting visit when he must've been a sophomore or junior in high school, and I was playing. He was even smaller then than he was when he showed up and I was like "this guy, really? Are you kidding me?" But no, I think Case told him that if he learned how to bunt and handle the bat, he'd play. We took that under our wings together and we bunted a lot, I can tell you that much. He's such a little fireball, he's confident and he's one of my favorite kids I'll ever coach.

Brooke Knight, Corvallis Knights manager: Steven had a great attitude. He was fighting a hamstring (injury) most of the summer he was with us, so he had some downtime on two different occasions. … But Steven, he could really bunt. I give these guys an optional drag at times and they were crashing hard on the third-base side, I mean pre-pitch they were down his throat, 60 feet away the third baseman was. Because he's competitive, he was like "I'm going to thread the needle toward the shortstop between the pitcher and third baseman." So, he lined out to the pitcher and I know he can really bunt. Most guys can't do what he can do with the bat in that part of the game. And I said, "what are you doing?" He's like "I was just going to thread the needle; I've done it before." And I'm like "God-dang man, there's not enough room for error there. You've really got to thread it; you've got to punch it through there." And he's like "yeah, I know. Probably not the right decision." So, I was like "next time, man, just drop it down, you're still going to beat it on the third-base side, or take it with you." It was interesting because that's a learning moment for me, too. I'm like "God, this kid's got so much confidence in his bunt game that he's going to hit it in a three- to- six-foot-wide window with extra velo to get it by those first two guys so he can trot on down to first." Kwany was another guy who knew his game, knew what he excelled at and put the hurt on.

Steven Kwan: (Director of player development Tyler Graham) also helped out with the hitting aspect. I remember in the middle of the year; it was St. Mary's when I started breaking out. That's actually close to where I live, so my buddies came out to see me play, and I got inserted in there because Jack Anderson had hurt his ribs in right field playing a ball off the wall. I think a combination of that — T Graham working with me, and my best friends and family from back home, all those things culminated in the perfect storm. I had a really good game there and then at Stanford, and I think my confidence started soaring. I didn't look back after that.

Kwan became the team's primary No. 2 hitter in mid-April. Against Yale, he flipped spots with Madrigal to bat leadoff for the first time since opening day. He remained in the leadoff role for the rest of his college career.

Steven Kwan: It was really nice for my confidence. Obviously, I was used to the number two hole. Nick would get on and I would bunt him over, KJ (Harrison) would hit him in. It was a pretty solid sequence. But when Case had the confidence to put me in the leadoff role, that made my confidence soar even more and gave me a little more freedom to be a baseball player. I could be more athletic, just try some different stuff. And I've led off my whole life, so I really appreciate Case having faith in me for that.

Pat Casey: Steven Kwan, he was a guy that I didn't think really ever had a lot of confidence in himself. He wanted to know what he needed to do to play every day, and I said "well, that's easy. You know what you need to do to play every day. Why don't you come back later and tell me what you need to do to play every day because I think you can play every day."

If you take Trevor Larnach and the impact he had on him, and you take a lot of the mental off-the-field stuff that Tyler Graham did with those guys ... you could go ask Kwan how important Larnach was to him, and you could probably go ask Larnach how important Kwan was to him. Kwan's work ethic, his dedication and the time that he put into doing that, is amazing. I give a lot of credit to the coaches that were around that helped him.

Nate Yeskie, pitching coach: He went through that same learning point with coach Casey, just trying to figure out who he was and how he was going about some things. Coach Bailey had some insight for him. As people say, it takes a village when it comes to helping guys, and they're right. Because it's not just the baseball side with these kids, it's getting their schedules and their routines down in the classroom, weight room and getting acclimated to new surroundings that come into play.

Zach Clayton, outfielder: One of my favorite people of all-time was Steven Kwan. That guy had such high energy and took me under his wing. We had a lot of conversations not only about baseball but about life and all that. He was a person that I really looked up to … and he was amazing at focusing on the little things. He wanted to be great, and he knew that it wasn't just going to be about doing all the fun stuff that everybody wants to do. Because obviously he was a smaller guy, he was never going to have the power, the flashy big hits. But he worked at his craft and started really becoming the player he believed he was, which was tough to get out. A battler at the plate, because he would rarely strike out ever. I think his focus on his craft was just insane.

Kavin Keyes: Kwan was always the guy in the middle of something. Whether it be hitting a home run at the right time or something else that he wasn't supposed to do, he was doing it.

Kyle Nobach: He was so good out there, running around and making plays. He did a really good job in batting practice with how he trained, just running routes. It really made him a lot better and a much better defender. He set that tempo in practice, and he hit and put in that extra work. That's how everybody was at Oregon State, they worked their butts off.

Oregon State cruised to the Corvallis Regional title by outscoring the opposition 27-3 over three games. But a bigger threat was heading to Goss Stadium for the super-regional round. Vanderbilt outlasted regional host Clemson to advance, setting up an SEC/Pac-12 matchup for a spot in the College World Series. The Commodores had a pair of top-end starting pitchers in Kyle Wright and Patrick Raby, a duo that Vanderbilt head coach Tim Corbin hoped could go toe-to-toe with Heimlich and Thompson. Pitching figured to be the main storyline entering the super regional.

But instead, a bombshell report emerged about a star OSU player's past. On the eve of Game 1, The Oregonian published a story detailing Heimlich's juvenile record. At age 16, Heimlich had pleaded guilty to one count of child molestation. The alleged victim was his 6-year-old niece; Heimlich was 15 at the time. Heimlich has maintained his innocence, claiming he only accepted a plea deal, which included two years' probation, to avoid the messiness of a trial. The case and subsequent fallout, which received considerable national media attention, are far too complex for an in-depth exploration in this book. The most complete coverage of the story to date can be found in S.L. Price's Sports Illustrated *cover piece,* Prospect and Pariah, *from May 16, 2018. For a look at the story from the perspective of Heimlich's immediate family, see Kerry Eggers'* Portland Tribune *writeup from Feb.*

FINISH

1, 2018, titled: Penalties paid, Heimlich ready to return for Beavers baseball. *It's a tragic saga with no clear answers.*

Heimlich addressed the team before the story was published and chose to step away from the field for the rest of the season. He issued a six-sentence statement prior to the super regional, closing the letter by saying, "I understand that many people now see me differently, but I hope that I can eventually be judged for the person I am today. I'm so proud of our team's accomplishments and don't want to be a distraction. Therefore, I've respectfully requested to be excused from playing at this time."

There were a wide range of reactions to The Oregonian's *Heimlich report locally and nationally. Some argued a person with Heimlich's record should not be allowed to compete in college sports. Others believed Heimlich — innocent or guilty — had already paid his debt to society and had every right to pursue his dreams. With an intense debate swirling outside the program, OSU's coaches and players did their best to support Heimlich and focus on the task at hand.*

Pat Casey: You're not a head coach for 31 years and don't face adversity. There are things that are difficult in coaching, and that was certainly one of them.

Pat Bailey: I didn't know about it until a couple days before it came out. I actually called up his high school coach who I'm really good friends with, Marc Wiese. And I just said, "hey Mark, did you know anything about this?" And he goes "when I found out about it, I cried. Luke Heimlich is one of the neatest young men I've ever coached." So, it was a shock to all of us.

Christian Donahue: Everything just happened so fast. One morning, boom, it came out. Next thing you know, it's all over ESPN. Next thing you know, it's on every sports website, news page, everything. I remember I was with my family at the time when the report came out. I think my dad opened his phone and he saw the article, and we were all just sitting there speechless for a good 10 or 15 minutes before we even said anything.

Luke Heimlich: It was a whirlwind, there was a lot going on. I was able to talk to the team beforehand, they knew everything and they had my back from the beginning. All those guys trusted me and supported me in what I was doing. Those guys are my brothers and I stay in touch with every one of them. It was obviously a tough time, but having those guys around me made it a lot better.

Trevor Larnach: I think coach Casey kind of prepared us for that in a way. Not that specific thing, but he always said while we were grinding with each other during practice and doing better and better and becoming a number one national seed or whatever it is, he always basically said "the better you do, the more people are going to try and shoot you down and the more people are going to try and come after you." That prepared us for what that whole situation was like because Luke knew it was coming before we did, and we didn't really know what that was all about. But when he brought us all into the locker room and told us, the demeanor of the team wasn't like "all right, screw this kid." It was more "all right, we were prepared for this. Teams are coming after us, people are coming after us because we're killing it. What do we have to do to support our guy, what do we have to do to keep being successful and what do we have to do to keep morale and our attitude at the highest possible level for success?" And ultimately, I think that's what we did. Every single one of us backed him up. I don't think there was one person in that group who was like "I don't know about Luke, man." It was all "whatever you need, Luke. We've got you."

Andy Jenkins, assistant coach: It didn't seem in-house as magnified as it did in the papers and the national stories. We certainly all knew what was going on. I thought Pat Casey and the way he navigated through what he believed and what he felt was right to do, and what maybe people above him were telling him to do, I felt he did a great job of doing his job, and that's being a leader of a team and a leader of young men and a father figure. It was definitely a distraction, definitely an unfortunate situation for our club and Luke, but I sat back and watched coach Casey really make some tough decisions and fight off some pretty good criticism. I don't think it fazed our team as much as it fazed people in the world and social media because I felt like we believed in a particular person and we were around him 24/7 basically. We're all family and some of us are fathers, and we respect Luke and who he is. Luke is a good kid and he showed me that every day. We went out and played for him down the stretch and backed him, and that tells you a lot about how we felt.

Pat Casey: We tell them from the very beginning in the fall that there's going to be all kinds of distractions, there's going to be all kinds of people that want to get inside our club, and you've got to learn how to navigate it. High seas make great sailors. It's not a question of if any type of adversity is going to happen, it's just when and how much. That's the way it is with college athletes when you play together for an entire season and you have 35 to 40 guys involved with your program. Something's going to happen that's going to be a distraction. There's a lot of great things that happen, and then there are some things that happen that you don't anticipate, but you know there's going to be adversity. It could be injuries, it could be grades, it could be off-field incidents, it could be tragedies in families. There are so many things, and that's why you become a team.

Pat Bailey: Case did a great job of talking to our team about it. I don't know about the exact situations of all that stuff that happened, I don't know if any of us will ever know. I know there was a really nasty divorce and there were a lot of other things going on, but what I do know is Luke Heimlich, while he was here, was a model citizen. He was a great teammate, he's a high-character guy and he's a wonderful young man. One of the things I've always said to people is in the New Testament they were bringing out a lady who had committed adultery to stone her to death, and Christ was writing in the sand and he said "let he who is without sin cast the first stone." And I'm not taking away from what Luke did if it did happen. If it did happen that's terrible and it's sad, but there isn't anybody in this world that hasn't made mistakes.

Jake Thompson: We all know Luke as a person, a baseball player, pretty much everything because we're all family. We all have to wake up at 6 a.m., hang out in the locker room, be at baseball all day, so we all know who he is. He told us his side of the story, and we all believe what we want to believe. I don't want to get too into that, but we were all together about it. Luke told us the story, we're all comfortable with his story and what happened, and it did not change anything we thought about him, it did not change anything at all. He was our teammate, we were there, we knew his side of the story and we full-on supported him and wanted to help him out as much as we could. It was huge knowing a lot of the things that would come with it, but it wasn't something that was going distract us, it wasn't something that was going to distract him because we all knew the story that he told us. I could be wrong, but we were firmly with Luke.

Zak Taylor: It was tough. I mean we all know the story and even to this day people still have their certain opinions and I understand that, but you can't treat a human being how he was treated. He sat us down right before that story broke and addressed us as a team. And I remember sitting in that locker from Day 1. We've all had his back, we've all had his back. I love Luke, I think he's an absolutely great human being, a great person, a hard worker, one of those guys I'd do anything for.

Steven Kwan: It was really hard, and I thought it was just very unfair. Obviously, I get that in the story you're going to take the victim's side in that, but the way he explained it and how the story was, I just wish more people would take the time to understand the whole story. It was really unfortunate how it all turned out. With the situation and the nature of it, people don't want to give it a full listen. They want to jump to conclusions, which I get, I totally understand that. I wish more people would take the time to understand the whole story.

Drew Rasmussen, pitcher: I think there are two sides to every story. It's a touchy subject, and when I talk to him I don't even bring it up. But like I said, there are two sides to every story. I think people read a headline and immediately jumped to conclusions. Being honest, until I lived through it, I would've been the same. I used to think life was black and white, but it turns out there's a ton of gray area. People love to jump to conclusions so fast now that they're not always willing to hear both sides out.

Christian Donahue: For me personally, it didn't really affect the way I looked at Luke. Because I'd known Luke for three years up to that point and I still don't think he did it. I don't think of him any differently because of it, and I don't think most of our teammates did, either. Luke's a great guy and everyone around the clubhouse loved him. I don't think it really affected everyone as much as it (could've) because of how tightly knit we were and how close we were as a family. It was just a thing where we were there for him, backing him up and trying to help him in any way because we couldn't even imagine what he was going through at that point.

Steven Kwan: Luke's been a great teammate, a great friend, a great person. I knew it would rally us even more. He was a teammate who needed our help, and we had his back.

Kyle Nobach: I love the guy and until this day I support him. I love Luke, and I think that's all we can say. We don't see Luke as that person, and it's really too bad.

Nick Madrigal: Going through it, we tried to be there for Luke. It was just one of those things where it was hard to deal with. Not only was it hard on the team, but it was really hard on Luke and I think that was the worst part. Because we all felt bad for him and tried to be there for him.

Drew Rasmussen: You're just worried about the guy. Obviously, it's tough to understand what he was going through. I would go to his room and check in on him. But other than that, especially at 21 years old, I didn't really know how to handle the situation perfectly and it was uncharted territory for all of us. I was mostly making sure he was doing all right, and trying to keep him in the highest spirits possible was basically all I was trying to do. Other than that, man, it's a blur how fast all that stuff happened. It's too bad for him, but he's grown through it and he's doing well now. It's awesome to see who he's become, even though he's had all that adversity in his life.

Jack Anderson: I missed so much stuff because I was in class all the time. For team meetings and stuff, I usually wasn't there, so I'd just ask someone. So, I had no idea what was going on at all, and I think Case found me at practice the next day and brought me into his office and told me what Luke told the team, that something was going to come out. I really didn't know the extent of what was going to come out until it did, and we were all kind of shell-shocked there for a day. We were pretty much worried about our brother, worried about Luke. We weren't too worried about him playing or not, we just wanted to make sure he was all right. Obviously, so much came from that moment, and we still had baseball to play. I think we tried to control what we could control, take it from that standpoint and let everything else go as it would. But yeah, that was definitely one of the crazier weeks for all of us to be in the middle of a national news story like that. It was crazy.

I think Case was probably up all night figuring out the best thing to do, whether to play Luke or not, having meetings. We could see from his face that he was going through a lot. I feel like we were just playing for him, too, because he was pretty worn out I think from having to figure out what's going to be the best thing to do for the program. I feel like that (situation) could be an ethics class for what should or shouldn't be done because it was so unique. And we were all playing the biggest games of our careers at that point. Max Engelbrekt was the only one who'd played in a super regional. I think once that Friday rolled around, we didn't even have to have a team meeting or anything like that. We knew it was go-time and it didn't matter who was playing, we were going to go out there and play our best and let the chips fall as they may. But yeah, that was a blur of a super regional. They were the biggest games of our lives, so we just focused on that, I think.

Max Engelbrekt: Selfishly, that was also during finals. So, we're all going through the same period of time where we have the most important week of the year, and for me I'm in grad school, so it's not exactly the easiest thing. I actually had to study for that stuff. That was just crazy. It was quite a lot to process, especially with us going into a super regional.

After the earth-shattering revelation, Oregon State still had a super regional to prepare for. The top-seeded Beavers (52-4) were going to have their hands full against Vanderbilt (36-23-1) with Heimlich in the fold. Down the Pac-12 pitcher of the year, the task would be even tougher.

Nate Yeskie: When everything surfaced and you're trying to take into consideration everybody that's involved, you're doing your best to really be in the moment at that time because everybody is going to process things differently. People had their versions of what happened, so we really had to galvanize ourselves as a group and come together and just say "hey, we knew when we got up today that we were going to be playing the game of baseball against another quality opponent. So, let's stay focused on that and focus on those things that we can control. Let's keep things there."

Nick Madrigal: I knew we had a lot of great and mentally-strong players on the team, so I wasn't too worried about it. There was almost a fire to us after it all came out that we were going to do it for Luke, go out there and play our game, so I wasn't too worried about it.

Cadyn Grenier, infielder: I've told this to a lot of people: the thing that impressed me the most about our team wasn't how good we were, it was how we handled that. And when Luke finally told us what the alleged story was and everything was happening, nobody skipped a beat, nobody did anything. We walked out of the locker room, went straight to stretch and nobody cared. We were just there for Luke, and nobody felt like it was going to affect us in any way, and it didn't. It absolutely didn't. We went about our business like we had a super regional to win, and it was the most incredible thing. Because I feel like at any other place that happens and guys are like "dude, what's going on? This is crazy," and now it's a distraction. We had all the distractions in the world for that series, and not one person skipped a beat. It was incredible, man. Still to this day I'm shocked how everyone ate it up and was like "whatever, we've still got a game to win."

Brandon Eisert, pitcher: I think it just brought us together. We all care about each other so much and we still had the goal in mind to win a national title. We were going to play no matter what, and that's obviously what he would want, too, for us to not get distracted and to keep pushing forward. I think that's exactly what we were able to do.

Jake Mulholland, pitcher: There was a quick moment where it was kind of weird, but once the lights go on and you're in the locker room, it's all about competing and being at your best. I think a lot of us had a lot of motivation as well. We wanted to play well for him.

Joe Casey, outfielder: We knew he'd want us to go out and crush it, and we did. He did so well for us that year and picked us up so many times, it was time for the whole team to pick him up. Our whole season was so amazing, we were still going to get the job done and go to Omaha.

Pat Casey: We were prepared to play and I thought we played very, very well.

With Heimlich sitting out, the Beavers needed to shuffle their rotation on short notice.

FINISH

Thompson, who threw the first game of the Corvallis Regional, was the natural choice to start in place of Heimlich. The junior right-hander had a full six days of rest and was pitching with extreme confidence.

Jake Thompson: Luke was supposed to throw that (first game) against Vanderbilt. I was doing homework, going around campus and stuff like that because it was a Friday, and I was trying to ignore the fact that we had the biggest game of our lives that night. We'd already talked. Luke was going Friday, I was going Saturday and Fehmel would be Sunday, if needed. I remember they had (Kyle Wright), who ended up getting picked fifth overall, and I figured Luke would go against him. So, I was thinking about Saturday a little bit, trying to keep my mind off of everything. Then coach Yeskie texted me and asked if I could stop by the office real quick, and I was like "OK, yeah, no problem."

Nate Yeskie: I'd gotten the phone call from coach Casey and he just said, "hey, we're going to need to start Thompson tonight. Get him ready, I'll see you at the park later." So, I hung up the phone … and brought Jake in, and the way our previous week had set up, Jake was on his normal rotation. And the way we were constructing bullpens at that time, there weren't any potential obstacles that we'd created for ourselves as far as would he be ready or not. We were anticipating throwing him Game 2, but because of the previous week it just lined up well for him. So, I looked at him and said "how are you feeling?" He goes, "great!" I said, "how would you like to start tonight?" And he goes, "I'd love it!" "Well, you're starting tonight then." He goes, "all right," and he didn't think anything of it. With him being from Florence, I said, "call your family, I'm sure they're going to be at the game tonight. Tell them that you're pitching so they don't show up in the fifth and they're surprised when you're out on the mound."

Jake Thompson: He said to not tell anyone I was starting because there were some things they needed to do with everything going on. So, I was like "I won't tell anyone and I'll be ready to go." At that point it was like two or three in the afternoon and the game was in four or five hours. So, I immediately left everything I was doing on campus. I went home, did my routine, got ready, ate what I wanted to eat, and showed up to the field.

Nate Yeskie: His development, his level of confidence, how he'd performed that year, he was ready for that moment. When I told him that he had the ball tonight, he put a big smile on his face and said, "all right, let's go!" And I said, "I love it, go get 'em. I expect at least seven out of you tonight." Just joking, I always tried to keep those guys on their toes. But what did he go, maybe seven and change that night? He was pretty good.

Jack Anderson: Jake pitched a hell of a game, and we knew Jake was going to be Jake. He'd figured himself out that whole year, so we knew nothing was going to change there.

Jake Thompson: I didn't get to pitch against Kyle Wright, which kind of sucked, but it was one of those games where I was just so focused. Like I knew it was the big time with everything going on with Luke and Vanderbilt was a great team. We always talked about how they were the guys to beat. I remember being so focused and it seemed like the game just cruised by.

Thompson worked an easy 1-2-3 top of the first and settled in from there, putting together another strong outing under the lights at Goss. He finished with seven strikeouts in 7 2/3 innings, allowing four runs on seven hits on a dreary, damp evening. The run support came early and often as Harrison belted a three-run first-inning homer off Raby. Madrigal added a two-RBI double in the second, and the Beavers tacked on a few more runs as the game progressed for an 8-4 victory.

Harrison's homer — a drive through the rain to straight-away left field — felt monumental in the moment. It was a clear signal that the previous 36 hours of chaos were not going to impact Oregon State.

KJ Harrison, first baseman: To be able to come up in a situation like that and do that was unbelievable, especially against Vanderbilt. They were a very, very good team and playing them at home, I was just looking for a good pitch to hit. Luckily I put a good swing on it, and it was definitely one of the coolest moments of my baseball career.

Andy Peterson: Jumping on them like KJ did, that was something special. I think I jumped eight feet in the air on that one, it was hard to hide the emotions.

Pat Bailey: It just let the air out of the balloon. Obviously you are playing Vanderbilt. They're a national power and we're a national power — and it's a huge game. They've got a bunch of guys that are going to be first-round picks, we've got a bunch of first-round picks. There was electricity in that stadium. I think when KJ hit that home run, it was almost like everybody took a deep breath, relaxed and focused on playing the game.

Christian Donahue: I think that right there set the tone for the whole series. For us it was like "oh, we're playing against Vanderbilt at home, super regional. This is about to be one of the biggest series we'll ever play in." And for KJ to come out and hit that, yeah, he just set the tone from the start. That was awesome.

KJ Harrison: I never try to actually think to myself "hit a home run." I just remember stepping out of the box and trying to relax myself because you get so amped up, especially when everyone is yelling and it's such a big-time game. To do something like that, it just felt good to get that first one out of the way.

Drew Rasmussen: I love KJ, man. He's just another fun-loving, awesome dude. It was a picture-perfect Corvallis day: 60 degrees, raining. Growing up and committing to Oregon State, it was everything you sign up for. Maybe you don't know it's coming, but once you've been there for two or three years, you couldn't have picked a more perfect environment to play in. Goss was rowdy. And KJ, I want to say he blew the roof off the place, but there is no roof. That place exploded with excitement and that was really just a snapshot of what the entire season was. We were able to put pressure on a great arm and eventually … we had so much talent on that team that you knew something big would happen at some point. And KJ happened to be the guy to deliver.

Harrison was a top-100 national recruit when he signed with Oregon State out of Honolulu's Punahou School as a catcher/infielder. A Day 1 starter at first base, Harrison went on to win Pac-12 freshman of the year honors in 2015. He was one of the most consistent hitters in the country from 2015-17, making the all-Pac-12 first team in each season as the anchor of OSU's lineup. Harrison hit a career-best .313 as a junior, finishing with nine homers and 43 RBIs while dealing with injuries to his thumb and ankle.

Andy Jenkins: KJ was another high-profile guy who came in that really could hit, that was his number one tool, and he had a huge arm. The catching stuff was a work in progress and we made it work a little bit, it was really nice having Logan (Ice) for some time as a defensive backstop back there and KJ shuffled into more of a first baseman. He was a very, very low-key guy, a hard worker. Him and Donahue with the Hawaii culture brought a little bit of fun to our program up in the Northwest. I know once a week our managers would put on some Hawaiian music. KJ was just a great kid and he played hard.

Christian Donahue: We were pretty close growing up, and even more close in high school. Then once we got to college, we roomed together for three years. So yeah, KJ is one of my best friends. I know him very well and we had a lot of fun times together.

Zak Taylor: KJ was great. I was really close with him and he was one of the older guys that kind of took me under his wing. I would always pick his brain a ton, especially working with him since we both caught and we both played first. I think he really helped to push me and prepare me for when he did go down. And I did play for a period of that season and that was my first time having a little bit of success at that level. I almost proved to myself and he helped instill in me that "yeah, I can do this, I can play at this level." It helped me too that it really doesn't matter where you're from, if you came from a smaller school in Oregon or wherever it may be, if you're good enough and you work hard, you can absolutely play at any level that you want to play at. You just have to put in the time beforehand and of course work your butt off.

KJ Harrison: We were playing Arizona State and I was catching. I threw it down to second base and the batter interfered and I hit his helmet, and I had a partially torn ligament in my thumb. And then in the (Civil War) series I rolled my ankle sliding into second. So yeah, I was a little dinged up that whole year.

The thumb had an impact for sure. It's a tough spot, especially because it was my right hand, which was my throwing hand as well. I had to sit out some games, but obviously towards the end of the season it felt way better because that's when I started to hit well again.

Steven Kwan: KJ was getting a little hot there, and that was the juice that we needed. Because a lot of our games had been one-run games, real close nail-biters and we'd always pull through. But KJ getting an early home run, getting us some momentum, it was like "we're really going to do this thing."

Jake Mulholland: That was so crazy. I think that was our first time playing an SEC team that year, so for me it was my first time ever playing an SEC school. You always hear what the national news says about SEC teams, so I was just so excited to be able to play a team like Vanderbilt, a very renowned program, very good.

I remember when KJ hit that home run, the stadium erupted and we were all going crazy. It was just a sense of, we belong here. This Northwest team that didn't even make it to the postseason last year, we can hang with these guys.

Steven Kwan: I mean, it's Vandy. They have a reputation that follows them, and they came to our yard and tried to do their antics. They did that stretching in right field between innings, and we're just looking at them like "really? This is what you guys are going to do?" We couldn't wait to shut them up. It felt awesome. SEC, Vandy, it was awesome.

FINISH

Nick Madrigal: Some of those guys ... it was a chirpy series. We talked back and forth to each other and we really wanted to beat those guys. But yeah, it was a lot of fun. Goss Stadium was rocking and the environment there was great.

Andy Jenkins: When you think about Oregon State and you think about 2005 when we clinched to go to the World Series for the first time since 1952, once we won we learned a lot about Omaha and we learned about where we were actually going. The teams that you watched on TV were LSU and Miami and Cal State Fullerton and Long Beach and Texas, and Vanderbilt's done a great job of getting their name in there for national recognition along with Oregon State. So, to have a high-profile team that's had success on the national level come into Goss, we definitely didn't back down as a fan base.

Michael Gretler: Those were fun games. Of course, it's Vanderbilt, they have obviously had a lot of success the last however many years and you want to play against the best. For them to come to Corvallis was cool because it's a little different than the SEC. But I think they'd be the first ones to tell you that it might be a smaller crowd, but man those fans are on top of you, they're in your ear.

Adley Rutschman, catcher: The energy was something. We'd seen packed crowds at Goss before, and I think one of the things that makes Corvallis special is that we have consistent crowds that are invested in the players' success and the team's success, but it was a different energy. That playoff atmosphere is just different.

Jake Thompson: I was having a ton of fun all game, but I remember getting taken out and I was like "wow, I can finally breathe now and I can finally relax, hang out and talk with people." And my team backed me up with (eight) runs, so winning that game just said "hey, we can do this." We'd beaten everyone all year, so winning that game set the tone for the next night when Fehmel pitched incredible.

While Vanderbilt turned to Wright — the No. 5 overall pick in the 2017 MLB Draft — with its season on the line, Oregon State surprised some by choosing to start Bryce Fehmel over Drew Rasmussen in Game 2. Fehmel had been used sparingly over the last month to give his arm a break, throwing just a single inning against Abilene Christian after leaving the rotation in early May. The layoff worked, and Fehmel was ready to re-enter the rotation for the postseason. Rasmussen, who had started the past four weeks in place of Fehmel, would be available to close Game 2 or start Game 3 if necessary.

Bryce Fehmel, pitcher: (My arm) wasn't feeling good, but it got better with time. I think some time off helped. Pitching 20 innings in high school and going straight to 100 caught up with me real quick, but a little time off helped it pretty good. I just tried to keep my mind ready for when my name would be called because I knew I was going to be called upon eventually.

I think it was that Thursday, Case and Yeskie let me know I was going to start. Once they let me know, I did everything I could to prepare my mind because I knew my arm was in better shape than it was before. I got scouting reports, I talked to Yeskie about what I needed to do and my mind. I was much better with my mental game. Preparing myself and visualizing what I needed to do on that given night was a big part of my process that game.

Pat Casey: We knew that (Wright) was an elite guy. We liked that and we kind of embraced that.

Bryce Fehmel: I knew he was going to be a top-10 pick. I knew he had all the filthy stuff in the world, but I also knew our lineup could compete against anyone. Our lineup didn't seem to care about who was on the mound, they just stuck to the plan and stuck to the scouting report. So, I had all the trust in them, and my job was to put up zeroes each inning and give our offense a chance.

Nate Yeskie: Case and I looked at each other after the first inning when Wright went up against our first three guys and I went "oof, man. We've got our work cut out for us tonight because this guy's got some monster stuff."

Cadyn Grenier: Once again, it was one of those things where it didn't matter who was on the mound, it didn't matter who we were facing. We had all the confidence in the world that we weren't going to give them anything and we would take anything we could from them, and that's exactly what we did. KJ hits that huge home run and from that point on it was over, the game was over. We weren't giving them an inch, they kind of just collapsed and we got on top of them and didn't let up.

For the second time in as many nights, Harrison delivered an early blow to ignite a sold-out Goss Stadium. Wright faced the minimum through two innings before running into trouble in the third, giving up the game's first run on a Kwan base hit. Madrigal followed with an infield single to bring up Harrison, who blasted a Wright fastball into the temporary bleachers above the left-field bullpen for a three-run homer. Oregon State — wearing its throwback gray pinstripe uniforms from the 2007 title team — was suddenly up 4-0 on one of the best pitchers in college baseball.

KJ Harrison: I couldn't believe that it went out when I hit it, especially against a guy like him. To be honest, when I was running around the bases I blacked out. I was just so excited and juiced up and amped up in that situation. Kyle Wright is an unbelievable pitcher and he's in the big leagues now. I played with him during summer ball as well, and he talks to me about it sometimes. It's funny with that kind of stuff, but he's a great dude and it was really, really cool to do that.

Andy Jenkins: To come out and throw the first punch against a top-10 arm was definitely something that lifted us, no doubt. KJ was kind of known for those big hits in big moments.

Zak Taylor: KJ was having such an incredible year, Wright was carving that entire year. And just to have two guys that are having these incredible years go head-to-head, I mean it was pretty special to watch. You could feel the competitive fire that was out there, and when your team comes out on top in that, that was pretty special to experience.

Michael Gretler: We came out of the gate hot both of those games, and KJ's home run off Kyle Wright was something. Here's a kid who's going to be drafted in the top five picks, obviously a great pitcher. The biggest thing I remember is just the team offensive approach those two games. You had Kwan working walks, Nick and Cadyn playing small ball, hitting behind guys, putting pressure on the defense and letting the big bats of KJ, Trevor and everyone else drive those guys in.

Bryce Fehmel: I was up-top in our locker room so I didn't see it, but I remember hearing it and feeling the crowd go absolutely crazy. I remember running down the stairs and the dugout was going crazy. Everyone was outside of the dugout waiting for him. Just talking about it gives me chills. So yeah, that was a big turning point in that game. I'm glad I was able to put up zeroes after that as well.

Nate Yeskie: KJ put that big swing on Wright in the third, our guys just started going and you could feel the momentum and the energy. Bryce kept getting better and better, and what people forget is Bryce was out of the rotation one week earlier. We had to take him out and give him a break, he was pooped from being in the rotation. That's just part of the stuff that comes with our job as coaches, to recognize when to push and when to pull. At that point in the season, Bryce was pooped. Taking him out in hindsight was a great piece for us and especially for him to kind of regroup, take a deep breath and get a second wind and get ready to go back out there. But he was good, good that night, man.

Fehmel was better than good, flummoxing Vanderbilt with his impeccable location and ability to change speeds. He gave up a pair of sixth-inning runs but Oregon State answered with three insurance runs in the seventh, all of which were charged to Wright. In his last college start, Wright was tagged for seven runs on eight hits in 6 2/3 innings. Fehmel looked like the first-round pick that night, wowing the Goss Stadium crowd with a 104-pitch complete game. The sophomore struck out a career-high 10 with no walks, giving up just one earned run on five hits. On the back of Fehmel, the Beavers secured their first College World Series berth since 2013. Final score: OSU 9, Vanderbilt 2.

Bryce Fehmel: I don't remember feeling anything in my body, I just remember staying locked in. The crowd was massive, the crowd was loud and it was probably one of the bigger games I've pitched in, in my life.

Brandon Eisert: Just an amazing performance from Fehm. I was out in the bullpen getting ready to go into the game if I needed to, and obviously I never needed to. He was putting on that kind of performance.

Nate Yeskie: Fehmel pitched I think one of the best games in the history of the program.

Trevor Larnach: Bryce looked like he could've fallen asleep on the mound because that's how calm and chill he was. And that's how he always is, he's a damn stud. That's what I say about everybody, Bryce, Kwan, KJ, Luke, I could name off all these studs and all these cold-blooded killers. And when it comes to Vandy, a big SEC team coming in with a top-five pick, and Bryce shuts them down like it's nothing, it just makes you smile and nod your head because our team doesn't really expect anything else, no matter who's out there. The coaches expect that, the players expect that, and that's how we all worked at our game. Watching Bryce, it was just 1-2-3, 1-2-3, that's what it felt like at least, and there was no touching him. I remember all these players on that team making themselves look like fools because of how untouchable he was and how on top of his game he was. And I can only imagine how his parents were feeling after watching him do that. It was a special outing; it was a special performance by him and the team. There's no amount of words I can say that will express the joy and the love and the feeling I get talking about these guys in those moments.

Jake Mulholland: Fehm was another guy who never let a situation say what he was going to do. No matter who he was playing, he was going to come out and give it his all every time. He's a very, very smart pitcher, knows how to throw to guys, really likes to learn scouting reports and how he's going to pitch to every single person. He definitely does his research and he just competes like no other. I was so happy for him when he went out and threw. He threw a complete game to go to the College World Series.

Drew Rasmussen: All he knows how to do is win. There was no fear, no nerves because we had a guy going that we knew was going to get the job done and our offense was going to take care of business, we were going to play great defense. We knew for teams to beat us, they were going to have to play basically perfect baseball.

The guy just gets it done. It doesn't matter who you're playing, where, when, what the weather's like. He's a gamer, he gets out there, he wins. And ultimately he's super competitive. He went out and threw a great game for one, but he also gave us the ability to rest a lot of arms and get back to where we wanted to be heading into Omaha.

Max Engelbrekt: I remember I was warming up some before. At that point, I'd kind of been boxed out since Mulholland and Eisert were so good. I was always there to come in if they needed help, but they never seemed to need help. So, I remember I was one of the first people to tackle (Fehmel) because I was down in the dugout when we did win. I was almost always in the bullpen until the game ended. So yeah, Fehmel had a funny year that year. He was quite good there, and he just kept pitching. He probably thought he was going four or five since we had such a good bullpen, and there he is pitching in the sixth and the seventh. All of a sudden it's the ninth and he's still going.

Jake Thompson: No matter what kind of year Fehmel has or what he did the game before, you're always confident in him. He's going to throw strikes and get the job done. And when it came to big games, he always seemed to be that calm, cool, collected guy that goes out there, competes, challenges every hitter. And before you know it, he's thrown nine innings. It goes by quick; his games are always quick. It was one of those things where whether he gave up five runs the game before or none, when we needed Fehmel, he performed.

Christian Donahue: Fehm would go up there and he knew what type of pitcher he was. He wasn't going to blow you away, but he could throw it pretty much wherever he wanted. He could keep it down, throw it up if he wanted, and he was a really good competitor, too. He wasn't backing down from anybody. For him to do what he did … it was just awesome to see him grind up there against an eventual top-five pick.

Jack Anderson: I think that's the beauty of baseball. Vanderbilt was a really good hitting team, but Bryce at home was tough to play with when Goss was playing like it was that day where you're not going to hit the ball out unless you really deserve it.

Cadyn Grenier: It was like "dude, it's right here. This kid can do this to one of the best teams in the nation, we're unstoppable." And at the time, we felt like we were.

Bryce Fehmel: I'm just glad I was able to perform on that given day and send us to Omaha. It was a pretty special moment.

Jack Anderson: The first few innings of both those games were kind of like a heavyweight battle. Once we got ahead, we just suffocated them. Vanderbilt had a brutal draw. They were in Clemson and then they came all the way to Goss. I bet they were frickin' fried from their week. I think we knew if we got up on them, we could take control of the game and not give them any hope.

I was just stoked that we got to wear those 2007 jerseys, those were my favorites. When I was growing up, those were the jerseys I watched on TV. The fact that we convinced the school, or whoever we needed to, to wear them was just awesome. Those are my favorites. I don't think we could wear them in Omaha, but we were able to get those by them. We probably broke a contract there or something, but at that point I don't think we really cared. I really don't know how that all came about, but I do know Bryce really wanted to wear them because he wore them when we were playing Utah earlier in the year. And I guess it was our team, our moment, who cares? Let's just frickin' wear them. That was definitely cool, it brings the program full circle to wear the same ones the guys before us did.

Jake Thompson: You don't really believe it's actually happening until after the fact. I remember the dogpile, and after the dogpile you don't really know what to do because none of us had really ever dogpiled like that before. It was just so surreal, like "holy smokes, we're going to Omaha!" It was something we'd talked about all year, and I think another big thing for us. The year before, everyone was like "don't talk about Omaha, let's just think about one game at a time" and everything like that. People were scared to talk about the results you want. When we went into the offseason and fall and then that year, we talked about Omaha all the time. That was what we wanted, that's what we were going to accomplish, and we told ourselves we were going there.

CHAPTER IV

WELCOME TO OMAHA

After dispatching Vanderbilt and getting in a couple of post-super regional practices at Goss Stadium, Oregon State took off for Omaha, Nebraska, with one goal: complete the historic season. Due to the fallout of The Oregonian *report, Luke Heimlich decided to stay in the Pacific Northwest as the team departed. He released a three-paragraph statement before the College World Series, writing "I'm sad to say I am not joining them because doing so would only create further distraction for my teammates, more turmoil for my family and given the high profile of the national championship, direct even more unwanted attention to an innocent young girl."*

Heimlich's absence did not come as a surprise following a week of intense scrutiny, but the Beavers lost another key player in the lead-up to the CWS. The day before play began at TD Ameritrade Park, head coach Pat Casey announced that Christian Donahue had been suspended for a violation of team rules. Donahue, who had found a home defensively in left field and was one of the Beavers' better hitters, declined to discuss details of the infraction on the record.

Christian Donahue, infielder/outfielder: A few days before we were leaving for Omaha, I got a call from Case. From everything that went down, I wouldn't be able to travel to Omaha. And I was suspended for 50% of the next season. The call was basically just that my season was done and I wouldn't be able to go to Omaha with the team. So, for me, it was really tough. It was probably one of the scariest phone calls I've ever gotten. My heart dropped as soon as he called me because I had gotten the news right before that. So, I knew Case was going to be calling at some point. It was a tough, tough situation. I made some decisions I wish I could take back. But everything happens for a reason, and I think it's only made me stronger. It definitely sucked, but at the same time it changed my perspective on everything and the way I go about life nowadays in not taking anything for granted.

Pat Casey, head coach: I didn't like that at all. I felt bad for C Boy. He really had a great super regional and we weren't able to take him due to team rules. I stay in touch with C Boy to this day — a great kid, great family. We always hope that we don't make mistakes, and sometimes we make mistakes at the wrong time.

KJ Harrison, first baseman: It was really hard. He's one of my really good friends and he works his butt off and he's a great player. It would've been really nice for our team to have in Omaha with us.

Christian Donahue: I was in Corvallis during the World Series. I couldn't bring myself to watch the games. I mean I'd turn it on here and there, but after a while of watching I'd have to turn it off and I'd just follow it on my phone.

Pat Bailey, associate head coach: That was just brutal. (Donahue and Heimlich) are both great young men and great teammates, and it was unfortunate. Christian's was obviously self-inflicted; it was one of those things that just happened. But I love Christian, he's like one of my extended sons. The Luke thing, Luke Heimlich was a model citizen here at Oregon State. He did everything right, he did everything we asked him to do, he's a great young man. I have nothing but great things to say about Luke.

Trevor Larnach, outfielder: Luke took himself out of the playoffs and the World Series, but we still were doing it for him and we were doing it for each other. That's how it always has been. I remember that meeting to this day. Luke, he was hurt, man. They took his soul a little bit. And for all the blood and the sweat and the tears that he shed for us and Corvallis, we knew that a lot of people in Oregon weren't going to support … or maybe they would've, but we didn't care. We knew who Luke was, we knew how he was as a person, how he was as a teammate, and we believed every single thing that he said in the locker room to us that day, and we took that to heart. We fought for him, we did everything we could for him, and coach Casey and the staff did the same. It was a collective effort from the whole team, the coaches, the players, the staff, everyone, to support him and back him up and win for all of us.

FINISH

Drew Rasmussen, pitcher: There was so much toughness and grittiness built into one of the most talented college baseball rosters of all time. We had a bunch of the right personalities that meshed together really well. We enjoyed playing together so much that we were able to leave the negativity off the field for whatever those two or three hours on Fridays, Saturdays and Sundays could possibly be. Because everyone is going through something. There are obviously different degrees and levels of adversity, but everyone is going through a little bit of something. Maybe it's back home, maybe it's with a girlfriend. I thought it showed a lot of maturity to be able to not allow that to affect our performance. To go out there, take care of business and get back and take care of our brother again.

Nate Yeskie, pitching coach: The way '17 had played itself out, it was next man up just because everybody was helping us win games in some fashion. Whether it be a pinch hit off the bench, Preston Jones scoring from second base on a wild pitch, there were just different ways of doing it.

Zak Taylor, first baseman: We kind of took it like there was just another target on our back, and I feel like we embraced that. If one guy goes down, that's when another guy can step up and have those opportunities. We took it in stride that way. Of course we were bummed for Luke, but we knew we still had a job to finish.

Leaving Donahue and Heimlich behind was a major blow for Oregon State, but the team had plenty to look forward to in the Midwest. First contested in 1947, the College World Series has called Omaha, Nebraska, home since 1950. After 61 years at Rosenblatt Stadium, the CWS moved downtown in 2011 to TD Ameritrade Park — a 24,000-seat state-of-the-art facility.

The CWS is one of Omaha's largest annual events, and the city goes all-out to support it. Players, coaches and fans are greeted with open arms at every corner of the city by locals. It's a true celebration of college baseball.

Trevor Larnach: I just remember a lot of us were saying, "man, we're really going to Omaha!" We were on the jet to go over there to keep fighting through our setbacks, our adversity or whatever you want to call it. We were going to keep fighting through it and keep fighting toward this goal that we've had since we all stepped on campus. Everyone was just excited, man. Excited to get it going, excited to get it rolling as a team and as a group. Yeah, we were missing a couple of our key guys, but that gave us all the will in the world to fight through it and do it for them. So, we were excited for it, and it was a crazy week to say the least.

Jack Anderson, outfielder: I'd never thought too much about Omaha. I knew I always wanted to go there, but once we were finally there … I knew it was hot but I walked off the plane and was just like "jeez, this is different." Because I never played baseball other than in Oregon growing up, I never played on any travel teams or anything like that. So that was my first real humidity experience.

Drew Rasmussen: Getting there, it was one of my first times experiencing a little bit of humidity, so of course it's hot. But other than that, the town is awesome. The fans … it's one of those things where even if the team that you root for isn't there, it's something every college baseball fan should experience. Because the atmosphere is incredible, you know you're going to see good baseball with the teams who made it. Nobody accidentally gets there.

Tyler Malone, infielder/outfielder: The airport is right there, so we hopped on the bus and we were rolling in and you see TD Ameritrade for the first time. Then you see the Oregon State banners up with the rest of the teams, and it just hits you like "dang, we actually made it here."

Jake Mulholland, pitcher: I had never been to Omaha, never been to Nebraska, never had been to the Midwest, really. It was crazy, we get on the plane and there's a bunch of people there to cheer us on the way out. Beaver Nation came out and supported us the whole way through, there was so much orange in the stands in Omaha. All the stuff we got to do, for a lot of people it's a once-in-a-lifetime thing. We were so happy that we were able to get there, but it's not over when you get there. There's a whole 'nother tournament going on, so you've got to separate the fun and exciting stuff from baseball and realize you're there, you're on a mission, you've got business to finish still. But Omaha itself was amazing the whole way through, they did a great job of making all the teams feel welcome and special.

Max Engelbrekt, pitcher: It was awesome. At that point I was done with school, too, and I just remember going out and I was like the first one who went out and sat in the dugout before we had practice. You have so much free time there and you really don't even play games that often, it's quite a lot of fun. It's unlike any experience that I've had playing baseball, or really anything else, because you have tons of people going to the game and then you have two days to do whatever — and you basically did that the whole time. I went to Zesto like every day for ice cream. You get to walk around and see people in Oregon State gear, obviously a lot of people come out for that. Yeah man, I'm glad I got to do it twice. It's funny to go there as a freshman and then a fifth-year senior.

Kavin Keyes, undergraduate assistant coach: When Danny Hayes caught that ball against Kansas State (in the 2013 super regionals), I mean that's what the dream was, to play in the College World Series. Hardly ever are you talking about winning it. I mean you are, obviously that's in your heart, but it's more about going to be a part of the College World Series. I'm not going to speak for everybody, but I was satisfied and I was happy to be there. We were going to the College World Series and we played great, we just fell a little short.

That was one of the things we talked about, the environment you get put in. The pictures, the signings, people saying, "you made it, you did it!" But you haven't done anything yet, so a big thing that we preached was, "hey, we came here to win. We didn't come here to kiss babies, we didn't come here to sign autographs, we came here to bring it home." That was a thing that (Andy Peterson) and (Nate) Yeskie talked about. Yeskie was a big part of that for sure, he's just the man. He was such a great coach to everybody.

Andy Peterson, undergraduate assistant coach: The few of us who had been there had to pretend like it's not a big deal, even though it's the coolest thing we've all ever done in our lives. You get to sit back and watch all these guys be giant stars, talk to the ESPN reporters and sign all of the autographs. It's fun to put the months and months of work in and getting to see them do all of that and be these big stars in the state of Nebraska for a month. You're just so unbelievably happy for the players.

We'd make fun of the guys for looking all big-eyed. I'm pretty sure it was (Steven) Kwan and (Michael) Gretler, we saw Jessica Mendoza when we were walking through the stadium one of the days and they were both like "oh my God, it's Jessica Mendoza!" And I was like "guys, act like you've seen her before. Play it cool." And they both go like "oh, you're right, yeah, yeah, yeah," and they just keep on walking. But they were all giggly and freaking out and I'm like "guys, Jesus, come on!" But deep down I'm like "oh, well I'm going to say hi."

Joe Casey, outfielder: I had gone as a batboy (Joe is the youngest of Pat Casey's four children) and a fan, so it was a different perspective going as a player. You just get to do more things and the experience is a little different. The experience of being a fan is also awesome there, you get to see certain things, but when you're a player it is really cool. I knew in 2017 I probably wasn't going to play because I was on the roster but hadn't played all year, but just being able to hit and take BP on that field, take fly balls on the field and walk through that tunnel was pretty awesome.

I think going as a player is obviously the best, but it's a different perspective because as a fan you get to watch the opening ceremonies, watch everything from the outer part of it. And as a player, you get to experience it in the dugout, on the field, all that cool stuff. Plus, you get to experience some of the stuff as a fan a little bit when you're a player because you get the passes and we get to go to the other games, and that's really fun. You play and then the next day you go shop around at all the cool little stores, hop over to the game, get a snow cone and go sit in the stands. I think it was awesome knowing what it's like to be in that dugout while watching a game.

Mitchell Verburg, pitcher: It is amazing no matter how old you are, no matter what year you are. It's a surreal experience, especially with guys you really, really love. I grew up with Jack Anderson and I remember watching him in high school (at Lake Oswego), he's actually my brother's best friend. Getting to experience that with guys like him, you really can't write it up any better. It's such a cool experience, you get treated like a big-leaguer for the week. It's something that for the freshmen, I now expected that. That was my expectation for the rest of my college career.

Jake Thompson, pitcher: Jack and I were the only two players left from our recruiting class. I remember telling him in Omaha "hey, we made it! Omaha is what everyone talks about when you come in freshman year, and we're here."

Tyler Malone: It's literally baseball heaven. There are so many things set up around the stadium, and it's super cool how the entire town itself just gets revolutionized for those couple weeks to have baseball take it over. When I was younger, me and my family went to Cooperstown for a tournament there and we were comparing it to that. But it was even more enjoyable because of the stage. I mean, it's the College World Series, it's the biggest college baseball stage you can be on.

Cadyn Grenier, infielder: It was everything that you hear about, and then some. Especially the first time. Casey always preached "hey, believe me. You want to go play there." Not just because it's the national championship, but because it's special, it is incredible. It's an unbelievable atmosphere, it's a lot of fun, and the words don't do it justice when you actually get the chartered flight and get the team hotel and warm up before your first game and have twenty-plus thousand people in the stands. It is incredible, man. I wish everybody that's passionate about baseball gets the chance to go experience it. Obviously not everyone can get the chance to play there, but just to go experience it because it was freaking awesome.

Steven Kwan, outfielder: Case says this one thing that I totally agree with. He says that the feeling of walking out from the tunnel and seeing the whole baseball field is just an unexplainable feeling, a feeling that every time it happens, it feels the same. It takes your breath away, it's an amazing feeling.

Michael Gretler, infielder: It's an experience that is right up there with anything for the coolest thing I've ever done in my life, the most special thing I've ever done in my life. It's the Mecca of college baseball I guess you could say, and Omaha does an unbelievable job hosting us. I just remember the excitement and looking forward to being there with guys that you've worked so hard to get there with. And obviously having gone through what we did my sophomore year in 2016, what we had been through that season and feeling like we were starting to get over the hurdle. There was so much excitement, and we really wanted to take it all in because it's hard to do. We didn't know what would happen the next year and we weren't thinking about that. It was like "let's enjoy it and go win the national title."

Joe Casey: It was important to have fun with it. I think we all treated it like it was serious, but we had to have a good time with it. Especially some of the guys who didn't play, like me, we were all joking around and having a little bit more fun during BP. When we were shagging, I was throwing too many balls to the fans and got yelled at.

Andy Jenkins, assistant coach: You're always just excited for the kids to get the experience. I think what separates the great teams is being able to enjoy those moments and enjoy what Omaha is all about, but also keep a focus on what you're doing and why you're there and not really get caught up in too much of the show, because there's a lot of it there.

Nick Madrigal, infielder: Everyone was excited to be there, but we knew we weren't finished just being there. I know that was everyone's mindset.

The format of the modern College World Series mirrors the regional and super-regional rounds. The eight participants are separated into two four-team pods with no reseeding from the original 64-team bracket (if the top eight national seeds made it to Omaha, No. 1 would open play against No. 8, No. 2 against No. 7, etc.). Each side of the bracket is double-elimination, and the two finalists then play a best-of-three championship series for the national title.

Inclement weather forced the traditional Friday evening opening ceremonies indoors, but the conditions were nearly perfect for Saturday afternoon's CWS opener between Oregon State and Cal State Fullerton. The Titans (39-22) placed second in the Big West Conference behind Long Beach State and made it to Omaha the hard way, winning on the road at the Stanford Regional and Long Beach Super Regional. OSU (54-4) had won 21 straight games entering the CWS, two victories shy of matching its early-season streak.

Pat Casey: We went into the World Series, and a lot of people just thought that you can't sustain this. It's difficult to keep winning and winning and winning.

Kavin Keyes: It doesn't matter if you're playing in a four-team tournament, the College World Series or whatever, it's always hard to show up for the first game right out of the gate. It's always hard to win that first game.

Andy Peterson: I grew up a Long Beach State fan and I hated Fullerton. I never got to play them in college, so that alone was special for me.

KJ Harrison: I still remember when I was standing at first base and they were doing the national anthem and the flyover with the jets. I was shaking because I was so excited and so amped up. It was electric and it was the coolest and best experience I've had in my life playing baseball. The atmosphere there was just unbelievable.

Trevor Larnach: We were the opening game, and it was the first time for myself really being in that type of atmosphere. Opening day, the stadium is always packed, everyone's excited, adrenaline is through the roof. And when you hear those fighter jets come over the stadium after the national anthem, there's a jolt of energy that goes through you.

Adley Rutschman, catcher: I remember that first game in Omaha, I was like, I don't know. Usually during games, once the first pitch or the first inning is done, the nerves go away. But I don't know what it was, that first game in Omaha, I had the shakes going for the first three or four innings. It was just a different thing. The field is so much bigger. It's almost like a big-league stadium.

Steven Kwan: My first at-bat, I couldn't even see the pitches coming in. I was going cross-eyed, seeing stars, I was breathing really hard, my hands were shaking. That was the most nervous I've ever been playing baseball. And I don't know if you recall, but I got a catcher's interference call because I was so late on a fastball I pieced up the catcher's mitt. I had never done that before in my life. I was like "thank God, I just got bailed out so hard!" It was just that first at-bat too where everything kind of rushed over me. We were the first game, the jets had just flown over, my heart was racing. I couldn't even see the ball that first at-bat.

Jake Mulholland: Game 1 of Omaha, we're all excited. It's a whole new experience, a whole new atmosphere when you've got 30,000 people there instead of three or four thousand.

FINISH

Max Engelbrekt: We're all pumped, we show up and we're down immediately.

Things rarely go to plan at the College World Series, and that's exactly what happened to Oregon State. Jake Thompson started in Heimlich's place for the second consecutive week but immediately ran into some trouble he didn't face while stymying Vanderbilt. Thompson walked the leadoff batter to open the game, plunked Fullerton's No. 3 hitter and then served up a three-run home run to Timmy Richards. The upstart Titans led 3-0 before many fans had settled into their seats.

Jake Thompson: Yeskie had gone to Omaha in 2013 and I remember him saying "hey guys, everyone is going to have to hit it twice to get it out of this ballpark." So, I knew he wanted us to throw strikes, attack the zone. He knows there will be nerves and everything like that so if we just throw strikes, everything will take care of itself. I go in and throw some really good pitches to the leadoff batter, he's taking them and I'm like "what is going on?!" So, I'm getting a little frustrated, I ended up walking him on a 3-2 count. I'm sure everyone in the dugout was trying to say "calm down, calm down." I ended up (hitting a batter) and the next guy comes up and smashes one to left-center over the fence. It just carried and carried and carried. I was like "holy smokes, if that guy hit that over the fence, he must've hit it so hard." And it didn't seem like he hit it hard which was crazy because Elliott Cary was in center field and I thought he was going to catch it no problem, just maybe a little bit deep. So, I was like "what is going on?" But that year the home run record for (TD Ameritrade Park) was broken, so something was up.

Mitchell Verburg: We came out and were a little lethargic. Jake Thompson had a tough first inning and we were down. But that 2017 team, we never gave up, we never thought we were out of the game.

Jack Anderson: I just remember being a nervous wreck in the outfield. It seemed like all the action was going to left-center, so I was over in right field like "oh boy, what's going on right now?" I'm thinking to myself that this was kind of like how Jake pitched the year or two before, and I was worried he would not be able to get out of the first or second inning. But he was able to figure it out and get a couple more innings in. Once we got over the scariness of those first few innings, it was like "all right, we're better than these guys. Let's get back to it and put something together."

Drew Rasmussen: It was unfortunate because Jake Thompson had had such a great year. He had a little hiccup and that's going to happen from time to time.

Jake Thompson: I struggled that game, and Yeskie later told me that he heard from the Florida State coach (Mike Martin) that I was tipping my pitches. And up at Driveline, I talked to a guy from Cal State Fullerton and he said, "yeah, we had every one of your pitches." So that sucked. … I'd been having success all year and I remember feeling a little bit down after that, but then we had this huge comeback.

The Beavers trailed 5-1 after four innings, but panic never set in. The team's resume was littered with come-from-behind victories.

Trevor Larnach: I think there were some nerves that game, just being in that spotlight and that situation for the first time. But once the dust settled, once our team recuperated, we were back to ourselves. As Nick would say, we were going to keep fighting until the last out was made, and that's exactly how we played every single game.

Pat Bailey: It was just a great example of how our guys were so used to winning and the relentless pursuit of excellence. We were pulling for each other, staying positive in the dugout knowing that we had plenty of opportunities to get back into that game. And let's be honest, getting used to winning, there's a fine point between winning and losing in college sports, especially when you're at the Division I level. So, I think at that point in time, we were 54-4 going into the World Series, I think we were so accustomed to winning that we just knew we were going to win that baseball game.

Kavin Keyes: I remember sitting there thinking the same thing I thought all year: there's no way we're going to win this game, and we did. Actually, by that point I did know we were going to win because of how many times it had happened.

Cadyn Grenier: I feel like that's how a lot of our games in Omaha went in the two years we were there. In a lot of those games, we were down and it was like "oh, the best team in the world doesn't seem like they have it anymore." And then it was like "ah, just kidding!"

Drew Rasmussen: I remember it being 5-1 in the middle innings, I was still in our dugout, I hadn't gone down to the pen yet. And I don't think I've ever seen a team down 5-1 have less panic. Especially in Omaha, you could think the moment would be too big and there'd be panic and chaos. The leadership from our position players was absolutely incredible, and the way they were able to stay calm and understand that as long as we took care of our side of things, it was going to work out.

I think that really puts all of the pitchers at ease as well. Because throughout that entire year, the days the pitchers weren't going well, the position players always picked us up. And the days the position players might've been struggling a little bit at the plate, the pitchers always pitched well. So, for them to not show any panic was huge.

Steven Kwan: It was one of those moments where it was like "OK we're down, but we're not out of this. We're not even close to out of this." The stadium was getting all loud, and I just remember thinking "oh gosh, you guys have no idea who we are. You have no idea what we're about to do."

Oregon State's comeback began with a stretch of scoreless defensive innings. Jake Mulholland took over for Thompson with two down in the fourth and promptly got out of the inning. The freshman left-hander proceeded to flummox Fullerton by throwing 4 1/3 innings of shutout, no-hit relief.

Nate Yeskie: At some point, I looked at Pat (Casey) and was thinking "let's switch it up, get a different look in here. Let's go left-handed and go with a guy that can maybe spin it a little bit more." They were really light against left-handed arms and we felt like with the way we'd swung the bats that year we were well within striking distance.

Jake Mulholland: I knew I wasn't the kind of power pitcher that Jake (Thompson) was. I have to be able to switch sides of the plate, throw up and down, back and forth. For me it was about locating my spots and letting my defense work, and I just wanted to get us back in the dugout and let our offense go to work.

Jake Thompson: He made me look very, very bad! But no, he was someone where if our starters did our job, we had Mulholland at the end of the game. And if we only went six innings, we could have Mulholland come in and be fine, he's going to throw strikes and get us out of there. It was so comforting that we could attack the zone and if we ended up getting hit around towards the fifth or sixth, Mully would come in and get us out of any trouble. Having a guy like that was huge and set the tone for our bullpen.

Bryce Fehmel, pitcher: Mully came in and really shut the door. Whenever Mully was in the game, we knew we were in a good spot.

Max Engelbrekt: The whole year he was just incredible, him and Eisert. I probably don't think they were underrated because they were so dominant, but when you can get that kind of production out of relievers and pick and choose when they pitch, those are extremely, extremely valuable arms.

Mulholland needed a little help in the sixth after issuing a four-pitch leadoff walk. The small-ball-oriented Titans opted to play for one insurance run and bunt the runner over, but Taylor Bryant popped it up in front of the plate. Adley Rutschman made a diving catch to secure the first out, quickly got to his feet and gunned down Richards at first to complete the double play.

Jake Mulholland: That was crazy. I had just walked a guy and they went to bunt to move the guy over, and he blooped the bunt a little bit right in front of the plate. Adley made one of the best plays I've ever seen: dives out like a cat, catches the ball and throws the runner out at first. That got everyone going. Little stuff like that, taking every play like it's the last one you're going to make, that's just who Rutsch was. He would've done the same thing if the score was 20-0.

Adley Rutschman: I remember being behind the dish and I don't know if he tipped off the pitch before, but I had a feeling that they were going to bunt. I don't know, it was just one of those instinctual things. I saw it go up and I wanted to make a play on the ball. I think it was a little bit of a momentum shift.

Nate Yeskie, to the Corvallis Gazette-Times after the game: Rutsch caught the hell out of it behind the plate, and the play on the bunt was spectacular. That's another moment that highlights his athleticism.

You look back at that point and it's a four-run lead, they're looking to stretch it so one swing of the bat doesn't tie it or beat you, and that's their style of play. They're going to try and get guys in scoring position as much as possible. For him to make that play and for that guy to get hung up that far, that changes everything. Especially after a four-pitch walk because two pitches later, nobody is on base.

Mitchell Verburg: Rutsch is an absolute competitor, he's one of the most competitive people I've ever met. The inning before he made that ridiculous diving play on the bunt, he got challenged by Nick Madrigal in the dugout and he started going off. He got pretty angry, but you saw the ferocious competitor come out. He went out there and he made that ridiculous play. All I can think about is his mind and what he was thinking in the moment and his ability to separate stuff in the dugout and make an amazing play that was huge in the moment for that game.

As is often the case in baseball, great defense led to offense for Oregon State. Fullerton replaced starter Connor Seabold with top arm Colton Eastman to open the sixth, and the Beavers loaded the bases with one out on three walks. Nick Madrigal brought home the first run with a sacrifice fly, making it 5-2. Next up was KJ Harrison, who battled for a 13-pitch walk that re-loaded the bases. *After another pitching change, the Beavers tied the game on back-to-back singles from Trevor Larnach and Jack Anderson. Just like that, Thompson was off the hook and the Pac-12 champions were back in business.*

Max Engelbrekt: I remember being in the bullpen with Yeskie because at that point Mulholland was in and I think I was warming up to go in unless we came back. Then we had that slow rally, and in those games you're obviously so much more into it than a regular-season game. I don't even really remember how it went down, but it seemed like we had the bases loaded forever.

Nate Yeskie: KJ had some of the biggest at-bats of the season. Going back to the supers, he hits the three-run homer off Raby, he hits the three-run homer off Wright, he hits the grand slam against LSU when we beat them the first game in '17. But what people forget is against Colton Eastman, who was really their best guy at the time — even though Seabold went in the (third round) and was pitching on Fridays — Eastman was their hottest guy. They were going to use him in relief, roll Game 2 guy out there in Game 2 and Eastman would start Game 3 had they won that game. He had KJ down early 0-2 and he threw him everything but the kitchen sink, threw him a ton of nasty stuff and KJ worked out a walk, which allowed us to get to Trevor, which allowed us to get to (Anderson) and play that inning out the way it did. The way that it went down, man KJ's at-bat was big at the time.

Jack Anderson: I remember being a nervous wreck my first at-bat, it almost brought me back to my first at-bat as a Beaver. It was my redshirt freshman year and I think I watched two fastballs and a curveball, three pitches, three strikes and I was out. And in (my first CWS) at-bat I got to 0-2 again and then I got hit, so it was like "all right, I've got the nerves out of the way now." After that I was feeling good, I think I was 2 for 2 at that point and I just really wanted to be up there hitting because I was feeling really good and confident in what I could do. It was 5-4 and yeah, I was completely in control and ready to go. Trevor got a hit before me so it was KJ at third, Trevor at first and we were rolling in that sixth inning. Once Trevor got that hit I was like "all right, it's my turn now." That was our mindset that whole year, we fed off each other and we would also put together at-bats and knew we were never really out of it. I think getting that hit in that moment, that was probably the biggest hit I've ever had. And I was slumping at that point because I hadn't had a hit in like a week and a half. So, that was going over my head that entire game until I figured it out. But in those moments, you've got to shut the brain off and just react. And they had good pitchers, they were a good pitching team and their pitcher had a cool mustache, but luckily I got it by him.

Jake Thompson: I don't mean to be selfish, but when you have that perfect record, you're just like "all I care about is not getting the loss!" Which is good for the team because obviously I want us to win, I'm rooting for us to win more than anyone else.

Brandon Eisert, pitcher: The rally that we had, it was how our team had been all year. Even if we were down, we were going to find a way to win, especially in that game. A couple things didn't go our way … and then the rally happened. We had that feeling like we had all year that we were going to find a way to win.

Drew Rasmussen: We stayed together; we didn't let little things affect us. You start watching how that game unfolds, and the next thing you know it's 5-3, 5-4, 5-5. We clawed our way back into it and then we had the lead. Obviously it was not the most ideal start, but once again it just showed the toughness that team had to not let adversity or negativity affect what we were doing. We were going to take care of our own business.

The Beavers finally took the lead in the eighth inning behind another two-out rally. Larnach singled and Anderson was hit by a pitch. That brought up Rutschman, who drove a base hit back up the middle to make it a 6-5 game. At the time of his at-bat, Rutschman was 0 for 4 with eight runners left on base.

Adley Rutschman: I think that (at-bat), I was sitting fastball and I just got back to what I was doing: fastball, adjust and hit it hard somewhere, make something happen. I got a pitch up in the zone and I just tried to crush it. A base hit up the middle, and I think I hit it pretty hard.

Andy Jenkins: That College World Series was kind of Rutsch's (breakthrough). As a freshman, we wanted Rutsch to be a lockdown catcher for a great staff. We knew he had the potential to bang the ball around, but we had some guys that already did that in the middle of the order. For me personally, I just wanted to win games and I wanted our pitching staff to be the best they could. As the catching coach, that was my message most of that year to Adley. But he's a worker, and obviously he's going to take pride in his offense. He started to be a little more aggressive late in the year and had a nice season, but the way he finished and what he showed going into the next year there in Omaha was that no moment was too big for him. The complete player was coming together.

Nate Yeskie: If there's anything we look back on and wonder sometimes, maybe we hindered his development offensively because we thought we had a very good offensive team and we just said, "hey, you're going to get your swings, you're going to get your hits, you're going to do everything that you can." But knowing he was a freshman, we shifted his focus to "handle that pitching staff right there. Try to catch as many shutouts as you can, make the most out of each one of those guys and we'll live with what comes of it." I look back and I read something not too long ago that he had one hit in Omaha in 2017, and it happened to be the go-ahead single against Fullerton. So, there were a lot of moments of what this guy was capable of doing that were hiding in plain sight.

Adley Rutschman: In Omaha freshman year I went 1 for (15). Freshman year was a tough year hitting.

Jack Anderson: What's so funny to me is that year I hit better than Rutsch. I was just like "how did that happen?!" But he was also an 18-year-old kid who didn't practice with us since he was kicking for the football team. The fact that he caught as much as he did and hit pretty well that year is a testament to the ballplayer that he is. That guy, I don't think he sees the big games and big lights as big games and big lights. He just goes out there and pretends like it's a normal game and doesn't let the drama and all the fans get to him. He was a highlight reel that whole World Series, and I think that boosted his confidence and allowed him to do what he did the next two years. But yeah, he was incredible that whole way. That's when Rutsch came into his own.

Steven Kwan: We were chipping away, chipping away. Jack had the tying hit, Rutsch got us ahead. I think we could all agree that we knew we were going to win that game.

Nate Yeskie: Just like we'd done all year, every guy held their own, did their part. Then we trotted Rasmussen out there in the ninth.

Mulholland needed only 45 pitches to get 13 outs in relief. The coaching staff considered leaving him out there for the ninth but decided to try a different look with Drew Rasmussen, who was fresh after not pitching in the super regionals. With Bryce Fehmel set to throw Game 2 of the College World Series, Rasmussen could be used in relief and potentially start another game down the road. The right-hander made the coaches look brilliant by striking out two in a dominant 1-2-3 ninth inning. Final score: Oregon State 6, Cal State Fullerton 5.

Drew Rasmussen: While I was coming back into games, we had talked about me throwing out of the bullpen versus starting, and how they wanted to shuffle me back into the rotation. Going into that game, starters for the most part will wear tennis shoes (on off days), they won't wear spikes. As we were headed out to the field, Yeskie just said "hey Ras, make sure your spikes are on today. We want to guarantee a win in Game 1." If going to me was what we had to do and that's what the situation presented, we were going to do it. So, entering the game, I knew there was a chance I was going to pitch. I tried to stay ready, stay out of the sun and mentally prepare myself for going into the game.

It was exciting, there's no other way to describe it. I was down in the bullpen and (undergraduate assistant coach) Ryan Ortiz was down there with me and he basically said "love this experience, enjoy it. But when you get out there, please take a look around, take it all in." Omaha doesn't happen for a lot of people and it can very quickly become a once-in-a-lifetime experience. So to get out there and actually experience pitching in a close game and getting the opportunity to close the door, it's an awesome memory to look back on and know I'll have for the rest of my life.

Max Engelbrekt: Drew was just unhittable. That was probably one of the more impressive innings I can remember. I mean I was a long way from it, I think I was warming up to maybe go in if Drew got into any sort of trouble. But he didn't, and that was amazing.

Andy Peterson: He was throwing FUZZ! Rasmussen showed up with a whole year built up in him of not being able to pitch.

Jake Thompson: He makes throwing 98 look easy. Watching from the side, it looks like he's throwing easy, trying to throw strikes and everything. Then you realize the radar gun says 97 to 98, and he's got this incredible slider. It's just like, "wow. This is our guy who is coming back from surgery and is going to be pitching as needed. Holy smokes we're really good."

Nate Yeskie: You have these conversations in-game. Pat (Casey) says, "what are you throwing him?" I said, "another fastball." He goes "man, at some point we're going to have to throw something different." And I'm like "Pat, we've been watching film on these guys and they can't catch up to anything that's above 92. Right now, I'm looking at that radar gun on the board, and it says 94 to 97 for Rasmussen, so we're going to stick with this."

Drew Rasmussen: Luckily the fastball was working because in the bullpen, I couldn't throw anything else for a strike.

Nate Yeskie: The nerves. People forget that was Rasmussen's first time in Omaha, too. For as prepared and under control as he was, it was still a new experience. How you process that is unique and you've got to watch how those things go. So, it's interesting, you get him out there in that thing and he's like a bull in the chute anyway. When you open that door, he's going to come out kicking. He pitched with a little bit of extra oomph on the fastball and it was working, so we just figured if it ain't broke, don't fix it.

Drew Rasmussen: I don't remember exactly how many pitches I threw or how many were fastballs, but all I can remember is we got down to two strikes with two outs and I saw a slider was called. I didn't shake Yeskie off very often, and there was no need to. He always called great pitches and called great games, but I remember sitting there going "heck no, there's no chance." And sure enough, we got a fly ball and it was on to the next one.

Nate Yeskie: It's so funny, you play that game in the middle of the year and it's not a big deal. A guy hits a fly ball at the end of the game, everybody is walking out of the dugout before the ball is even caught. But you get into Omaha and when the ball gets hit in the air, you're watching it the whole way making sure whoever is underneath it squeezes it home just because outs, they're hard to come by when you get into those types of situations.

Andy Jenkins: We had our backs against the wall right away against Cal State Fullerton, showed that relentless will to win ... and found a way late in the game. I don't think there was anything crazy offensive, there was no big bomb that game, it was just chipping away at-bats and getting base hits that were rolling through holes. And next thing you know, we came out on top.

Pat Casey: It was a great character win. Anytime you get to the World Series, you have seven opponents that have won a regional and have just won a super regional. So, it's not like anybody you're playing isn't playing well, it's not like anybody you're playing isn't worthy of being there. It's difficult to win in the World Series. The more you can relax and the more you can play the way that you were accustomed to playing all year, the better you're going to do.

I'm the fortunate one who got to go to six of them over the last 15 or so years, so I guess it was a little easier to say "just sit back and be the club that we are, relax and play." And for the most part we did that.

Jack Anderson: I just wanted to get to the zoo. I'd heard Joe Casey talk about it, so I always wanted to go. I knew that if we won the first two, we were going to have a couple days off, go to the zoo and it was going to be sweet. So, once we beat Cal State Fullerton, it was like "all right, one more. One more until the zoo!"

Next up for Oregon State (55-4) was No. 4 national seed LSU, a 5-4 winner over Florida State in its College World Series opener. One of college baseball's blue bloods, the six-time national champion Tigers (49-17) shared the 2017 SEC regular-season title with Florida. It was set up to be a showdown for the ages on a Monday night in Omaha.

Andy Peterson: There was a lot going into that game of "how good are the Beavs? Can they beat this LSU team?"

Bryce Fehmel: LSU is always an unbelievable team with a great lineup and usually a great starter on the mound. My job was to just put up zeroes, give our offense a chance and stick with the scouting report me and Yeskie had come up with. Pound the zone, switch sides of the plate, change speeds and let my defense work.

Nick Madrigal: We were always looking to play LSU I would say. It was on our minds and we wanted to show them how great we were. That was another series that was pretty chirpy. Those guys were confident in what they were doing, but we were confident in what we were doing. We just had different styles about it. We were those hard-nosed guys who were going to get out there and do everything we can, and we believed they were a little bit flashy, and different things like that.

Steven Kwan: My favorite thing from that game was getting interviewed about the fake bunt I would always do (on the first pitch of an at-bat). It was a reporter for ESPN who did the announcing, and he was talking about how "oh yeah, Kwan, fake bunt, most obvious thing in baseball. He'll do it every single time no matter what." And I remember that LSU team we were playing, you know, Kramer Robinson, the second baseman (Cole Freeman), all of them, just big ego guys, pumping their chests and stuff. So, I remember thinking that if I could get a bunt down, it didn't even have to be a good bunt, I knew they were going to be feeding into that and thinking "oh, he's going to fake bunt. Screw this kid, let him do his little stupid antics," and I'd catch them off guard. I told Andy Peterson about that and he was fired up, and he goes "yeah, get it down and let's do it!"

Andy Peterson: We had talked about it the whole night before, just joking around like "hey, are you going to do it?!" And he's like "yep! First pitch, I'm totally doing it. I'm going to bunt. I'm doing it, I'm doing it." And I'm like "oh, you're totally taking it. You're not going to put it down." And he's like, "you want to bet?"

Steven Kwan: I tried to make it a soft bunt, my adrenaline was just pumping and it turned into a hard push and I was like "oh God, this is a bad bunt." But like I said, nobody was expecting it. The second baseman wasn't even close to covering first, and that was just an awesome game. My next at-bat I had like an eight-chopper double because the first baseman was in making sure that didn't happen again. I knew playing into their egos would get it going.

Nick Madrigal: I remember someone asked him, "when did you decide you were going to do that?" And he said that it was hours and hours before the game, maybe it was back at the hotel when he decided that he was going to lay it down. It was a great way to start off the game.

Andy Peterson: That's as big of a spark plug as you're going to get. Steven Kwan bunting is the coolest way you can start a game, for me at least. But yeah, I told him he was going to wuss out. But of course, hot-headed Kwan, he does it. And as soon as he gets in he looks at me and I don't think he said, "I told you," but he wanted to.

Steven Kwan's opening-pitch bunt was a sign of things to come for Oregon State, and LSU. Larnach promptly plated Kwan with a single up the middle and the Beavers were off and running. Tigers starter Eric Walker exited in the third with an arm injury, and OSU feasted on the LSU bullpen. Larnach drove in two more runs in the fifth before Harrison delivered the knockout blow — the first CWS grand slam in TD Ameritrade history — to make it 8-0 one inning later. The Beavers continued to pour it on in a 13-1 runaway, extending their winning streak to 23 games.

KJ Harrison: I was just looking for a good pitch to hit in that situation, and I was going to be aggressive early with the bases loaded. It was the same feeling as Vanderbilt. After I hit it I was like, "wow, this has a chance!" I was rounding the bases, it went out, and I blacked out. All I know is I was excited and I remember looking up to all the fans and pointing at them. They asked for a curtain call, and that was the coolest thing I've done in my baseball career. To do it for the team and come through in that situation was unbelievable.

Jack Anderson: I was on-deck when KJ hit the grand slam. I was like "all right KJ, get a hit or something. Knock a few runs in for me so I can be a little looser up there," because I was definitely a little more nervous than I usually was at that point. I just remember watching that whole at-bat. I was already zoned in watching the pitcher. Once he hit that, I remember my at-bat being like, "who cares?" No one in the stadium was paying attention to me at that point because they were all freaking out over the grand slam. I was still thinking about KJ's grand slam when I was up there.

Steven Kwan: Obviously, KJ's grand slam was awesome, the first at TD Ameritrade. I did not think it was going out. That was such a low, line-drive trajectory. I was like "OK, I know I'm scoring from second base easily," so I started jogging and when I saw it go out, I was really surprised. I was like "oh my gosh" and the whole Beaver section was just roaring. Again, in our heads we were like "this is how the whole year has been going, we're going to win this whole damn thing."

Michael Gretler: That was special. It was another one where from the get-go, we were banging out hits and scoring runs. What was the final score, 16-1? Am I adding too many runs? Every year that goes by I'm probably going to add a run just to make the story sound better. But no, that was awesome. Being from the West Coast, you hear so much about the SEC and it lights a fire under your ass because you want to show them that we know how to play pretty good baseball, too. And obviously, we knew they had a great team.

Trevor Larnach: For me personally, when it comes to playing SEC teams, I don't think there's anything better than beating their asses and making a statement about it, too. Because we played Vandy, we beat them two games in a row and that was fun and all. But when we get to the World Series and we're playing LSU ... and we came out and pummeled them and won 13-1. That was our impression of two SEC teams right at the top of that conference, and we felt on top of the world, man. Because for one we made a statement through each of those games, Vandy and LSU, and we knew we were the best, even though we didn't have all of our guys.

Andy Peterson: It just didn't stop. We got that first run and it absolutely exploded. You could see them getting depleted and we're getting even more hyped up.

I mean winning like that, nobody can ever expect that. You're going to assume that in the World Series, every game is going to be a dogfight. But I think that was fun for all of us, especially doing that against LSU, who we had history with in the past of having some good games and not coming out on top.

Nate Yeskie: What's kind of been known as their style of baseball, we played it back at them. KJ hit the grand slam and about blew the lid off the place. Bryce was good and kept getting miss-hit. A lazy fly ball here, a two-hopper there, and we played clean.

Adley Rutschman: It was like the Vanderbilt games, it just felt like we were rolling. We got back in our groove and the jitters were out from that first game, and we were rolling at that point. Obviously Fehm was dealing that game, too. He could do no wrong.

FINISH

Nine days after his complete game in the super regionals, Fehmel tossed eight innings against the Tigers, giving up only two hits. He allowed a solo home run in the seventh but nothing more, striking out three with three walks. It was quite the turnaround for Fehmel, who had lost his spot in the rotation due to a tired arm just six weeks prior.

Pat Casey: I think that he had to go back in and find himself and say "wait a minute. I believe in Bryce Fehmel, I believe in myself. I have to quit doubting myself." And everybody has a game where they don't pitch the way they want — I don't care who it is. I think that he started doubting himself, and when you start doubting yourself, you start putting pressure on yourself. And when you start putting pressure on yourself, you start losing your stuff. When you start losing your stuff, you lose your confidence. When you lose your confidence, your teammates, they feel it. He was way too good of a kid, way too good of a competitor to doubt himself, and I think that's what turned it around for him.

Michael Gretler: That guy, it doesn't matter what he's doing, he's going to find a way to win, he's going to compete. He's not that intense, rah-rah guy, but he'll get locked in and he dictates the flow.

When he's out on the mound, he's not as fiery as someone like Luke or Jake Thompson. But he controls the game, he controls the flow of it. Things are going to happen the way he wants them to happen. He's just a great guy to have on the mound, and obviously he turned in two special pitching performances back-to-back in games against the SEC and great baseball programs.

Adley Rutschman: It was like a video game. You say, "I want the ball here," and I probably could've sat on a knee the entire game and he would've been within three inches of it every single time. It was crazy.

Bryce Fehmel: You just do whatever you can to keep them off-balance. Off-speed pitches early in the count and trying to sneak a fastball by them whenever I can. And it worked out for us on that given day. Yeskie definitely knows what he's doing with every team we face, so I had all the trust in the world in him and what he'd come up with for us.

I don't think I had more than a strikeout or two in that game, so being able to pitch with the defense we had was a big advantage of mine. I wasn't an overpowering guy. It was about getting the ball in my defense's hands so they could toss it over to first base and we could go hit.

Jack Anderson: At that point, everyone on our team was like "we are who we are.

We're not some fluky (55-4) team." We meant business taking it to LSU like we did that game. After that game, for me at least, it was about more than just having fun in Omaha. We knew we could win this thing with or without Luke and Christian and whoever else was hurt. That sparked us to really have that feeling of "we're in the winners' bracket now, and it's ours to lose."

Pat Bailey: That was a fun game to be a part of. Unfortunately, we had to play them two more times, but that's baseball.

Max Engelbrekt: It's hard to think about that game without thinking about what came next because we … you know, it was the last time we won. I guess from that year's standpoint, it was the pinnacle of the year. KJ hits the home run, it ended up being a complete blowout. We just killed them. It seemed like we were going to win the World Series, it seemed like this was the year.

There is ample downtime at the College World Series, particularly for the teams that start 2-0 in bracket play. Oregon State embarrassed LSU on a Monday night and didn't play again until that Friday. With three full days off, the team was able to enjoy some of the non-baseball elements of Omaha. The Beavers took a zoo trip — the Henry Doorly Zoo and Aquarium was named the world's best zoo by TripAdvisor in 2014 — and spent some time at Boys Town, a non-profit organization dedicated to helping at-risk children. There was also plenty of time to practice and enjoy the fan experience at CWS games.

KJ Harrison: Obviously we were feeling great coming out 2-0 in Omaha. We got that extra rest to rejuvenate the team, rejuvenate the arms to get their stuff ready. Those games are as much mentally draining as they are physically, so to be able to have that extra time to regroup and get our minds right was awesome.

Jake Mulholland: We practiced, we still had work to get in. One of the days we ended up going to the zoo as a team. A lot of us had our families in town, so it was nice being able to go out and grab a bite to eat with your family and stuff like that. We went to Boys Town and got to hang out with some kids one of the days. That was really fun. Just going out and trying to give back a little bit as well was pretty cool. Some of the things you do are a little bit bigger than baseball, trying to make a kid's day, hanging out with people. But you know we're there for a reason, so all the fun stuff you're doing, you still have to know that you've got a game coming up in a couple days. You don't want to get too crazy.

Jake Thompson: We had those (three) days off, and that's when I talked to Yeskie and he told me how I was tipping my pitches and it was on the scouting report for other teams. I found out that when I was throwing a slider my glove was like this, when I threw a fastball it was like this, that sort of thing. So, once I realized Fullerton had a huge advantage going into that game … and it was something I could fix pretty easily, I gained back my confidence just like that.

Jack Anderson: Those few days were great. We were just hanging out. I don't think we ever lost sight of what our goal was. I think there's a bit of that rest versus rust thing that everyone likes talking about in baseball, football or basketball. LSU, we weren't sure if we were going to play them, but I think we had a pretty good idea that they were the best team on our side, and if we did play them they were going to have their number one guy going against us.

Trevor Larnach: We had three days off, and most of us didn't like that. We didn't like the fact that these teams were getting at-bats and getting innings in and fighting for survival while we were kind of just on vacation for three days in Omaha, sitting on our asses. It was great to get rest and bring some more pitching into the picture because you don't have to worry about innings. But I think we came back a little bit asleep and off guard. I think we got too comfortable, and I think that took our attitude away from feeling that "we're the best and dominating these SEC teams and whoever is in our way" to thinking "we're 2-0, we can chill out," and all this stuff.

Pat Casey: For me, I don't think (the extra time off) should make any difference whatsoever. If it made a difference for somebody, they'd have to explain to me why, you know what I mean? You've got three days off, you get to practice, you get to watch other teams play, you're fresh. We've already played 60 games, it's not like we've got to stay in some type of rhythm. But you know, if it affects somebody, it does. But I don't think it should, I don't think it did. I think we played a very good LSU team.

Sure enough, LSU played its way into the bracket finals by dispatching Florida State. To reach the championship series, the Tigers would need to beat Oregon State, which hadn't lost consecutive games in more than 13 months, twice. Thompson was back on the hill for OSU while LSU turned to ace Alex Lange, a right-hander with a killer curveball who was drafted 30th overall by the Chicago Cubs. Thompson pitched valiantly and allowed three runs in 6 2/3 innings, but Lange limited the Beavers to one run on two hits in 7 1/3 innings as LSU forced a winner-take-all bracket finals game the following day with a 3-1 victory.

Jake Thompson: I knew the guy I was pitching against was a first-rounder, and he was always a top pitcher in the nation. I told myself that whole week that I was going to out-pitch him.

KJ Harrison: He was their guy and he was an unbelievable pitcher. I played with him on Team USA so I knew him from before, and he was coming at us. It was just a back-and-forth game; a couple things didn't fall our way and it was obviously a hard situation for us.

Pat Casey: We just couldn't score at the right time when they had Lange on the mound. We faced a guy that was a first-rounder and felt like we were right in the game.

Drew Rasmussen: Tip your cap. A great arm pitched well against a great offense, and unfortunately we couldn't get the job done. You knew LSU was a really good team so you tip your cap, and we tried to get refocused going into the next game.

Michael Gretler: We didn't get the offense going the way we wanted to right off the bat. Obviously Alex Lange pitched a great game and yeah, that first game it was like "OK, whatever. Tough game, we've had a couple of those this year, let's just get ready for tomorrow."

Jake Thompson: I think back all the time that I would take my stats over (Lange's) stats any day and how I should've won that game, but it is what it is. ... I ended giving up six hits and (one) walk and he gave up (two) hits and (four) walks. I told Yeskie that I will take my pitching performance every day and believe I'm going to win that game over his pitching performance. You would think that many walks would get you out of there pretty early by giving up some runs.

Nate Yeskie: Jake didn't deserve to lose against LSU. He made the adjustments; he was throwing the ball well that day and he had a lot of success. It's just a funny game. But Jake made those adjustments, we confirmed what we had thought, so we just worked on getting that better and it obviously paid some dividends because that outing was certainly better than the first. And that tells you how good his stuff was the first outing. He still didn't really get scuffled; he just made a couple bad pitches and was still throwing some quality stuff. If you throw it where you want and how you want, it doesn't matter if they know it's coming or not.

Brandon Eisert: That's how baseball goes sometimes. Two good pitchers dueling it out, and we came out on the wrong side of it.

FINISH

Jack Anderson: I think we played fine; it was a great baseball game. Things just didn't go our way, and we didn't know we could video review! That was brutal.

With the Beavers down 2-0 in the bottom of the third, Michael Gretler stroked a one-out double and Cadyn Grenier followed with a walk. Kwan then sent a laser to left field that caromed off the foul line on the padded wall just below the foul pole — a clear fair ball. Kwan's hit was ruled foul by the umpiring crew and Oregon State did not challenge the reviewable play. The Beavers ended up scoring one run that inning, but the damage could've been far greater.

Steven Kwan: My ball off the left-field wall, that was pretty crazy because I didn't think I could hit a ball that far opposite field. I didn't think I hit it that far or that well. I saw it tailing down the line and I remember just giving up on it because I was close to first base and I almost missed first base, so I had to look down and make sure I touched it. And once I got going, they called it foul.

Andy Jenkins: A ball was hit by Kwany, and I'm looking at two pretty good runners and what I'm (considering) is am I going to send these guys? At third base ... you follow the ball, but you also want to know your runners and try to anticipate what you're going to do, sending them or holding them up. The ball kicked left and next thing you know, everybody is yelling.

Steven Kwan: Cadyn's rounding second, it hits the wall, the umpire says it's foul, Cadyn puts his arms up and I did, too. I was like "oh man, that was so close. I thought it was fair." And Cadyn is super adamant, he's going nuts over there at first, trying to get someone's attention. Cadyn had a perfect view of it because he was on first rounding second and he saw it hit.

Cadyn Grenier: I was on first and when Kwan hit it, I just took off. I started running, I was rounding second and when it hit the wall and I just kept going. Then I look up, they say foul and coach Jenkins was kind of like "hey, that was a foul ball." And I was like "dude, are you sure?" And he didn't really know.

Steven Kwan: Cadyn told Jenks to challenge it, and Case and Jenks started talking about it. I guess I ran back to the plate and we just lost the opportunity to try and challenge it. It all went by super quick.

Cadyn Grenier: When we didn't challenge it, I was like "OK, they must've seen it hit foul. I was running so I obviously didn't see it right." Because I thought it was fair so I kept running, but I attributed it to not seeing it right because I was running.

Pat Casey: When you read the things you can appeal, it says fair or foul ball beyond first or third base that hits the ground first. So, in all actuality, the NCAA said the crew chief was the one who should've reviewed it because the rule doesn't say the fence is part of the ground, but apparently by rule it is. I've never read anything that says the fence is part of the ground and I'm sure that's in there. Had they said in the rules "fair or foul, hits the ground first including the fence," then we obviously would've challenged it. But when the third-base umpire indicated that it was foul, he was the crew chief I believe, he was the one that had the right to appeal it and so did we. It happened so quickly, what I should've done was call timeout to talk to Kwan at the plate to see if he thought it was fair or foul and to appeal it, but I just trusted that it was ... something (the crew chief) should've appealed and something we couldn't appeal. But we could've, we should've.

Andy Jenkins: When you have guys on first and second or a guy on first, I wasn't just staring at the ball like the guys in the dugout. What I did see, it was not an obvious this or that. I wish I would've done more, I'm sure Case wishes he would've done more, but a lot of times people on TV see a lot more than the people down on the field. That's just an interesting part of really that rule change and us not having the ability to do that in the Pac-12. Looking back, I certainly wish I would've been more aggressive, even if there was a little doubt, saying "Case, we've got to review this." And we didn't do that, but I still think we were in position to win that game. There was a lot of ballgame left.

Nate Yeskie: If you're going to put in instant replay, just have somebody in there that's watching the thing and can buzz it down. They do it in Major League Baseball now. In society, things happen after the fact. Something happens, then we work to fix it. We just were not ahead of it in that sense as a sport as a whole to have the capacity to do some of those things. There were some questions on what was the ruling, what could be challenged, what couldn't be challenged. In the game the next day, it felt like there were seven challenges. People were challenging everything just because they knew from watching the night before.

Jack Anderson: When Kwany's ball hit the wall, Kavin Keyes ran up to watch it because we didn't have a TV in (the dugout). He ran up into the locker room, saw it hit the line and he sprinted his ass back into the dugout. One pitch had already happened and the ball was going back to the pitcher, and he was like "challenge it, challenge it, challenge it!" And we were all like "what?" And he said "it hit the line, it hit the line!" But it was already a pitch or two late.

FINISH

Kavin Keyes: I was up in the clubhouse; I don't remember why but there was a reason why I was up there. The play happened, so we're watching the replay and I'm ready to go down and sprint because I know it's a big deal. So as soon as I saw the replay and the ball hit fair, it hit the line, I sprint down. When I get down there, I yell to the batter's box "Kwan, step out!" I yelled that as loud as I could. Everyone looks over at me like I'm an idiot, and I'm like "what?" Someone says, "a pitch has already been thrown," and I'm like "no! That ball was fair!" Case comes over and goes "that ball was fair?" And I go "yeah, it was fair." There was nothing we could do at that point; it was just one of those things. There wasn't a whole lot of experience for anyone in that replay department. You look back at it and you can go "well, why didn't you challenge it?" But it was so new and there was a delay upstairs, Kwan could've stepped out like 10 times but there was no way of planning for that. It was just one of those things where I was up there, sprinted down, tried to make it on time and just like when I played, I wasn't fast enough.

Cadyn Grenier: You get done with the game, you lose, you get back to the hotel and everyone is like "dude, why didn't you challenge it?" And I'm like "what are you talking about?" People are sending me screenshots and all that good stuff and I'm like "wow, that was clearly fair." I couldn't believe it was a blown call and that we didn't challenge it, but there's only so much coach Casey could've done.

Jack Anderson: It took the wind out of our sails when that all happened with Kwany hitting it off the wall.

Pat Casey: You always go back to wondering if we had put a run on the board in that particular inning how that would've impacted the game.

Nate Yeskie: They already had their pen up; Lange was in trouble. The game was just going to take a different shape altogether … and you've got options to play the game a little bit differently. That park, at times, when it's a two-run lead, it can feel like four, four can feel like eight. In '18, Zak Taylor hits the base hit against Arkansas in Game 3. I looked at Bails and I go "that's like an eight-run home run," and it was 5-0. The game just plays itself different.

Jack Anderson: The next day during BP, I was out in left field because I was playing left at that point. Case walked out almost like a zombie and just stared at the line at the wall. I was looking at him, looking at the wall and I didn't want to say anything. He stood there for a minute, looked at the wall and then turned around and left. I was like "yeah, that wasn't too good." I remember that vividly.

Jake Thompson: If they'd called that ball fair, I think we win the national championship.

Bad breaks aside, Oregon State still had another chance to punch its ticket to the College World Series finals. LSU's top three starters — Lange, Walker and Jared Poche — were all unavailable, forcing Tigers head coach Paul Mainieri to go with bullpen arm Caleb Gilbert. Rasmussen was initially announced as OSU's starter, but the coaching staff made a last-minute switch to Fehmel, who had thrown superbly against LSU five days prior.

Jake Thompson: They were discussing whether they wanted Drew or Fehmel, and we were going to feel great with either one of those guys out there. Fehmel had just shut these guys down, so we were feeling pretty confident.

Drew Rasmussen: I was preparing to start. Case called us into his office and just said "hey man, this is what we're noticing. Fehm had a great outing against them last time and we want to roll him out there. As soon as we feel like he's in trouble, we'll make the switch and turn the ball over to you for the rest of the way." We had so much confidence in our team that we were, I don't want to say we were looking to the future, but in a winner-take-all game to go to the championship series, we also wanted to set the table going forward should we win so we had enough arms on the backside. It was a last-minute switch but there was no lack of confidence in our team. Nobody had a problem with that.

Pat Casey: I think that anytime we make a decision, the decision is based on what's best for our team. And whether it was because we felt like Drew wasn't going to be able to get us deep into the game, or because we felt like we wanted him to pitch behind Bryce, whatever it was. Obviously, the decision is always based upon what gives us the best opportunity to win. And we thought (Bryce) gave us the best opportunity to win. We felt he had pitched really well against them, so we thought he was the right guy, had the right stuff, was the right matchup. And so, that's what we do. I don't think we ever second-guess those decisions once we make them, nor do we second-guess him.

Nate Yeskie: There were times when we were both back-and-forth about guys that we felt like would be better suited for this or that and hindsight is always 20/20 with regards to certain things. People had reasons for why one guy should start, this guy or that guy, how you're going to navigate certain games. At the end of the day, when the head guy makes the call and says "these are the decisions we're going to make," you go with that, you live with that and you move on. Bryce was certainly capable of getting those things handled and taken care of.

FINISH

Bryce Fehmel: I think I found out about two hours before game time. The coaches were still debating on who was going to start, and I found out about two hours before the game. I'd prepared my mind the day before as if I was going to start, so I was ready. I was ready to go, I just didn't have the same stuff I did the first game.

Fehmel got through the first inning unscathed before running into trouble in the second. He retired the first two batters but issued a two-out walk followed by a double. Michael Papierski then ripped a three-run homer to put the Tigers on top.

Brandon Eisert took over for Fehmel one inning later and Rasmussen finally entered the game in the fourth with Oregon State down 5-0.

Pat Casey: I think (Fehmel) gave us a great effort. I think he missed a couple pitches that had they gone our way, particularly on the guy that hit the three-run homer, we felt like he made some pretty good pitches to him prior to that. And here again, he was a guy that when you get to the World Series and you're pitching on fumes … guys have to step up. Just like Madison Bumgarner coming out pitching in the World Series, throwing 100-some pitches on two days' rest. It's what you do to win the ring, man.

Bryce Fehmel: On a stage like that, adrenaline and nerves will kick in. Once game time started, I didn't notice any type of fatigue. It was just about going out there, competing and trying to make pitches.

Nate Yeskie: Fehmel gave up a home run early, and it almost seems like in those types of elimination games, whoever scores the first crooked number is really in the driver's seat. So we were fighting an uphill battle from there.

He left a couple balls up, we got in trouble and we didn't swing the bats the way we were capable of. The zone got stretched, a lot of things didn't go in our favor and it just became too big of a hole to get out of.

Drew Rasmussen: I felt great playing catch before the game, felt great in the bullpen. Velo was pretty good that day. It was hard to complain, everything came out pretty well.

Rasmussen kept the Beavers in it, allowing one run on three hits over the final 4 1/3 innings. The problem was offense, and Oregon State could not find a solution. Gilbert took advantage of home plate umpire Greg Street's unusually wide strike zone, primarily using his fastball to record out after out. He surrendered just two hits — one a Gretler solo homer — in 7 1/3 innings, finishing with seven strikeouts to one walk. As frustration mounted in OSU's dugout, Gilbert appeared to get stronger and stronger.

Pat Casey: We were obviously dialed in the first time we played them. The second time we played them, I thought either team could've won. We just couldn't get anything going and were facing a guy that was real, real good. The final game was just different, man. We felt like … we needed to get some baserunners. There were some situations we could've had some baserunners and it was a difficult day with handling that part of it. If you have a game where you don't play very well, which happens in baseball, you certainly don't want it to be in that particular arena. We just didn't play as well as we could've.

Pat Bailey: When we lost that first game to LSU, it was almost like driving a car down the road and you need to stop and get some gas because you'd end up running out. It seemed like we ran out of momentum, it was just a really weird feeling.

Jack Anderson: It was the first time all season I think we played scared. We'd just lost for the first time in God knows how long, and if we lose again we're done.

Jake Thompson: At that point, I'm feeling like I could've done better the day before. So, I'm like "please, win us this game and I will pitch the next game, we're going to win that and then we're going to win the championship. Just give me another chance."

You have this group of Beaver fans, but then everyone else in the stadium is hoping we're going to lose because we were this Goliath of a team. People thought this can't be real, they're going to lose it at some point. It just had that feeling that everyone was watching us and hoping we were going to lose this game, and that sucked. But that's what we'd faced all year and we thrived on that.

Michael Gretler: That (third) LSU game was where I really remember a complete shift after the first couple of innings in the dugout and the emotions in the dugout. There wasn't the energy, the air was sucked out of the dugout. It's tough to explain because we hadn't had a dugout like that the entire year. It was quiet, everyone kind of felt like we were walking on eggshells, no one was really talking after those first couple of innings. We were like "what the hell is going on?" It was just weird. We weren't getting any hits, and seeing guys like Trevor and Adley, who probably hadn't argued with an umpire all year, turn around and argue strike-three calls, and Kwan jumping up-and-down after he thinks he took ball four.

It was just a very different feel in the dugout after those first couple of innings, and we weren't able to get over that hump. Obviously having seen the TV and the strike zone and all that, I'm not going to use that as an excuse, but it's tough. I think we were a team that really took ownership of that team offense. Kwan was going to give us a good first at-bat and either walk or give us a single. Nick and Cadyn were going to move guys around and put pressure on the defense, and the big guys in the middle were going to drive them in. It felt like that was taken away from us, and I think that's why the mood in the dugout shifted so much because we felt like things were out of our control, which obviously isn't a great feeling. And to their credit, LSU put pressure on us and took the lead, hit a couple home runs, and we weren't able to flip the mood and light a spark. There was never a spark in that game. It was definitely not a fun dugout.

Pat Casey: I don't really know what the mood was. I don't think our team has ever not been competitive, I think guys were frustrated. I think there were some pitches guys felt like they couldn't reach, couldn't swing at, that were called strikes, and I think that got some guys frustrated. I think there was some frustration from that, I don't think there's any question after I looked at it that there were pitches that they just couldn't reach. So, I do understand the frustration, but I don't think we ever lost our competitiveness. People see into things whatever they want to see. If you're winning and the dugout is jumping up and down and you've got all kinds of enthusiasm, well, you're a great team then. And if you're behind and it's 102 degrees out and guys have a towel wrapped around their neck and are focusing or concentrating, maybe people are thinking "hey, they look a little dead." You play 60-some baseball games, it's not like you're at the circus every day. There are ups and downs and certainly if anybody would've felt like we weren't being competitive, we all would've stood up and said something. But it was a day that ... their guy was good. He was throwing the ball 93, 94 miles per hour and was able to throw it where he wanted to, and we weren't able to do the things we wanted to do.

Steven Kwan: I told myself "if this is how the zone is going to be for both sides, we'll just have to adjust." But seeing it from center field, it was not a fair zone. Fehm was pitching that game and it was against Michael Papierski. There was a (0-1) pitch that was corner-black, pitches that we struck out on, he called it a ball. I was like "OK, that was kind of suspicious." I thought that one was there, and (three pitches later) he hits a home run. I don't want to make excuses but damn, it was hard. And you can't complain as a batter because that just makes the zone even worse for you. But I knew when me, Gret, Trev and Rutsch were all complaining about the strike zone, which we never all do, it was like "man, we're going to have to figure something out."

Bryce Fehmel: It's part of baseball. Umpires give and take, it's not up to me and that's what they're there for. They're there to call balls and strikes, safe and out. I was just trying to make pitches in the right spots, and it didn't go my way that day.

Trevor Larnach: That game just didn't feel right, man. I wouldn't go as far as to say there was an agenda being pushed against us, but that's what it felt like. I played the outfield that game and I remember Bryce throwing these pitches and he wasn't getting calls. Nothing was getting called for him, and meanwhile our guys are going down left and right not swinging and it's like "that's not right." Being there in that position, it didn't look right. It just felt off, man. It didn't feel like we were given a real proper chance. Even though we were in the winners' bracket, it didn't feel like it was an equal opportunity, almost. And that's the only thing I can say, everyone has their different opinions. Everyone is going to say "make your adjustments to the zone" or whatever, but when you've got your pitcher out there working his ass off and he's constantly coming back into the dugout ... saying "those pitches are F'ing strikes" and we're getting laid out by pitches left and right that are in the other batters' box, you can't help but say "what's going on here?" That's what it comes down to, it didn't feel right and it felt like there was almost an agenda-type deal.

Pat Bailey: Well, let's be honest, if a pitch is eight inches off the plate and it's a fastball that the umpire calls a strike, you have no shot of hitting that pitch. You might be able to change your posture, reach out and foul it off, but you've got no shot of hitting it. And one of the things that we've done over the years and I think we've been really great with is from Day 1 we talk about managing the strike zone and controlling the zone and getting pitches in your damage zone and just being patient at the plate. Everything in that last game went against what we teach philosophically. And I don't know if we would've won or not, but the umpire's strike zone that game was the worst I've seen since I've been coaching.

Tyler Malone: From an outsider's perspective, people were probably like "oh, didn't you just get up on the plate?" But we are such patient and selective hitters that it's hard to get out of that. We get so locked into a certain strike zone and we all have such a good understanding of the zone that when you start getting calls out of that zone, it's hard to adjust because it's very instinctual. You have such little time to decide if you should swing at a pitch or not, and because it's instinctual you are just checking off those pitches. It's like "oh, ball," and then we hear it's a strike and now it's an 0-1 count instead of a 1-0 count. Counts in baseball are huge ... and you just get put in a hole. I don't want to make it an excuse or anything, but it's definitely a hard thing to adjust to when it's something you're not used to.

FINISH

Nate Yeskie: The strike zone, people say you've got to make adjustments and this and that. But you can't make adjustments to things that are just unaccounted for, there's no way to do certain things. We ran into Florida's coaching staff after the game. I've known (head coach Kevin O'Sullivan) for years and he said, "we've got guys in our league where I have to make adjustments to my lineup accordingly just because I know how the game is going to be called with regard to the strike zone." It just, it was an unfortunate circumstance because maybe if it's called straight, who knows? Maybe that team is playing for a second title in '18 as opposed to their first as a group.

Steven Kwan: Greg Street, that was just a terrible zone. I thought it was overall so very unfortunate. It took the bats out of our hands, didn't let the baseball players decide the game, which is very unfortunate. It definitely didn't work out how we wanted it to.

Max Engelbrekt: It was kind of anticlimactic because we were playing from way behind. I don't think I was going to pitch in that game because I'd already thrown a bunch the day before, so really all you can do is hope. And they were good. Their starter who was (normally) a reliever pitched (7 1/3) innings and Zack Hess pitched well.

Those two games, they just flew by, and that was it. You could kind of tell. It's just hard to come back when you're down four or five runs. It really ended in a hurry. It seemed like we should've won, but we got beat. I mean they were really, really good, but it was pretty abrupt to be three wins away and in a really powerful position, then not win again and have it be over in about 24 hours. It was crazy.

Zack Hess, a hard-throwing 6-foot-6 freshman nicknamed Wild Thing, picked up the save in relief of Lange by striking out four of the five batters he faced. The right-hander was back at it the next day, working 1 2/3 more scoreless innings as LSU stunned Oregon State 6-1 to secure a CWS finals berth against SEC rival Florida. The short-handed Beavers' magical run had come to a swift end.

Nate Yeskie: When it was over, everybody is just looking at each other like "no. We haven't lost back-to-back games all year, so this couldn't have really happened. This doesn't make any sense. We're playing tomorrow, right?" It had such an abrupt, out-of-nowhere finality to it.

Tyler Malone: We had never lost back-to-back games, so even when we lost that first game, it's not like we were panicked or worried or anything, we were just ready to get to the next game. And after we lost the next game, it was just shock. Not the shock of not being in the World Series anymore, it was shock because that was something we had never gone through before because of the success we'd had in the regular season. It was a super tough pill to swallow.

Nick Madrigal: There were a couple plays that could have gone either way. Kwan's hit down the left-field line that was fair that they ruled foul, there were just a number of things that could've went our way. I remember it being tough, especially after the series. For the ball to not bounce the way we wanted and to lose two games back-to-back, the first two all year, was very, very tough. I was in shock for a while after that and after the season ended. I always wanted to be a part of the teams like Darwin Barney to say you went back-to-back and things like that. Once that option left, there was a lot of anger and frustration.

KJ Harrison: We'd had such a great year and we were putting good things together; we'd started 2-0 in Omaha. But they were a great team and they were hot, and it was obviously devastating and heart-breaking. The hardest thing is you get so close and you get a taste of it, and to not come through was very difficult to handle.

Max Engelbrekt: It came so fast and just to know you're never going to play again there was pretty crazy. I'd known Yeskie for five years playing at that school and he'd become a pretty good friend. All the juniors, I'd played with them for a few years and lived with a lot of those guys. And really the whole team, it's hard to have relationships like that. And to know you're done playing there was just crazy.

Jake Thompson: We didn't have Luke there, which would've been huge. I mean if we would've had Luke, we would've cruised through that and made it to the championship series no problem with all our arms rested. By not having Luke there, we started running out of some pitchers and we had to think more strategically.

You win those first two games and you don't really think about that. Then you lose a close one and the second one you don't play as well as you should've played given some factors, then you look back and you think "if we had Luke and Donahue, that changes everything." It's a woulda, coulda, shoulda type situation.

Cadyn Grenier: We didn't have Luke, and we felt like that was a big loss. It didn't help that our pitching staff was on short rest, they were trying to do everything they could to make up for that and we just felt like we weren't getting a lot of the same calls. I'm not going to get too much into it because everyone knows about the umpiring and the calls that were made, but obviously those were huge moments in those games and it ultimately ended up being our downfall in some sort of way.

FINISH

No. 2 national seed Florida went on to sweep LSU in the championship series for its first national title. Oregon State shared third place with TCU, matching the program's 2013 College World Series finish.

While falling short of the ultimate goal, the 2017 Beavers still put together one of the most prolific seasons in college baseball history. OSU went 31-1 at Goss Stadium and finished with an overall record of 56-6, matching the 1975 Texas Longhorns for the fourth-best winning percentage (.903) of the CWS era. Numerous team and individual school records were shattered along the way during a season that can only be described as extraordinary.

Pat Casey: It really doesn't (make sense), and I say that humbly and I say it for them. I'm not sure what our record was going into the College World Series, I think it was 54-4. I don't care if you played in a smaller conference that wasn't a Power 5 conference, I don't think you'd go 54-4. I can tell you how it happens: character and will and camaraderie and sacrifices guys make, all the things sometimes people think don't matter and kind of pooh-pooh. Some people think "I've got to get Mr. Joe Tool player, the five-tool player. I've got to have the guy that runs, throws, hits and does it all in order to win." Here again, I go back to that fabric of the team and what guys were willing to do that year and the sacrifices of playing different positions and not being an everyday player. Talent is, without question, a part of that. The pitching was phenomenal. We really had an unbelievable blend in addition to having very talented players, but talent doesn't get you to 54-4. The intangibles are what made that happen, what's inside that locker room, the fabric of what's inside the uniform, not the fabric of the uniform itself, and I always like to tell guys that. I said, "the one thing those guys don't have, they don't have you, they don't have the real guys. That's what they want, they want you, they want real guys. Because the uniform don't play, it's the man inside the uniform." Those guys embodied what it meant to be someone that maximized their abilities together. Not individually, but together. Closeness, character, you name it, all the things that some people don't think count, don't think get on the field. They get on the field, they count, there's no doubt.

Tyler Graham, director of player development: I would say the number one word that comes to mind about that team is family. Those kids absolutely loved each other, they all had a mission and they all bought into Case's mission of doing anything it takes to win. When you have a strong bond like that team had, it was incredible to watch. Because baseball is a tough game and in a lot of cases the best team doesn't win. I think it just shows the character and the will that team had. With all the close games we had and we were able to come out on top in a lot of those games, it was something that I don't think any of us will ever forget. It was a magical season and it's probably not going to happen again where a team only loses four games in a (regular) season. There was a lot of magic, there was just something special about that team that's hard to explain.

Pat Bailey: Probably the craziest thing about (2017) is we were 14-1 in one-run games, and I think that is the key to going 56-6 that year. I mean it's just crazy how many one-run games we won versus what we lost, that will probably never happen again.

I think it's even more amazing what we did considering that everybody only has 11.7 scholarships to give. With the 11.7 scholarships, you are very limited in terms of the number of players you can get, and you've got to hit the right guys.

Bryce Fehmel: It's unbelievable to look back on it and be like "damn, we really had two 23-game winning streaks in one year?! That's impossible." But just the vibe we had in the clubhouse and at practice … whatever we were doing, we felt like we were going to win before we even stepped on the field.

Trevor Larnach: We knew we were the best. It didn't shake out that way, but that's how the attitude was and that's how it always has to be no matter what your record is, no matter who's on the field, no matter what the situation is, what the score is. You've always got to feel that you're the best, and that's how we felt and that's how we played. Baseball's baseball, it's going to happen. We didn't win it that year, but the fact that we made statements like (beating LSU 13-1), for a young team in our class' sense, that really kept the ship sailing.

Andy Jenkins: It's a great lesson in sports and in life when you're that good in the regular season and you don't come out on top. Sometimes it's a little bit of luck, a little bit of the baseball gods not being on your side, and unfortunately we came up just a little bit short.

Jake Thompson: It was such a great group of guys … and I knew most of those guys were coming back. It was like "holy smokes. If we just did that, what are they going to do in 2018?!"

Pat Casey: There was just a tremendous motivation coming home on the plane to think about what we were going to do next year when we got back.

Trevor Larnach: We moved past it when we were on the plane. I don't think anybody was really sulking over it or anything like that. It was a pretty shitty feeling at the time. We'd just got our hearts broken; we didn't do what we wanted to do obviously. We got cut short and the game that we lost on just didn't feel like an actual opportunity for us to move forward. After that, we were bitter about it and to say the least, we weren't happy about what happened. But once we got on the plane, I think Nick did a pretty good job of already looking forward to the next year.

Steven Kwan: Nick brought the whole team together, the returners, and he said "you guys, savor this feeling, remember this feeling. Because this is not the same feeling we're going to have next year. Work hard this offseason and right when we meet up in September, let's get going." So that was the lasting impression I had in my mind.

Bryce Fehmel: We knew we came up short after an unbelievable year, and we had almost the same team coming back. It was pretty much the same mindset going into that offseason as the year before. You just put your head down, get to work and we knew we'd definitely have another chance the following year.

Jake Mulholland: Looking back at it, that was one of the best things for us. It was kind of similar to the 2016 team not making it in at all. The 2017 team not finishing really helped our team prepare for the next year.

CHAPTER V

RUNNING IT BACK

Much like the previous offseason, Oregon State's core remained largely intact. The Major League Baseball Draft did some damage, as KJ Harrison (third round, Milwaukee Brewers), Jake Thompson (fourth round, Boston Red Sox) and Max Engelbrekt (40th round, Washington Nationals) all agreed to professional contracts. Outfielder Elliott Cary, utility man Andy Atwood and reliever Mitch Hickey headlined a small group of players who transferred elsewhere in search of more playing time.

For three of the Beavers' more prominent players — Christian Donahue, Luke Heimlich and Drew Rasmussen — the summer of 2017 was filled with uncertainty. Rasmussen was taken 31st overall by the Tampa Bay Rays, but a post-draft team physical revealed an issue in his repaired right elbow. The draft signing deadline passed without a deal in place between the two sides. Rasmussen wound up returning to school and underwent a second Tommy John surgery that would sideline him for the entire 2018 season.

Drew Rasmussen, pitcher: We lose in the College World Series, which is demoralizing. It sucks, you're so close to winning a national championship and so close to realizing all the work and effort you put in. Getting to the final goal and having it all taken away there at the end really sucked; it was tough and it was difficult. We flew back to Corvallis and Tampa Bay was really nice. They gave me two or three days to pack up my house, all my stuff. They flew me out there, I got an MRI one of the first days down there, went through my physical and all that stuff. The next morning, I got called and they said, "hey, I think we're going to do a second MRI on your elbow."

FINISH

So, I started piecing things together that something probably wasn't right. To what extent, I didn't really know. I'd played catch the couple days I was back in Corvallis because I was preparing to go play for Tampa's short-season A team and kick off my professional career. It turns out I had blown out my elbow again at some point along the way, and Tampa Bay decided to not offer me a contract. They sent me to see Dr. Keith Meister in Arlington, Texas, for a second opinion. And he confirmed what the MRIs had said.

Nate Yeskie, pitching coach: Rasmussen's deal was just a horrible unfolding. Major League Baseball gives you an area of time to turn in your medical reports, and he was penalized because he turned his in too early. Had he'd waited like an extra three days to turn them in, it would've fallen within the period of time that whoever selected him, if they would've decided to basically medical him out and say "all right, we're not going to sign this guy," well they're obligated to offer a minimum of 60% of what the slot's value is (Rasmussen's signing bonus slot value was $2.1 million). He got penalized for turning in his homework early, that's essentially what happened.

Drew Rasmussen: I stayed in contact with Dr. Meister and he was always upfront. I did some research on Tommy John experts in the country and Oregon State baseball was more than willing to help. They took care of everything expense-wise for getting my second surgery. I went home and I worked for the offseason to be able to afford going back to school and living and all that kind of stuff. From there, I got surgery on Aug. 23 and started the rehab process in Corvallis again and just moved in and prepared for my senior year. I knew I was going to be around the team and around the facility all the time … and went into the fall of 2017 preparing to graduate and knowing that I wasn't going to play at Oregon State that year. I was able to focus on school a little bit more and tried to be a good leader and keep a positive attitude around the team and work hard in the weight room. Obviously, for personal reasons, and as a team leader.

All the guys on the team were great to me in 2018. They were sympathetic to my situation and were the same fun-loving group they always were. I think getting to go back and be around the team, see familiar faces and the people I loved, I think it really helped ease the blow. And on top of it, my family, my (now-wife's) family, they were great about helping me through the situation. Just checking in, making sure everything was going all right. I mean it's pretty hard to say I've had a hard life, but that was definitely the most difficult situation in it. All the help and the support I was given from Beaver Nation, the Oregon State community and on top of it friends and family, it was incredible. I was ultimately able to graduate on time and experience more of student life than what I had previously.

Nate Yeskie: He wasn't on the roster, but he was a part of what we were doing. He was getting his work done. He went through his procedure to get himself right and he was there pulling for the guys and staying engaged as much as he could in the things that he could control, all the while trying to help our guys get better and learn. If you look at guys like (Grant) Gambrell and (Kevin) Abel who he felt had big stuff, he tried to give them insights on what he went through as a freshman and how he could help them get better. I remember he watched Gambrell throw for the first time and he just shook his head and went "I've got to get better." I said, "what are you talking about?" And he said, "this guy's got better stuff than I did at the same age. If this guy works as hard as I do, I'm going to be out of a job, so I've got to get better." That's the beauty of Ras, he's always looking for an opportunity to get better and he utilizes his time in the weight room to get it done.

Max Engelbrekt, pitcher: From a college standpoint, his career numbers are less impressive than you would think because he unfortunately got hurt twice. But of guys I ever played with, nobody threw that hard and had that good of a fastball and was literally that strong.

Drew Rasmussen: Talk about going from a first-round draft pick to the College World Series to losing in the College World Series to finding out I was hurt. In life there are peaks and valleys, and unfortunately that's the way it goes sometimes. Being able to roll with the punches and make a positive out of a negative situation and keep your head up and keep fighting. I mean, that's ultimately what defines you in your life and your career. I was never able to get an exact answer or exact reason (for what happened), but that's all right. I'm feeling healthy now … and I'm just trying to take this thing and run with it as far as I can.

After sitting out the end of the 2017 season, Heimlich's status moving forward was also unsettled. A projected early-round pick with one year of college eligibility remaining, Heimlich was bypassed by all 30 teams in the MLB Draft. Oregon State President Ed Ray issued an 11-paragraph statement prior to the CWS, agreeing with Heimlich's decision to step away from the team. Ray also wrote, "if Luke wishes to do so, I support him continuing his education at Oregon State and rejoining the baseball team next season."

The university announced a new policy in February 2018, requiring all students to self-report felony convictions and registered sex offender status moving forward. The accompanying press release stated: "Going forward, a university committee will conduct a confidential case-by-case review of each of the self-disclosing students' situations. (OSU vice president for university relations and marketing) Steve Clark said OSU's dean of student life then will determine any extracurricular engagement and participation limitations or requirements needed for safety involving a self-disclosed student. The dean also will provide support to self-disclosed students in their engagement activities. Clark also said OSU's director of Public Safety periodically will meet individually with each self-disclosed student. ... 'Where there is not a safety risk posed by the student participating in an activity, OSU will support the student's participation in programs and activities, and their success,' Clark said."

Pat Casey declined to comment on the details of the proceedings, but Heimlich returned to the team for fall practice. The Beavers were getting another season from the reigning Pac-12 pitcher of the year and willing to deal with any potential distractions that came with it.

Luke Heimlich, pitcher: I didn't know right away, it was kind of an ongoing process, but Casey supported me 100% and he basically told me "we're going to have you back, don't worry about it. We'll take care of business on this end." I went home that summer for the first time. I stayed in Corvallis the two summers before that, so I went home that summer for about a month and a half and just worked out at home and got ready to come back in the fall.

Nate Yeskie: With Heimlich, we'd talked to a couple clubs and he was going to be a first-round pick. It was pretty much a foregone conclusion. It was just about which team was going to be the one that took him, because a couple teams wanted him there in the middle of the first round.

Jack Anderson, outfielder: After 2017, once he didn't get drafted, we weren't sure if he could play. There was still a lot going on behind the scenes where it was like "should he play, should he not, what should we do with Luke?" I felt terrible that he didn't get drafted and didn't get the dream he was hoping to have and deserves, but he came back and I was kind of like "well, it's good for us!" I mean, it's the best pitcher in the nation and we've got him for another year. I think it was for the best that he was around the Beaver family a little bit, and it definitely didn't hurt having him. He was the same Luke as always out there ... and you just knew he was going to do what he had always done in his career at Oregon State.

Kyle Nobach, outfielder: I was actually hurt when the whole Luke situation was going on so I had spent a lot of time around Luke, I tried to spend a lot of time around him. Clearly everything he was going through was just insane, very hard to deal with. There were a lot of emotions, his image and all this stuff, so he dealt with a lot and I tried to be there with him through that. As soon as we figured out he was coming back, I think all of us were very excited.

Nick Madrigal, infielder: Luke was one of the best pitchers, if not the best pitcher in the country. To have him back, no one expected that. But we were excited to have him on our side and knew that it would elevate our team to be even better. It was great to have him there, and he was close with everyone on the team. So, it was nice to have him there not only on the field, but off the field as well.

Trevor Larnach, outfielder: The coaches always stressed that pitching is what will win a national championship. To have a guy of that caliber come back to make you better in the fall and the winter and to have him back as a teammate, it's a satisfying type of feeling because you have your ace back. He's going to come out, give his all and dominate because that's what Luke does. It was also just another guy we could play to win it for because he didn't get the opportunity to go to the World Series the previous year, and we needed him. We knew we would've won it if we had him, so it was a huge, huge uplifting thing to get him back, and we were ready to go.

Facing a lengthy suspension to begin the season, Donahue had multiple options moving forward. Pat Casey helped him get in touch with the Chicago Cubs, who wound up signing Donahue to a free-agent contract.

Christian Donahue, infielder/outfielder: Everyone was in Omaha and literally right after the news came out that I wasn't traveling with the team, NAIA teams started calling me and saying, "hey, if you're not going back to OSU next year, you're always free to come here." Five or six NAIA teams called within like 10 days of when the news came out, that was crazy. So, we started weighing our options because I didn't get drafted, either. It was either go back to OSU, sit out half the season and just play half a season, or go NAIA and hopefully do good enough to get picked up in the draft. It wasn't until the World Series was done … Case had been in contact with the Cubs' scouting director (Matt Dorey), and he was the guy who hooked up this whole Cubs deal. I will forever be grateful to him for that and helping me out with everything that happened.

Pat Casey, head coach: I just felt like C Boy was a great kid. C Boy worked his tail off and he was one of the funnest kids I ever got to coach. He came to work every day, and I don't know a lot of kids who go through their entire time and don't make some type of mistake anywhere. Sometimes something happens where people are aware of it, other times something happens and nobody is aware of it. C Boy was in a situation where I didn't feel like he needed to be reprimanded and punished the following year. I thought missing the College World Series for any young man that put in the time and effort he did was plenty of penance. I just thought he was a great kid and

FINISH

I wasn't going to give up on him, so therefore I didn't. I called every organization that I could call and talked to a lot of my friends and talked to a lot of guys that wanted to go to bat for him. Some organizations were unwilling to take on C Boy and there were a couple that were, and I'm just happy for him.

Pat Bailey, associate head coach: The Cubs love him. They love the way he plays the game and how he goes about doing things. His family is an unbelievable family. His younger brother, Jordan, (signed with Oregon State in 2019). Christian is just a great young man.

Christian Donahue: I owe everything to coach Case.

The 2016 NCAA Tournament snub provided ample motivation for Oregon State moving forward, and the same thing occurred following the team's back-to-back losses to LSU. The 2017 Beavers will forever be on the shortlist of greatest college baseball teams to not win it all. The 2018 squad had no interest in joining them.

Pat Bailey: You have two choices when you fall short of a goal. You either pull your pants up, buckle them up, get going and learn from it or you have a pity party, and I think that's just not the personality of this coaching staff, not the personality of this program. Case did a great job postgame (after LSU). I remember him saying, "right now it's really hard, but in a week or so we'll look back and see how amazing of a year we had in 2017." But I'll tell you what, when we came back in the fall, our practices in the fall of 2017 were amazing. I don't think we had a bad practice the entire fall. And then going into the springtime, we were on a mission. You could see it in the way our guys went about their business, the way they acted on and off the field, the way they walked around campus. Everything that they did felt like we were championship material.

Morgan Pearson, assistant to Pat Casey: The intensity was a little different in practice. We weren't trying to prove ourselves. I just feel like the identity of the team was a lot more concrete in '18. We knew who we were and we knew no one could beat us when we were doing what we could do.

Luke Heimlich: I think everybody was motivated. The last season didn't end the way you wanted. Everybody wants to win the last game of the year. It's one of those things where you were close and our team was really good, but ultimately we didn't accomplish what we wanted to accomplish.

Cadyn Grenier, infielder: We felt like we had that taken from us. We didn't feel like we lost those games, even though we did and there are definitely things we could've done better. But we felt like we were robbed of a true chance of making it to the final, and that was the taste in everyone's mouth. But when everyone got back onto campus, it was like "yeah right, we're back. Look at this team!" We knew we were going to be at the top of the Pac-12. We knew we were going to have a chance to go back to Omaha.

We had that bad taste still, but it was towards the back of our minds. We were out for blood that year, and that was the best thing. We all knew what had happened, but we weren't focused on it.

Brandon Eisert, pitcher: I think with all the guys we had returning, we knew we were going to be a good team, and obviously we had the goal of winning the national title. Just the other day me and (Steven) Kwan were talking about how in scrimmages we would split the team up and have half the talent on each team. We were like "those teams even at half strength were incredible teams." When we got to put them together for our regular season, it was just remarkable how much talent we had.

Zak Taylor, first baseman: It was the most motivated I've been going into a season. You had a group where for a lot of those guys, it was going to be their last year, their draft year. I knew this was going to be our chance to win this thing. We had the talent, and I knew if we just stayed healthy, we were really going to make a run — and that's a good feeling. Getting knocked out by LSU, that put a sour taste in our mouths. You just go back to that moment all the time throughout the offseason, especially if things get tough or you get in a mode where you're beat up, your body is sore, you go to that and use that as fuel. I feel like we really did, we took that to heart.

Nate Yeskie: Their singular focus was "listen, we're going to win this thing. We ain't out for anything more than winning the whole thing. You can have the conference title, you can have the batting title or the ERA title or the Pac-12 player of the year title. Those are nice, but those are the booby prizes. We want the big one at the end." I think the abrupt fashion in which '17 ended just changed the whole focus and dynamic up another notch for that group to really catapult themselves into the 2018 season.

Jake Rodriguez, assistant coordinator of baseball camps: I remember coming into the locker room the first day of practice in the fall and the guys, they hadn't done this in the past, but in the locker room there's a huge picture of the trophy from when they held it up in 2007, and on the trophy you can see where it says 2007 national champions. When we walked into the locker room, one of the players had taken a big piece of tape and put 2018 over it. So, when you walked in every day, you saw the national championship trophy with a 2018 on it.

Adley Rutschman, catcher: I know, for a lot of the guys, it felt like the (two LSU losses) never went away. Like we came in the next fall, and it was a lot of the same guys. Except for a couple dudes, it was mainly the same guys. And the whole year ... for the new guys, it was basically trying to explain to them what we felt and what our goal was. We had enough guys that year that had the same feeling and were willing to put in the work to make that year special.

The batch of newcomers included talented freshmen pitchers Kevin Abel and Christian Chamberlain, junior-college arm Dylan Pearce and a pair of undergraduate assistant coaches in Ryan Gorton and Bill Rowe, both of whom played for Casey at Oregon State. Chamberlain, a left-hander, entered the program as a two-way prospect from Reno, Nevada, while the right-handed Abel was one of the nation's top pitching prospects coming out of San Diego's Madison High School. Pearce, a graduate of Crater High School in Southern Oregon and Southwestern Oregon Community College, was a lifelong Beavers baseball fan.

Kevin Abel, pitcher: North Carolina was my dream school growing up. I had seen them play on TV when I was a kid and got to visit the school when I was in either eighth grade or as a freshman when I was out there for Team USA stuff, and I loved it. It's actually pretty similar to (Oregon State). A lot of brick buildings, history and things like that. It's funny, when I came here on my visit the first time they had a video playing in the Omaha Room, and it was of them beating UNC back-to-back years. It seemed fitting since UNC wasn't interested in me.

UNC was the only school I had ever emailed myself, saying that I really want to play for your school. My travel ball coach even, when we were playing in a tournament, started me against a team that had six UNC commits knowing the UNC coach was going to be there. I threw well and my coach went up to him and was like "hey, my kid that just pitched really well wants to play for you." And he was like "no, not interested." I think they already had their class filled up or had already made their decisions, I don't know. I never really got that far. It was just not going to happen, so I found somewhere else to play.

Bails had watched me in a couple tournaments in Arizona and Southern California and I was invited during my sophomore year of high school to go to the pitcher/catcher camp that's held (at Oregon State) in January, or at least is traditionally held in January. So, I went and that was the first time I got introduced to Yeskie. I went on a tour of the campus and everything. I threw my bullpen part of the camp, and right after that Bails and Yeskie said they were going to offer me a scholarship, which was crazy. I went over to my mom and was trying to hold back tears, I was like "mom, I finally did it. I'm going to go play Division I baseball," because that was something I had been told that I would never be able to do. So, that was a big relief I guess just hearing that. I was offered a scholarship, stayed in touch with them but I was still looking around, I wanted to make sure I made the perfect decision for me. A couple other schools were interested. They offered, but nothing compared to OSU. They had everything: the winning legacy, the great coaching, the best pitching coach in the country, all of that. It was a no-brainer to come here, so I committed my sophomore year.

Dylan Pearce, pitcher: The presence and the atmosphere the program gave off was unbelievable. It was the team of my dreams. I had given everything and dedicated my baseball life to play for this team. Just showing up and seeing how the guys were, being on the field and being surrounded by the coaches and the players, the feeling was almost indescribable. I felt like a little kid going to Disneyland for the first time. It was like "oh my gosh, I'm here. I've made it, I'm here." And then we just got down to business.

Christian Chamberlain, pitcher: The standard was set really high as soon as we stepped on campus. I was both a pitcher and a hitter coming in, so I was up in Corvallis pretty early with all the other pitchers. You knew what the Oregon State culture was as soon as you were on campus. The bar was set higher than anything I'd ever been a part of.

Kyler McMahan, infielder/outfielder: It was better than I ever could've imagined, walking in as a freshman and seeing what I had seen on TV for so long and how accepting the guys were. They made you feel part of the team and it was time to get to work so we could get back to the College World Series because they had that nasty taste in their mouth of not pulling it off and not finishing it. Come 2018, there was no screwing around. We were getting to work from Day 1.

Zach Clayton, outfielder: As a freshman coming in I knew that we were a really good team and that we were going to be contenders for the national championship. But it was just like, it felt like those guys were your brothers. Like you didn't see those guys as the superstars that they actually are. There was a family feeling and we were playing for each other rather than we were only playing for a national championship. It seemed like there was so much more than just baseball going on.

Ryan Gorton, undergraduate assistant coach: I was just impressed with how professional they were. Pretty much all the starters had routines that they would stick to and go hit on their own either before or after practice. They were always trying to get more ground balls, staying late. When I got there, at least with the starters, there wasn't a ton of coaching that had to be done because they knew what they needed to do. That's a pretty good testament to the rest of the staff for bringing them up to speed when they were young.

Bill Rowe, undergraduate assistant coach: I came aboard in December, in the middle of that offseason, so I didn't get to see those guys throughout the entire fall. I came in as the newcomer mid-offseason, so it was a little bit different vibe for me compared to what I'm used to. Obviously there was a bunch of really skilled players on that team, and it was really easy for me to come back and be around Case and (Tyler) Graham and people like that. But in terms of the players, it's difficult when you're the new coach and there's a bunch of really good players on the team and they know they're really good. You need to develop a trust at first. So right when I got there in December it was really about getting to know the players, just waiting for them to learn enough about me so they could decide for themselves whether they wanted to trust me as a coach or not. Obviously, the skill level was really high. You just saw a lot of players who were gifted with physical abilities that only a few college baseball players really have. I noticed that right away, and noticed a lot of the similarities between the way those players and the way that our team acted back when I was on it in 2006, just in terms of how many people were upstairs in (McAlexander Fieldhouse) getting extra work on their own time and how many guys were focused on the one goal of winning a national championship from the very beginning, which is also what we had in 2006 coming off a disappointing finish in Omaha the previous year.

Jack Anderson: That offseason was a new role for us being the big dogs on the block and everyone was going to put a target on our backs. We tried to not really change anything we did from that summer before and kept that same mindset where last year was last year, no one deserves anything this next year. I think we were definitely more experienced; we knew what we needed to do to be ready for the season. We definitely had that veteran leadership. At that point, most of our players had been in the program for three or four years and it was kind of a player-ran team, which it should be when you have good coaches and they can give the keys to the players their junior and senior years.

Zak Taylor: I've never been on a team that was more tight-knit than that group, 100It was nice because the majority of that team was our junior class, and you had some of those key seniors like Jack Anderson, Michael Gretler, Kyle Nobach and Luke. It really tied everything together; that helped so much. We literally did everything together and we really held each other accountable more than anything. Of course, the coaching staff was awesome. But when it came to getting stuff done every day and getting our work in, we were on each other more than I would say the coaches were on us. We held each other accountable and that was the reason why day in and day out we were so good. We all knew our whole entire goal was to win a national championship. We knew we had the team, we knew we had the talent, we had the experience, too. So, I think all those factors played in.

Jake Mulholland, pitcher: We were on a mission to finish. Obviously, in 2017 we had a little bit of motivation because we didn't do that. So in 2018 instead of breaking (huddles) on "Beavs" or "together", we started breaking on "finish" because we knew that was the goal and that was what we were there to do. We really wanted to show people who we could be, so we broke on "finish" and we took games one game at a time up until there weren't any more.

With so many leaders in the program, Pat Casey decided to do something that he'd never done before: instead of a group of captains, the Beavers would only have one. Nick Madrigal, a co-team captain in 2017 with Rasmussen, was the clear choice.

Pat Casey: Nick's a humble guy. He's the silent assassin. He is always wanting to win. He is after you. But he was never a vocal guy that wanted to act like "hey, I know how to do it." He just likes to play. I think (being the sole captain) was really good for him, and it was good for us. I think that he needed to be the guy because there were so many other guys that could've been a captain along with him. We could've named five guys captain, and I didn't think that was the way to go. You could talk about Grenier, you could talk about Rutschman, you could talk about Fehmel, you could talk about Larnach, you could talk about Heimlich. There were so many different guys that it just felt like this was going to be really, really good for Nick and this was going to be really, really good for our team.

I think he was a great captain. He did things and said things and led in ways that he may never had done if we had not named him the sole captain.

Kyle Nobach: Nick was our leader, he really was. He took over a lot of things and we did a lot of things on our own. We had captain practices and optional things that were player-ran. Nick ran a lot of that stuff and set the attitude and the message.

Trevor Larnach: He was coach Casey-esque, man. If coach Casey said something,

Nick … it's not that he was quiet, but his attitude and the way he carried himself was definitely the way of a leader, nothing less than that. He would say stuff when it came down to it. If something was BS and shit wasn't getting done or whatever it was, he'd bring us to the side and he'd either hold himself accountable or put us in check with what we needed to be doing because he's a leader at heart. I think that comes from his mom and his dad raising him. Him and coach Casey, it's the same type of mental attitude, same type of mentality, and it was perfect. It couldn't have been more perfect. Because Nick might be the smallest guy on the field, but upstairs when it came to the mind, he's the biggest. And that's all that mattered to coach Casey, your mind and your will and your mentality.

Nick Madrigal: It was something that was a huge honor and something that I wanted, but I also knew that even if they named me the sole captain, there were so many captains on that team so the whole responsibility wasn't just on me. I remember guys like Michael Gretler, Kyle Nobach, Cadyn, the list goes on and on. There were so many leaders on that team and we all made each other better. So honestly, I didn't want all the credit for being the captain because I knew that that team was special and there were so many people who made each other better.

Ryan Gorton: Nick was a leader by example. He had a routine where he would get to the park at 11, 11:30 a.m. every day and hit, do his whole thing for like an hour before everybody else showed up. He went about his work in a professional way, and to couple that with how good he was on the field, everybody wanted to follow him and do what he did. My first year was his junior year, and I think he became a much better leader and more personable and charismatic with the guys the longer he was in the program. I think he realized he was the best player and people looked up to him, so he needed to add that vocal piece to it a little bit, which he did. I remember the first game we lost that year to Cal State Fullerton, Nick wasn't even playing but when we got back into the locker room, he was the first one to step up and say something about what needs to be done. I thought that was pretty cool for a guy who doesn't typically say a whole lot and wasn't even playing.

Madrigal wasn't in the lineup for the Cal State Fullerton rematch because the leading candidate to derail Oregon State's season — injuries — reared its ugly head a couple of weeks prior in Surprise, Arizona. On the second weekend of the year, Madrigal suffered a broken left wrist while sliding into home plate against Ohio State. The reigning Pac-12 player of the year would miss the next seven weeks of action.

Nick Madrigal: Gosh, I remember feeling so locked in in the box down in Arizona.

I was feeling good in the warm weather there, and it was just one of those freak plays. I went for a hook slide at home plate and my wrist kind of jammed in there. I remember immediately popping up and knowing something was wrong. I thought it was a stinger at first but it would not go away, so I knew that something was wrong. I tried to shake it out but had to come out of the game.

Morgan Pearson: When it happened, I was standing next to Case in the dugout. Nick slid in and it didn't really look bad at first, then somebody came sprinting down to us from the other end of the dugout to say "hey, Nick's done, Nick's hurt." So, Pat said, "we've got to get Nick some X-rays quick." The previous summer I had interned with the Texas Rangers, and we were playing in Surprise and I knew all the guys. I knew the trainers, the big-league medical staff. So, I made a call to a guy named Jamie Reed, the senior director of medical operations for the Rangers and said, "hey, we've got Nick and we might need him to get pictures of his wrist." I remember we took Nick out of the game, and we got him up getting pictures within 10 or 20 minutes of his injury, and that was really big. The Rangers took care of Nick, they helped Nick with that.

Pat Casey: I can see it happen right now as we're sitting here talking. Nick never wants to come out of a game, and it was really, really too bad, man. If it's going to happen, it happened early enough that we got him back and that was the only good thing. But I remember him sliding in there and catching his hand on the ground. We were told after the game. He had an X-ray there and we thought it was negative. And then later on we were told it was fractured.

Michael Gretler, infielder: To see someone like him go down and not be able to go out on the field, it's devastating. You're thinking "here we go, we've got all this talent and we've got everyone ready to go." Then he breaks his hand and we're all like "oh, gosh." Having been through it and seeing guys like Drew Rasmussen get hurt the first Pac-12 (road) series my sophomore year, it's not easy.

Nick Madrigal: I wasn't sure how long I was going to miss, but I knew if there was a chance I could be back for the season — even the slightest chance — it might make everything better. But it was tough for a while to not be in there and just be on the sidelines because I'd never sat out that many games in my life. It was all new to me.

Brandon Eisert: It was definitely tough, but as a team we still had the talent to keep moving forward. Obviously, you want him to be able to play, but even when Nick was hurt he was still such a big part of the team. Just leading us in the dugout, making sure everyone was ready to go, that kind of thing. We knew we were going to get him back.

FINISH

Ryan Gorton: We were like "well crap, there goes our best player." But Andy Armstrong filled in and played awesome, and we didn't miss a beat. It was fun to watch the rest of the guys rally behind each other and not leave it all on Nick's shoulders.

The Beavers' top backup infielder was Andy Armstrong, a sophomore capable of playing second base, third base and shortstop. Armstrong, from West Salem High School — about 35 miles north of Goss Stadium — didn't see the field much as a freshman, but was ready to fill in for one of the best players in the country.

Andy Armstrong, infielder: Nick slid into home plate, came off the field and was holding his wrist and wincing pretty bad. In my mind, that's pretty serious, and in the back of my mind I was the next guy up. I can remember getting my hat and my glove and I knew I was going in and was probably going to have to play for a longer period of time than I had at Oregon State.

Michael Gretler: Andy Armstrong did an incredible job of stepping in and staying ready. Here's a guy who probably didn't think he was going to play a whole lot. But there wasn't a day that went by that he wasn't taking extra ground balls or extra swings, and that's a testament to him and a testament to the program. That's what it takes to have success. You never know when your time is going to come. But when it does come, you better be ready for it because the (sixth) game of the year when Nick Madrigal goes down, you've got pretty big shoes to fill, right? If you haven't been preparing, you're going to let your team down. (Armstrong) obviously didn't let that happen and filled in nicely.

Cadyn Grenier: That's about as bad of a spot as you can put somebody into. You have Andy Armstrong, who had barely played at all in his college career, and he has to now fill in for the best college baseball player on the planet in Nick. People are like "well, he's not going to produce what Nick would." And you can't expect him to. But the job he did for those several weeks was amazing, and I felt like it kept our team going where we didn't feel like we'd lost our best player. We didn't feel like we'd lost our most highly-touted guy. (Armstrong) did a fantastic job at trying to fill those shoes as much as he could.

Nick Madrigal: Armstrong, I already knew how much talent he had. He was already a strong player and worked really hard. A lot of people on the team didn't notice that he would come early, stay late, and he worked hard. He would take a lot of ground balls and hit. He's somebody who probably would've started and been the guy on any other college team in America, I truly believe that. But for how much talent we had on the team he was kind of that extra guy that filled in here and there. But when he stepped in, he almost didn't even skip a beat. He had a great couple series and did a lot of things well for the team. Honestly, I always believed in him and knew he could get the job done. And yeah, when that happened I was so happy for him and the team. It was tough sitting on the side, but I was glad we weren't losing. It made things a little bit better.

Andy Peterson, undergraduate assistant coach: There was nobody that worked harder than Andy Armstrong his freshman year. Every single day, I had to stay after and hit him ground balls until I said he was done. Every single day he wanted ground balls before and after practice, it was so constant. It was one of those things where he almost started to make everyone else look bad. So all of a sudden a few more people were staying afterward to take ground balls and showing up early to take ground balls.

Obviously, you've got Cadyn and Nick and Gretler, so it was good luck as a freshman. But the kid just worked his tail off and it was fun to see him be the starting shortstop (later on) because he absolutely deserved it. The second he showed up, he did more than everybody. You had your freaks of nature in guys like Cadyn, Nick, Larnach, Rutschman and those guys. Then you had your dirt dogs in Nobach and Gretler and Kwan and Armstrong and Jack Anderson. I think it was the perfect mix of freaks and grinders.

Armstrong started the first four games after Madrigal's injury and was ineffective at the plate, going 1 for 13 with a pair of walks. Then Kyler McMahan received a couple of starts before the Beavers turned back to Armstrong, who went 1 for 2 with an RBI in his next start against Portland. He stuck in the lineup from there, and hit .361 (26 for 72) with 17 RBIs, 12 doubles and two home runs over the next 20 games until Madrigal returned.

Andy Armstrong: I had to fill in for the best second baseman in the country. I struggled at the beginning a little bit … and (Kyler McMahan) actually came in for me at second base at one point. Second base was mine, and then it got taken. But next thing you know I'm back in there at second base, playing against Cal State Fullerton at home. I had a double off the wall to score the tying run, and it took off from there.

I'm a big believer in momentum, and I just think that really got the ball rolling for me. I went on a hot streak there for 15 games or so and I don't know, I just found myself in a routine. I was very, very strict in my pregame routine and right before the game and everything I did. Some of that is because you need structure to perform at your best, and another part of that was just superstition. It was very stressful I must say because at this level, it's about performing. And you're not just going to roll the baseballs out there and play. It was very stressful for me going into a series and stuff like that because I was trying to help the team. I wanted to play at my best level and I found myself in this really strict routine, all the way down to listening to the same list of songs right before every game, and that never changed. I think that's what helped me best, continually practicing my process down to the little tiny details.

Nate Yeskie: Andy Armstrong was maybe second or third on the team in doubles at the time (Madrigal returned). If you just play his numbers out and give him the same number of at-bats as everyone else, he leads our team in doubles by a wide margin.

Pat Casey: (Armstrong) could always defend. He was always going to be a guy that could defend and he swung the bat pretty good during that period of time for us. He was excited about playing and he did a great job for us.

Andy Armstrong: (Coach Casey and I) never sat down, we never had a one-on-one conversation about "this is what you've got to do." I just think Case has a lot of faith in the players that he brings in or you wouldn't be a part of the program. That's the way I looked at it and I assume that's the way they looked at it as well.

My approach to it was "this is my time to help the team. Obviously, Nick is out, and I've got to fill in." I never really thought about having to play in his shoes, I just thought that it was time to play my game and help the team. I put together a good stretch of games and helped us win, and looking back on that, I'm really proud of the fact that I had the opportunity to go in there and play and the coaches and my teammates had faith in me.

Madrigal had his cast removed in late March, but wasn't close to returning to the field. It didn't dampen the All-American's spirits.

Nick Madrigal: It felt like it was the longest time ever from when my cast got put on to all the rehab and everything. I remember being in the dugout and just seeing all the behind-the-scenes stuff from all the coaches and seeing how much it seemed like they worried and how fired up they would get in the dugout. Being on the field you never saw any of that, but they were constantly going back and forth at each other and were so fired up during the games. I remember making a comment to someone and asking them "are they always this fired up? They've got to relax, we've got this."

Pat Casey: Shoot, you lose one of the best players in the country, you're not excited about it. But none of that was ever going to keep us from saying that we were going to come out and play the way we wanted to play. I think you're concerned about that way more in the office than you are on the field. We just wanted to get him healthy, we wanted to get him prepared. We have a huge obligation because we know he's going to be a professional. You have to have everything done right, and it was, and he came back as fast as he could. It just tells you what kind of a guy Nick is.

Jeremy Ainsworth, trainer: Obviously, injuries are part of the game and bound to happen at some point. With Nick specifically, the things for him were his continuous drive to want to get better, do everything he could to get better with rehab and treatment and everything like that. And his ability to still have an enormous impact outside of the lineup on the mindset of people, and his ability to understand the game and elevate people even though he wasn't playing. That was a tough time for him I would assume because you're not on the field and he's such a competitor. But he was able to focus some of that energy elsewhere and help bring other people up.

Morgan Pearson: Nick, he never felt bad. He never felt sorry for himself. That was a big thing that really impacted me being around Nick was he never felt bad about the situation, he never felt sorry for himself that he was hurt. He didn't miss a practice. He was always there and this contagious attitude with Nick was just unbelievable.

Steven Kwan, outfielder: (Not having Nick) was definitely a blow to the team. He was our leader, but he kept a good attitude. He was never down, he just kept saying, "keep it going boys, I'll be back. Keep growing, keep doing what you're doing, and I'll be back when it matters." He kept our spirits high; he kept his own spirits high. I lived with him, and it wasn't a show. He truly believed we were going to be fine, and obviously we were. I would say that was great leadership from his point.

After a 26-game absence, Madrigal finally rejoined the lineup April 19 for the Civil War conference series opener. He was his usual self, going 2 for 4 with an RBI, while playing perfect defense at second base. Armstrong remained in the starting lineup at third base for the next six games, but returned to a backup role when his bat cooled down.

Nick Madrigal: I think we were targeting the Civil War, it just ended up working out that way. There were times there when it wasn't feeling the best. So I was waiting for it to start feeling a little bit better and it never did up until the very last second. I was just thankful to be able to play again that year and be a part of that team.

I remember the crowd gave me a nice welcoming back, everyone was on their feet. It was something that made me feel really good because I put a lot of hours into thinking about that moment of being back on the field and being with that team. There was a lot of physical therapy and things like that, so it was a really nice, warm feeling for me to be back on that field and get that ovation.

Luke Heimlich: (Getting Madrigal back) was a big deal. He was playing really well to start the year and he was still a key part of our team the whole time. Once again, it was the same thing with Drew. He got hurt, but he wasn't away from the team. He was with us every day, and he did everything he could to get back as quick as he could. Nobody questions Nick's ability. I think he missed a month and a half, two months. He didn't take any live at-bats the week before he came back and he was just like "I'll be ready to go this weekend." And then his (second) at-bat he hits an (RBI single) and it was like "all right, this kid's good."

Andy Armstrong: I look at it from a team standpoint. My role was now to be the backup to Nick again. Obviously, everyone on the team wants to play, wants to start, things like that. So yeah, I was champing at the bit to get back into some games but I was obviously excited to have Nick back because those were our best guys right up the middle. It felt good that he was back healthy to get going again. There were some mixed emotions there because I felt proud of myself for the job I did when the team needed me the most, and once he got back in there it was cool to see him get going again.

Jake Mulholland: Armstrong knew he was probably only going to play for those six weeks or so, but he took that role, he wore it and he did as good as anyone could've asked him to do. He helped us out and he contributed a ton and helped us win a bunch of games. And when Nick was ready to play again, Andy was always there whenever he was needed, whether it was to get a bunt down, be a defensive replacement. That's just always being ready when your name is called, even if you're not playing right now. I think that was one thing guys did really well — knowing that they're probably not going to play, but just in case, they're always ready. It didn't affect them. When they got to the field every day they still worked like they were the best player on the team, even if they didn't play at all. I think having a bunch of guys who are doing that kind of stuff is really huge for a team because it can't just be nine guys, it takes everyone. And in 2018, it took everyone.

By the time Madrigal returned, Trevor Larnach had established himself as one of the top all-around hitters in the country. Larnach batted just .157 during his injury-impacted freshman season, but bounced back nicely as a sophomore, hitting .303 with three home runs, 48 RBIs, a .421 on-base percentage and .429 slugging percentage. Always capable of belting long home runs, Larnach turned himself into a consistent power threat during the offseason. He homered in three of the Beavers' first seven games in 2018. The 6-foot-4, 210-pound slugger wound up with 19 home runs and 77 RBIs as a junior, while slashing .348/.463/.652 en route to All-America honors.

Trevor Larnach: I started working with (Tyler) Graham on the side my sophomore year and got deeper and deeper into it as the year went on. Got really deep into it with the mental game, mindset and work ethic in the cages, practice, everything. I'd say it all came together, and at that point it was more of me just being in the flow state more than anything else. Because I knew that I couldn't have done anything more to put myself in the best position to be successful and be prepared. And I think that's how I showed. I'm not trying to be cocky or anything, but that's how I felt. I always knew what I was capable of doing. My freshman year I knew what I could've done. My sophomore year I knew what I could've done better, and even my junior year I know what I could've done better. But there's always this voice in the back of my head knowing what I'm capable of doing if I miss an opportunity or miss a pitch, whatever it is. When it came to opening day of my junior year, I couldn't have been more prepared for that season.

Steven Kwan: It was crazy. I knew Trevor was going to have a really good year because T Graham, when he was working with me, it would always be me and Trevor together. So, Trevor was working just as hard if not harder than I was the whole time, and he was making huge adjustments to his swing, too. Leading up to it, he was hitting some balls far, really hard and really far. So, I was like "OK, he's going to have a really good year, I'm really excited." I remember he put one out to dead center, and center is deep in Surprise. I was like "holy cow, this is nuts," and he just kept doing it, it wasn't a fluke. Him and Nick went back-to-back (in the opener) and I looked at Gret and went "yo, we're going to be nasty this year."

Ryan Gorton: That kid hit in the cages every single night for at least an hour or two with Steven Kwan. He was just really smart with it. He'd always ask questions, really good questions, some I wouldn't even know the answer to. He was really a student of hitting, he took it really seriously and tried to get better in every aspect, whether it was his swing, his pitch selection or approach at the plate. He was always trying to get better, and that's what it's all about. You've got to put the time in. And obviously he's big and strong too, there's no denying that.

Joe Casey, outfielder: That guy probably spent more time in the cages than anyone that's been here. He got after it and that's what totally made him better. He was a great guy off the field too and a funny guy. He liked to mess with the guys and be a jokester about it. But that guy spent so much time hitting and working on his game, and it paid off.

Luke Heimlich: We all knew he had the power. We'd seen it in BP, we'd seen it since he showed up. But it was just getting him to be consistent in his swing and get the ball in the air a little bit more. There's no purpose hitting ground balls when you can hit the ball 500 feet. He made a couple adjustments and felt really good going into the season, and things started clicking.

Pat Casey: Trevor Larnach went from being a guy who was a part-time player as a freshman to one of the best offensive players in the country by the time he left. I'm not sure I've had any hitter evolve more from his freshman year than Trevor Larnach.

You could take (those opening games) down in Arizona and take a picture of every box score and say that this is his development. That would explain it all. He hit every ball on the screws, it was as impressive of a hitting display as I've ever seen. He absolutely was phenomenal, he hit everything that they threw. His demeanor, his makeup and his belief and everything about how he perceived himself and the game changed so much. The physical ability was always there. Even when he was a freshman and going through some times where he struggled, I said he would put up Michael Conforto numbers, I believed that. His transformation was phenomenal.

Pat Bailey: Trevor for me is the consummate professional. He's very organized, he's very self-disciplined, he's a relentless worker. He ended up being a great student. He wasn't a great student in high school, and he was a great student here. But his daily routines that he has for himself are going to take him a long way in professional baseball. I'd be shocked if he didn't make the majors with how much self-discipline he has, how hard he works and how much he improved while he was here.

Kyler McMahan: With guys like Trevor and Nick and Cadyn and Rutsch and all of them, all of those guys are just … you would think walking into a program and meeting someone like that, they are going to be above and beyond arrogant. Like they know what they need to do, they are going to get drafted and they are going to move on. But that wasn't who they are. They are all very personable people and even though they had their unbelievable seasons, nobody on the team had any idea how good they were doing until everything was over and we'd go back and look at it. It was just smooth and normal and they were used to it. They were so composed. They wouldn't show off, they wouldn't go out and tell people their stats. They just went out and played every day with their head down and never brought emotions into it. I think that's the best thing that I could've learned from my years with Rutsch and Trevor and Nick and Cadyn. Just watching how they work and how calm they are and how composed they are. They know what the goal is and they know how to get there and they're going to do everything they need to.

Adley Rutschman also took his offensive game to another level in 2018. While struggling at the plate as a freshman in the Pac-12 and Cape Cod League, Rutschman was making some mechanical adjustments to his swing. He didn't return to the football team that fall, and began to see positive results in the winter, setting him up for a sophomore breakthrough.

Typically batting fifth in the lineup between Larnach and Michael Gretler, Rutschman went on to earn All-America honors by hitting a team-best .408 among regulars with nine home runs and a school-record 83 RBIs. His on-base percentage (.505) and slugging percentage (.628) were equally impressive, but Rutschman became best known for his late-inning heroics, frequently coming through with game-tying or go-ahead hits. The nickname "Clutchman" was thrown around, and it stuck. Rutschman had two seventh-inning, go-ahead doubles against Hartford, and tagged Portland for another the following week. In early April, Rutschman produced back-to-back walk-offs in extra innings against Nevada. The first was a dropped fly ball in center that allowed Cadyn Grenier to score from third, and the second was a play for the ages. With two outs and nobody on in the bottom of the 10th, Rutschman hit a line drive just in front of Nevada center fielder Cole Krzmarzick. Instead of playing it on a hop, Krzmarzick went for the diving catch. The rest is history.

Preston Jones, outfielder: We're playing Nevada, and Rutsch had two walk-offs. I think their center fielder had a pretty rough couple of days. I remember that because I was just thinking "wow, what can't this man do? Now he's got a walk-off inside-the-parker."

Kyler McMahan: I swear half the team was already out of the dugout before he was even rounding second base because we knew that something special was going to happen. That inside-the-parker was absolutely the most insane thing that I've ever seen, especially having it happen at home and having all the fans go ballistic over it.

Adley Rutschman: The game before, too, the center fielder, he dropped the soft line drive that I hit. And obviously the next game, I was trying to hit a home run that AB to left field. I was hoping to get a fastball or something early in the count and be able to trot around the bases, but I think it got on me a little bit more than I expected and I ended up hitting a line drive to center. I just remember, because it was a line drive to center, it was still in my line of sight to where I could see what had happened, and to see him dive and miss the ball, I got excited. I was like "oh my gosh, all right." So, I was rounding second base and I saw they still didn't have the ball, and then I put my head down and looked at third base just to see if he was going to send me or not.

FINISH

Andy Jenkins, assistant coach: When you coach third base, there's always the one ball each year where the center fielder dives and the crowd, which we always have, gets real excited. As Adley was rounding second base, really you have to trust yourself and not what you hear. You make your decision based on your training and what you like to do out there and if it's a smart decision and not an emotional decision. An emotional decision would be listening to the crowd because everybody wants to see an in-the-park home run and the crowd is very close, the players were almost on the field. You just have to lock in and make a good decision, and I felt with where the ball was and where Adley was, it was the time to send him. A lot of good things had to happen for them to get him out.

Steven Kwan: I still remember his face rounding second into third, just his running form. Again, that was one of those feelings where we're like "oh of course that happened, we're nasty. This would happen, we believed this would happen." And to see it happen in that kind of situation, it was like "all right, this kid's nuts. This kid's insane."

Preston Jones: It was wild. I think that cemented who he really was, what kind of freak athlete he was and how great of a baseball player he was.

Andy Jenkins: Rutsch is a good athlete. When he's got to go right-to-left or run 90 feet, he's going to go pretty good. I think what works against him is catching all the time and being down there. And it will probably get gradually worse as his career goes on. But you can never forget what kind of athlete he was in high school and being able to play football. He's real good in the weight room and works hard, so when he gets an opportunity to take an extra base or score from first or an inside-the-park home run, he certainly was somebody that could do it.

Adley Rutschman: I remember I was very tired by the end of that. That was a long run for a catcher after innings of catching. Definitely a crazy series between those two games. If you tell that story to people, they're like "what? No way. I don't believe you." That's usually the reaction you get.

Ryan Gorton: Clutchman! The guy just delivered. He had an uncanny knack to stay calm in the big situations and his batting average in the seventh inning and later that year was ridiculous. Honestly, I don't know how he did it. It was incredible. The guy was absolutely incredible in the big moments to be able to center himself, not get too high or too low, and to stay locked in and focus on what he needed to do.

Adley Rutschman: None of my teammates would really say or call me (Clutchman), which I enjoyed that they didn't. I would've felt kind of weird if they said that, and if they did say it, it would be more jokingly than anything. It was one of those things that I didn't like to think about too much just for the weird thought of like maybe I would've lost whatever the weird magic was that year. I don't know, I feel like it was just one of those things where whenever a situation becomes tighter or you need to make something happen, I feel like my focus is always able to sharpen a little bit more during those times. I just put a little more focus into what I'm doing and I try to stay relaxed and let my instincts take over during that time, and I guess it worked that year.

Steven Kwan: I mean, gosh, we all knew how good of a player he could be. I played with him on the (Corvallis) Knights his incoming freshman year and just seeing him bloom, it wasn't a shock to any of us I would say. He was another one of those really hard workers. He was piecing it together, and I would even say he was on the back burner behind Trev and Nick leading up to that point. Like those guys were doing it flashy, but he was just being a really good hitter. I mean obviously he's just an unreal player.

Zak Taylor: I don't think people really take it under consideration just how hard it is to do two sports. And I know he was only kicking, but still. The amount of time that you're spending bouncing back between the two, it's just hard. Most college athletes specialize in their one sport, so I think that took a lot off his plate where he could really make some changes. And I would say he made some pretty good changes.

Adley Rutschman: The thing for me was I didn't even realize how much work I was putting in between both baseball and football. It was the only thing I knew coming into college, because everyone said "oh, there's a huge workload coming into college," so I was just expecting that going in. When I would go to eight o'clock football practice to noon, and then go to lunch and then one to five for baseball and basically my whole day was just football and baseball practice. Then we'd travel for football that Thursday or Friday. I didn't know anything else besides that, so I didn't know it was that much work. Once football season was over and I committed to just baseball for the rest of the year, I remember thinking back during the baseball season like "wow, that was a lot. That was probably way too much for me." And I didn't really make the strides I wanted to in baseball, or in football for that matter, just because I was splitting time between the two and I couldn't fully commit to either one. That was basically the reason why I quit football, because if I'm going to do something, I want to do it 100%. I don't want to be half in, half out on both of them. And baseball's my love, so it made the decision pretty easy for me.

There's a couple things (that contributed to offensive growth as a sophomore). Naturally, getting a year older, having a year of experience in the Pac-12 and a year of experiencing hitting college pitching, I think for most guys that's going to help no matter what. You add that component along with the mechanical adjustments of me basically slowing down my load to allow myself more time to see the ball. And be adjustable to different pitches, and then also messing with my barrel path to allow myself to be in the zone longer — dropping in deeper as some hitting coaches would say — and just being able to be on plane longer.

I've always had decent power, but it allowed for that to show a lot more. I gave myself more of an opportunity to hit for power because of my mechanical changes. It wasn't like I got a ridiculous amount stronger or anything, it was the mechanical adjustments and understanding how guys wanted to throw and being more a student of the game per se.

Pat Bailey: I think the coolest thing about Adley is not just the character, the work ethic, the self-discipline and all the other pieces, it's his humility. He's really humble. If you talk to him he always seems to deflect and talk about teammates and other things. He does not like talking about himself, and he's just a great young man. I'm so fortunate to have gotten to know him better by coaching him and being a part of his life.

Dylan Pearce: Rutsch was my roommate. I lived with him for two years along with Preston Jones, Mitchell Verburg and George Mendazona. When I first met (Rutschman), he was kind of a quiet guy, didn't really say much to me at all. He was still trying to get used to me, and I was with him. Then after about the first week I was there, I got to know him. He's a laid back, just a gooby, goofy guy. He has his own unique personality, so he was great to get along with. As soon as we started talking, we clicked and found a lot of common interests.

I think the reason why he is so good at what he does is because he stays so focused on one thing. I love the guy to death but I think he's the worst multitasker I've met in my life, and I think that's what makes him so good. Because when he's in the moment of something, he's in the moment and is so focused on what he does, whether it's catching, hitting, throwing a ball down to second, nothing is going to knock him out of the zone. The man, it's almost impossible for him to breathe and be on his phone at the same time.

Rutsch is just a good guy. He's always there for you, always there to talk. He wants the best for you at all times and is always trying to give a helping hand or opinion on what he sees.

Mitchell Verburg, pitcher: I love Rutsch. Me and Rutsch were roommates for three years. He's my best friend. I think he ruined every other catcher for me because I expect every catcher to be like Adley Rutschman: cannon arm and a brick wall, and that's just not realistic because he is an unreal player. It was a pleasure, an absolute honor throwing to him for my first three years, and maybe one of these days I'll get back to him. That's what I'm chasing.

Zak Taylor: I grew up around Adley and his family, and it's nice because I don't think a ton of guys get the chance to ... you grow up as athletes and you start to really develop skills and know that you can play beyond high school, we were both in that camp. And then to think that we both went to the same college and coming full circle now, he's the one guy I continue to work out with during the offseason. It's just nice to have the dynamic where this guy is one of my best friends that I'd do anything for, and we still get to enjoy the game we love and we still have that same passion. I cherish that, and I cherish all those moments we get to spend with each other.

Jake Mulholland: He's a great leader. He didn't care who you are, if you played every day or were never going to play here at all. He treated everyone like they were important and he wanted to get to know every single guy on the team because he believed it would make the team better if we were closer, and it obviously did. He cared so much about the person as well, it wasn't even about baseball all the time. He wanted to hang out with the guys outside of baseball, wanted to get dinner with you, whatever it was. He really embraced the family aspect of this team.

Jake Thompson, pitcher: He was a little bit quiet as a freshman and I hate that I didn't get to play with him beyond his freshman year. Seeing how he went from this quiet freshman, a guy who had all these skills, it was like "just give him a year to put it all together." And obviously he did more than that, he's just incredible. He's definitely one of those guys who came in very, very talented, and grew a lot from seeing how everyone went about their business and everything like that. I personally think that he came in at a perfect time, set our pitching staff where it needed to be and helped set the tone for 2018. Everyone did incredible that year and I watched a lot of those games and rooted them on.

Luke Heimlich: Most of my senior year, his arm was bothering him, or at least for a little bit. Some weekends he would only catch my game, and then he would play first or DH. I remember talking to him and being like "hey, if you need a week off ..." and he would go "no, I'll be fine." You could never tell if he was hurt, he always had the same attitude showing up. He was just a freak athlete, making ridiculous plays. I remember one specific one against (Stanford). They popped one up in foul territory by our dugout and I'm running over there to try and make a play, Adley's running over there. He catches it and hits his head on the cement corner of our dugout. Adley makes the play, kind of falls back into me because I'm right there. So, I catch him and look at him and am like "dude, are you all right?!" And he just looks at me and is like "yeah, what do you mean? Of course I'm fine." I was like "dude, you just hit your head on this cement corner," and he's like "oh no, I'm fine." So, I'm like "I guess this guy doesn't feel anything."

Adley Rutschman, to the Corvallis Gazette-Times after the game: I enjoy those plays, I really do. It's fun for me getting some action besides just catching and blocking.

Michael Gretler: I remember we were down at Arizona and before practice, Case got a scouting report from a team we'd played. He was going through it, not really calling guys out but he wanted guys to accept it as a challenge. Adley had obviously gotten off to a good start, but it was funny because he got to Adley and it said "switch-hitter, not a threat." It literally said not a threat, which is pretty funny now. I remember Larnach would flip Adley so much crap about that, saying "yeah, you're not a threat, blah, blah, blah." I'm sure that report was off his freshman year or whatever and at that point I don't think he was hitting .400 or anything, but looking back at that it's even funnier because of how he finished the year. It's weird, because there wasn't a time where it really clicked like "oh my god, Adley is doing incredible." He was just so consistent. He hit from both sides of the plate, he would drive in runs, he hit with power, he'd get on base, he'd have good at-bats. I don't think anyone realized how good of a year he was having until the World Series. And then everyone looked at his whole year and it's like "oh my goodness, that guy's had an unbelievable season." At least for me, maybe other guys followed the stats more than me.

Ryan Gorton: I always wondered, was that really in the scouting report or was Case just saying that to motivate you? Because they did the same thing when I was playing, and I'm pretty sure it was just to motivate me. I don't think my scouting report actually said some of those things, but maybe it did. Who knows?

Adley Rutschman: At that time, I think I was hitting like .350 or something. I was hitting very well at that time, so when I heard that I was taken aback a bit. I was like "really, that's the scouting report?" I was a little bit upset when I heard that. I don't know if the coaches planted that there, or if that was actually the real scouting report that they acquired, but either way it worked.

Kyle Nobach: Case was holding this piece of paper that was basically a scouting report, except it wasn't a real scouting report. He was making it all up! Each guy, he was just saying stuff almost in the way to piss you off a little bit. He was doing it to get under your skin and get you going a little bit. I remember in particular him talking about Zak Taylor and it saying he had the longest swing in the country. Case was just making up some of the most absurd things. He was a maniac about some of this stuff but I'll tell you what, it worked. He had everyone buy into the fact that we were all together, and if anybody was doubting anything we believed in, it was not OK.

Pat Casey: Well, I can't tell you everything. If I told you everything … nah, I'm just teasing! I would tell you that if you have an opportunity to maybe let's say elaborate on a scouting report and add to it something that may inspire somebody … if you take the body of it and twist it just a hair, it might sound a little better. If I thought I could maybe get under somebody's skin just a little bit to maybe ignite the fire, there's a possibility I might've done that.

Ranked No. 2 in D1Baseball's preseason top 25 behind reigning national champion Florida, Oregon State won its first 13 games of 2018 entering a marquee non-conference home series with Cal State Fullerton. The Titans were off to a rough 3-8 start but had plenty of talent back from the previous year's College World Series team. With ace Colton Eastman on the mound, Fullerton took advantage of three OSU errors to earn a 5-3 Game 1 victory. Pat Casey was ejected in the seventh inning for arguing a check-swing call with third base umpire Mark Buchanan. During the heated exchange Casey got a little too close to Buchanan and briefly made contact with the umpire, triggering an automatic four-game suspension.

Pat Casey: I was a little frustrated with some of the calls and the way the game was going when I ran out there and argued with him. In the report it said the bill of my cap touched the bridge of his nose, so they suspended me for four games.

It really has nothing to do with anybody individually when you go out there and argue with an umpire. I just thought that, in my opinion, I think there was a drag call that was missed and a check-swing I felt differently about. I think there was a fair or foul ball that happened, it was a while ago. But you're in the heat of the battle and my energy level and my excitement level took me out onto the field.

Dylan Pearce: The umpires really were not on our side, and it was going back and forth. We could tell it was getting on them, and they were nagging us over everything constantly, over and over. There were some routine things that were causing that game to get blown, and I was just like "what is happening?" Case went out to go and back up our guys. The umpire turned around and Case … you're not allowed to touch him in any way, but the umpire completely and totally overreacted and was very immature in that way, I believe.

Jack Anderson: I've seen Case get even more fired up than he did with that, but the contact was the thing that got him. Because he's been close to saying that he's ready to fight someone, let alone argue with someone. It definitely wasn't the fieriest I've seen him, but his brim just got a little too close to Mr. Umpire, I guess.

Pat Bailey: I never saw the bill of Case's hat hit the guy on the nose. And the other thing is, if it just touched him, so what? I thought it was ridiculous that he got suspended for four games, but the rules are the rules.

Jake Rodriguez: I remember Case coming into the office talking about "I didn't bump him, I didn't bump him!" Everything's on tape now, so we had the tape and it showed the brim of his hat almost coming undone because he went into the guy so hard initially.

Bill Rowe: I freeze-framed the video of him when his hat is touching that guy's (nose). I always get up in someone's face and say, "you realize how close you have to be to have the bill of your hat touch someone on the face?" Like that's crazy close! And to have somebody like Case come up to you like that, I can't believe that that umpire didn't need to change his underwear after that.

I've now been around him and around people he's played with long enough to know that's the kind of player he was, too. Hearing some of the stories from him back in the minor leagues from some of those guys, it's just one intense individual. I think in 2006 we saw a little bit more of that and as the years went on it mellowed out, but it still comes out. He definitely has a fiery passion within him that's never going away, that's for sure.

Ryan Gorton: When Case got ejected, one of the guys who works for the school who used to be the baseball liaison, Roger Ely, he made Case a hat where he cut the front of the bill off of it. He gave it to him as his umpire arguing hat, so he wouldn't get tossed again.

Pat Casey: It's not something where I go out there thinking I'm going to get close enough to the guy where the bill of my cap is going to touch the bridge of his nose.

That was just an odd deal. When you're suspended for making contact, it makes it sound like you wrestled with somebody when in the report it said the bill of my cap touched the bridge of his nose. That's really hard for me to imagine being a coach that had been doing it for a long, long time, that that would be the answer. But when you have things that they say like, "well, we can't do anything about contact. It's in the rulebook," it makes you feel like they have to have some type of imagination or better judgment to use common sense. Because in his own words, the bill of my cap touched the bridge of his nose. Four-game suspension, that's pretty rough. But you know man, it was what it was and we just moved forward.

Casey could not recall a previous suspension during his coaching career. He was prohibited from attending the final two games against Fullerton and the first two games of Oregon State's Pac-12 opening series at California. Pat Bailey acted as head coach until Casey was eligible to return.

Pat Casey: I don't think I felt good about it. I don't think I had been thrown out of a lot of games over the last 10 years, I typically don't go out to the field unless there's something I feel is really important. I think that's just maturing a little bit and being around the game a little bit. I probably was disappointed that I wasn't in uniform. I certainly didn't hold anything against Buchanan. I don't think of those things from a personal standpoint, but you never want to not be around your team.

Ryan Gorton: Looking back, it's a funny thing to think about now, Case making contact with the umpire. How do I say this? … we weren't shocked by it. But nobody was nervous that we didn't have Case there or anything. Everybody knows how to play good baseball. And it was more or less business as usual. I mean for sure we didn't feel the presence of Case in the dugout, but it was a pretty veteran team so it didn't affect the players too much, luckily.

Jack Anderson: That was so funny, it was kind of like putting a puppy in the corner. Case loves the game so much, and taking away being a coach and being there for the players and him just watching from afar, I think that was the worst thing you could possibly do to that guy in that moment.

Nate Yeskie: With Case being suspended for a while, we had to captain the ship with regards to how we were going to do things during games. We talked to Case before games and we talked to him after, but in-game there was nothing he could do.

Dylan Pearce: It was definitely weird. Case just has an aura to him and a presence to him that circulates around everybody. You know he's there, you know he's watching and I think that's why so many of our guys would step up as high as they did, because they knew they were playing for, in my opinion, one of the best coaches in college baseball ever. Just being able to be around him makes you step up, and having him there it was like "man, we've got to do everything right." But we still knew when he wasn't there, all of our guys were so driven and so professional in everything we did that it didn't matter whether he was there or not — we were going to do what he taught us to do. We knew that he wasn't there in the dugout, but he was certainly at home watching the games.

Pat Casey: I just walked all over campus and would click my phone and see who was ahead. Hell, I'd get close enough to the stadium where I could hear it, but I couldn't be anywhere where they could see me at the stadium, I couldn't be on the premises. I could come back and watch a little bit of it on TV, so I made it work.

Oregon State came back to win the final two games against Fullerton and headed to Berkeley, California, a few days later. Casey stayed at the team hotel for the first two games of the Pac-12-opening series.

Jake Rodriguez: Friday night, we're getting ready to leave and we're having a pregame coaches' meeting; Case isn't in uniform yet. And then we go to leave for the bus and Case is down there in full uniform saying goodbye to everybody and wishing us luck. We come back and he was waiting for us in the lobby to congratulate us on the 4-3 win, and he's still in uniform. We just could not believe it, it was hilarious. And it was the same thing the next day.

Michael Gretler: I remember going to Cal and he was suspended the first two games. We get on the bus to go to the games, and here Case is dressed in his full uniform, giving us high-fives to get on the bus. And sure enough, when we get off the bus back at the hotel, the guy is still in his full uniform and you're like "what the hell?!"

Pat Casey: The guys uni up, I'm going to uni up, man!

Ryan Gorton: It just shows you his level of commitment and how much he cares. Because I'm sure some coaches would've been like "ah, I can't coach today" and would've gone to the bar and had a good time or something, whereas he was still living and breathing every breath with us.

Pat Casey: It was funny, I had a guy that was one of my best buddies in minor league baseball who was from Cal. A guy named Jeff Ronk, and he came back and got honored. He was on the club that went to the World Series in the '80s. He stuck his head in the dugout and said, "hey man, where's Case?" And someone said, "oh man, he got suspended." And he goes "ah man, nothing's changed," and he laughed. So, of course Bails and the coaching staff had a good time with that one.

Kyle Nobach: I had a knee scope right when we got home from Surprise, so I was out for two weeks. We had the home series against Cal State Fullerton and the next week we went to Cal. And I didn't travel with the team because I'd just had surgery. So, I was in the clubhouse watching the game on TV when Case got hosed against Fullerton, then they went down to Cal and I was at home hanging out. Brad Brown, who was our video guy, he set up this stream using Zoom. He set it up for coach Casey to watch the game at Cal in the hotel room because it would've been an NCAA violation for him to be there while he was suspended and the games weren't on TV. I believe there was no way for anybody in the country to watch those games except for Brad's programming. So, I was watching this game back home along with coach Casey, and he was in full uni! He had met the team prior to them getting on the bus, and we watched like the first three innings together. Brad texted me and was like "hey, Case has no idea that you're on this conference call." I had to mute my audio because I could talk to him through the conference, so Brad was just like "don't press any buttons, don't press anything." I couldn't hear Case, but I could see him.

Jack Anderson: I mean Case, technology. He had no idea what was going on.

Pat Casey: I don't recall watching, but they had it set up so I could hear it live. I don't know if they had it set up where I could watch it. The Fullerton series, I know that that deal obviously I could see it, and there was no way I could sit and watch it.

Michael Gretler: I heard this story where it was the first inning of that (Saturday) game, we had the bases loaded with two down. I grounded out and we didn't score any runs, and I guess Case back at the hotel was just like "I can't watch!" Who knows what he did after, probably went on a walk in his uniform or whatever.

Kyle Nobach: Andrew Vaughn then hit a homer against us early in the game and Case's screen went black, I didn't see him the rest of the game. And what happened was Case got so pissed off when Vaughn hit that home run that he pressed the power button, and he pressed it so hard that it actually broke the screen on the tablet.

Pat Casey: I don't know who set it up, but I was able to get Parker on the radio. That lasted about an inning and I seriously was so very ... it was just so odd and so different and so trying that I walked all over the hotel. Up, down, outside, inside, outside and then I would go on that game tracker on my phone and see what the score was, and I'd get off it really fast.

Jack Anderson: It took him less than like 20 minutes to not even be able to watch the game because he was so competitive and couldn't stand not being there. He couldn't bear having no control over what was going on out there.

Michael Gretler: It just shows how much passion he has; he cares so much about us. He can't be there, but he's in his full uniform and wants to be part of the battle. As funny as it is, it definitely shows the type of person he is as well.

Cadyn Grenier: Case was only there to coach; he was only there for baseball and to help us develop as people and baseball players. When the competitive side of him gets taken away and he can't be on the field, especially for something as stupid as the thing he got suspended for … for him it's like "my whole entire life's passion of baseball is being taken from me right now when I've got this group of guys, and all I want to do is see them succeed." I know for a fact that killed Case.

Pat Casey: That was tough, the Cal deal was tough, because you can't go anywhere. I didn't care for that a bit. It was odd to me and I didn't think it would be that way. I thought "oh, I'll sit down and watch the game and I'll really be able to evaluate the players and learn from it." Nope, couldn't do that.

Pat Bailey: At the end of that last game, I took the lineup card, I wrote 4-0 on it, signed my signature and handed it to Pat and I said, "I'm the only coach in the history of Oregon State University that's undefeated. Do not get suspended again."

Jack Anderson: At that point we were all old enough and kind of our own coaches, so we didn't have to be coached too much during the game. But it was funny … Bails went (4-0) when Case was gone so we were like "all right, he's got it. He's undefeated, Case! I don't know, maybe you should hang out a little longer back at home?" We were messing with him and stuff.

Nate Yeskie: We played well those first two games at Cal. When Case came back on Sunday I was joking with him on the bus ride to the park, I said, "if we lose, you might have to go back into suspension."

Pat Casey: Tells you how much they needed me!

Pat Bailey: I just think Pat is such a competitive person that he probably had a hard time watching the game the whole time. And those games were all really close, so that was probably really hard for him. I've never been around a person that's more competitive than Pat Casey. And I thought I was a really competitive person. But I can be honest with you, he's more competitive than I am.

I'll tell you a funny story. He said to me one time that the difference between Mitch Canham and Darwin Barney is Mitch Canham in a war would cut a guy's throat and go on to the next guy. Darwin Barney would be right behind him in the war, would cut a guy's throat and he'd hold his hand while he died before going on to the next guy. That's the difference between Case and me. And I hate losing more than anything, but I'd hold that guy's hand probably. That's just our personalities.

Pat Casey: The house I grew up in, my father was extremely competitive. My brothers were extremely competitive. I am a very, very competitive person by nature — very, very competitive in just about everything I do. I just feel that you're doing an injustice if you coach a sport in which they determine a winner and they determine a loser and they keep score, and you aren't willing to compete to be the team that wins that contest. I just think that's an injustice for anybody to say, "hey, I do a good job, we're real positive all the time and we have a good time." I think maybe that's what you do at a very, very low level when they don't keep score, maybe you do that in a sport I'm not aware of. But in this sport, at this time, and the uniform I'm in with them, we put it on together for one reason, and at that particular time it's to win that game. Now that isn't the only thing that matters, but on game day when we're playing a game, the only thing that matters about that game is that there's a winner and there's a loser. And if we're going to play it, we're going to play it to win.

Some people show up to play the game, other people show up to win the game. I always expected our guys to show up to win. You win the pitch, you win the at-bat, you win the inning, you win the game, you win the series, you win the league, you win the natty. In my opinion, there's absolutely nothing wrong with being that competitive … and this has nothing to do with not being relaxed, either. Some of the greatest competitors in the world do it free and easy. But that deal inside, that burning fire inside to win has to be paramount in order for you to have sustained success, and I don't care what it is.

Anyway, I was unable to ever put the uniform on and go out and say, "hey you know what, I'm just going to go out and have a good time." It wasn't that way with me. I don't need someone to tell me "hey, you've got great kids" and "hey, you guys really took care of the hotel" and "hey, you were very courteous on the plane," but you lost all three games. I think you can be very courteous on the plane and take care of the hotel and be very nice and kick somebody's ass. That's why we play, that's why we practice and it would probably be something that wouldn't be very truthful to make them work as hard as you make them work and tell them that winning and losing doesn't matter.

Oregon State swept California and then took two of three from Washington for its 14th straight Pac-12 series victory. Prior to the Washington loss, the Beavers had won 80 of their last 87 games (.920 winning percentage) overall dating back to 2016.

The defending Pac-12 champions were long overdue for a rough weekend entering a road matchup with Utah, and the trip to Salt Lake City turned into a series from hell. The Utes, who went on to finish last in the Pac-12, scored 24 runs over three games, defeating OSU twice. The pain didn't stop there. The following week at Arizona, the Beavers led 5-2 late in the series' rubber match, but were unable to hold on. OSU was suddenly 4-5 overall in its last nine games after losing just six times the previous season.

Luke Heimlich: Utah was the best team in the world when we went to face them. Some of us still joke around that Utah was the best team we faced all year, like they were just incredible when we went to play them.

Brandon Eisert: It was hard to tell what exactly was wrong. Utah certainly wasn't my best outings and we had to get back to making pitches — I don't think we were doing a good job of that. We were leaving pitches over the middle and not making the quality pitches that we knew we could. I think it helped us reset a little bit and showed us that things weren't going to come super easy. We weren't going to win every single game like we did the year before and cruise.

Nick Madrigal: I think there were some tough breaks for us. We didn't get the big hit in the big situation like we did the year before and, I don't know, things just didn't go our way. We had all the talent, so that wasn't the issue. But baseball is one of those games where sometimes things don't go your way, and I really think that's all it was. I don't think there was any worry or anything like that from the guys on the team. But yeah, there were some games where we could've done some things differently. That's mainly what I remember, we didn't do the little things at times during the games we lost.

Nate Yeskie: Utah, that was just a funky, weird deal. We hit into so many double plays that weekend as a whole (nine). It seemed like we couldn't do anything right.

Pat Bailey: Utah was a nightmare, honestly it was. We so underachieved that week, it was so frustrating to see us play the way we did. And it was an anomaly. We knew that, the players knew that, and that's just baseball. I've been coaching for a long time, and I can't remember — other than 2017 — not having one weekend like that. It was crazy to go the entire year and not have a bad weekend, and it's the only time in my coaching career where we didn't have a weekend like that. I remember coaching at George Fox the year we won a national championship and we had a bad weekend. So, you're going to have weekends like that, and I think how you respond to it is a lot more important than what happened, and I thought we did a great job of responding to it.

Bill Rowe: Because you're playing Division I teams, all it takes is for one team to really put it together for a weekend and for you to not be quite on your game. When you're Oregon State, every team treats that weekend as their biggest weekend. And we'd talk about this amongst the team, that you're going to get everybody's best and they're coming out, trying to beat you harder than anybody.

I can remember when I played for UC Santa Barbara (before transferring to OSU) and we went to Long Beach State when they were a top-five team and we swept them at home. It wasn't because they played poorly, it was because magic happened. I wouldn't say we played our best games at Utah, but they looked like the best team in the country that weekend. Sitting at that field and watching them play against us and how strong they were, you learn from that and you realize you need to be able to bring your A-Game even when you're playing a team you don't really expect to be a premier program, because they're coming for you super hard. You can't let off the gas at all because there's a chance you're going to get them at their very best. That's what Long Beach State got from us at Santa Barbara and that's what we got from Utah when we went there.

Nate Yeskie: When teams were playing the '90s Bulls, the (Bulls) knew whoever was coming to the arena that night was going to give them their best effort. I think that's where we were at, because we'd won so many the year before. The real types of competitors want to measure themselves against real competitors, so teams would come into our place and we'd go into theirs, and there were teams that really wanted a piece of us and were going to give us everything we could handle.

Pat Bailey: I thought that weekend was a defining moment for us. It could've destroyed us because we played really bad there. I mean it was bad, bad baseball. We took that as a learning lesson and we just said, "that isn't who we are and what we're about." I've got to give coach Casey and our entire staff and our players a lot of credit for that.

FINISH

Andy Jenkins: I think you're glad that happened. It was almost a little too good to be true in 2017 when you look at it. I mean to be (54-4) and you're rolling into the World Series and there's a lot of hype, I think a betting person would tell you we were not going to win in that year just because of the dominance that we had all year. I think those hiccups were good — facing a team that wanted it more, wasn't as good as us but found a way to get two of three. Utah was definitely a humbling time, and I think those were good growth experiences for our team in 2018, and our staff.

Pat Casey: We didn't have Nick, that part of it wasn't good. We were probably number one or number two in the country at the time, so everybody wants to beat you. Everybody is throwing out their best effort. It wasn't like we were playing somebody that wasn't energized. I remember Abel struggling down in Arizona when we had the lead. I remember Mulholland coming in and struggling a little bit. So, it was frustrating.

The Utah result raised eyebrows because the Utes sat at 4-19 overall entering the series. Offense-oriented Arizona was a different story. The Wildcats were typically dangerous at home and possessed another formidable lineup. Bryce Fehmel stymied Arizona in Game 1, a 6-2 Beavers victory. Heimlich and the bullpen got hit around in the second game, but the Beavers were poised to win the finale with Abel on the hill in relief protecting a three-run lead. Abel worked a 1-2-3 sixth and struck out the side in the seventh, staring down a lively Arizona dugout after the final out. Abel went back out for the eighth and loaded the bases with two walks and a hit-by-pitch. All three runners wound up scoring, and Arizona walked it off against Jake Mulholland in the ninth.

Kevin Abel: I had been pitching well. They got real chatty and said some things that I thought were against the rules to do. So, after I got out of a big inning I didn't say anything, just shot them a look to show I'm not here to mess around and I'm not going to get bullied around. I didn't say anything and I just walked off.

Andy Jenkins: Kevin Abel was on the mound. An addition to an already great team, a freshman kid that was coming in, highly-touted. He really liked to strike guys out and stare in their dugout, he had been doing it all fall. And as a coach, you like the competitiveness, you like the confidence. But he did it in a way at Arizona that was not the time to do it. He looked in their dugout and kind of flexed on them, and he woke up a good team. Then he came out the next inning and was wild and erratic, and we ended up falling apart. I remember going into the locker room at Hi Corbett (Field) and seeing guys take their wrist tape off saying, "how did this happen?"

I know a lot of the guys were pissed off and not happy with Kevin at the time, and I didn't know if Kevin was going to be able to recover on this team from that because of how many guys that we had that were great players who really wanted it. Michael Gretler and Nobach really shouted at him, and there were some words said, some uncomfortable feelings, and we all got on the bus and went home. What I'll tell you is from that moment, Kevin Abel grew up. He started thinking about what he was doing, he started controlling his emotions, how he pitched, his body language.

Michael Gretler: I remember me and Adley and Nick and Kyle, all those guys kind of being "hey, you don't need to do that." We were up (5-2) ... and that's not how we play baseball here. That's not the Oregon State baseball way, and I think that was a turning point for him which obviously paid dividends down the road. It was just a learning point. Here's a young freshman who probably wanted to be in the starting rotation, didn't get a lot of opportunities, and I think that was a clicking point for him.

Jack Anderson: When he had that blowup in Arizona, all of us were like "get this kid away from the mound." He was an unreal talent, but he just didn't have it. For him, it was a strikeout or walk kind of thing. His stuff was filthy, but he was getting in his own way there for a little bit.

I think that's why he didn't pitch for two or three weekends in a row after Arizona. It was like "let's cool him down and put him in his place a little bit, let him know that he can't do what he was doing out there, walking guys and taunting players and stuff." I think that was a good wake-up call for him.

Kyle Nobach: I came up to him in the airport and I was pretty fired up at him, everybody was. And he knew it and he figured it out. It wasn't that we didn't like Abel as a person, we were just fired up about the fact that "hey man, we're a team here. We're not going to do things intentionally that are going to hurt our team." And Arizona was dead man, they were dead. The momentum of that game shifted. That was not the right thing to do in that moment. We probably would've beat Arizona and took that game, and they came back and were fired up.

Trevor Larnach: Kevin was young. He was a freshman that year and there was a lot of pressure on him being a huge pitching prospect, and I'm sure he was putting a lot of pressure on himself. But that wasn't the sole reason we lost at U of A or Utah, it was a team effort and a team thing.

Kevin Abel: When you're out there it's man on man, you've got to stand up for yourself. You have to be the bully. (Yeskie) was all about it, but our conversation about that was after you do that and stand up for yourself, you've got to direct your energy into our guys and getting our guys fired up again because all I really did was get them fired up. I didn't bring any negative energy to our team, but I didn't build up any more energy to match them. That was what we mostly talked about, but he had no problem with it. It's FU when you get between the lines, there's nothing civil about it. … The media and other people made it a lot bigger deal than I thought it was.

Nate Yeskie: I think he's often overly criticized for it because … he didn't say anything, he just shot them a look. They were kind of defeated at that point, and when he shot them a look they got going. Actually, one of their guys (relief pitcher Robby Medel) got thrown out that game. I saw Cadyn Grenier grow quite a bit in that moment because he had stopped and really tuned everybody and everything out. I remember him squatting down next to Abel just saying "hey, not right now. That's not the time."

A couple guys were really heated and there was some volume and intensity from some guys, and here's Cadyn really trying to help him out. Cadyn, I've always said he's one of those guys where you can't judge a book by its cover because it's a great book. When you get to know that guy, he'd do anything for his teammates. I watched him grow and learn and try to help Kevin through those moments, and that's what Kevin needed. And Cadyn probably saw what he himself needed when he was a freshman and just thought "here's a chance to do what maybe somebody could've done for me at some point." And they all go through it. Sometimes you have what we call expensive experience, and you don't want that when it costs us something. You want inexpensive experience, where it happens to somebody else and you learn from it and go "well, OK. I'm going to make sure that doesn't happen to me." But for Kevin, it was one of those moments where he was revisiting what he did earlier in the season, which was really Jekyll and Hyde, and he was starting to come out of it. That was maybe a defining moment for him for sure.

Ryan Gorton: We ended up losing that game, but it was a huge learning moment for Kevin. Between the undergrad (assistants), we'd said all along that he was going to be the key to our season. Because Luke was really consistent, Fehmel was really consistent, our bullpen was OK and we needed that third starter. We knew Kevin had the stuff, but at the beginning of the year he probably wasn't ready for the big moments. I think that game was really a turning point for him. He learned to control his emotions better and just be more in control of himself and not let the game take over.

The wounded Beavers returned home from Arizona at 24-6 overall. They were 7-5 in Pac-12 play, trailing UCLA, Stanford and Washington in the conference standings. Oregon State had tumbled from first to ninth in the D1Baseball top 25 with another difficult road series coming up at No. 19 Missouri State.

Trevor Larnach: Every time we'd lose, if it was an away series we'd be in the airport and all of us felt like we were coming home from a funeral. That's just how Casey would look at losing. He didn't like that, none of us did.

Zach Clayton: That week of practice after those two tough series, we came back and had a heart-to-heart as a team. It looked like we were starting to fall apart a little bit, but after that it seemed like we got even closer as a team. We realized what we were fighting for, and that's when everything turned around.

Jack Anderson: We were really good and then we went on that slide against Utah and Arizona, and it was kind of like "what is going on right now? We are way better than this," that kind of feeling. We weren't used to it because we were used to winning so many games. We weren't used to the game of baseball doing what it does and going on those little losing streaks. I think that was the best thing that happened to us, honestly, losing those games and feeling what it felt like to lose a couple games in a row, have Kevin struggle, have our hitters struggle at certain times individually. We weren't the same machine we were the year before. And thank goodness we weren't, because it made us look in the mirror a little bit and figure out what we needed to do to take it to the next level, the level we didn't even make it to in 2017.

Luke Heimlich: I think one of the biggest things for us was we knew we were good; we'd had success the year before. We knew we could come back when we were down, so anytime we did fall behind … there were no nerves. The coaches would start trying to pump us up, but it was always just like "we've got this." We were all older, there was a good group of seniors and then all the juniors, the first-round picks and draft picks that year, we were all very mature on that team. So, if things didn't go our way, there was never a doubt that we would come back. We weren't freaking out, we weren't turning on each other, it was a very calm and trusting team.

Jake Mulholland: That is when we knew how good of a team we were. And I think for a little bit there we just showed up expecting to win, which is never good. It was like maybe a three-week thing where we didn't play at our best because we expected to win, and after that Arizona series I think it all finally clicked for us. We had to bring it back and take every game one step at a time, and I think we carried that on right after that series all the way through Omaha.

Bill Rowe: The biggest thing that stood out to me about that team was there were so many good players that if one didn't really have a good game, there were enough other people to pick them up. I'd say Luke Heimlich was a really good example of that because there were many times he didn't have all of his pitches. I'm not even sure there was a single game during that regular season where he did put it all together. Yet he still was dominant enough to work with what he had and the rest of the team could pick him up with good run support. And if he didn't get it, he would find a way to use the one pitch that he had that day and make it really effective. It's one thing to have a lot of talent. It's another thing to find a way to win with what you have, and that's what makes a championship program.

Nate Yeskie: It was a good wakeup call for our guys to go "all right, here's some adversity." And we learned how to deal with it accordingly, and that's when we went to Missouri State and started playing really well.

Jake Rodriguez: We went to Missouri State and battled some crazy weather, and we had a hit-a-thon. I don't think we missed a barrel the entire time we were there. I think the first day we were there it was about 100 degrees with 100% humidity and the last day we got snowed out. So, it was quite the midseason trip to the Midwest, but the bats were hot and we had a great trip.

Luke Heimlich: I think the Missouri State series was the turning point for our team. It was terrible scheduling. We flew there for a non-conference series in the middle of the year, we only got two games in. It was just not ideal at all. Long travel, terrible weather. I started the Friday morning game; it was humid and like 75 degrees and I was wearing short sleeves. That night our game got canceled because the NCAA has a rule that you can't play below 32 degrees, so our game got delayed that night because it was so cold, and that morning I was pitching in short sleeves. But we just played really well. We had (eight) home runs in the two games, we got an extra day off since we only played two games. I think going back there, it all started to click and we were feeling better about ourselves.

The wild Midwest conditions reinvigorated Oregon State's bats. The Beavers scored 27 total runs in the weather-shortened two-game series, winning by scores of 17-6 and 10-2. Larnach and Tyler Malone both homered twice, while Armstrong, Grenier, Gretler and Rutschman went yard once apiece. The eight home runs came in the first 11 innings of the series.

The Missouri State road trip was also the turning point for Heimlich, who was 7-1 with a 3.31 ERA entering the series. The numbers were solid, but Heimlich had not dominated opposing batters as consistently as he did the year prior. It was certainly understandable. The Oregonian report had thrust Heimlich into the national spotlight, and he also had the pressure of living up to his unrepeatable 2017 numbers. Heimlich regrouped from a rough outing against Arizona to strike out 10 at Missouri State, beginning a streak of seven consecutive outings with double-digit strikeouts. The old Heimlich was back.

Luke Heimlich: At Missouri State, I pitched all right. I went six innings, gave up (three) runs, had 10 strikeouts and somehow I got Pac-12 pitcher of the week. I don't know how, it was ridiculous. But I remember Case said something at practice. Like, he never acknowledged any of that stuff and it's just one game, it's not a big deal at all, but he said something like "nice job, congrats." Because I think he knew I still had some nerves and was trying to get my feet back under me that season. So, I made a sarcastic remark back like "yeah, I don't know how I got this one." And Case was just like "well, maybe because you're the best pitcher in the country, so they thought you deserved it." And I was kind of like "oh yeah, you might be right." So that game, obviously the 10 strikeouts help you feel good about your pitches again. That started my run of however many weeks in a row of double-digit strikeouts.

Nate Yeskie: I had a guy from the Pac-12 Network tell me that in all his years in baseball — and this guy played in the big leagues — he said "I don't think I've seen anybody better than that." And it all started in '18 at Missouri State. He scuffled a little bit here and there, and we made an adjustment. He had been throwing two side sessions between his starts — typically most kids will throw one. And he hadn't been very good. I just thought "maybe we should try something different here." It was his idea in '18 to do it, and I said "hey, why don't you get back to just doing one a week? We let you do it your way," and I typically allow kids to have a big say in their development because they've got good ideas. You want to empower those guys; you need them to give you feedback. But we had gotten to a point where I think we'd exhausted it and it just wasn't working so I said "let's get back to throwing one a week." If you go back and look at the box score, he threw (six innings) and struck out (10). He threw better than the line score indicated, and then it was just bang, bang, bang, bang, bang.

Luke Heimlich: I switched back to my old routine a couple weeks prior to (Missouri State). It was just one of those things where I would throw Friday, Sunday I would take off, and then Monday the team has off. But I'd go in, throw a bullpen and lift. Monday to Friday is still five days, that should be a normal starter's rotation, so for my senior year I just wanted to get on the mound one more time during the week and throw at like 70%. So, on Wednesday I would get up on the mound and throw some pitches light. For me, I probably shouldn't throw pitches at 70% because I'm not doing that in a game, so there's no point to get a feel for my changeup at 70% because it doesn't replicate a game scenario. I also don't like flat grounds because there's no point throwing on flat ground when I don't pitch on flat ground. So, after that, I was getting up there in innings and Yeskie was just like "hey, let's cut back on the throwing a little bit. There's no need to get on the mound a second time between starts." And I was like "all right."

Pat Casey: He always had great stuff. I know the Utah game he was out there and they had his pitches and he was frustrated with his performance. I think he was putting a lot of pressure on himself, thinking that he had to match the numbers that he put up the year before, which you could never do. Never could you put up the numbers he put up again, so I think he was chasing that expectation level. It hurt him for a while, and finally he had to get back to saying "hey man, I've got to be who I am."

Brandon Eisert: He was always the same. He was always going to compete and I think he just got back to what he had been doing in the past. Yeskie always told us to get back to the basics, look back at what you've done and what's made you successful. That's probably something he did both with Yeskie and on his own. Just look back at what had made him successful and not trying to do too much, not trying to recreate what he did the year before, and move forward from there. I think there may have been a mental roadblock just trying to live up to the past year, and he realized he didn't need to have that same exact stat line. I think that definitely helped him.

Dylan Pearce: There are guys where something just changes, and that happened to me in the earlier part of the season. With him, I don't quite know what changed, all I know is that it did. I know he never gave up or let himself be down. He'd work as hard as he could whether he had just thrown the worst game of his life or the best game of his life. If he had just thrown a four-hit shutout for eight innings with 12 strikeouts, he would come back in early in the morning and get his breakfast, get his treatment and run. And if he had done horrible and gotten pulled after the fourth or fifth inning, he would still be right back in there with his breakfast, his lifting, his training. He did 100% on the field and off the field.

In 21 appearances as a senior, Heimlich went 16-3 with a 2.92 ERA, while striking out a single-season school-record 159 batters in 129 2/3 innings. He was again voted Pac-12 pitcher of the year. He was a first-team All-American, and was the College Baseball Foundation's national pitcher of the year. Heimlich finished his college career as Oregon State's all-time leader in strikeouts (385) and tied for first in wins (36, with Ben Wetzler).

Andy Jenkins: Every time Luke went out on a Friday night, he was certainly going to give you a chance to win, and there was also a chance you would just need to score one or two runs. And when he's not on, he still has the ability to wiggle out of jams and pitch to contact. He's one of the best pitchers I've seen, certainly at Oregon State. And by the end of the year, the numbers didn't lie. He was a horse for us.

Steven Kwan: I remember him coming back for our 2017 fall and winter, we were doing some scrimmages and he came back with this slider. I knew after that, it was done. This guy was going to be unhittable. Watching all those balls from center field move, watching him live on the black corner on the outside, man that guy was just special for sure.

Dylan Pearce: It was insane watching how good Luke was with basically two pitches. He didn't really have a changeup when I was there, it was mostly just a fastball and a slurve. He just knew where to throw it, when to throw it and how much to take off and how much to put on. The man absolutely destroyed people. He filled up the zone phenomenally and knew how to pitch, flat out. There's a reason he was the best pitcher in college baseball for two years. His stats speak for themselves. The man was unbelievable and it was so cool to watch him go out there and absolutely carve everyone that he pitched against.

Bill Rowe: I played first base defensively at a lot of those practices when guys were working on getting their leads and working on their pickoff plays, and I can tell you Luke Heimlich could pick off anybody he wanted to. A lot of times he'd do it out of spite. If he walked a guy, he'd be so pissed at himself that he'd be like "I'm picking this guy off," and he would. He always knew the right pitch to do it on, the right time, it was close enough to that balk move where no one would call it, but it would fool you. To have that in your back pocket was such a weapon and just showed what kind of pitcher he was.

Kyle Nobach: He's an absolute animal for enduring the things that he did and accomplishing the things that he did. It's a self-image shattering because people look at you in a certain way, and he was still able to compete at the highest level and be very dominant. So, I don't know, he was an All-American two years in a row, he's an absolute great human being and everybody loves Luke.

Christian Chamberlain: Luke took me under his wing from the day I stepped on campus. He was an outstanding leader, always doing things the right way whether it was on or off the field. He was also everyone else's biggest supporter.

FINISH

Luke to this day is the best pitcher I've ever seen live. Obviously, there are some big-league guys (who are better), but they'd be neck-and-neck with him. And Fehmel is by far the most accurate and most competitive person that I've ever seen.

While Heimlich received the lion's share of the headlines, Fehmel put together a strong junior season as Oregon State's No. 2 starter. Fehmel made the all-conference team, going 10-1 with a 3.19 ERA in 20 starts. The Beavers had Heimlich's power on Fridays and Fehmel's pitchability on Saturdays. It was the perfect combination.

Luke Heimlich: Fehm was a third baseman when he showed up, and not a good third baseman. Not a good hitter, either. He would have to show up, take infield, take BP and then after practice was over, he would go down to the bullpen and do some of the Driveline weighted balls, do the recovery, do the throwing program. I was usually staying late, cleaning up, getting some work in or whatever, so seeing him being committed to both sides of the ball … I mean most everybody is leaving to go home, and he's finishing his day as an infielder and then going to get his work in as a pitcher. I was just impressed with him and his work ethic from when he first showed up. His success was no surprise. He always had the right attitude, never had a negative attitude, was always going to be positive out there and was always consistent. That's who Fehmel is.

Brandon Eisert: He came in as an infielder and ended up as a pitcher, an extremely successful pitcher at that. It's crazy to think about that. I mean, he's extremely competitive, would do whatever it takes to win. Obviously coming in as an infielder and switching to pitcher, he was willing to do whatever the team needed. He just wanted to win, and that was the only goal he had in mind. Nothing really shook him, either. Whether he had a great outing or a bad outing, he was always the same old Fehm.

Dylan Pearce: Just because he didn't have the dominant stuff, he had to do something that would make up for that. He was so focused on what he did and he knew "hey, this is what I have. I'm going to come to the table, I'm not going to be throwing hard, I'm not going to have elite, elite stuff, but I am going to have elite location. I'm going to fill up the zone and I'm going to compete on every pitch, no matter what."

He would come in and he wouldn't be blowing it by everybody and he wouldn't have the most wipeout off-speed, but he could throw any pitch in any count in any location and would do it constantly. He was rarely walking anybody, would start ahead and stay ahead. That is what I think made him so deadly when he threw. That was one of the most important things for our team, knowing that when Fehm comes in that he's going to be getting down to business. He's not going to be getting into full counts, he won't be walking a bunch of people or getting hit all over the place. He was just constantly filling up the zone.

Steven Kwan: I lived with Fehm and he takes that work ethic and does the same stuff at home. Everything he does has an intention to it; he has an amazing eye for detail. It wasn't even a surprise to me that every time he went out there, he was just carving guys up. He is the definition of a pitcher.

Pat Bailey: For Bryce to go over his career, I believe he finished (33-8) for us, that's a great example of pitching. You don't have to throw 95 miles per hour to win a lot of baseball games, you just have to be able to add and subtract and move up and down, in and out of the strike zone. Bryce's record, if you just watched him warm up you'd go "how in the heck can that guy finish (33-8) at Oregon State?" And he won some huge games for us, some really big games. I remember when he threw against Vanderbilt. I just think about a lot of big games he won for us over his career that were really, really important games.

Jack Anderson: Other than (Luke and Bryce), our staff was pretty young. I think looking back at it, Yeskie didn't let those guys sleep without believing in themselves. There were those bumpy roads along the whole way in the regular season with the bullpen, and it seemed like it was the first Beaver team where the hitters were leading the pitchers rather than the pitchers saving the hitters. It was literally the first time I can think of where that was the case because that just wasn't the brand of baseball we played as much.

Times really had changed in Corvallis. Oregon State possessed arguably the nation's top lineup and two frontline starters in Heimlich and Fehmel. But the team had been unable to settle on a No. 3 starter, and faced bullpen questions behind Brandon Eisert and Mulholland. If the Beavers were going to challenge for a College World Series title, a couple of arms needed to step up. Abel and Chamberlain, OSU's acclaimed freshmen, seemed like the most likely candidates.

Nate Yeskie: If we had any question going into '18 with our roster, I guess it was who was going to win that Sunday job. We thought (Grant) Gambrell was ready to take that next jump. We knew Abel had some good stuff but just needed to maintain some consistency. That was our Achilles' heel. If you look at a lot of our losses in '18, I think they were on Sundays where we just didn't close the gap or separate if we had certain leads.

FINISH

Michael Gretler: The coaches tried to plug a lot of different people in there and no one was really stepping up and embracing that. Obviously, guys wanted to, it wasn't like they weren't trying. But it's tough, it's the Pac-12 and after you probably beat teams the first two games, they don't want to get swept. People probably think your Sunday starter is your third-best arm or whatever, but if you've got two guys going on Friday and Saturday and you're going to hopefully win those games, then your guy on Sunday better be ready because those other teams don't want to get swept.

Bryce Fehmel, pitcher: Sundays were our kryptonite. It always felt like we had a tough time winning on Sundays. But we figured it out in the end. We were a younger staff with some of those freshmen coming in, so we had to stick with them and let them know that it's a long season and they would get their chance in the end.

Kevin Abel: We knew those two days (with Heimlich and Fehmel starting) that we were going to win for sure. We always believed we were going to win on Sundays, but we knew it was going to take the whole team. I guess going through it for me, I just wanted to figure things out so I could help the team. Because my whole fall coming into the season was "these guys just won 56 games, they didn't lose much, so they don't really need me. They can go back (to Omaha) without me just fine." So, if I wanted to be part of it, I was going to have to bust my ass and really earn it. That was my whole mentality the entire time until I felt like I was a benefit to the team almost.

Pat Casey: That three starter was just a wildcard. And that was odd because we really, even that year, won a lot of games. Obviously, we wanted to get Abel in that hole, and at the end of the year he gave us some good starts. But until he got ready to do that, it was a wildcard for us a little bit.

Abel and Chamberlain both pitched well in spurts during the first half of the year but wrestled with consistency. Midseason conversations with Pat Casey and Steven Kwan helped get them on the right track.

Christian Chamberlain: I hit pretty much all fall but I knew coming in that pitching was going to be the route I would head in later in my career. I'd say it was probably 70/30 with me pitching and hitting in the fall, and after winter break is when I finally put the bat down. It was a mutual decision, obviously it's a pretty tough lineup to break into. I was a lot more confident in what I could do on the mound than what I could do at the plate at the time.

Me and Abel both came out of the chute hot and struggled a bit in the middle of the year. Coach Casey and Steven Kwan sat us down on separate occasions and talked to both of us and said that if me and Abel could figure our part out that we would win the national title. After that, it was a huge turning point for both our team and me and Kevin personally.

Steven Kwan: I want to say it was in May, I talked to both of them and I said, "yo boys, if you two figure this out, we're going to win this whole damn thing. Keep chugging along, doing what you're doing." And Chamberlain brought this up a couple times, I remember it really fondly with him. I just knew that if we could get those two rolling that we would be unstoppable. And obviously, it was huge from them. Chamberlain's got a Major League (breaking ball), he's disgusting. Abel's got the same stuff, changeup, (curve), fastball. Those guys were unreal and with Kevin getting the mental game and focusing up on that and Chamberlain just grinding away, I knew we were unstoppable.

Nate Yeskie: They went through their freshmen growing pains. Some of it was fair, some of it was unfair just because we knew the level of play guys like Luke were at, what a guy like Mulholland had accomplished his freshman year. We get caught up in those comparisons with what guys should and shouldn't be able to do. But both of them had big stuff, roundhouse overhand curveballs that were different from other guys on our staff. They could both strike anybody out at any time if they really set their mind to it. You go back to some of those things and you look at it and go "all right, here's where they grew, here's what they did." We had a midweek game against Oregon, I look up at the radar gun in Eugene and it says 95 on the scoreboard (radar gun) and I'm like "that can't be right." We check after the game and sure enough Chamberlain was up to 95 and we're going "holy cow, man." Because when he came in he was 87 to 91, kind of in that range, a little erratic. Then all of a sudden, one day things just started to click, and that weekend against Washington State it was the same deal. He was 93 to 95.

Jake Mulholland: Watching those guys throw and not having maybe the immediate success that you always want for guys, it didn't change the way that they worked or the way they went about everything that they did. Sometimes you make a good pitch and a guy is going to hit it, sometimes there's nothing you can do about it. But when you can shut everything off and compete, when you're on the mound and that's the only thing you're thinking about, good things are going to happen.

Kevin really just started believing in himself. We did, so why shouldn't he? He took that on — all these guys believe in me and think I can get it done, so I can. And the same kind of thing with Christian, they both really believed in themselves and that's when they started dominating basically. We were not going to win it without both of them.

Christian Chamberlain: We had all the pieces, but we were just missing a couple key arms. Obviously it was going to take a lot more than just Luke and Fehmel to get us through a whole College World Series. Other guys did have to eat up innings, and at that point no one else was really doing it, and Eisert and Mulholland were getting the brunt of the bullpen innings. Pretty much me and Kevin had the next-man-up mentality and realized what they were saying could be true.

For me it was about confidence. I had a lot of self-doubt when things went south for me personally in the middle third of that year. They reminded both of us I'd say, and I just came out with confidence and after that it changed, from Washington State on.

Nate Yeskie: I think they had been through enough battles that they started to realize some things. And our older guys, much like they were when they were freshmen and wanting to perform and validate their value and their existence with the teammates based on their performance — the Greniers and Madrigals and Larnachs were beyond that, and Gretler has always been beyond that — where it was "hey, how do I help this younger guy get better?" That nucleus of guys did such a good job of helping the younger guys get through those growing pains. That's when they started to turn the corner a little bit there. I think that had a huge impact on how and when those guys developed.

Kevin Abel: A big turning point in the pitching staff I think was after the Utah and Arizona series. We had lost two out of three to both and it wasn't necessarily because we weren't hitting the ball. We really, really took it upon ourselves as a pitching staff to say, "this is enough." We really bought into being selfless and doing whatever it took to make sure we won the game, to make sure we held them to zero or one run every game.

The stat we really honed in on was our comeback zeroes. Anytime we scored, the next inning they will get zero runs, no matter what. We started keeping tallies of how many comeback zeroes we had, and that really I think helped boost that sort of focus in our pitching staff. And you saw guys really step up later in games after our starters came out.

And yeah, things just started to click. People got more comfortable in the roles they were in, getting either moved into or moved away from. Christian was throwing the ball then, too. Izzy was throwing it well, Dylan was a consistent guy out all the time. Guys were getting confident and comfortable knowing what their job was and how we were going to attack hitters, and we took off with that.

Dylan Pearce: That was a huge thing for us. We knew that whenever we had a big inning or our guys scored, it was so important that we came back and backed up our lineup that just did their job. We needed a zero, every single time. And that was something we would write on the board. We would score and it would be "OK, the next pitcher that comes out, you need to put up a zero." It was a personal goal for our team to throw up as many zeroes as possible.

Brandon Eisert: We knew our offense was going to give us run support, and what we needed were comeback zeroes to keep momentum in our favor. Because at times we maybe got a little bit too relaxed, thinking that our offense will support us even if we give up a run here or there. Those comeback zeroes were something we needed and I definitely focused on it the rest of the year.

Oregon State ran away with the 2017 Pac-12 title but found itself in a heated race in 2018 due to its midseason mini-swoon. Stanford, Washington and OSU all had a chance to win the conference entering the final day of the regular season. The Huskies and Cardinal were facing each other, while the Beavers hosted playoff-bound UCLA.

OSU and Washington both won the first two games of their series, but Stanford and UCLA rebounded in the finales. First place went to the Cardinal (44-10, 22-8). The Beavers finished second (44-10-1, 20-9-1), followed by the Huskies (30-23, 20-10) and Bruins (36-19, 19-11). OSU was undone by going 3-2-1 against Utah and Washington State — the Pac-12's worst teams — and 3-6-1 in series finales.

Kyle Nobach: That was a bummer. We definitely wanted to win the Pac-12; I mean we wanted to win every single game we played in.

Jack Anderson: We wanted to win the Pac-12 just as bad as we wanted to win anything else. The Utah and Arizona series laid those dreams to rest a little bit, and we lost the last Stanford game that we needed to win. We didn't overlook the Pac-12 or anything, we were just thinking "all right, we want to win the Pac-12 and then we want to get to Omaha." Once we got out of that Pac-12 championship race, it was Nick and Case saying, "hey, who cares? We've already got one of those rings, that's not the ring we were really wanting to get when the season ends."

Nick Madrigal: We knew our sights were set on something so much bigger. There wasn't really any disappointment for a couple days or anything like that. We kind of … everyone knew what we were going for that year, it wasn't just the Pac-12. So yeah, I think it was a bummer for a second, but we didn't skip a beat after that.

FINISH

Nate Yeskie: Our eyes were on the prize of winning the whole thing. It's not that we didn't care about the Pac-12 title, but that just wasn't our focus. We'd won the Pac-12 title and not won the national title. When you start the year off, your focus is on dogpiling at the end of the year.

Bryce Fehmel: We didn't have a (23-game) winning streak that year, but we were still able to go out and win on almost a daily basis. We didn't win as many games, but we were in every game that we played. To have a chance to win every game is special, and to be able to fight back and win some of those games was huge. It just shows the type of heart we had and the team we were. We weren't going to give up no matter what the score was, no matter who was on the mound or at the plate. We always had a chance to win.

Nate Yeskie: We knew going into the year that there was no way we were going to go single-digit losses. We weren't going to put together some ridiculous 58-4 record on the board and win the whole thing. We said, "don't be surprised if we lose more games but we win that national title." We just knew how to deal with adversity a little bit more I think.

Michael Gretler: It was a very different year than the year before. I almost remember more from (2017) than 2018, which is funny to say. In 2017, it felt like we dominated every team we played. And in 2018 we were thinking we were going to do the same thing, and obviously things didn't work out the same way.

To be honest, I don't remember a whole lot other than (Nick getting hurt). We had our ups and downs throughout that whole year, I can't even remember who won the Pac-12.

Jack Anderson: Case would always bring up the 2007 team, how at some point during that season Darwin and a couple of the other leaders were talking about how "oh, this isn't the same as last year." And Case told them "yeah, it's a different team. There's a lot of the same guys here, but you guys need to figure out as a team who you are because the 2006 team isn't the 2007 team. No matter how many guys are still there or how many new guys there are, you have to find your own identity as a team." I think that's the thing we were trying to figure out during the regular season. We knew who we were, we knew we were good, but I don't think we had the same fire in our belly that we did in 2017 because we were jaded from 2016. We weren't OK with losing, but I think we knew winning all these games in the regular season didn't mean as much. It was more about getting these young guys experience and putting them in tough situations.

Because we knew we were going to make the tournament, but we wanted to push the envelope there to make sure we were ready for the moment in Omaha that we weren't ready for the year before.

CHAPTER VI

CLEARING THE MIND

By this point, attentive observers may be hungry for more details of the vague "mental game" discussed by Kevin Abel, Trevor Larnach, Jake Thompson and others. This chapter, a glimpse at the teachings of Alan Jaeger and Tyler Graham, is for those readers.

Jaeger has been a staple of the baseball training scene since the founding of Jaeger Sports in 1991. Jaeger Sports, based in Southern California, focuses on arm health, arm conditioning and mental training. Jaeger, a former college pitcher, is credited with being the Godfather of long toss and a bona fide mental guru who has coached the likes of Barry Zito (2002 American League Cy Young Award winner), Dan Harren (three-time All-Star) and Andrew Bailey (two-time All-Star).

Alan Jaeger, Jaeger Sports: When I was a junior in college at Cal State Northridge, I had gone through a very difficult, challenging time, and it was basically all mental. This is a time when there really wasn't … I mean there were technically sports psychologists, but if you can imagine 30-plus years ago compared to now, it's hard to explain how not mainstream it was. For probably a good 20-year period, I'd almost say that if the term sports psychologist came up or the mental game came up, unfortunately there'd almost be a stigma around it like you'd have to have a problem. And I'm not saying I didn't have a problem that I needed to work on, but I think it just unfortunately got painted as a negative stereotype.

I fortunately put two and two together, I don't know how, but I ended up seeing someone who was literally a sports psychologist and he was amazing. He actually had a hypnotherapy background as well and he did wonders for me. Another thing that helped a ton and was really the next major piece to my life was when I switched my major over to psychology. I felt like I wanted to know what happened to me because that essentially ended my season. You could say it ended my career. I really just was curious what happened to me and why. I guess I wanted to know the why behind it. So, I switched my major to psychology and in one of my upper-division courses my professor was really unique and interesting and outside the box. Our class sort of went from the West to the East and one day he told a Zen story, and I had no idea what Zen was. I asked him afterward where he got that from, and he mentioned a book called *Zen Flesh, Zen Bones* by (Paul Reps). That eventually led me on to Alan Watts and a book called *The Way of Zen*, and that just really rocked my world. I got heavy, heavy, heavy into Zen and meditation. I did get my degree in psychology, but I really pursued more heavily the Eastern arts and Eastern philosophy, Zen being the primary. Zen comes out of Daoism, so Daoism was also a big piece of this as well. And then at some point in the early '90s I got heavy into yoga. I guess long story short is that I was hit very hard by a challenging experience, enough to end my career.

When something traumatic happens to you in your life, a lot of times it's a major growth opportunity. For me, fortunately, it got me on my path. At the time it was devastating, because I dreamed of playing as long as I could. And don't get me wrong, I still played for a good 25 years in adult leagues, but that's sort of the core. I think the tenacity, the determination, the interest level was off the charts for me to really delve into what happened. I challenged myself by writing a book, it took me four years. The book, called *Getting Focused, Staying Focused*, came out in 1994. That, to me, I don't know if you'd call it a graduate degree, but for me those four years, it felt like a radical shift in my life. I just feel like once I came through that period, came out the other side of it, I started feeling a completely different state — a healthy state, a productive state, a state of heightened awareness and more of a feel of flowing with life rather than stressing out about life. The last piece to it is you get to a spot … well first of all, I guess I was meant to be a teacher because it feels very natural to me. But there was this part of me where I went through this difficult time and I was fortunate to work through it and seeing a sports psychologist was a key, key piece. I think at the end of the day, when you feel like you've discovered something that's life-changing, you're inspired and you want to share. That to me was a massive catalyst. Not only had I found this life-changing experience, but I was eager to share it with people.

At the time, I assumed everybody I was going to deal with maybe was going to be dealing with something super traumatic. But as it turns out, 30 years later, the average person … just wants to be more relaxed or more clear-minded or less stressed. For athletes, they want to learn to be more in the present moment and less distracted by the future or the past. This is a common theme in life of course, so I feel like I did heavy-duty work to get to a point where it was really clear to me that the things I had learned through trial and error, through other people, through books, through writing my book … I got to a point where I really trusted the process, I trusted what I had gone through. And you don't know until you've gone through it, but fortunately early on when I started dealing with players or teams, the feedback was just awesome, and you can feel that. You can tell the difference between someone paying you a nice compliment versus someone who you feel has really been affected.

A longtime admirer of Oregon State's program from afar, Jaeger had never worked with a Beaver when he was introduced to pitching coach Nate Yeskie at the 2014 American Baseball Coaches Association in Dallas. The two hit it off and stayed in touch.

Nate Yeskie, pitching coach: Alan and I had a lot of mutual friends but had never connected face to face. One night after I received an award, Alan had been there and we had a chance to connect. We formulated a friendship in January of 2014 and Alan and I became very, very close moving forward. He's just been a great resource. He's been around baseball for many, many years; he's influenced the likes of Barry Zito, Clayton Kershaw, there's a long list of very, very talented individuals.

Alan Jaeger: Nate's the reason why I came up to Oregon State. Nate and I have become extremely close, and his wife Brittney and daughter A.J., they are like family to me. It's ironic because I have been in the baseball field for so long, but I'd never met anybody from Oregon State over the years. And they've always had such a perennial, first-class, top-ranked program. It was just one of those things.

I had become friends with a gentleman named Liam Carroll, who was the head coach and basically general manager of the British National Team. I'm at the ABCA Convention and Nate was getting an award. Somehow it came up and Liam said, "oh, I know Nate really well." He knew Nate from (working at UNLV). So, I asked him to introduce us, and Liam Carroll introduced us. I really wanted to meet Nate, I didn't know if he was interested in meeting me or not, I didn't know if he knew who I was. As it turned out, as you know with Nate, he is a bear for details and he really wanted to break down long toss and things like that. We became fast friends.

Nate Yeskie: Alan's just, he's really a great spirit. He's a great spirit and he wants everybody to succeed. It's funny when he goes out to UCLA and you see Andrew Moore is going up against James Kaprielian, and at some point Alan may have talked to both of those kids about how to help them get better because he's an open source and open format for everybody just in the sense that he's got books out there, he's got a website with information on it and he's accessible. Alan's great for baseball, he's kind of the guy who provides a different perspective on things. I think his influence on myself helped trickle down to some of these other guys, and they were able to formulate relationships as well. Alan is just great for the game of baseball, great for kids and is a great human being. I can't say enough good things about him. As that relationship began to grow and blossom, we crossed paths a couple of times. I think we were at UCLA one weekend and he came out to say hello. He's based out of Santa Monica and as we got to know each other more and more, he got closer to our program and got to know some of our players.

Alan Jaeger: It was probably in '16, I was at spring training and (Oregon State) opens up down there in Surprise for eight games. So, I went out there and met up with them, and Nate invited me to come down and talk to the pitchers in the bullpen. He had me stay in the dugout during the game, just hanging out, and that's really where it started. It was a good, slow burn and at some point, just from being around the program, I got to be around Case a bit. And I think he got comfortable with me. I would see them in Surprise and see them in L.A. It was sort of like that, and when the thing really ramped up was (in May 2017). I went up there for six days and really lived at the field with the guys, we had a daily meeting. I was with that same team both in Surprise and then in (April) at (UCLA), so I had probably already had four different meetings with them over the course of those two years. So, I went up there in May and was there for their series against Washington State right before regionals. I think that's where things shifted a lot because I was there for six days and I got to know a lot of the newer kids. Even though we did a lot of stuff up there then, when we met with the guys the next February in Surprise, some guys had graduated but a lot of the core guys returned, and I had such a great relationship with them. And then I saw them again at (USC) in '18, so I guess that would really be the crux of it.

It took time for most of the players to fully buy into Jaeger's teachings, but one staff member was eager to learn from the beginning. Tyler Graham, Oregon State's director of player development, lettered for the Beavers from 2003-06 and famously caught the final out of the 2006 College World Series in center field. The Montana native fought his way through the minor leagues and was called up to the Arizona Diamondbacks in 2012. Following an injury-prompted retirement in 2014, Graham began his coaching career as an undergraduate assistant at OSU. His curiosity about meditation and the mental side of baseball took off not long after.

Tyler Graham, director of player development: I had a teammate (Brock Bond) that had a major concussion and had to quit playing. He was right on the verge of making it to the big leagues and had a major concussion. He got hit in the head with a ball, and he ended up becoming a meditation teacher in California. He had asked me several times to try it, to do it, and I kind of did what everyone else does to me now: just blew it off and didn't really think much of it. Because I hadn't heard a lot about it, I hadn't researched it, I didn't know a lot about it. We were playing UCLA in 2015 and he was teaching Transcendental Meditation in Beverly Hills. So, I took an Uber and went and did a little two-day course with him and learned how to do it. I promised him I'd do it for two weeks and give it a try, and I did. I saw instant results just in the way you feel, how calm it makes you, how focused it makes you. It takes away anxiety, it does multiple things that really helped me out. Me going through that with him personally and knowing how much it affected my life and my mind, I just felt like it was something that I had to share with the players because it was something I wish I'd had when I played. I think it would've made a world of difference, I know it would've made a world of difference, because I struggled with the mental game like everyone else going through the minor leagues. It's really hard. And without it, it's really had to be successful.

I dealt with anxiety all the way through the minor leagues. I think a lot of people do. They just don't like to talk about it. It's something I think a lot of people have in their daily lives and something I know a lot of athletes have because there's a lot of pressure playing on big stages and there's a lot of money involved if you make it to the big leagues and have a good career. I felt it take away my anxiety, I felt like I was calm. It's a lot easier to talk to people and have good conversations. I really noticed it with tough conversations, it wasn't as uncomfortable to have the tough conversations because it really frees your mind up so you're not thinking about what everyone else is thinking, what everyone else is doing. It really allows you to focus on what's going on right now, and all that noise about the future and the past kind of got taken away. It was an amazing thing that it could happen that fast. It took away the daily anxiety that you would have from everyday life, just thinking about the past and the future. That was probably the biggest part of it.

Alan Jaeger: What's beautiful about Tyler is when I got up there the first time, when we met for the first time, he told me that he already had a background in meditation. A lot of times when I go to schools or wherever and do my training with them, I'm sure they'll do their best to continue on. But I knew with Tyler's background, and that he was so fired up and inspired and bought in, that he wanted to take advantage of every second.

He and I would have hours and hours of conversations about all this stuff and broke it down and set it up, and obviously he put his own spin on it, but we just broke it down to where he felt comfortable leading them through a meditation.

Tyler Graham: I didn't start (leading meditation sessions) until the '17 season. I think Michael Gretler might've started before and maybe Jake Thompson a little bit, but there weren't too many kids doing it in '16. I knew about it, but it wasn't until Alan came in and really talked to me about how to implement it in a team setting that it really started. I know all the kids really trust Alan and they respect Alan and they know he's a great guy and a really smart guy. He was a huge, huge part of getting kids to buy in and actually do it. Without Alan, I don't think a lot of kids would've done it.

Alan's been a huge mentor for me in different ways to get kids to buy in, different ways to teach it, different ways to do it and different ways to explain it. I'd say my old buddy and teammate Brock Bond and Alan Jaeger were the two guys that definitely got me onto meditation, and I owe them a lot.

Alan Jaeger: T Graham had a meditation practice that was optional, but it was available every single day at Oregon State after I left that year, starting in 2017. That was his gig, and it was cool. ... Not to mention the stuff he and I talked about, whether it was about the process, queues. He's such a sharp guy and he also was able to basically be a full-time sports psychologist up there. He is a massive piece. From my perspective, he played a huge role in the mental part of the game for these guys … and being the great hitting coach he is, of course.

His strong desire and big-time buy-in to the mental game, I mean here's a guy that played (nine) years professionally, played in the big leagues and played on a national championship team. This is a guy who's been there, done it and understands where these kids are going. I just can't tell you how passionate he is. He's so, so bought into the mental game and feels that it's a game-changer, a life-changer. I think the fact that he was up there full-time around these kids, man what a gift for these kids to have him around.

Tyler Graham: We would meditate every day before practice, and I would encourage them to do it on their own at night as well or in the morning when they wake up. The best times to do it are right when you wake up or in the middle of the day. I tried to get those guys to do it more than just at the field, and I think a lot of them started to do it more as they saw positive results with it.

Basically, you try to inform them of what it does and give them scientific research of different effects that it has, different things that it takes away. You give them information of all the athletes and all the successful people out there who have done it. Michael Jordan, Kobe Bryant, LeBron James, Tiger Woods, Oprah Winfrey. Phil Jackson made it mandatory for the Lakers to do it on the championship teams he had. All the proof is out there that it works and it's an essential part of success. Pete Carroll says it's one of the main reasons why they made it to and won the Super Bowl in (2014). There is a lot of different research from really successful people out there. I think the facade is just that a lot of people are good because they're talented. But if you're in the realm of athletics and sports, we all know that talent will only take you so far if you want to get to the highest level. I think everyone would agree that the guys that make it and the guys that have sustained success are the guys that practice the mental game. And without it, you really can't do anything about it. You can be aware that you struggle with the mental game, you can be aware that you don't deal with failure very well, you can agree that you have a ton of different thoughts and have negative self-talk. All the problems are out there right in front of you, right in front of everyone's face out in the open, but not many people are willing to put in the work to battle those issues. Without a calm, clear, focused mind, the athlete just isn't going to reach their full potential. So, I try to inform them as much as I can with scientific research and different people that have done it, stories about it. It takes a lot of time for kids to buy in, but you start with a few guys that really buy in and a lot of kids start to see their success.

Alan Jaeger: The meditation, the process, building their process ... this is where T Graham gets a boatload of credit because these guys obviously leaned on T Graham. I think the fact that breathing and meditation were brought into their culture, the fact that we talked about a process and the visualization, the mental drills, doing the mental drills, credit to T Graham. I think it helped to have T Graham being a constant resource up there, a resource that was there before I came up, a resource they trusted and relied on before they met me. And the fact that whatever I brought, T Graham was able to facilitate and implement that and have the buy-ins from the program to where he was able to do his thing with them because I think he already had such major credibility and was a great hitting teacher for them regardless. I just think it was a combination of me being around to present some new ideas, and Tyler there to pound it in and be resourceful.

Tyler Graham: The first guy who started doing it was Michael Gretler. It really changed the way he went about things.

A Pacific Northwest recruit from Tacoma suburb Bonney Lake, Michael Gretler made 32 starts as a freshman in 2015 and batted just .171 with an OPS of .448. Gretler began receiving hitting instruction from Graham that fall and improved his sophomore slash line to .339/.391/.441 in limited at-bats. The following February in Surprise, Gretler added the next piece: meditation. He went on to win the starting job at third base and slashed .301/.364/.468 with five home runs and 33 RBIs in 57 starts. Turning down the MLB Draft, Gretler came back for his senior season in 2018 and earned all-Pac-12 honorable mention for the second straight year with even better offensive numbers (.305/.379/.473, seven homers, 51 RBIs).

Michael Gretler, infielder: It really started off with T Graham early in the fall (of 2016) working with the hitters individually on mechanics, maybe some swing changes to try to get a little bit more out of each of us. And Alan Jaeger, a great guy, unbelievable guy, he came down to Surprise on one of our first days down there before the season started and led us through a team meditation session ... and it really hit me that year. I had done it a little during my freshman and sophomore years but I didn't really think too much of it. But for some reason, I don't really know what it was, T Graham and I were like "wow, we really need to find ways to incorporate this into our daily routines," T Graham especially. So, Tyler headed it, we would do it before every game, home, road. We started a group text and sent it off to the whole team, then some regulars started coming. We'd send texts to each other like "bus leaves at one, we're going to go into conference room A at 12:30."

Alan Jaeger: Gret's the first guy who came up to me at USC or somewhere, maybe it was Surprise, and he was probably a sophomore at the time. He was interested and open-minded and just wanted to be a sponge and learn. He loved the meditation, he looked forward to it, he got a lot out of it and he wanted to really make it his own and become his own meditator. Gret wanted to apply it to everything. He wanted to apply it to hitting, to defense, and it became a way of life for him, which is powerful. Gret's easy, man. He was one of those guys who was just hungry and wanted it and was passionate and excitable and interested.

Michael Gretler: It really helped me slow the game down. Even when you do meditate, like the first game of the College World Series, everyone's nervous, everyone has those butterflies. But it's more about learning how to accept it and move past it rather than dwell on it. If you're human, you're going to get antsy or a little bit of anxiety or a little bit of stress or nervousness. What are the tools you have (to combat that?) Everyone's different, Nick probably has something else. But for me, the meditation piece was something I could always go to that if I did it before the game or did it in the morning, when shit hit the fan later on during the day or in the game, I had a tool in my toolbox to counter that.

You can't think negatively, the game is way too hard and will eat you up if you do that. Meditation gives you the tools to get rid of those things and keep them out of your mind.

Tyler Graham: Gret was just really hard on himself. He didn't deal with failure very well. Like all of us playing sports, it was really tough to deal with failure when you've been good your whole life, and then you come to a top-notch program and for the first time, you fail. Most kids aren't prepared to deal with that. I wasn't prepared to deal with that in my career, and I struggled as well. I think pretty much everyone struggles with that at some point. He knew he needed that, and I think he's just the kind of kid that will do anything it takes to get as good as he can. He's one of the hardest workers I've ever been around and one of the most coachable kids I've ever been around. He was open to any kind of information that would help him out to have sustained success. Because a lot of guys can have limited success, they can have success, but just not consistently. That's what we were aiming for, to have that sustained success, and he saw instant results with it. He was the first guy that really started to buy into it. He was a team leader, and having a guy that everyone respected and wanted to be around, it was huge that it worked for him and he could also help other kids buy in as well. It takes a lot of people, it's not just one person that makes this stuff happen. The players have a huge, huge role — just like Alan did — in getting this thing going.

Alan Jaeger: When I was up there for that six-day period in May 2017, Michael and I had already developed a very good relationship. We had talked on the phone and we became like friends because he had bought in, and he said to me "I'm having a hard time with this two-strike pitch off the plate. I can't tell if it's a strike, it's on the black or just off the black. I'm swinging at balls I shouldn't and I'm letting strikes go by that I should be protecting."

I basically told him about some mental hitting drills, some visual drills … I wasn't allowed to touch a ball, but through the powers that be, Gret did these drills where he'd basically track balls and you work on. Without going into too much detail, you really get a better understanding of the strike zone. Because you're not swinging, your awareness is really high. We really hammered this drill to where he was identifying with yeses and nos balls that were balls and balls that were strikes. The drills in general helped him have a clearer and more relaxed mind at the plate, which of course helps him as a hitter in general, and he had his own process as well. So, we had a bunch of things working with him, and after the first at-bat of that Friday game, I was next to Tyler. Tyler and Gret were really close, Tyler knew everything about that kid, his body language and swing. I didn't know as much of that obviously, but Tyler told me after that first at-bat — and I think he actually walked that first at-bat — Tyler basically said, "that's the best at-bat he's had this year," or "he just looks different." Anyway, he went on to have an unbelievable series (5 for 7, five RBIs), and I know one of the main things that made it unbelievable was he walked (four) times. I think those drills really helped him a lot. His discipline at the plate was good, I think he had to take a tough two-strike pitch he knew was a ball that first at-bat, and for him it was probably like winning the lottery. He saw these drills come into live action, so that was really magical.

Because Tyler is so close to these kids and knows them so well, I would not have been able to know that. But Tyler basically said "it's the same guy, he just looks so much different at the plate, his approach is different, he looks more relaxed." And obviously based on the results, it was a cool thing because Gret, it was probably causing him some stress and frustration. To help him feel so liberated, it goes back to what I said before. The one thing we all want to do as teachers or friends, you want to help. It's just cool when you see it in real time. That was a real cool moment with Gret, and that's something he and I can talk about for the rest of our lives. That weekend series really shifted it for him.

Michael Gretler: Tyler did an incredible job and when Alan came in, he would do an incredible job of opening it up to everyone. They never said "everyone's going to do this," because it's not for everyone, everyone has their own thing. But we left it open to the group and I think T Graham played a big role in telling guys "hey, you need to do this." He probably pulled Steven and Trevor along and said "hey guys, you might already be having success, but try this, stick with it and you'll have even more success." So, I think T Graham was the main one to (recruit guys), and he might've been like "hey, look at what Jake Thompson's doing, he's having a great year."

Alan Jaeger: Tyler would be feeding me guys to talk to. Like he'd say "hey, it would be really cool if you'd talk to this guy." So, what ended up happening was I'd have private phone (conversations) with various guys, so that was cool.

Tyler Graham: Jake Thompson was another guy Alan and I worked with. He had struggled for three years and was a super-talented pitcher, and he just could never get through three, four, five innings. He would always implode. Once he learned the mental game with Alan, and just what I learned from Alan and continuing that with him at school, you saw major changes in his success.

Jake Thompson, pitcher: Before I worked on (the mental game), when I was doing really well, I expected at some point that I was going to struggle. Maybe I had just thrown a shutout, I'm pitching really well, but when is the struggle going to happen? Then I'd go out another game and think about when the struggle was going to happen. But (in 2017), I would go out thinking that I was going to pitch exactly like I did the previous weekend: dominate, dominate, dominate. I got that through my head, and before I knew it, it was the end of the regular season and I hadn't lost a game.

Alan Jaeger: I think the main thing with Jake is pretty universal. My goal with all the guys is to get them into what I call their process. I just want to know what two or three things they want to focus on on the mound or at the plate, and master that and become aware that if the mind wants to go into anything other than those two or three constants, they are variables. And variables, another word for a variable I use is drama or distraction, and I basically say "look, you're not a bad guy if you go onto these variables, but you've left your process. And you told me that if you do A, B and C, those are the keys to you making the best pitch of your life, well then there's no reason for you to leave it." Basically, that's what I laid out with Jake. I had him identify his keys and like everybody else, hopefully they really see "OK, I've just got to be great at sticking to these keys," and also to have the awareness that if you leave these keys, know that you're not a bad person, you're just now entering the world of drama and distraction and future and past.

And then the second piece to it all, which I think becomes really important to keep as a foundation, is some kind of mental practice or meditation. So, with all these guys, I've told them all the same thing. I'm going to give you what I think is the best advice and you'll channel it the way you need to. Unless you're in a zone 24/7 and living that way already, maybe you don't need to do any kind of mental practice if you're just flowing with life. But a lot of guys, if they have this tool available to them to try and work on really getting quieter, getting more relaxed, more clear-minded and also learning how to detach from your thoughts, knowing your thoughts are the ones that are going to take from that other process at some point in life, when they're on the mound or at the plate or in the grocery store or when they're in class. It's really very universal for all the guys. Yes, the process is different for some guys. Like anything else, you talk to some guys a little bit differently, a little more this and a little more of that. But it's really universal.

Tyler Graham: Alan talked to (Thompson) personally and got him with the process of what he needed to think, something to reset the mind. He gave him a solid process to focus on, a couple different words that he can think on the mound to kind of reset. When he was aware that he was thinking the negative thoughts, he would step off, look at something in center field and come back to a couple of words, a couple mental queues that would get him to throw the best pitch of his life on every single pitch. The meditation is just the out-of-practice practice for the in-game process, and that's what Alan brought to the table. The kids that bought in really saw a lot of success.

Alan Jaeger: One story that I really remember vividly was Jake came up to me when I was out there for those six days and he started on Sunday that year. He came up to me before the game and said, "hey, can we do a private meditation before the game?"

And I'm like, "sure." So, we went into the players' lounge and I took him through a very deep session. I knew what his three keys were for his process … so during the game, again I'm in the dugout for the week, I remember throughout the game I'd remind him every so often, I think breath was one of his words, commit, whatever they were. It was just fun because I felt like we had this strong connection that we built before the game, and it was fun throughout the game. I didn't really need to say much because he was so dialed in, but he threw a complete-game shutout, a (two-hitter), punched out (five) and walked (two). And it was more than that, if you looked at him on the mound he had this presence about him that was just so strong. It's fun for me because I felt like he was living his process, he was living his meditation and as a teacher, someone who is giving someone information, that's what you hope for as a teacher, that they use it to their advantage.

That was really a special deal, to this day it's one of those things that still stands out. Because a lot of times I might work with a client and then they'll pitch and, unless they're on TV, I'll hear after the game in maybe a phone call how it went. But this was in the dugout, at the game and it was sort of different that way, kind of living it with them. You become like a mother hen at that point, you want to see the players do well.

Michael Gretler: I remember one day that first year in Omaha, me and Jake meditated on the floor of T Graham's bedroom at the hotel. Fast forward a year, and we're in the conference room before the final game of the national championship and there's eight, nine, 10 guys in there. And that's awesome, it's guys wanting to improve and make an impact.

Tyler Graham: It was pretty cool to see a few kids buy in early, you get a few more the next year and it builds from there. … Gretler and Thompson started it that first year, and the second year the main group of guys was Gretler, Zak Taylor, Adley, Trevor, Kyle Nobach, Kwan, Abel.

As documented in the previous chapter, inconsistency plagued Abel through the first half of the 2018 season. The talented freshman entered May with a 5.72 earned run average in 28 1/3 innings. His strikeout numbers (45) were high, but there were too many walks (26). Something needed to change.

Kevin Abel, pitcher: I was just in my own way. I was letting other things affect what I was doing, like the last pitch, the last hitter, the last outing, things like that, letting these thoughts and things crawl into my head. That was really crippling me from being the pitcher I could be.

FINISH

Tyler Graham: I just asked Kevin if he was open to talking to Alan. He had a prior relationship with him in high school, so that was good. When I heard that, I was very optimistic that he was willing to put in the work with the mental game. He was willing to talk to Alan, and they had a long conversation, maybe more than one. And soon after that is when it really started to click for him. He started to have longer outings and he could sustain his success for longer and longer on a weekly basis.

Kevin Abel: I had known Alan while I was in high school, just because he's down in the Southern California area. I had used his J-Bands and things like that, so I had talked to him like my junior year and senior year when I'd go up to UCLA or USC to watch Oregon State. Yeskie would introduce us, get us together to have a conversation. I had known him and had many conversations with him. T Graham was the one who orchestrated it because T Graham follows Alan's meditation. He got me his number and we would talk about ways to develop something personal for me, that was the big thing. Yes there are things out there that people have come up with, but it was about making it meaningful and more appropriate for what I needed. That was developed over a couple phone calls, we really got it nailed down and it ended up working pretty well.

Alan Jaeger: Kevin falls into the category of T Graham sending me a text, as he had done with other players. Really that was it, he just said "hey, if we can get Kevin going here, he can be a horse." Of course, Ty was right. If you look at the timeline, I know the week we started talking he was not in the rotation, he was not the weekday starter even, but his first inning after we started talking was against Oregon on a Tuesday.

However it came about, we were on the phone, and I've actually told this story before because I think it's so important to see that if you can simplify things even if you're going through a tough period, you can start to make pretty fast adjustments just by changing the way you think about things in a more advantageous way. So, with Kevin, I did the same thing I do with everybody. One, we identified his process. The question I ask every person is what two or three things, if you did consistently before this pitch or during this pitch, would lead to the best pitch of your life? And I'm literal, I don't mean sort of the best pitch of your life, I want to know the best pitch of your life. If you need to, go back to the best game of your life and think about it. I'll often give the players an analogy of what I use because a lot of times it's very similar for pitchers because a lot of pitchers want to do the same things. One is they want to have a target they're focused on, they want to commit to the target. Sometimes they want a mechanical piece in the middle there, and now with the popularity of the word breathing and breathe and things like that, a lot of guys use breath, which is good of course because I always talk about how the breath is happening now, it's a present moment symbolic move as well, very powerful. So, I said to Kevin, "first, we're going to figure out what your process is. I don't know how much meditation you're doing with Tyler, I don't want to get into that, I don't want anyone to feel guilty. But look, the major piece of this is having a meditation practice each day so you can let some stuff go, you can start to plant some of these new messages and new focuses that we're working on. We want the mind to start defaulting to your process and start defaulting to being quiet rather than thinking."

This all is why mental practice is so important. Both parts are huge, having your process but also having mental practice. The thing about the process is usually guys can cement that pretty fast because it happens so often in bullpens and even catch play and of course on the main mound. Kevin was all-in, man. We broke his process down, he told me he was going to do the meditation religiously, which for me was maybe 10 to 15 minutes, twice a day was sort of how we start. We want to get at least one meditation in per day.

Kevin Abel: We use the meditation to really focus on our breathing because if you're thinking about breathing, you're not really thinking about anything. But when you are just laying there and you have a thought come in about "it's cold today," you acknowledge it, move it to the side and go back to breathing. It's about redirecting your focus, and when you do that it really helps it go away, your brain forgets about it. Maybe you make a bad pitch and you get all upset with yourself. You acknowledge it, understand what you learned from the pitch and how it can affect the next one, deep breath, reset, and just go back to being focused on what the next one is.

Alan Jaeger: So we laid out his process. It was basically my process plus a mechanical piece in there, and he agreed. I said, "if you do these things, do you agree you'll make the best pitch of your life every pitch forever?" And he basically said, "yes, if I can do these things." He bought in, he believed it, he trusted it. Now I'm not saying it's easy to pull off right away, but part of Kevin's makeup is he's just determined and he's the kind of guy who wants to vet things, and if it makes a lot of sense, he's in. And it made a lot of sense to him, and luckily he had an outing the next day, so he had a chance to practice his process and trust those things and understand that if he leaves those things, he's just going into distractions and the past or the future or some other thought.

Kevin Abel: My pitch-to-pitch process is just three simple keywords or phrases: breathe, stay tall and commit. Breathe is to remind me to relax and really focus on my breath. Stay tall is sort of my mechanical queue that I use to help maintain my posture so I can rotate, keep everything in line. And commit is my attack word, that trust and confidence to understand what you're doing, and then you have to fully commit to it. Because if you throw anything with hesitation, it just seems like it doesn't have as much to it and hitters can see it for some reason.

I'd say it took one conversation with T Graham and Alan, and I believed in it wholeheartedly. I mean I'd read about it before, but I wasn't really educated on it. So, once I was, it made absolute sense. It took me a while to develop the practice and be able to use it all the time. Like when I first started doing it, I'd maybe do it 10% of the time. And it just took that really, really slow progression to develop it to where I was doing it 95% of the time, 99% of the time. And when you have that sort of focus for an extended period of time, generally you will have success.

The first good outing I had where I was using (my process) pretty well was the midweek Oregon game. Then that carried over to Washington State, and then to USC. That one was tough because when you look at it, it looks like I didn't perform very well. But that was actually the first time where I was pitching and just didn't have my stuff. That was the first time in the bullpen I remember telling myself "it's going to be tough today." And I was more proud of that outing than any other up until playoffs when the games really meant something because I knew I didn't have my stuff, but I still made it work for almost five innings and battled through it. That was what I hadn't done previously when I didn't have my best stuff, I kind of cashed it in and was throwing everything all over the yard.

Tyler Graham: Kevin obviously came into Oregon State as a huge talent and had a lot of expectations and a lot of weight on his shoulders from being such a successful and highly-touted high school pitcher. This game is hard enough as it is when you're going good and when you're confident. With him you would see a couple good innings, you would see him dominate for three or four innings, it was similar to Jake Thompson. He was similar to Jake Thompson in the fact that they were dominant, dominant pitchers, but when the negative thoughts started to get into their heads, you could see both of them start to get off track a little bit.

Once Kevin developed a process with Alan and used meditation, you saw major, major results. That was probably one of the coolest things I've ever seen … because when you make physical changes either with pitching, hitting or fielding, those changes take a long time, sometimes years. For him to buy into the mental game and have it work pretty much instantly, he wasn't to the point where he was at the end of the season, but you could slowly see him climb the mountain. Each start you could see him get a little bit better, a little bit better and a little bit better. It didn't come in big waves, it came in small waves at first and gradually started building. And by the end of the year, he ended on top of the mountain.

Alan Jaeger: The rest is history. I just really believe what he did is his default changed to where instead of whatever he had been thinking about to that point, it shifted to these basic constants that he believed were the keys to him making the best pitch of his life, and he was diligent to his meditation process. Like Gret and the other guys, he wanted to meditate. He was feeling the difference, he was seeing how it was translating. We didn't even really talk a whole lot. We talked a few times, maybe three times over the course of the first week or two. After that, there might've been a text here and there. That's again where Tyler was so key, he was there to be a grounder in there, a reinforcer. I just think Kevin got this thing so quickly and bought in so quickly and saw how it was affecting him so quickly that there was nothing else for him to think about in a way, and I think that's where guys get locked in and get into that quote-unquote "zone" state. There's an absence of thought, an absence of future, an absence of past. There's only an immersion of what's happening now, and his process was an immersion that can become unconscious. In other words, there comes a point where he's probably not even thinking about his process on the mound because he's now living it. You first teach someone to ride a bike, then they're just riding the bike.

With Kevin, it became a self-fulfilling prophecy. I think that's the full story with Kevin, it became him. And like Trevor in a way, though I don't know Trevor's story quite as well, I just feel like it's a cool story because it says that you can be going through something that feels stressful and distracting and blah, blah, blah, and then to sort of change your mentality and add in some mental practice as well, it's amazing how it can shift a human being. And in Kevin's case, the way things were going up to that point compared to what happened the following weeks, I guess the word would be transformational.

Abel had thrown only 2 2/3 innings in the previous three weeks when he took over in the second inning of Oregon State's May 1 non-conference game at Oregon. Fresh off a conversation with Jaeger, a revamped Abel tossed 6 1/3 one-hit, shutout innings of relief as the Beavers clawed their way back to a 4-3 victory. It was the beginning of a magical stretch for Abel, who closed the year with 1.36 ERA in his final 11 appearances, striking out 63 with 20 walks in 53 innings.

Gretler, Thompson and Abel weren't the only Beavers to embrace the mental game. Graham and Jaeger also reached Steven Kwan, Larnach and many others in a variety of ways.

Trevor Larnach, outfielder: I started working with T, I want to say it was towards the end of my freshman year. We were definitely in contact my freshman year; he was the first base coach that year and he helped with the outfielders and all that. Me and him gradually got closer and closer together through my freshman year, and at the end of that year we started working together in the cages and stuff like that. The real, real work started my sophomore year when I first got back to campus. Because my freshman year, this doesn't knock any of the coaches who were there at the time, but I was listening to four or five coaches at once on hitting, trying to be coachable, and you just can't do that. I learned that the hard way, batting .100 or whatever it was that year. I learned that and took it to the side and said "I won't be doing that again." I stuck with the one person I thought would help me out the most and I connected with the most. Me and T Graham in a lot of ways have the same kind of work ethic. We're always trying to get things right, we're always trying to get things down to a T, we're always trying to get better and better and better. Once he came into the picture the end of my freshman year, my sophomore year was when the real work started, and we learned more and more and more together as we spent more time with each other. That's where it all started, really.

Tyler Graham: Trev is very hard on himself as well. He was obviously a really good high school player, a big prospect coming into college and he had a negative attitude at times like all of us do when we're not having success. He didn't really know how to deal with failure, and I think the biggest thing for him was just learning how to deal with failure, learning what to do when things aren't going good and where he could put his mind.

Alan Jaeger: I think this is a powerful statement on the mental game: the first time Tyler wanted to lead a meditation as a group, Trevor didn't really want to do it. Tyler told him to come in and he could just sleep if he wanted. To me, this sort of epitomizes how powerful the mental game is and sometimes guys don't buy in right away, and I think it's a healthy picture to let people know that maybe people aren't going to buy in right away, but don't give up on it. So, when Tyler was doing these optionals every day, he and Trevor Larnach are very close and he said to Trevor "come in and try this out." And I think Trevor at first, I don't think it was his thing. Trevor was very talented and was successful, but Tyler more or less said "hey, you can come in and you can just sleep. Just come in and give it a try, and if you don't like it, sleep."

Trevor Larnach: I couldn't have been more out on that idea. It got brought to my attention that there were some benefits to meditation, that I should try it. And T Graham, along with Alan, pretty much had to just drag me in there against my will, and I couldn't thank them enough for doing so.

Alan Jaeger: So long story short, to tell you the effect meditation had on him ... Trevor Larnach was waking up at 4 a.m. so he had the time to do a 40-minute meditation that included some visualization. I believe he was doing this twice a day, and it just tells you how much the mental game can impact people, that he went from not really being sure if he wanted to do it to it becoming a major staple. Can you imagine getting up at 4 a.m.? In the offseason, the offseason! He didn't have to be anywhere. To me, it gives people a snapshot of how some people are maybe like, "what is this mental game stuff?"

Trevor Larnach: That whole thing happened, they got me into it and ever since then I've been hooked on it, and I think it's made a world of difference. I think the other guys that still do it can attest to that because it's something baseball players need, and honestly I think it's something everyone needs. Maybe not everybody, but people who have a hard time relaxing or are uptight about stuff, I think it could really help them and it doesn't hurt to try it. Don't take my route with it, I thought it would hurt. Definitely just try it. You never know what kind of benefits it will bring or how it will make you feel. It was a thing of trial and error, but it ended up being something that's far greater than just one session back then for 10 minutes. Sometimes it's turned into sessions for me that have gone for an hour, have gone 40 minutes, 30 minutes, now it's kind of a steady 20 minutes. You just have to find what you like.

I'm very blessed to have T Graham as a mentor because he's one of the individuals that you'll rarely find when it comes to learning all these different things and to help distribute information to help guys out with getting better and progressing and developing as a player. When T started talking with Jaeger about meditation, me being hard-headed, I was like "no, I'm not going to fucking meditate. What do you think this is?" He basically said "just try it, man. Just try it." So, I tried it. I was a huge anxiety-driven guy freshman year for the most part and sophomore year somewhat. But once I started doing that, I think it really played a big part in calming me down a little bit when it came to before the game, during the game, after the game, all that stuff. I've done it ever since, and I personally think more guys should do it.

Steven Kwan, outfielder: I honestly would credit all of how I've developed as a hitter to T Graham. We actually started working together at the beginning of my freshman year, and it took a whole year and a half for me to put everything together. We had to break my swing down, talk everything through, drill work, drill work. I was in the cages after practice every single day for hours, and it was hard because I wasn't seeing the results I wanted but he told me to keep sticking with it. He's an awesome person because there was never a time where he was like "ah, I don't feel like hitting today." He would hit with me after practice every single day. The guy knows his stuff. Even though he's a high-energy guy and he shoots all this stuff at you, he knows his stuff. I would completely credit all of my hitting abilities to him. He's a really caring guy, so I'm really appreciative of him.

Tyler Graham: Kwan had major self-doubt as a freshman, and even his sophomore year he dealt with that early on. It's just a constant, everyday talk. Just little things, a constant message. That's why I think Case is so good, he has a constant message that you can never be too good and you never have any limits on yourself. He made that message clear every single day, and the more the kids hear it, the more it starts to become a reality.

Steven Kwan: That was also an introduction to meditation for me. I actually talked to Greg Warburton, who was kind of our baseball psychologist at the time. He talked about meditation, but I was just like "meditating? That sounds like some yogi kind of stuff, third eye awakening kind of stuff." It sounded tacky and cheesy to me. But with T Graham pushing it on me, and we were also really close to Alan Jaeger, so I gave it a try. I remember that first time we walked through it, I felt so calm and quiet at the plate. I think that also contributes to me being able to see the ball really well at the plate and controlling the strike zone. T Graham was a huge advocate of that for sure.

T Graham just told me how it would help for the baseball aspect, and Alan explained it from the ground up, what it does for the body, the science behind it. He had a very good understanding about it, and he walked us through all of it. I still talk to him because of it. He's super helpful and a friendly guy.

Zak Taylor, first baseman: T Graham, I love that guy. I started really hitting it hard with him my junior year. Me, Kwan and Trev, we would hit with each other a ton and we'd all hit with T all the time my junior year. My big thing my junior year was really working almost like on visualization more than anything else. It got to the point during the season that we were doing a ton of drills because I wanted to be as comfortable as I could in the box, as loose as I could be. I tracked a ton of pitches and formed a better understanding of my zone and where I want to hit pitches, and just worked on my approach in general. That was a huge part.

Mitchell Verburg, pitcher: Working with Tyler, he does a great job and he really cares about our performance and our mental process. He really helped me clear my head on the mound. I've always been very, very competitive. But during my injury, I was a mental head case. Just worrying, anxiety. I started working with Tyler in the middle of the 2018 season when I hit a lower low, and it really helped me eliminate my anxiety and calm me down. It took a long time to master it, I would say I haven't mastered it yet, but to be an amateur at it took a while because it's a tough process. It really helped me a lot (in 2019) when I was going good, and it actually helped me a lot when it was going bad because it helped me reset my brain and get back into my process.

Tyler Malone, infielder/outfielder: I started working with T Graham the beginning of my sophomore year. Meditation is super cool because it always forces you to be in the moment and recognize the thoughts that are going on in your head. We learned that thoughts aren't necessarily bad things, it's just about what you decide to give your attention to. Because if you give your attention to negative thoughts, of course the negative thoughts are going to consume you. Or you can address that there are negative thoughts taking place and basically redirect them into positive thoughts. You feel super relaxed and super peaceful in the moment, and that's something that helped me a lot in the World Series. That's honestly the best I've ever felt.

T Graham was great because we not only worked on hitting stuff, but a lot of it was just mentality and a lot of mental aspects that guys deal with but don't necessarily know how to deal with. The team was doing a lot of meditation stuff and it was a good group, a good corps of people who really started to work with T. By the end of the year, a lot of the starters were doing his stuff. Nick and Cadyn kind of had their own thing and you just let them do their thing because they're beasts, but a lot of dudes were doing it.

Kyle Nobach, outfielder: Tyler Graham was somebody who really helped me and influenced me and still does to this day. He taught me a lot about the game and how to play at Oregon State. I actually started working with him before I ever played at Oregon State. In the fall, I hadn't played in games, I started going to the cage every single night, I was just working on things, and he'd mentor me, tell me things I needed to work on, teach me to swing. It's something I really fell in love with and something we still talk about to this day. His love of hitting, his passion for hitting and his mindset, he taught me the attitude it takes to play at Oregon State. I wouldn't say it was completely Tyler Graham, but we spent a lot of time together.

Jack Anderson, outfielder: T Graham was kind of the first coach to really show an interest in me and give me time to work with him, and he was just like that with everyone. I was thankful that he offered that to me, a "hey, let me know if you want to hit" kind of thing just because he was Tyler Graham in my mind. I started working with him sophomore year with Nobey … and we would always hit with him, so I got to know him, and that was really before he got to really understanding the mental side of the game and it was us kind of figuring things out.

I think that was his first time really coaching, so he was learning new things, working with us and helping us with the mental aspect of how to coach the game. Then he got into meditation and that was really the first time I had worked on that as well. I didn't do it as much as those other guys because I was usually meditating in my own way per se, I was more low-key and focused on what I needed to focus on.

But I remember, it was hilarious, I was kind of on the fence with all the meditation stuff during that year. I was like "ah man, that seems like a lot of time to do before the game," because I just wanted to go out there and play. Then we got to the championship and I was like "oh gosh, I need some meditation right now!" I was freaking out. That was the first time in like a couple months where I went to T Graham and was like "dude, I need some help right now." And he was like "dude, OK, sounds good." That was the cool part about T Graham, man. He threw a lot of stuff at us, and it was up to us to figure out what we needed to learn and take from what he was saying. That helped me so much and he was just one of those guys you call up and he'd give you advice because he'd been there and done that. He was pretty valuable behind the scenes with everything.

Kyle Nobach: I meditated before every single game. Looking back now on what I've learned, I've met with a lot of peak performance coaches and people that teach the mental skills of baseball. I think it's important as a coach to develop how to help guys think on a baseball field because it's not easy. You've got to keep things simple and you've got to have a certain technique and a certain way of getting to a state where bad thoughts are bad in your mind, good thoughts are good and no thought is best. So, getting to a place of no thought on a baseball field, when you just understand things so much … it helps you.

Dylan Pearce, pitcher: I'm very close with T Graham. I've been fishing with him and I talk with him all the time about mentality stuff. Same with Alan, I am close friends with Alan. He's a great guy and he's helped me a lot.

Bill Rowe, undergraduate assistant coach: When I was a player, Mitch (Canham) and I were fishing at these ponds out here in Corvallis multiple times per week. So, I kept that tradition going and brought a lot of players out fishing like Dylan Pearce, Zak Taylor, Kyler McMahan.

We're going to the same ponds and catching the same fish, and I think that's such a special thing for those players to be able to travel five minutes and escape completely and focus totally on something other than baseball, but still talk about baseball if you want while you're out there. I think that type of mental medication is really what helps when you're doing everything else you possibly can. The fishing thing seems to be where it works for athletes, it's easy for them to turn everything off and let go, and that can be difficult to do for these guys.

Dylan Pearce: With Alan, I mainly ask him about stuff like long toss regimen and what he'll do, and also some pitch-forming kind of stuff. I talk with both T Graham and Alan about mentality. They are big into meditation. I'm not a meditation kind of person, I don't thrive in that type of area. I'm a big visualizer and a visualization kind of person, so I will like to sit alone, by myself. I don't want to hear anybody talk or anything like that and I just want to breathe and visualize what I'm doing, and that was a thing where they said "hey, that's totally OK."

When you're doing that visualization, they were giving me options and mental things to do where at times, just as a normal person if you believe or have the things they were telling you to believe, you might go "oh man, you're super cocky." But no, you've got to have that in order to be successful. You've got to walk in and go "I'm the best, period. I'm better than everybody here. No one can stay in my way, no one is better than I am." You have to have that mentality. It's not that you're coming out to people that way, telling them they're trash or anything like that. You have that inside of you knowing that you can take on anybody, and that's what built that strong mental preparation for coming into the games.

Zak Taylor: Alan Jaeger was a huge part, too. I think him and T Graham worked hand in hand, especially on the mental side of the game, developing a process for when I was hitting in the box. I think working with T Graham and Alan really helped me take my game to the next level because that postseason, I played pretty well. I prepared so much and I visualized myself in those moments so much that when it actually happened, it had already happened thousands of times because I had already put myself in those moments. When you visualize something, your brain can't tell if that's just make-believe or if it's reality. So, for me especially, the more I can visualize, it's like the more I'm doing that over and over and over. I'm getting those repetitions of being there without actually being there, so it's like tricking your brain that you have all these reps in a sense. For me, that was huge.

Alan Jaeger: Zak, like Gret the year before, came up to me at USC and was very similar to Gret. He was so interested, almost like you could tell he was saying "hey, one day I'm going to coach and I want to start getting ahead of the game on this." I think maybe he mentioned he was going to be a sports psych student or he was into psychology already at that point, but he was just interested and fired up and wanted to talk. So yeah, we talked at USC and I probably gave him my number. We started breaking down his process and we spent enough time together where he was a sponge and wanted to learn all this stuff. He got into the meditation like Gret, he wanted to do it every day, he wanted it to be part of his world.

Jake Mulholland, pitcher: Alan was big on the mental side of the game, which is something I had never really heard before he came around. Just the importance of visualization and being able to be present is huge in baseball. Being able to flush what just happened and bringing yourself back to the present moment is one of the biggest things I was able to learn pretty early on, and that was something Alan really tried to hammer into us when we'd talk to him. We'd meet with him and visualize almost every day in Arizona in 2017 before I had even played here. He was really good at helping guys be in the present and getting them to be at their best.

Kyle Nobach: Alan would come out and we had multiple conversations and mental conversations about how to think in-game. It was very simple because the game isn't easy. You've got to keep things simple and you've got to play under control. It's a game of emotion and that can kind of take over, but you've got to be able to focus on one thing and be under control, smooth and easy. When there's 30,000 people in the crowd, for me, I just need to calm down. Because I was fired up, I was ready to go. It was good competition, so you need to get to a place where you're not thinking about that, you're not worried about the other team.

Dylan Pearce: With a lot of guys, I saw not so much their performances shoot up, but definitely their attitude when they were in the game did. They seemed so much more relaxed. When something bad would happen, you could definitely see them let that go a lot more, and that would just allow them to ease into things and not be so pressured with what they were doing.

Tyler Graham: None of the kids really have it coming into college, right? Nick Madrigal is probably the only guy I've ever seen that just had it coming into college as a freshman, because it's a tough game going from high school into a big program. You're on the big stage, and not too many kids have a strong mental game coming into college. Everybody needs it, and Nick was probably the only kid I've ever seen as a freshman that had that mentality, the inner confidence, the self-belief and was able to deal with failure. He's one-of-a-kind in that sense.

Besides Nick, there really aren't too many kids that didn't need it. Adley already had it, too, he was very similar to Nick. Adley meditated too and it probably helped him out, but Adley was one of the most mentally-strong kids that I've ever been around. He was on a similar stage as Nick in that they already had a really good mental game and were able to be the same guy whether they were struggling or weren't struggling. They always had a good attitude and they always believed in themselves, those two were pretty special in that sense.

Adley Rutschman, catcher: I really was drawn to (meditation), just from the standpoint of how I felt after doing it. I was able to make it personal, you were able to make it for yourself. As you get better at it, you're able to find out "OK, what do I want to get out of this and how do I want to go about every single session, what do I need?" That's what I really liked about it. Just so much right now with social media and your phone and everything, life gets so busy. That 20, 25 minutes every day that you're able to relax in your thoughts is huge.

Trevor Larnach: At least six or seven of the starters were doing it. And when it comes to that team, most of the starters and the guys who were really putting in the same kind of work were on the same page of things. Obviously we all had the same goal and everything, but to have six or seven guys before the game doing that because we think that it helps us goes to show that our whole team was willing to do whatever together to better ourselves.

Tyler Graham: (Head coach Pat Casey) was all about it. He let anyone do it, he was into it, so a lot of credit goes to him, too. Because you know, old-school coaches didn't have that back in the day so it maybe isn't necessarily their belief system, but Case was completely open to it and supported it. Without his support, we probably wouldn't have gotten any of the kids to buy in. ... Yeskie was definitely into it, he supported it as well. The pitchers that did it saw big results.

Trevor Larnach: Coach Case was pretty old-school, pretty hard-nosed, and I'm thankful for that because honestly I think you need a little bit more of that nowadays. That style of coaching, that style of teaching, I loved it, personally. I think it brings the best out of people. Some people may think otherwise. As far as meditation goes, he was not really affiliated with that. But when it comes to winning and if it's something that helps us win, he's not going to do anything against that. He's never going to say anything against that because he's a guy that will do anything to win, and I think that kind of mentality really rubbed off on our team, especially myself. When you've got something that has science backing it up and a lot of successful people do it, why not try it? And if it helps you perform at the highest level and you win, I mean I wouldn't argue against it, either.

Pat Casey, head coach: Tyler was hired as our player development guy. And that player development guy is there for the players' needs, mostly off the field. Mentally, how does he help them? How can he help them with the things they go through that aren't at the field? How can he help them with their social life mixed with their student-athlete life with the rigors that you go through in the sport of baseball, missing so many classes? How do you get a guy to handle times when they don't play well? So, I think he had a vital role in helping those guys from a mental aspect, and of course he had such great respect because he was a big-league player and he played with his tail on fire. I think there are a lot of successes that guys had that had a lot to do with how he helped them mentally understand what they needed to do and how they needed to do it. How to play the game, how to be ready to play the game, how to prepare to play the game, how to handle adversity. I think he was a valuable part of what we did.

BOB LUNDEBERG

CHAPTER VII

PLAYOFF GOSS

Selection Monday always represents the beginning of a new college baseball season. While their Pac-12 title defense fell short, the 2018 Beavers still possessed a resume worthy of a high NCAA Tournament national seed. Oregon State was rewarded for its strong body of work with the No. 3 overall seed behind No. 1 Florida and No. 2 Stanford, the Pac-12 champion. The ESPN telecast unveiled the bracket region by region, starting with the Gainesville Regional in the top-left corner and ending in the bottom-right with the Corvallis Regional. After sitting through the first 15 four-team pod announcements, the Beavers finally learned their opening-round opponent would be regional No. 4 seed Northwestern State. The next team revealed was No. 3 seed San Diego State. By that point, a few people in the Reser Stadium club level viewing party knew who the No. 2 seed was going to be.

Nick Madrigal, infielder: Going through the selection show, we wanted LSU. That was the team we wanted.

Dylan Pearce, pitcher: We hadn't seen them pop up yet. It was in the back of our heads, but not really. When the Corvallis Regional finally popped up and LSU came up on the screen, we were freaking out. We were so excited and we were like "YES! We're taking it from you guys."

Tyler Malone, infielder/outfielder: It's like something you see in books or movies. They were coming to Corvallis, and we were totally ready for it.

FINISH

Nick Madrigal: To see it unfold the way it did, we couldn't have written it up any better. Everyone on the team was so excited when their name was announced that they were coming to Corvallis.

Cadyn Grenier, infielder: We were sitting in the room just itching for that name to be called in our bracket. And LSU was good again, there's no doubt. They made the playoff, they were good again. They may not have been as good as they were the year before, but we were sitting in that room and we just ate it up. Like normally when that happens, people only cheer when your name gets called. But no, no. We cheered when LSU got put in our bracket. That's how that was, and that's the team we wanted to see.

The first baseball meeting between Oregon State and LSU came in 2012 at the Baton Rouge Regional. The host Tigers won both matchups, including a 6-5, extra-innings victory in the regional final. The teams faced off again in 2017, and the Beavers dismantled LSU 13-1 at the College World Series. But the Tigers got the last laugh by upsetting OSU twice to advance to the CWS finals, ending the Beavers' dream season.

LSU lost a few key pieces to the draft and wasn't the same monster it had been the year before. Still, as a college baseball power, LSU won two of its final three SEC series and made it all the way to the SEC Tournament final. For their efforts, the Tigers were shipped west for a potential matchup with the vengeful Beavers.

Michael Gretler, infielder: When they announced LSU, that place went pretty crazy. Obviously, having played them the year before … it was for sure a different team, they'd lost a lot of their starters, but hey, it's LSU. They ended our season the year before and we wanted to definitely end their season in 2018.

Steven Kwan, outfielder: Oh God, it was awesome. I'm usually used to being very PC and non-controversial, but I guess since I'm not on the team anymore I can say this with a little more pride. When we saw their name in our regional, we started bursting out cheering. I remember that all of our answers to the media were supposed to be "oh no, we're just excited that we saw our name there." But everybody on the team was pumped we were facing LSU again, like this was our revenge tour. That was the absolute first thing on all of our minds. We didn't want to stir up any trouble with media stuff, but we were thrilled, thrilled to play LSU.

I think it was Nick who made sure when we were talking to the media to try and not amp things up, don't make a big deal about it. I remember watching Fehm in an interview, and he was talking about how all the cheering was about the (selection show being over). We were all teasing him about that and were saying, "nice, man. Way to lie to them! Like dude, how did you think of that?!"

Bryce Fehmel, pitcher: Hey, that was right. We got to go home after the selection show! We were stoked to get another chance to play them since they'd knocked us out the previous year. I'm sure the selection committee did it on purpose, setting them up with us, and I'm glad they did. They were the one team we wanted to play again.

Nate Yeskie, pitching coach: I had a feeling it was coming when I saw they weren't going off of certain things. There's always a, I don't know if you want to call it a grenade or a party popper, that goes off on that board where it almost seems like there's a hidden agenda in there, somebody is trying to poke the bear with a stick.

Jack Anderson, outfielder: We almost couldn't believe the committee put them there because there were always conspiracy theories and we'd always think "oh, LSU always gets the best draws." Then we saw them at our place and were like "well this ain't a good draw for them, that's for sure."

Trevor Larnach, outfielder: I knew that those boys didn't have a chance when they were in our bracket because of how our year had ended. They couldn't have landed in a worse spot. Not only is it our home field and it's our regional, just the energy and the fire that really lit under us after we saw their name in our regional, you can't really describe it. I don't think there was any preparing them for that series.

Pat Casey, head coach: I was thrilled to get another shot at them, I can tell you that. I can also tell you that we probably sat back and said "hey, that's a pretty tough draw," for getting a team coming in the way they were playing.

Jake Mulholland, pitcher: Maybe for just a minute you've got those butterflies that they're coming because it's "that team," but honestly once the game starts, once the lights go on, it doesn't matter. It can't matter. Because once you start worrying about your opponent, you know who they are, that's a slippery slope. There obviously was some excitement that it was LSU, but you can't let it carry over into the game. That was one of the things the coaches really talked to us about because they could tell we were excited, but they told us "hey, it doesn't matter. We're playing the game of baseball, and it's going to be who plays the game of baseball the best."

Brandon Eisert, pitcher: We were excited for that chance to play them again and sort of get that revenge but in the end, it didn't matter who we were going to face.

We had one goal in mind. It could've been any other team and we would've had that same motivation.

Before a potential rematch with LSU, the Beavers first needed to get through a different Louisiana team — Northwestern State. Bryce Fehmel was his usual self, as Oregon State cruised to a 9-3 regional-opening win over the Demons. Earlier in the day, LSU — playing its first game west of Texas since 2010 — took care of business against San Diego State to set up the regional showdown OSU wanted. On a perfect 75-degree evening for baseball, an all-time record crowd of 4,009 people packed into Goss Stadium for the College World Series rematch between the Beavers (45-10-1) and Tigers (38-25).

Ryan Gorton, undergraduate assistant coach: It was probably the most electric I've seen Goss. There was just an energy in the stadium because they had a pretty good section of fans that came who were really loud, and our fans were trying to drown them out and be even louder. It was under the lights and it felt like a football game, honestly. Just with the pregame hype, and you could feel there was a buzz in the stadium.

Bryce Fehmel: The energy in the dugout, the energy in the crowd, it was just a surreal feeling to have that home-field advantage against that powerhouse of a program.

Pat Casey: The crowd was as excited about us playing them as we were because everybody remembered that they had beat us the year before. To get LSU to come to Corvallis, Oregon, and play baseball was awesome.

Nick Madrigal: There was definitely a lot of motivation behind what happened the year before. We were excited, and once we got to the games for that series, all the fans were rocking. Everyone in the dugout was definitely hyped up for that series. It was probably the best atmosphere I saw in Corvallis during my time there.

Jack Anderson: Especially the first one, we were just ready to rock. There've been some big games at Goss, but I think there was a bit of that vengeance, vendetta kind of feel. Everyone was fired up for us, but there was also a little bit of stink for LSU that brought it to a life. They were kind of our rival for the year, so the fact we got to play them at home was pretty cool. I'd definitely never heard Goss like that before, at the beginning of those games.

The pitching bout was also set up to be a dandy — Luke Heimlich against LSU ace Zack Hess, who had closed both of the Tigers' College World Series victories over Oregon

State the year before. Heimlich didn't get to face LSU in 2017 and was not at his best in the Corvallis Regional.

Andy Jenkins, assistant coach: We were pretty excited to get Luke that opportunity to pitch against them and go at them, which he didn't get to do in 2017. Luke had a great year, and I think the emotions of everything that happened with Luke and the emotions of having a powerhouse come into Goss … Luke wasn't very sharp, and I think it took him a couple innings to get going. He probably pitched one of his weaker games, and he was so good that year that even in his weaker games, he still got outs. I remember one double play in particular that was back to him with the bases loaded that shifted the momentum a little bit.

Luke Heimlich, pitcher: I was really bad that weekend. I walked the house and … I think I threw like 50% balls. It was just not a good day, I felt very out of whack, but I got a couple lucky breaks. I got a comebacker (in the first inning) and almost threw it over Adley's head at home, but he made an incredible play to catch it, tag home and throw the guy out at first that got me out of the inning. There was another lucky time when they popped up a bunt. And obviously the offense took care of business, so we were never super nervous because we jumped on them early, but I was very out of rhythm that game.

Pat Casey, after the game: The first thing Luke's going to tell you is that he didn't throw well, and that's the sign of a great competitor when you don't feel like you threw well and you give up one run.

The key to the game, the key to the whole thing was … the exchange that Rutschman made on the double play in the first inning. (It) was unbelievable. To catch the ball over his head, because (Heimlich) didn't make a very good throw, the exchange he made to turn the double play was huge. That guy is a freak athletically. Then the play that Luke made when he dove for the ball on the bunt and was able to from his knees throw the guy out at second base … young guys thrive on momentum, and those things are huge.

Nate Yeskie: Heimlich wasn't sharp but we played pretty well. We stretched it out late and it got completely out of hand, went just berserk offensively.

Heimlich still battled his way through seven innings. He gave up a single run on six hits with three strikeouts, four walks and two hit batters. It was plenty good enough on a day when Oregon State exorcised some demons by roughing up Hess and Caleb Gilbert. Hess was tagged for nine runs in 3 1/3 innings while Gilbert allowed three in 2 2/3 as the Beavers piled up 15 hits in a runaway 14-1 thrashing.

FINISH

LSU licked its wounds and knocked off Northwestern State the following afternoon to earn another shot at OSU in the regional final. The rematch didn't go any better for the Tigers. Steven Kwan led off the bottom of the first with a home run and the Beavers rode Kevin Abel to a 12-0 shutout to clinch the Corvallis Regional title.

Pat Bailey, associate head coach: We smoked them twice, they weren't even close games even though they had a very talented team. Them being the team that beat us the year before made it even more fun because we went from them dominating us for two of the three games we played them (in 2017) to us dominating them that two-game series.

Steven Kwan: It was satisfying, very satisfying, seeing (Tigers head coach) Paul Mainieri over there. LSU was just helpless. It didn't matter who they sent out, we were putting a beating on them. It never got dull because LSU had that little pocket of fans and they were loud, like they travel well. It was cool because we were beating them up, then fans would start cheering to try and get some momentum going and Goss would just drown them out. It was awesome.

Nick Madrigal: We were excited for that matchup all year long. For it to get there, we weren't surprised it ended up that way just because of all the talent we had. We knew those guys couldn't compete with us that year, we had way too many guys from the year before to let them do that to us again. So yeah, going through it, we felt like there was no way they were going to come into Corvallis (and win). We tried to embarrass them almost, that was our thing. For it to end up the way it did, that was good.

Trevor Larnach: The sole factor was we just wanted revenge, dude, and that's what we did. We didn't take them lightly and we didn't stop. I think the scoreboard would reflect that.

Jack Anderson: That was a blast playing those guys. And I think they were hurt, weren't playing their best baseball, too. So, we took it to them and made sure they enjoyed themselves out on the West Coast for the first time in a while. I don't see them wanting to come back for a bit.

Kevin Abel, pitcher: As far as my favorite wins from that season, I'd say the LSU win was my favorite because it was (at Goss Stadium) in front of the OSU fans with that atmosphere and the energy they brought. It was something I had never seen or been a part of, that's for sure. I mean walking down from the bullpen and hearing the O-S-U chant louder than ever, knowing what LSU had done to OSU the year before and how much it meant to all of the older guys who were on the team last year to really make a statement against them, it was just a lot of fun and something I am very grateful to have been a part of.

Making his fifth start of the year, Abel was sensational in the regional finale. The freshman worked eight-plus innings and surrendered three hits with eight strikeouts and a walk. Oregon State had finally found its No. 3 starter.

Pat Casey: He just kept getting better and better. When he pitched against Stanford, he got us into the (fifth) and was lights-out before he got into a bit of trouble. He kept getting better and better, and that deal against LSU was dominant. From that point forward we knew, and he knew, that he was a Friday night guy and he was going to be a real guy.

Cadyn Grenier: Obviously that whole year our Sunday mixture of Abel and Grant (Gambrell) was turbulent at times, and that's why they kept switching off. We didn't really have a true one between the two, but when Abel started to pitch better, and came out shoving like he did against LSU and later on, you're just like "dude, what is this?! You just gave us a pitcher who has been absolutely average the entire year, and now he's a superstar? We just added this to our team? Dude, this is like an early Christmas present!"

Nick Madrigal: I remember his stuff, he was on from the beginning. The dugout was hyped up because going into that, we weren't sure. Kevin had some good starts, some glimpses of being really good but up until that game, we weren't really sure. For him to perform on the biggest stage of that year to that point was definitely something everyone was excited about. That was a huge moment in the season to see that.

Nate Yeskie: People talk about the Mississippi State game and the Arkansas game, but I still think the best game he threw was in the regional against LSU. He was flat nasty that night. Luke was maybe a little jittery the night before against those guys and just the way the whole thing played itself out, that was when Kevin really started to turn the corner for me.

After the fourth inning, Abel threw a curveball to one of their guys and I saw Paul Mainieri in the dugout, his spine kind of stiffened a little bit. He turned his head and neck slowly to look at somebody else like "oh, man. If he gets that thing going, this thing's over." And they were scuffling a little bit, but Abel didn't throw a curveball until about the fourth inning. When he racked off that filthy one, I think they went "uh oh, we're in for it tonight."

Kevin Abel: I knew they were a good team, but we had done a lot of research and things like that to figure out how we were going to attack their hitters and how well my stuff played into that. I don't want to give too many things away to SEC teams, but I guess if you go watch film you'll see how many changeups I threw to SEC teams because they don't see it that often in their conference. They just see (hard fastballs) and 82 mile per hour sliders all the time. Knowing that really helped, and all I had to do was make pitches and things were going to happen behind me.

Jack Anderson: Kevin had come in in relief (against UCLA) the previous week and pitched pretty well. We really had no other viable option at that point for that starting role, so I think we were like "all right. Whatever we were thinking about, whether it was positive or negative with Kevin, we need to rally behind him. Because he's going to be our guy in regionals and super regionals." We knew he had the stuff, and I think the growth he made in those weeks between Arizona and the regional, it was just crazy how much more mature he looked on the mound and how he went about his business. That's a testament to Yeskie, Luke and Drew (Rasmussen), who wasn't even pitching, and some of the other leaders on the team. Kevin could've very easily put his glove down, it was a fork in the road. He could've worked his tail off like he did, or just let it go and gotten ready for the next year. But he decided to take the harder route which was working his tail off to get better those next few weeks. The results speak for themselves over that next month and a half. He pitched some of the best baseball I've ever seen.

Oregon State outscored LSU 26-1 over 18 uncompetitive innings at the Corvallis Regional. Paul Mainieri said it best in his final postgame press conference of the season: "They obviously have a much better team than we do this year."

Offensive explosions had become the norm for OSU during the 2018 season. The lineup featured the most dangerous top six in the nation. Kwan would lead off, followed by Cadyn Grenier, Nick Madrigal, Trevor Larnach, Adley Rutschman and Michael Gretler. A combination of Jack Anderson, Tyler Malone and Kyle Nobach filled the seven and eight spots, depending on matchups, while Zak Taylor held down the No. 9 role. With no holes in the lineup, OSU set numerous offensive school records, including runs scored (518), hits (753), doubles (151), home runs (67) and total bases (1,145). The Beavers led the Pac-12 in those same categories, and also led the conference in batting average (.321), slugging percentage (.488) and on-base percentage (.416).

Cadyn Grenier: My junior year, we probably had one of the best college offensive lineups ever. And there were a lot of guys in there that weren't top-tier draft picks and stuff. But in college they were just as good as it gets, and normally you don't expect those guys to be that way.

Everyone played up to the level of the person before or after them in the order, so we didn't have a true seven, eight and nine who were easy outs. We had guys who were going to get after it and make you work to get them out, and we felt like we were the only team in the world that had that. We didn't feel like other teams had a one through nine where you had to worry about the eight- and- nine-hole hitters hitting. They were just there to draw walks and get guys over or something. But not our team. Our team was nine studs.

Trevor Larnach: It was a joke. I put it on myself to take over KJ (Harrison's) spot, but I remember each game I'd look at that lineup, top to bottom, and I would laugh. You couldn't even compare us to another team because it was just a joke. That, mixed with the pitching ... I've always said that if we had our sophomore year pitching with our junior year lineup mixed with KJ and (Christian Donahue) and a few other guys, it would've been even more ridiculous. You're never going to have a perfect world, but the fact that our numbers were what they were, you just look at it and are like "oh my gosh. The fact that you've got to face this team as an opponent is pretty ridiculous."

Pat Casey: It just had so much balance of what you need in a lineup. It had speed, it had power, it had diversity. We had guys who could slash, guys who could bunt, guys who could hit home runs. It had experience, and you had people that were interchangeable, you had people that could hit in different spots, and it was really nice.

Jack Anderson is a great example here again. Him and Nobey, you could play either one of them in left field or either one of them in right field. Both those guys would get on base. You had a really experienced hitter in Michael Gretler who was really overlooked because so much attention was being given to the draft and people who were going to go high. And those guys should've got that attention, but he was overlooked. He was in the background driving in 50 runs and playing his fanny off at third base and being a huge inspiration and leader for our club. Steven Kwan, his ability to get on base and his ability to get into good counts and force pitchers to work ... everybody had a niche. We certainly, in the middle, were outstanding. We could just hurt you in a lot of different ways.

Steven Kwan: I always tell people that I had the easiest job. I just had to get on, I didn't have to produce in any way. I had to get on, make sure in my at-bats I swing at strikes and I'll get hit in by everybody behind me, and I stuck to that. I was very fortunate because I think a lot of pitchers were like "we can't walk this kid because now we have the brunt of the lineup coming," so I got a lot of fastballs. Obviously I had Cadyn behind me, and Nick, so I got a lot more pitches to hit than I think I normally would've been able to. But gosh, it was clockwork. I'd get on and have so many guys behind who could absolutely rake.

Nate Yeskie: Against LSU in '17 in the World Series, Kwan push bunts to start the game that we win and he's 3.65 (seconds from home to first). In '18 in the regionals, he starts out the game down 0-2, he hasn't swung the bat. He works it back to 3-2 and on the ninth pitch of the at-bat he hits a home run, and now we're up 1-0. So, you look at how he advanced as a player.

And getting Gretler back was huge, huge. I've had coaches in our conference tell me that he was really an unsung hero, and I'd be hard-pressed to think that in the last 10 years of our conference there's been a better third baseman. Michael was Steady Eddy over there and just a calming influence because his personality was different than Cadyn's, Cadyn's was different than Nick's, and then you had Zak Taylor on the other side who was coming into his own and just a really good college baseball player. He kept getting a little bit better every day, a little bit better every day. People forget this, and I tend to remind them at times when I remember, that Zak is a year older than Adley and they're from the same high school. So, Zak would always take a shot at Adley here and there just to keep him straight and let him know like "hey, listen kid. When we were in high school, I was the top dog and don't think those things have changed because we're here now and you may be putting up better numbers or hitting higher in the lineup." They had that funny dynamic between them.

Zak Taylor, first baseman: That lineup was awesome, it was so much fun. I didn't really think about it that much at the time which is probably better for me. You don't realize until afterward just how good some of these guys really are. But I knew my role in that lineup and I feel like I really embraced that, especially during that junior season. I was all-in.

But oh my gosh, it was so much fun to be a part of because top to bottom, guys had different skills in their bag, they knew the players they were, they didn't try to do more than they knew they could do. You have that awesome combination of those gritty guys on your team like your Nobachs and Jack Andersons, then you've got your superstars with Rutsch, Trev, Cadyn, Kwan leading things off. It was fun, it was fun. … When we went into games, we knew we were going to bang a little bit and we were confident. Those guys really helped build me up and build my confidence up and make me believe "absolutely, 100% I can do this." I was probably the least talented guy in that lineup, but I had so much confidence, especially going into the postseason. I don't think I've ever had more confidence, just because of my supporting cast.

Dylan Pearce: Still to this day, I have never faced a batting lineup that had the presence, the feel and the control of the batter's box as that lineup. The lineup for Oregon State in 2018 was so deadly. I mean you're starting it off with Steven Kwan, Cadyn Grenier, Nick Madrigal, Trevor Larnach, Adley Rutschman and quite a few more. Those guys just ran that lineup, and it was so cool to see those guys work. They were unbelievable to watch and see how good they were. Throwing against those guys in practice definitely sharpened my skills, not only in the pitches that I threw but in the location I threw them just because I was facing such a high-caliber group of guys.

Pat Bailey: The thing that's amazing about those guys is how well they manage the strike zone. Oh my gosh, I mean (Kwan, Larnach and Madrigal) were three of the best guys I've ever seen since I've been here in terms of managing the strike zone. Everyone had different issues. Nick's issue with managing the strike zone was, because he had unbelievable hand-eye coordination and hardly ever struck out, sometimes he swung at pitches that he shouldn't have swung at and didn't hit them as well, but the ball always touched his bat so he got himself out every once and a while. Nick is an aggressive-type personality, you're not going to see Nick ever have something like Kwany's junior year where he ended up with (50) walks and (18) strikeouts. Nick won't strike out that many times in a season, but he's not going to walk (50) times, either.

When you look at Trevor Larnach, if Trevor came back from an at-bat and walked up and said "Bails, that ball was four inches off the plate. It was on my knees but it was four inches off the plate." If I went and looked at that on video, that ball would've been four inches off the plate. That's how good he was at seeing the baseball. So, after he started playing for us a lot and I watched more video, I never argued with him when he said a pitch wasn't a strike because I knew it wasn't. That's how good he was at seeing and managing the strike zone.

With Kwany his junior year, we were probably 10 to 15 games in, and I said "I know your deal is to get into counts, but you can't start out 0-2, 1-2 all the time. There have to be times when you see a pitch early where you have to go after it. Because everybody knows you don't swing at the first pitch, so they throw it right down the middle for a strike. I LOVE the fact that you manage the strike zone, but every once in a while when you get a pitch to hit, you've got to strike it." And I think at the time he was probably hitting about .270, and he ended up hitting (.355) that year. But all three of those guys, they are as good as anybody we've ever had here at managing the strike zone. When we got pitches to hit we didn't miss them, especially down the stretch. From when we played San Diego in those midweek games, from that point on, oh my gosh. We were just hotter than a pistol offensively.

While the majority of the team had immense success to begin the year in Surprise, Arizona, Kwan went hitless in his first 11 at-bats and was batting .231 after six games. Pat Casey never considered a different option atop Oregon State's lineup, and Kwan got back to his old ways before long. He went on to slash .355/.463/.457 as a junior and earn first-team all-Pac-12 honors along with Bryce Fehmel, Grenier, Heimlich, Larnach, Madrigal and Rutschman.

Steven Kwan: My three years, I actually always did terrible in Arizona. I don't know what it was, I don't think it was anything, I just didn't play well in Arizona. My third year, I went in with a boatload of confidence and it started happening again. I was like "geez, come on, this can't happen again!" I started losing some confidence, it was obviously my draft year and I never thought I was going to get drafted until the Cape (the previous summer) when some teams were talking. I was like "oh, how typical of me. I get so close and now I'm going to start blowing it."

But I remember Case had a really good talk with me, it was maybe the second week in Arizona. He goes "Kwany, how we feeling today?" And I'm like "uh, I'm hanging in there, coach. I'm working on it, I've got you." And he goes "all right, well I'm going to let you figure it out. You're going to be batting leadoff the next day, and the day after that you're going to be batting leadoff, and the day after that you'll be batting leadoff, so just keep working on it." And hearing that, it helped my confidence so much. It didn't matter how I was doing. He was going to keep giving me an opportunity to figure it out. I wasn't playing for my job, I was just able to really hunker down and get back to it. And I think a couple weekends after that I started getting back on track. Case was really the help I needed there.

Pat Casey: He had earned that position. He had proven himself and Kwany was a guy that was really hard on himself. He wants to be a perfectionist. He wants to be the best, and he was more upset at himself feeling like he wasn't helping the team than he ever was that he wasn't getting hits. So, I just said "hey Kwany, the nice thing about you is you can go read that lineup card every day and you're going to be at the top of the order. You're going to play every day because everybody goes through times where they don't swing the bat, it just happens to be a little bit early for you." I never doubted that guy at all, and his confidence level went through the roof. I think by the time we got to conference, he felt like he could hit anybody in the country and anybody in any league, including the big leagues. That kind of stuff rubs off on people.

Pat Bailey: I think the biggest thing for Steven is that he's a really talented guy, he just needed to believe it. Once he got going his sophomore year ... he's probably the best leadoff hitter I've ever had on any team I've coached or helped coach. Kwany was a real key to our team those last two years in terms of the great job he did getting on base to be a set-up guy for the people we had behind him.

Pat Casey: He was just an unbelievable leadoff guy because he could do it all. He could push, drag, hit the ball in the gap, hurt you with a home run every once in a while. He played the heck out of center field, he energized us, always played with energy, man. Those guys are important to have at the front of your lineup. Those guys can get on base, they've got speed and can turn singles into doubles, doubles into triples. Kwany, he was special.

Since its inception, the Major League Baseball Draft has been held in the middle of college baseball's postseason. The 2018 draft began Monday, June 4, the day after Oregon State finished off LSU at the Corvallis Regional. Madrigal was expected to be a top-five selection while mock drafts had Larnach going in the middle of the first round (43 total picks) and Grenier, who played through nagging leg injuries for much of the regular season, landing anywhere from the back end of the first round to the third. Grenier was the 2018 Pac-12 defensive player of the year and received the College Baseball Foundation's Brooks Wallace Award as the nation's best shortstop.

The Detroit Tigers took Auburn pitcher Casey Mize with the No. 1 overall pick. Georgia Tech catcher Joey Bart was next off the board, followed by Wichita State infielder Alex Bohm. The Chicago White Sox snagged Madrigal with the fourth pick, making him the highest-drafted Beaver of all time (Michael Conforto previously held the honor by going 10th overall to the New York Mets in 2014). Larnach went to the Minnesota Twins at pick No. 20 while the Baltimore Orioles selected Grenier 37th overall. For the first time in program history, OSU had produced three first-round picks in the same draft.

Kyle Nobach, outfielder: That was absolutely incredible, it just gives me the chills thinking about it. The whole team was there ... and that's why Oregon State baseball and the organization is what it is. Every single person within the organization had a relationship with one another. It didn't matter up and down the chain of command, we were one family. We sat in that room and watched three kids have a moment that I don't even know if the top 1% of people could experience what they got to do. It was incredible and a powerful moment for them.

Drew Rasmussen, pitcher: It's the greatest thing ever. You spend so much time together that their success starts to feel like your success. You're always pulling for these guys, you want them to play well, you want good things to happen to them. So, to see all three of those guys get picked up, especially because the entire team was there in our players' lounge, hanging out watching the draft together. To hear their names called and just being able to surround them with love, happiness and joy, it was awesome.

Nick Madrigal: Leading up to draft day, it made things a little bit easier that we'd played (the day) before. It took my mind off of things, but it was an exciting time.

One thing that's funny about draft day, I can't remember if we had a workout or something before, but earlier that day I was actually just hanging out at the house and I knew my family was around, but I forgot what time the draft started. So, I was hanging around at the house and my girlfriend was over at the draft party. She texted me like "where are you at?" I think I had taken a nap at the house, and I almost missed the beginning of the draft! I raced over to the stadium, I mean I was there in plenty of time, but I had no idea what time the draft was starting. It was one of those things we look back on and laugh about now. So, I didn't catch any of the previews before, I saw a couple things when I got drafted, but leading up to it I didn't see all the draft previews that day or anything.

There was a lot of hard work that went into that moment and it was nice that my family traveled down, I had my brother there. And when the draft was going on, there were cameras there and the whole team was there for us. It was just a very exciting moment, and I was glad I got to share it with my teammates and my family. It was almost like a sigh of relief because I always thought about that moment after my high school draft came and went. I always hoped that I could be in the first round and hear my name called on TV, stuff like that. I worked extremely hard for that, and for it to actually happen really was a sigh of relief. One of the best decisions of my life was to go play for coach Casey and the staff there and all the guys that we had.

Pat Casey: I told Nick in high school "if you're a first-rounder, I'm going to pat you on the tail and say 'go get 'em.' But if you're not and you really believe that you are, all you've got to do is show up and show them how wrong they were." And man, he did. Not only did he show them that he's a first-rounder, I had a big-league team tell me that if they had the first pick that year, they would've taken Nick Madrigal one-one. That's amazing for a guy his size.

Jake Rodriguez, assistant coordinator of baseball camps: From the time he got here to the day he left, he earned everything. A very hard-working guy and a leader for his teammates. ... I talk to him probably almost every day, so him and I are really close. When he comes to Oregon, he stays with my wife and I, so we're really close with him and it's a great relationship. I'm a huge Cubs fan so having him play for the White Sox is a little tough on me, but other than that I'm really excited for him and his future and he's just a great person. I'm lucky that my son Tony will be able to look up to him as a baseball player and as a person.

Trevor Larnach: Draft day was nerve-racking for me. Nick didn't have to wait too long, but it felt like I had to wait three hours for my name to be called. And it wasn't just nerves for me, it was also very joyful. Obviously your family and yourself and your teammates work their hardest, and to see something like that is like a milestone being checked off, but at the same time it's rewarding at that point. We were all super stoked and happy for each other.

Nick Madrigal: That day, getting chosen, hearing everyone's name, it was great being able to celebrate with them. I was happy that I was next to Trevor. Being there, he was so anxious to get picked and I was anxious for him, and Cadyn as well. It was funny, I was almost more nervous for Trevor to get picked than I was. We were all hoping to hear his name called soon, and when it finally happened it was such a happy moment for everyone. Because I knew how hard Trevor and Cadyn worked throughout the three years together. And Trevor in particular, he transformed his swing so much and I saw him on a daily basis doing the little things, working on his swing. When a lot of people were at home doing other stuff, he was in the cage really trying to perfect his craft. For it to pay off for him, it was really cool to see.

Cadyn Grenier: Obviously, we knew Nick was going in the first five picks — that wasn't a secret. And we knew Trevor was going not too far after him. For me, I wasn't sure. I didn't know what was going to happen. We were hearing a lot of mixed things, a lot of guys saying "oh, he's going between 30 and 40" and some guys were saying "hey, he's probably not going until 40 to 50." We didn't know, so I didn't really watch. Once Nick was drafted, I turned on the Golden Knights versus Washington Capitals Stanley Cup Finals game. I had my own TV in the players' lounge and I was just sitting in front of it watching hockey. I wasn't watching the draft, and when Nick was drafted we were all obviously super stoked, and for Trevor as well. But we all knew that was going to happen, so we were there for them. And when it started getting closer for me, I was getting calls and I still didn't know if it was going to happen. Then they called my name and it was a surprise to everybody, which was super cool. I feel like it was cooler for me to not know than being a Nick or a Trevor where they knew they were going in the next two minutes.

Pat Casey: I had multiple scouts tell me "one of those guys will leave after their freshman year if they don't play short." I just marveled at how people don't think about other things that are important besides getting to play a position. They didn't know how much Nick and Cadyn wanted to win, they didn't know how much they both wanted and needed to be a part of a structured team, how much they cared about their teammates and how much they made winning and their teammates more important than playing the position they wanted. That's where they were underestimated, and they were both rewarded for that selfless style of play and attitude.

I'm just really proud of those guys for what they meant to Oregon State baseball and how that's going to affect their futures. I think there are a lot of guys at the professional level who were blown away that they both stayed and became what they became and gave up that ego of "hey, I have to be the guy playing shortstop." They knew what was more important and if they made that more important, meaning the team, that they would be rewarded for that individually. And they were by being first-rounders.

The MLB Draft continued the following day with rounds three through 10, and three more Beavers came off the board. Kwan went in the fifth round to the Cleveland Indians, an on-the-mend Drew Rasmussen was picked up by the Milwaukee Brewers in the sixth and the Pittsburgh Pirates snagged Gretler in the 10th. No other Beavers were selected when the 40-round draft concluded the next day.

The timing of the MLB Draft is less than ideal for college players on postseason-bound teams. For some, the draft and a professional future can get in the way of focusing on the season in progress. That was clearly not the case for Oregon State's draftees, who looked sharper than ever against LSU.

Pat Casey: I just feel like if getting drafted is a distraction, then you probably shouldn't have been drafted. (The draft) is what it is and you know what, good for you. But I don't feel like it ever really had an effect. Sometimes you have a lot of guys drafted, sometimes you don't. If you look at (2018), we had three guys in the first round and they didn't let it bother them. Guys like Larnach, Nick and Grenier, it was just like "OK, good. Let's go to work. The most important thing we're doing is what we're doing at Oregon State, we'll worry about the draft when we get done with winning a championship." And they played like that and approached it like that. I just think you go through enough pressures as a college player that it shouldn't distract you.

Drew Rasmussen: The coaching staff did a good job of making sure that our heads were always in the right place. I don't know if the coaching staff does it intentionally but from what I can remember, for the most part, most meetings with scouts and that kind of stuff get done before the season starts. You might have a meeting here or there during the season, but for the most part the scouts are very respectful and allow the players to just take care of business and focus on the field and ultimately compete. Our coaching staff did a really good job of protecting us and allowing us to focus on taking care of business every weekend.

Cadyn Grenier: I learned in high school that I couldn't play to the draft. I played with some guys in high school that felt like they had a chance to get drafted so they played to the scouts and had very sub-par years and ended up not getting drafted, and I didn't want that to happen to me. So, I had learned throughout high school that the only way I was going to play as good as I possibly could was to do everything I could to help the team win. That always made me play better, so I knew if I just did that the rest would handle itself. It helped that the only thing on my mind was that I wanted to win a national championship. I figured that was going to be my last year at Oregon State as long as everything happened in a good way, and all I focused on was "hey, all these dudes here, most of us are probably going to be gone next year. We have one more shot at this," and that's all we focused on, that's all we wanted.

Trevor Larnach: (The draft) is there, but for me it was just about how I went about my business on the field and off the field. When I say that, I mean the philosophy I have is doing everything right — on and off the field. Which means if you prepare as much as you can, everything will take care of itself once you get on the field. I think if I didn't give my all or if I didn't do something that I knew I could've gotten better at, I think it would've eaten away at me during the games and it would've started popping up in my head. But that never really was a thing because I tried to prepare myself so well for that season and it just let the floodgates open.

The ironic thing was I got drafted by Minnesota that week and then three days later we're playing a Minnesota team, so it was kind of two tests at once. How are you going to handle the draft and how are you going to handle playing a team from Minnesota next weekend?

The Corvallis Super Regional was set to be a battle of the rodents. No. 3 national seed Oregon State was set to face the 14th-seeded Minnesota Golden Gophers (the NCAA began seeding the top 16 teams, in order, in 2018. Previously, only the top eight received national seeds). Minnesota (44-13) won the Big Ten regular-season and tournament titles and went 3-0 hosting the Minneapolis Regional, defeating UCLA twice to advance. Big Ten baseball is often overlooked on the national stage, but the Golden Gophers were a complete team intent on shocking the world.

Kevin Abel: At first I remember thinking "damn, how in the hell is Minnesota good at baseball?" But they definitely belonged there and they were a very, very good team. It was a lot of fun to see the punches go back and forth, and each team just wearing them. Nobody was budging.

Pat Casey: Minnesota was extremely good. I'm telling you what, that team was loaded.

Zak Taylor: I always tell people that if we didn't play them in a super regional, I think they would've been one of the eight in Omaha for sure. I thought they were one of the better teams we played that year. They just had some dudes, especially on the mound, and their whole entire lineup was very balanced. I feel like they were pretty similar to us. Sure, they might not have had some of the star power that we did, but at the same time it was a very well-coached team that did things the right way. I think that's why we had such a good series with them.

Nate Yeskie: They had a deep, older, experienced lineup with an edge.

Ryan Gorton: I was super impressed with them. They were a veteran club and I thought they had really, really tough players. I know their second baseman (Luke Pettersen), he dove for a ball early in the second game and dislocated his shoulder on it. He actually made the stop and made the throw home to prevent (Madrigal) from scoring from second base. The trainer comes out, pops it back into place, he walks around a little bit, says "OK, I'm good," and plays the rest of the game. That was pretty impressive to dislocate your shoulder like that and stay in the game.

Andy Jenkins: Minnesota reminded me of an old Oregon State team from 2005 that I played on that got to play in the postseason and was going to be another story in college baseball. We certainly had a test. I don't think they had any monster players that year where it was "wow, we have to pitch around this guy." They had a lot of left-handed bats, they all looked the same, they were going to beat you if you missed over the middle and they played pretty good defense. They were just a northern school that certainly spooked us a little bit.

Jack Anderson: I always commend those teams up north. They kind of had that same mentality that we do, they keep them in that hitting bubble all season long and they're ready to play baseball when it's time to go. They were a hard-nosed team. I didn't know much about Minnesota baseball, but I thought they were a pretty doggone good team. Those were some nerve-wracking games because the year before (the team felt) mostly just excitement against Vanderbilt, and the next year it was more like a "we can't lose" type of thing instead of excitement to win. But I also think we were hitting our stride at that point.

Heimlich got the start in Game 1 and was back to his usual self despite the disappointment of going undrafted for the second consecutive year. It didn't come as a huge surprise to Heimlich, who tried to temper his expectations entering the draft. Taking the mound a couple of days after the draft was "the best possible thing that could've happened," according to Heimlich, who excelled at separating baseball from day-to-day life off the field.

On a dreary Friday evening at Goss Stadium, Heimlich worked a 1-2-3 top of the first with two strikeouts and was immediately staked to a 3-0 lead when Larnach and Rutschman launched back-to-back homers in the home half. Pitching with the lead, Heimlich put up zero after zero until a Toby Hanson solo shot in the eighth. He got the first two outs of the ninth and was poised to finish off his first complete game of the season, but Nate Yeskie wanted to give the two-time Pac-12 pitcher of the year a proper sendoff in his final home start. Yeskie walked to the mound and made a pitching change, allowing Heimlich to be hailed with applause as he left the field. The crowd demanded a curtain call, and Heimlich obliged.

Luke Heimlich: That was an awesome moment, just kind of encompassing my four years. Goss, Corvallis, all those people, it was always a great town. I loved being there, I still consider it a second home. I had a good outing and being able to finish it like that at home … I remember Yeskie came out to take me out with one out left in the game. I was like "come on, just let me finish!" But it was a cool moment, and I know that's what he wanted. He told me, "enjoy this, walk off, tip your cap to the people that have had your back." So, I walked off and tipped my cap, I didn't know what to do. I'd never done that before so I waved the hat briefly and walked into the dugout. Then I just sat down, started thinking back on the game. I was tired, I threw (124) pitches. And someone came up to me and was like "dude, go back out there! They're chanting your name." And I was like "what?!" I wasn't even listening or paying attention so I didn't realize it at first, but then I went back out (for a curtain call), and it was a surreal moment.

Cadyn Grenier: Getting to walk off the mound like that, it was incredible. We were standing there on the mound, Yeskie came up and he pretty much said to Luke, "hey, you're about to get a huge ovation. Eat it up, man. Enjoy it." We just stood there and it was incredible, the support that they gave to Luke. We all looked at each other, Nick and I looked at each other and were like "wow, that's amazing. That is so cool."

FINISH

Nate Yeskie: I think I had a similar conversation with (Ben) Wetzler when he came off the mound against UNLV in '14. I had it with (Jake) Thompson the year before in '17 because in all likelihood he wasn't going to pitch on that field again. You just become more aware of those moments the more the years go by that I do this, and you want those kids to be able to stop time and enjoy some of those moments. For our fan base, the way they'd supported him and done the things that they had to get him through some of the days that he had, I think it was a nice way for them to say "thank you," and for him to repay the thanks and acknowledge them.

Nick Madrigal: I always knew that Beaver fans were different than most. They are so aware of everything that's going on, on the field and off the field. For them to show how much love they have for Luke … everyone got on their feet and Luke got a little bit emotional, and I think a lot of other people got emotional just because it was that powerful of a moment to be there and hear the crowd roar for him. It was much needed at the time and I was just happy to be a part of it and see that happen because it was a really special moment.

Nate Yeskie: And Luke was really good that day. One of the national sportswriters told me that some of the hitters on the other team were coming back just confused. Their coach (John Anderson) kept looking at them like "what's the problem?" They were thinking his fastball was going to bounce, and they're like "out of his hand, there's no way that's going to be a strike." And then it's a strike at the bottom of the strike zone. He was a man on a mission to get that thing done because he didn't get to go (to the College World Series) the year before, so he was going to do everything in his power to make sure we went back, and he was going to be a part of that. He was really good, the curtain call was a neat moment for those guys to be able to enjoy that. Anytime you can be a part of that, whether you're a player, a coach, a fan, it's special, those types of moments. Because they don't happen very often.

Heimlich struck out nine with no walks in his final Goss Stadium start, an 8-1 Oregon State victory. There was minimal drama in the opener, but the second game of the super regional provided plenty. The Beavers trotted out Fehmel, while Minnesota turned to freshman right-hander Patrick Fredrickson, the Big Ten pitcher of the year. Fredrickson exited in the sixth with a 3-2 lead and handed it off to star closer Max Meyer, a 6-foot, 165-pound hard-throwing freshman righty with a wipeout slider. The Golden Gophers were going to ride Meyer for as long as they could.

Steven Kwan: I think that was one of my favorite games I ever played at Oregon

State. We battled, we grinded through that game, and I still tell everybody that Max Meyer is probably the best pitcher I ever saw in college. That guy was disgusting.

Nate Yeskie: We'd seen tape on Meyer and we'd heard "that guy's pretty good, he's different. It's not something that you've seen in college in quite some time."

Pat Bailey: I had a chance to see Meyer on video, but in person he was even better. It was the best arm I saw all year long. Just between an electric fastball and a plus, plus breaking ball, he was really good.

Michael Gretler: It felt like I was having flashbacks of facing Kyle Wright. That kid was electric.

Jack Anderson: Oh my God, he was so good. I've never been so defeated going against a guy. He was so dirty. I came up in some big spots and struck out, and I was like "why can I not hit this guy?'" I felt like I had a hole in my bat. I was getting nervous, they were kind of in control of that game.

Preston Jones, outfielder: After that series, everyone was talking about their closer. It was like "shoot, he's one of the best pitchers we've ever seen." He definitely showed that in the super regional because I think those first couple of innings he shut us down before we finally put some good at-bats together.

Meyer, who would later become the No. 3 overall pick in the 2020 MLB Draft, struck out a pair in the top of the sixth (Minnesota was the designated home team for Game 2) and worked around a two-out Kwan infield single in the seventh. Fehmel had already thrown six solid innings when he issued a walk to open the seventh. Instead of going straight to the pen, Oregon State's coaching staff left Fehmel out there to face No. 2 batter Ben Mezzenga. The Golden Gophers were likely to bunt for a shot at plating another insurance run, and Fehmel was one of the country's top fielding pitchers. Fehmel got two quick strikes on Mezzenga, taking the bunt off the table. In a rare mid-at-bat pitching change, the Beavers then brought in strikeout specialist Christian Chamberlain to finish off Mezzenga. Chamberlain proceeded to strike out the side in the seventh and fan two more in a scoreless eighth.

Bryce Fehmel: I believe in what the coaches do and their game plan for each series. I could field my position fairly well, so I think that was the main part of that. If they did decide to bunt, I'd be able to make a play, make a decision to get a lead runner out if I could. To bring him in with an 0-2 count and get us out of a jam, and continue doing what he did for the next (two) innings, it was just remarkable to watch a freshman compete on that stage.

Christian Chamberlain, pitcher: I remember warming up in the pen and feeling really good. Coming onto the mound, it was raining pretty good and I hadn't thrown in the rain too much at Goss. I tried wiping my hand to dry it off on my pants and my paints were waterproof, so that didn't really work. Then I tried to throw a warmup pitch and my first warmup pitch went about halfway up the backstop. I was kind of freaked out, but then the rain stopped a little bit, calmed down. And from that first pitch on, I was dialed in and locked in. I knew I wasn't going to get beaten up that day.

An 0-2 count, it was a little funky. I had the same thing but reversed in Game 1 of the finals against Arkansas. It was honestly easier because Fehmel had done most of the work, I just had to go in there and throw a curveball. Obviously Yeskie was calling great pitches for me at the time and I was confident in everything I was throwing. I knew that everyone had my back and if I went out there and just competed, I'd put us in a good position to come back and win.

Nate Yeskie: A big spot for (Chamberlain) was in the supers against Minnesota. We were thinking about going right-handed and Pat (Casey) had asked me at the time, he goes "want to go right-handed here?" We were thinking about bringing Dylan Pearce into the game. And I said "nah, I think he's OK." We felt like Pearce was a good matchup, we were chasing a run at the time and we wanted to leave it where it was so if we had to use him the next day, we could. We didn't want to get caught firing all of our bullets too soon. So, Chamberlain goes (back out in the eighth) and punches out Eli Wilson, who was good against lefts, and then chops the next couple of guys. He made it a little dicey one inning but he got through it, and that allowed us to play it out the way that we did.

Protecting the one-run lead, Meyer got Madrigal to ground out to open the eighth before issuing a walk to Larnach. Rutschman then singled, but Meyer fanned Gretler for the second out. Next up was Nobach, a fifth-year senior who'd redshirted in 2017 due to injury. It was the biggest at-bat of his college career.

Kyle Nobach: I was DHing that day and I remember striking out against Meyer, coming back to the dugout and I was fired up. I was walking up at the top of the dugout the entire time because he struck me out and I was just sitting there thinking "dude, I'm going up again and I'm going to have another chance. I'm going to get a hit, I'm going to get a big hit." I was feeding myself positive things and believing in what I was saying to myself.

Ryan Gorton: We'd driven that pitch count up. Once he got around 50, 60, 70 pitches, it was a little bit different, a little bit easier for us.

Nate Yeskie: That lineup would just wear your ass out. We forced their hand a little bit there. We felt like when they took Fredrickson out, it was an inning too early. They pulled the trigger on it and they had to, they had to.

Kyle Nobach: Meyer was really good, really good. I remember striking out on the slider and when I came back up again I had a plan where if that slider started at me, that was my mental queue as a hitter. I was sitting on that slider, I knew he was going to throw it to me because he made me look stupid with it earlier. I stayed inside that thing and barreled it up and it went right through that hole. I just remember that stadium erupting and I was like "here we go, man!"

Nobach shot a 1-0 slider into right field, bringing home Larnach to tie the game. Meyer came back to strike out Anderson, but the momentum was firmly with Oregon State heading to the ninth.

Pat Casey: Maybe one of the biggest moments in OSU baseball history is Nobach's hit down the right-field line off of Meyer. We're talking about a guy who is 96 to 98 miles per hour, and once again an electric atmosphere at Goss.

Trevor Larnach: If there's anyone you want to come up in a situation that's major pressure, you need major heart and major grit. It's going to be guys like Nick, Kyle, Adley, I mean I could go on. Kyle, that kid, he's special. I love him. Me and him have always seen eye to eye with each other with the way we work and the way we go about our business. Case isn't wrong saying that, man. That hit that he had set the tone for the rest of that game and really, really helped us win that series because obviously it was late in the game. He came up to the plate and knew he was a beast because he always says he's a beast, and it was awesome.

Brandon Eisert: To get that momentum is a big thing, giving us that energy. And that's something Nobach did for us all year, just bringing energy. And when he was able to get that clutch hit, it relaxed everyone. It got us back into the mode of "all right, we can do this."

Adley Rutschman, catcher: I'm good friends with Max Meyer now, and I talked with him a lot about this when we were with Team USA shortly after. I remember he had already been extended farther than he'd ever gone that year because he's one of the best pitchers I've ever seen in college, hands down, maybe the best. And he was just on fire that night, too. We had guys swinging and missing at pitches that usually we'd hit, but he was absolutely gross that night. He was pushing that four-inning mark and his pitch count was higher than normal. Kyle got that one hit off him and then they had to pull him out. We got more excited when he was out of the game.

Jake Rodriguez: That's probably my favorite memory from watching college baseball. Because you know Kyle Nobach, he's about as intense as it gets and the guy gets even more intense when the lights turn on and you can't settle the guy down. I remember him pacing throughout the dugout and you're just trying to talk to him and calm him down. He knew that he was going to get another opportunity to face Meyer and when he came up and hit that ball to right field, I think I started crying. It was the coolest thing I think I've ever seen because that was a guy who battled injury after injury after injury, and he comes up in that big of a moment against a guy who was absolutely dominating. Meyer had everything going that night, and Kyle comes up and just hits a line drive to right field.

Zak Taylor: What people don't understand, too, especially at night sometimes, it can get funky with the lights at Goss. And on top of that, you throw basically the best closer in the country at him and Kyle, mentally that guy was probably tougher than anyone, especially with the things he'd gone through. For him to be able to have that moment was so special. He was one of my roommates that year, so we were really close and just seeing the fire that he had when he got to first base, it ignited everyone. When you get a guy like that going, there's a trickle-down effect for the rest of the team.

Kyle Nobach: The emotions were really, really high. Everyone was excited. I would say (2017), the year I redshirted, I wouldn't say I wasn't part of the team, but when you're doing it and you're on the field and helping these guys win, it was pretty special to contribute to a team. It was amazing, it was crazy.

Nobach's career arc differed greatly from the typical Pac-12 starter. A 2013 graduate of Marysville Pilchuck High School near Seattle, Nobach played one season at Everett Community College before transferring to Oregon State as a walk-on. He butted heads with Pat Casey during the fall of 2014 but figured it out by that spring, earning a starting spot in the outfield. Nobach slashed .317/.377/.447 as a sophomore and .280/.379/.380 as a junior, fighting through knee pain that would come and go. Dead set on gutting it out in 2017, Nobach was talked into redshirting at the last second to heal up. He underwent an arthroscopic chondroplasty to smooth damaged cartilage in his left knee, and the procedure was a success. After months of rehab, Nobach was fully cleared midway through fall practice and the 5-foot-10 outfielder played in the first three weekends of the 2018 season. By that point his other knee was feeling a bit iffy, and Nobach tweaked it while stepping off an elevator. An MRI showed loose bodies in his right knee that would require another arthroscopic surgery with a recovery time of up to eight weeks. Nobach was back on the field in two weeks, going 3 for 3 with a home run, two doubles and four RBIs in his return against Washington. Knee issues weren't going to keep the redshirt senior out of the lineup.

Kyle Nobach: When I came back (the first time), I think sometimes as a player my biggest weakness was that I would go too hard at things. I was playing too hard and I didn't really know how to tone it back at times. I'd be running into walls and doing things that probably weren't the best for my entire body. Once I hurt my knee, I think I overcompensated for a while and ended up having surgery on my other knee. That was a different struggle.

We played UW the week I came back, I DH'd. I think I had two doubles and hit a homer that game. I was basically going through the season playing every couple of games and then I'd get my leg drained out. I got it drained right before the World Series, 70 milliliters of fluid. My knee kept getting swollen, but I was just playing. They drained it and I was good to go.

Pat Casey: That guy had so many injuries, had a chance to say "you know what, if I play I'm taking a chance of not being able to walk. I've got tendon on bone." But the guy would just not go away, he would not give in. For me personally, when you see guys do that that are not maybe typically the guys that had all the accolades or come from areas where they are visible, his situation was that he had to earn everything that he had. I just can't tell you how proud I was of him and still am.

Joe Casey, outfielder: That man's a psycho, but I love him. He always has your back. When we needed him at the end of (2018), he came up big.

Ron Northcutt, director of baseball operations: One of the guys they all loved to get on was Nobach, and Nobach would take it and give it right back. He was very intense, too. I am so, so proud of him and so happy for him. But Nobach, he was targeted most of the time and he could take anything. They'd get him a little excited at times which would fire him up, and then all the guys would get fired up.

Pat Bailey: Case has such a fun personality. I remember when Kyle was here his first year, we were upstairs hitting in the batting cages and Kyle is just struggling, he's thinking way too much. And Case goes "hey Kyle, why don't you take your head and stick it in a jar and stare at it for an hour." And Kyle comes out and I won't repeat what he said because there were some expletives in there, but he says to me "Bails, what did Case mean by that?" And I say "Kyle, he means empty head, full bat. Quit thinking and just hit."

Pat Casey: It was something along those lines. I believe I told him that I had his mind in a jar and I could read it for him. Of course, Nobey was an over-thinker, so when you get him frustrated he would just get tied up in knots. I always had fun with that. I'm sure he wanted to come down on the other side of the L-screen and knock me out.

Kyle Nobach: He told me to cut my head off, put it in a jar and stare at it all weekend. At that point in time, I was like "what the heck does that even mean?" I don't know, Pat was interesting. At first I was just a young boy, I didn't know how to handle somebody saying things like that to me. I would say he never really doubted me, but he would say that he doubted me because he knew it was going to get inside me that I was going to prove him wrong. That was deep inside my soul, and that was the mindset. I think that related right back to the (2016) selection show, that was our team's attitude. Pat had a way of getting people to believe in that.

Joe Casey: One day us outfielders were playing pretty bad, we were throwing over the cuts and doing all this. My dad said something to Nobach, and Nobach chirped back at him, and my dad said to Nobach, "just go home!" He's at home plate and Nobach is in the outfield and they're yelling at each other. And Nobach goes "I don't want to go home!" He sounds like a little kid saying he doesn't want to go home from practice. My dad says back, "just get out of here!" And Nobach doesn't say anything after that, and when we came in from the outfield they went and talked about it and weren't yelling anymore. It was funny, they went from yelling to a dad/son moment.

Kyle Nobach: Man, we were doing cuts and relays in practice and the outfielders were making bad throws, it was all of us. I think Case was actually yelling at Jack, and I was just so fired up because I hadn't been on the field in a while. I wouldn't say I was necessarily mad at Pat — I was fired up and ready to go at practice, I just had a lot of energy. Once he said something to us, I was fired up so I said something back. And I didn't go home because I cared way too much.

He gets you to fight, you know what I mean? He wants to get you to be better and play better, that's what Pat Casey did. He pushed you as an individual and he was absolutely incredible at that. He showed me a lot of things and inspired me to do a lot of things and taught me different lessons.

Pat Bailey: Kyle is one of my extended sons. He's a funny guy and honestly Kyle was one of the guys who was easy to tease because he took things so seriously, but he had a great personality.

Pat Casey, after the Washington series in 2018: (Nobach) just never goes away. He's Rocky, knock him down and cut him ... and he just keeps coming back. He is a special guy.

Nobach's clutch hit felt like a game-winner, but in reality Oregon State and Minnesota headed to the ninth locked in a 3-3 tie. The Beavers loaded the bases with one out in the top of the inning against a weary Meyer, and Minnesota finally went to the pen. New reliever Jackson Rose struck out Larnach on three pitches for the second out, but Rutschman ripped a 1-2 fastball back up the middle to plate a pair. As always, Clutchman delivered.

Adley Rutschman: I had two strikes and he tried to throw a fastball by me. I remember I got on top of it and kind of top-spun it through the middle. And they were shifted over, the second baseman was shifted over, and it got through. And that was just ... I'd rather not play extra innings if we don't have to. I was very excited about that.

Nate Yeskie: The legend of Clutchman continued to grow. He's going to be Paul Bunyan by the time he's done. People are going to think he walked around campus, he was 20 feet tall, he had an ax and he had a blue ox. Forty or 50 years from now, that will be the legend of Adley Rutschman, he will be Paul Bunyan.

Steven Kwan: Rutsch's hit was nuts, just because of the buildup and how that whole inning was. I've talked with Trevor a lot about this. Not to disrespect Rutsch or anything, but I feel like in some clutch situations Rutsch would get out and Trevor would come up clutch. But I remember in that inning, they brought in a righty and Trev went down on three fastballs. Now there are two outs and Rutsch is up, and I remember thinking "oh, it flip-flopped. Trev normally comes through, but now it's Rutsch's turn." And that's exactly what happened.

Trevor Larnach: First of all, when I do something like that, I feel like I've completely failed my team and my teammates. It's something nobody wants to experience, it's something I never want to experience again, but it happened. But that team, I don't think people understand how good every single person in the lineup was, whether it was the first batter or the ninth batter. When you failed, there was always someone backing you up if you didn't get the job done, and I was very fortunate to have Rutsch behind me. He just had stupid numbers that year, and that's a testament to how much he works, how much he believes in himself and how much he wants to win for the team. I was just thankful Rutsch was hitting behind me because he got my back a lot of times, it wasn't just that one time in super regionals. There were plenty of times I didn't get the job done and he ended up doing it. It was really sucky for me, but at the end of the day you don't care because if your teammate gets the job done and you win, it doesn't matter if I went 0 for 4 or whatever. Obviously I don't want that to happen, but when you have a team like that and you're constantly winning, it makes playing the game that much better.

Steven Kwan: Rutsch grinded it through, we got two runs … and I knew it was Omaha-bound.

Rose later hit Gretler and Nobach on consecutive pitches to force in another run, giving Oregon State a 6-3 lead heading to the bottom of the ninth. It was Jake Mulholland time, and the left-hander struck out the side to secure the Beavers' second consecutive College World Series berth.

Christian Chamberlain: I remember that if it stayed tied, I was going to have to come back and throw another inning or two. It was kind of up in the air whether it was going to be me or Mulholland going out there for the ninth. Obviously Mulholland had a little bit more experience closing, so they went with him. As soon as he came into the game, I knew it was over.

Nate Yeskie: Really the thing that stands out to me from that day outside of Chamberlain was we get to (1-2) on (No. 3 batter Terrin) Vavra, and his dad was a hitting coach for the Minnesota Twins. I talked to a guy going into it and he said "hey, now this guy is good. He's going to think along with you. You're not going to surprise him with anything, so as many different looks you can give him, the better, because he's going to think along with you and he's not going to get caught off guard by too many things." So, Bails had looked over to me at one point, it's (1-2) and he says "what are we doing here?" We've got Mulholland out there and I said "we're going to throw him a changeup," something Jake could do to left-handers. It was just a completely different look that he didn't do very often, but when you asked him to he could execute it. So, he throws that pitch in there and sure enough, he strikes Vavra out and now there's two outs. They've got their big DH (Toby Hanson) coming up who they've moved up in the order from the nine-hole to the four-hole. He comes up and Mulholland strikes him out to end the game, and here we go.

Steven Kwan: That game was crazy. We persevered through all of it, just crazy pitching, timely hitting. I mean, ooh. It's funny because they have that game on YouTube, the full game, so sometimes I go and watch that back and it just gives me chills.

Nick Madrigal: Those were a couple cold games in Corvallis. The stadium was packed, but it was not easy playing them. They had a good team that year.

Jack Anderson: I feel like that second game took a year off my life.

Pat Bailey: I think coach Anderson at Minnesota does a great job. They are always very good, and we've played them a lot since I've been here. They are always a disciplined team, they do all the little things really well.

Those two games were real battles with Minnesota. Those were tough, tough games. And to win both of them and know that we're going back to the World Series was just a kick in the pants.

Cadyn Grenier: Minnesota was a really good team. I think they might've caught us off guard a little bit, we didn't think they were going to be as good as they were and they had some awesome pitchers. We definitely had to grind in some of those games, but just like a lot of our stories from games, we had some guys come up absolutely huge. Guys that weren't the Nicks and Trevors and me and all the guys who were getting drafted. Guys came up huge when the team really needed them to.

Jack Anderson: I think winning the second game that way was huge because we were down the whole game, and in the seventh or eighth inning we figured it out and got the win. Going into Omaha winning a game like that is kind of the way you want to win instead of just winning some blowouts before you get there.

Trevor Larnach: It was a crazy series and a lot of fun being it was the last regional and super regional for a lot of us, but it was a test because that was a team that was hungry for the 'chip. They were prepared and they'd had a great season, but we knew we weren't done, man. And we knew we had a huge goal and something we wanted to finish.

Ron Northcutt: Every guy that we ever brought in on a recruiting visit, the coaches and myself would all have our rings on. Case and I had national championship rings on. Every guy who saw that would tell me "that's why I'm here." I remember after winning the super regional in '18, Larnach said to me "it's time to go take the natty!" And I'm going "what in the hell is the natty? Oh, duh Ron. The national championship."

FINISH

Nate Yeskie: I remember seeing the looks on Nathan Burns and Kevin Abel and Christian Chamberlain's faces. They're freshmen and they're going to Omaha, and for Luke to be able to go … the whole thing was just so unique on so many different levels because when you're recruiting kids and talking to families, you're telling them that this is a possibility. But somewhere in the back of their minds there's still doubt because there are 300 college teams playing baseball and only eight get to go, there are a handful of other coaches telling them the same thing that they think it's going to happen. But the part for us is we knew it could happen.

Andy Armstrong, infielder: We didn't dogpile after the super regional because while it was still special to go to Omaha, it wasn't as special because we expected to get back there.

Dylan Pearce: There was only one dogpile per year, and that was it. We made that clear. When we were about ready to close it out and win the game, everybody was like "do not dogpile, period. Do not dogpile. Act like you've been there. We can jump up and down, but we'll have our dogpile soon enough when we get to Omaha." And that was it.

BOB LUNDEBERG

CHAPTER VIII

RETURN TO OMAHA

For many Oregon State players and staff members, the College World Series was a return trip. But several people were going for the first time, eager to finally experience the grandness of Omaha after hearing all about it.

Kyle Nobach, outfielder: We got a charter flight out to there, so it was a little bit different of a feel. I remember flying into Omaha, and that was absolutely incredible knowing we were going to the middle of the country to play baseball. Growing up, all everyone ever did was play baseball, and now I'm going with a bunch of guys to play for a national championship. It was just an absolute dream come true for me. I remember watching Mitch Canham and Tyler Graham when I was 12 years old, 13 years old. I remember seeing Pat Casey and Darwin Barney and Joey Wong, all these guys, Jacoby (Ellsbury) and (Andy) Jenkins. I watched these guys at home because of Mitch, mainly. I would go over to my grandparents' house, and my grandfather would always read the newspaper and there'd be pictures of Mitch because he went to a rival high school of mine. I loved Oregon State, so it was a huge dream of mine knowing "hey, I'm going to be not just a part of that, but a whole organization with history." It was just amazing to say I got to go to Oregon State and play in the World Series because it was a goal of mine that I had watching Mitch do that and all those guys do that together. So, when we went to Omaha and showed up, it was awesome.

Ryan Gorton, undergraduate assistant coach: (The College World Series) was why I came to Oregon State as a player. I looked at (2018) as my second chance to get back there, and holy crap was it worth it. The place is unbelievable. Even walking outside around the stadium, everybody is there for baseball, everybody has their team's hat or shirt on. It's just a great place for baseball fans of any background.

Kevin Abel, pitcher: I loved the city, getting to go around the area and eat. That was something with Yeskie and I, if we weren't talking about baseball, we were talking about food. So, he made sure to give me a list of restaurants to go eat at with my family. And it was very, very good, I can tell you that. The steaks over there are a little bit different.

Dylan Pearce, pitcher: Omaha was a dream of mine. I believe every collegiate baseball player should experience it, or at least be able to go to something like that. It was unbelievable. We landed there in Omaha and we were so excited. I was like "oh my gosh, I'm actually here." Then we had to report, go get our pictures and go out and practice on the field. We all got dressed and it didn't hit me until we started walking down that tunnel. It opened up, you see the lights and the field and I had to sit there and take it all in. It was absolutely a dream come true and I just sat there for a bit. It was an emotional day for myself, and my dad as well. He had always talked to me about that since I was a little kid, and that was something that was so huge for both him and I just to be able to see each other there, in that position.

Luke Heimlich, pitcher: I could talk to people about the town, get an idea of the situation before, but ultimately Omaha is its own thing and you can't really prepare for it unless you've been there before. I was excited to get down there, and having that first day of practice on the field was great. Just getting out there, seeing the place. Basically, every journalist that was there asked me the same question: what's it like going to Omaha after not going the first year? Within about 15 minutes, I got pretty tired of answering that question.

I was just focused on playing baseball. I was probably a little blunt, probably should've tried to perk up a little bit and put on a better front, but I wanted to play baseball. I was there to win a national championship, so I wasn't really worried about anything off the field. My focus was on getting ready and having a good couple weeks in Omaha.

Pat Casey, head coach: For me, every time I headed to the World Series after the first time, I think it was the same, man. I know what we have to do, I know how difficult it's going to be, I know how I want to practice, I know when we want to hit. It's pretty regimented for me in my mind, my job was always I think to get guys to understand that you just do the things that got you here. You play the way you play, it's no different. We make Ameritrade our home, but we play the way that we play and we try to get them into a routine that emulates what we do, and we just stayed with it.

In 2017, Max Engelbrekt was Oregon State's lone player with College World Series experience. Nineteen Beavers saw the field during the team's four games at the 2017 CWS; fourteen were back for the return trip.

Andy Armstrong, infielder: I think it makes it even harder to win the World Series when you have a team that's never been there before. The second time, you know what you're getting yourself into and you know what to expect. You've played in that stadium before, you've played in front of that many fans before. I guess your comfort level does go up, so I think that makes it easier to just play loose. When you play in front of a lot of people and on a stage like the College World Series, you're excited. You want to play, you want to get after it. I think having that excitement sometimes can steer you off course a little bit because you're so amped up. I think because we knew what it was like to play in Omaha, it was a little easier to take it like a normal game.

Zak Taylor, first baseman: I think it made all the difference. I think you need to have some of that experience going in, especially if you're trying to make a run to win the whole thing. There's a certain element that I think can be a little overwhelming at first, just because it's a big stage. Like for us we pack out Goss, but Goss holds what, thirty-five hundred people? Maybe four, and that's putting bleachers in the outfield and things like that. When you get into a stadium that's 25,000 people, and of course they're not all our fans, so it's different. You're playing in front of a big league-type crowd, but it's still that college atmosphere. And that's where it's fun. I'd always rather play in those big games in front of a ton of people, there's more behind it and the excitement, it just flows. It's a fun, fun atmosphere to play in.

Michael Gretler, infielder: The second year felt much more like a business trip. We knew what to expect, we knew what kind of shops were around there, the whole fan experience. We'd done that, we'd experienced that, and those are just distractions, right? Obviously, when you're there you want to experience it, and I think we all experienced it the first year we went. But that second year was a completely different feel from a business standpoint. It was like "we're going to have a good time, but we're not going just to see what things are like. We're going to win the trophy and bring it home to Corvallis."

Cadyn Grenier, infielder: We, as the older guys that had been there, knew what we had to do to keep the younger guys focused and how to not let them get caught up in the moment. We didn't care that we were there, we just wanted that national championship. All the great stuff that goes on at the College World Series, we pushed it to the side and kept our mission to "hey, this is a business trip. We're not done yet." And especially with a lot of the same guys that had that taste in our mouth from getting kicked out the last year, we were not about to let that happen again.

Trevor Larnach, outfielder: I think having that experience of umpires getting in the way our first year really allowed us to learn that we can't rely on anybody but ourselves. We had a different mindset and we didn't let it bother us. We knew what we needed to do; we knew what to expect. We knew what would happen, what could happen and what will happen and we just didn't back down.

Jake Mulholland, pitcher: The experience helped a lot. Because a lot of teams when you get to Omaha, you're happy to be there, right? You made it, you're in Omaha, it's really easy to think "we did it!" But that's just when a whole new tournament starts. I think in 2018, we were not happy to just be there. It didn't matter that we were in Omaha, it meant nothing. We didn't go to the zoo that year, we eliminated all distractions and were there for baseball. That was what we were telling the guys who hadn't been there, we're on a mission here and this is a business trip. I think we kept that mindset and that mentality all throughout Omaha, and I think that's what really helped us to get through it.

Oregon State's pre-tournament schedule was a carbon copy of 2017's. The third-seeded Beavers (49-10-1) had the first Friday morning on-field practice at TD Ameritrade Park and were set to play No. 6 North Carolina (43-18) the following afternoon in the College World Series opener. The other half of OSU's bracket featured a matchup between underdogs Washington and Mississippi State, both of which advanced to Omaha by winning road regionals and super regionals.

Unlike the previous year, Mother Nature cooperated Friday night and the traditional opening ceremonies were held at the park. The Beavers took in the festivities before heading back to the team hotel to get ready for the next day's highly-anticipated showdown with North Carolina. The two programs had not met since facing off in consecutive CWS finals the previous decade.

Bill Rowe, undergraduate assistant coach: It was super surreal for me being back there again, but also because we played North Carolina in 2006 for three games. In 2007 they played them for two and I was a spectator there, so that was a trip watching all my friends beat the exact same team on the same field the next year. And then flash forward 11 years and the very next College World Series game I'm watching live is Oregon State versus North Carolina in a new stadium as a coach. That whole journey from being there as a player to being there as a coach ... I remember having butterflies as a player that first game in Omaha, but that feeling as a coach of being in that stadium watching that against the same team and the same coach (Mike Fox) across the field was really weird.

Pat Casey: Having Tyler and Bill in the dugout, that in itself reminded me of (2006 and 2007). That is the thing that was on my mind, when I knew that they were there and I was there and we were playing North Carolina. That's what brought up the memories for me, it was less about North Carolina and their uniforms and things like that.

Especially before the game, you get a little bit of time before you actually play the game, guys are in the dugout. So, there was a lot of nostalgia going on there, that's for sure.

Jack Anderson, outfielder: Our side of the bracket, I thought it was tough. North Carolina, they're always going to be good and it was a surreal feeling playing them in Omaha after watching the 2006 and 2007 teams play them. That was definitely cool, being in pretty much the same situation facing North Carolina in those moments.

Christian Chamberlain, pitcher: Game 1 against North Carolina, we lined up for the national anthem. As soon as those jets rolled through, it rattles your ribcage. I've never had the chills more than that.

Jack Anderson: It was cool that we got to play the first game both years, because of the flyover. The flyover is something I'll always remember, those are some of the coolest pictures I've seen and some of the best memories I have, just the flyovers at TD Ameritrade. Pretty freaking cool, man.

The first game of the College World Series featured a pitching matchup between Luke Heimlich and big North Carolina right-hander Luca Dalatri. Neither lasted long. Dalatri couldn't make it out of the first inning, exiting with an arm issue following a Trevor Larnach RBI triple and a four-pitch walk to Adley Rutschman. Heimlich never settled in, and was replaced by Brandon Eisert in the third. His opening pitch wound up being a sign of things to come for the Beavers.

Jake Mulholland: First pitch of the College World Series, ground ball right at the shortstop. (Grenier) boots it, guy on first and we're like "oh no, what's going on here?"

FINISH

Ryan Gorton: I was like "hmm, that's really how we're going to start?" Because normally we don't make any errors. A first-pitch error to our best defender, what the heck?

Michael Gretler: The first pitch of the game was an absolute rocket to Cadyn. He wore it off his chest, picked it up and the guy beat it out. I had an error that game, there were a couple passed balls here and there. It was just an ugly game, not what anyone had thought it was going to be like. And yeah, we were punched in the face right off the bat. It was hot, there were some guys getting into it with each other in the dugout which you don't like to see, but at that point of the year and in that point of the game it was obviously frustrating. It was hot, we were losing, everyone's mad, everyone's upset, things aren't going our way. That game was tough, but at the same time we did fight back.

Luke Heimlich: I struggled from the beginning. I kind of felt the same way I did during the LSU game at home. It wasn't really anything about the situation, it was more my delivery, rushing myself. I was probably excited, amped up for the situation. It was hot out, big stage, first time being there. So, I was just rushing, I wasn't as relaxed as normal and I was maybe trying to do too much on a big stage. Personally, I was very below-average that game, but the team battled to keep it close. It was tough for me to hang the bullpen out to dry like that, knowing it's going the be a long week and we've got a lot of games ahead. You want to try and conserve arms, and that just wasn't a good way to start.

Jack Anderson: North Carolina was just a good team, a good hitting team. They got on Luke early, which we weren't used to at all. I think that was a punch to the face in the beginning, like "oh, they're hitting our best guy pretty good right now."

Dylan Pearce: It was rough. It was very hot and it just took a lot out of us, I don't know. Pitching did not go our way and it went downhill from there with errors, pitching and not getting our bats fully alive. That was just a tough game.

Oregon State, which had only one defensive error in its previous eight games entering the College World Series, was sloppy in all phases on a muggy and windy Midwest afternoon. The Beavers committed three errors, left 11 runners on base and had multiple base-running blunders in an 8-6 loss.

North Carolina, champion of the ACC Coastal Division, was used to the sweltering heat. The Beavers weren't. Official records list the first-pitch temperature at 93 degrees with 19 miles per hour wind, but conditions on the field were much harsher. Constant wind gusts and extreme humidity took their toll on OSU's players during the 4-hour, 24-minute slog, the longest nine-inning game in CWS history. In the bottom of the first, Larnach unloaded on a ball to dead center field. The stiff wind was blowing straight in, and Larnach had to settle for a triple off the wall instead of a two-run homer. Outfielders from both teams had trouble navigating the breezy conditions during the marathon game.

Ryan Gorton: Trevor hit maybe one of the hardest balls I've ever seen and it didn't go out of the park. The wind had to have been blowing 40 miles per hour straight in.

Trevor Larnach: Fuck I wish the wind wasn't blowing in just so I could've seen how far it would've gone. Because I remember the wind was blowing in at 20 or 25 miles per hour and I couldn't have hit that ball better, sitting on it and everything. I just wish the wind wasn't blowing because that probably would've been one of my favorite hits in college. Nonetheless, it still was since it gave our team the lead in the beginning.

Ryan Gorton: I was playing catch with Luke before the game, and he had the wind at his back as he was doing his long toss. Adley would throw it to me, and I'd throw it back to Luke. Me and Adley could hardly get it there because the wind was blowing so hard. I had to throw it as hard as I could. I normally throw it 180 feet and I was probably throwing it 120.

Jack Anderson: It felt like I was playing in a convection oven where it was 100 degrees outside with like 20 mph winds. I remember in the outfield, I almost passed out in the middle of the game. I'd never been so close to passing out before, and I was just like "this is not good." We were wearing the black jerseys. The heat, I've never been so hot in my life. I think that was the first time the elements got to us a little bit where we were just dog tired for whatever reason.

Kyle Nobach: It was hotter than hell, man. It got so hot at one point that I literally — because I was playing left field that game—would go up to the clubhouse when I wasn't hitting because there was AC in there. I just needed a second because it was so damn hot in that dugout, I think it was 110 degrees in there. We were all dying, too.

Nate Yeskie, pitching coach: Everything was weird, everything was miserable. Maybe some of our guys tried to do too much. And maybe (we) went to too much effort or too much tension to get things done.

Adley Rutschman, catcher: It was a weird-energy game. I mean guys were nervous but it wasn't how it was the year before. It was more like "why are we feeling this way, why is this happening? We've done this, what's going on?" That type of thing. We started out terribly in that game, we had a couple errors and the pitching was just not exactly what we'd hoped for during that time.

Ryan Gorton: I remember Nick and Adley getting into it in the dugout during that game, just trying to spark something. We were down and needed something and two of our alphas in the dugout started going at each other. I don't necessarily know if it helped for that game, but it showed the fight that we had and the passion everybody on that team played with.

Nate Yeskie: A lot of people don't remember this one, but Adley and Nick got into it against North Carolina. We were scuffling, and I mean Adley was ready to probably Hulk out and turn green there for a second. But Bails came up, he and I were trying to mediate this thing and finally I point at Nick and say to Bails "you take him, I've got this one." So, Bails and Nick go down the other way. And with Adley, I can see whatever I'm saying isn't registering, he's looking right through me. It's just not there. And then finally I get him back and it's like "OK, there you are, there you are." And I said, "I get it, everyone's frustrated right now, but that guy out on the mound, he needs you." And he just goes "OK, I've got it." And he did, he had it from that moment on, and we saw what unfolded over the next handful of games from there.

Kyle Nobach: The heat definitely got the best of us, we weren't playing well, our emotions got high. We were bickering with each other and it wasn't like us, but it was hot! Tensions were high. I think everybody understood that if we lost the first game, the chances of us winning it all weren't very likely. I think what happened was there was a passed ball and Nick didn't really like that Rutsch didn't run hard to it. Nick said something to him and they got into it a little bit, but in a way that was almost something to fire each other up and we fed off it. We never took things personal within the team. Whenever we talked with each other, it was never personal. It was always out of love and using each other to have willpower.

Trevor Larnach: That was the hottest game of my life ... and I felt it, man. I was in right field and it was pounding the side of my head. Personally, I thought North Carolina was the best team we played in that tournament. And that's not to knock any of the other teams, but those guys came out and played their asses off every single game until the last moment, and they were hard to deal with. They were a good team.

Steven Kwan, outfielder: I thought North Carolina hit really well that day. I think we beat ourselves in certain aspects, but they were a good ball club. I remember I botched a ball in center, it was just sloppy play. I let the ball snake on me, it got by me and a couple runs scored. It was very uncharacteristic of us, and I think that was a wake-up call for us. Because we had been on auto-pilot again just moving through, we had that cockiness to us like "we'll figure it out, we'll be fine." So that was a really good gut-check early on in the tournament.

Cadyn Grenier: We made a couple mistakes, myself included. Those little things that we had been super good at all year came back and bit us in the butt, and obviously North Carolina played well enough to beat us. It was tough, that one hit us hard because we were so good and so confident. To lose the first game and know that the toughest thing to do is go through that losers' bracket and make it out, it sucked. It was like "man, I don't know. This is going to be really difficult." And by the next day, we were all fine again.

Nick Madrigal, infielder: That was a crazy game. Coming down to the last inning, so much emotion in the dugout. I remember there were frustrations from the coaches' side, from the players' side. There were ups and downs and I remember after that game just being so mad and so shocked. I think a lot of people were shocked, that's the best word to describe the team after. The locker room was quiet and I remember saying a couple things to the team about how "this isn't the end of us. We can do this, it's happened before." But yeah, it was definitely a punch in the face.

Andy Armstrong: It was pretty hard at the time because I think for a moment there, everybody was like "oh no, this is going to happen again." But I remember in the locker room Nick Madrigal said "hey guys, we're not done. We're just going to have to do it the hard way." I think everything shifted right then. You know what, we're not done, it can still be done, and we turned it on from there.

Trevor Larnach: Even though we lost, our morale wasn't down. We knew what we had to do, we knew how good we were, we knew the history of Oregon State when it comes down to something like that. We were just going to take advantage of the opportunity that was still in front of us rather than dwell on what we didn't do.

Pat Casey: It's tough to win games. We're playing Game 1 and it's 115 degrees in your dugout and they're good, they're good. They beat us. We didn't play great and some calls could've helped us out maybe, I don't know. You just know that it's not easy to win at the College World Series. The thing about the College World Series though is it's not like you only get one shot. You actually get more than one shot if you get to the championship deal, and we've proven that you can lose and lose and still win.

I think we were all disappointed. The only thing I told them was, "hey you know what, men? The good thing about this is we get to play again. Now I will say that we'll have to play better than we did today," because we just did not play well, and that didn't have anything to do with how good they were. They were talented as heck, and we didn't play well. We had some opportunities we didn't seize on, and we didn't pitch well. I think they were just like I would've expected them to be after we lost a game in conference, they were unhappy.

Pat Bailey, associate head coach: I thought we were really upbeat, and I think that had a lot to do with the attitude of our coaching staff and Case as a head coach. I mean, what can you do? There's nothing you can do to change it. You can sit there and mope but it's a new day, there's nothing you can do about the past so let's focus on the present and get after it.

Bryce Fehmel, pitcher: I remember coming into the locker room after the loss and Case doing what he does, just motivating us to stay in it and letting us know that we're not out of it. We had all the trust in the world in Case, and how he went about it and how he believed in us was a big part of it.

Pat Casey's message carried weight because the 2006 Beavers were also an experienced group that won a national title despite losing their College World Series opener. Director of Player Development Tyler Graham and undergraduate assistant coach Bill Rowe were both starters on the 2006 team that made history by winning a record six CWS elimination games.

Steven Kwan: T Graham was on the 2006 team that had to grind through that same thing. We were a little down and he was like "hey boys, we did the same thing. Why can't you guys do it?"

Michael Gretler: I remember T Graham pulled us aside and he goes "you guys played arguably your worst game of the year, and you still had multiple chances to win the game. You guys can beat anybody here." When you lose the first game, it's a long road back, a long road back, so I think that reinstalled that confidence in our minds. We could still do this; we don't need to worry or think about anything other than the next game. It was a big help when T Graham said that. It was like "yeah, he definitely gets it."

Ryan Gorton: After we lost that first one, it wasn't like I didn't think we could win the rest of them. Bill Rowe was my roommate the whole time and he was on the 2006 team that did the exact same thing, so I think there was that comfort knowing that Case has been here before, this program has been here before, it can be done. All you have to do is play good baseball because we knew we were really, really good.

Bill Rowe: With players like that who are very smart, you don't have to shove it in their face. You show them you don't care by not caring yourself. I'm not grabbing the whole team and being like "look guys, we did this back in 2006 and we can come back from this." It's like they can see in the way that we're acting that there's literally no concern because we know if they play the game they're capable of playing, there's nobody who can beat them. I think getting that feeling from a coach is way better than having it thrown in your face, so T Graham and I weren't concerned about it and we basically went through the exact same process the next day. I mean we were treating every game like it was do-or-die, it didn't really matter that our backs were against the wall.

Jack Anderson: All those thoughts come into your brain like "all right, we've got that first loss now. Crap. Now we've got a real journey to get to where we want to go." But even after that first loss, I think the memories of the 2006 team are forever embedded in Oregon State baseball. It's one thing to see it happen, another team doing it and coming back. But it's another thing when it's your own program and you really believe "hey, they did it so we can do it, too." That's the mindset we had, that it was 2006 all over again. I think that propelled us, and we knew we were good enough to do it. As long as we could pitch the way we needed to, we were sure going to hit. And the next game, Huskies. Oh, man. Now we really, really can't lose to these guys. No way.

Losing teams don't have time to dwell at the College World Series, and the Beavers were ready to move forward the following day. The 149th Oregon State University commencement ceremony ran concurrently with the baseball team's game against North Carolina. Sunday morning, a special edition commencement was held at the team hotel for seven graduates in the program. OSU had the highest team GPA of the eight CWS participants at 3.27.

To avoid the dreaded two-and-barbecue showing in Omaha, the Beavers (49-11-1) needed to get through regional rival Washington (35-25), a first-time CWS participant. OSU had won five straight regular-season Pac-12 series against the Huskies, and there was still plenty of bitterness from the 2016 NCAA Tournament selection process.

Kevin Abel: We knew Washington was going to be tough because the Pac-12 is just tough. When that style of play goes against each other, it's really about who gets lucky that day.

FINISH

Andy Jenkins, assistant coach: I remember thinking about 2016 and how we didn't really have a fond place in our hearts for UW when we played them the next couple of years.

Brandon Eisert, pitcher: Going in, we knew there was no way we were going to lose to Washington to get taken out of the World Series, or else Case probably would've made us walk home.

Trevor Larnach: He might've walked home if anything.

Jack Anderson: It's like the butterfly effect. Would I ever hear from Case again? (Pat Casey's oldest son) Jon Casey would've disowned everyone because Jon didn't like the Huskies more than anyone. There was definitely that feeling of "wow, we're playing Washington!" I mean, hats off to them. They played their worst series against us. We kicked the dog out of them. So, to see them there, we knew they were playing much better baseball and we definitely couldn't take them lightly. But yeah, it was definitely like "if we lose this game, everything we've worked for is just down the frickin' toilet, man. No way this is going to happen like this." Either they were ending our season or we were ending theirs.

Kyle Nobach: We didn't sit there and think "hey man, this is going to be the last game." I wasn't at least. I was thinking "hey man, we can win this damn thing!" I truly believed in my heart that every single person sitting in that locker room believed that, too.

Jake Mulholland: Washington came out playing really well, took an early lead on us and it did not look great.

Trevor Larnach: The energy was not there at the beginning of the game for whatever reason. It almost felt like we were laying low, we were just not really into it or whatever it was.

Nate Yeskie: We were dead in the water. I mean we were flat, dead, throw in any other adjective that you want. The team looked unenthused, we weren't playing well and it was almost a "here we go again," because that's the same dugout we'd been in the year before when we got eliminated.

Luke Heimlich: We started out a little flat and people were thinking about the day before. It was the same thing I'd felt (in Game 1). Obviously nobody wants to lose, so you start trying to put it on your own shoulders and make something happen. When you're pressing like that, baseball just doesn't work well. You've got to be calm; you've got to see things as they come to you.

The underdog Huskies plated three runs in the third off Bryce Fehmel and led 3-0 after four innings. Oregon State was dealt a crushing blow early when Steven Kwan tweaked his left hamstring in the outfield. Kwan stayed in the game for a bit but eventually took himself out after grounding into an inning-ending double play in the third. Plagued by the hamstring injury for the rest of the College World Series, Kwan was mostly reduced to a pinch hitter moving forward. Nick Madrigal took over the leadoff spot while center field duties were primarily handled by Preston Jones and Jack Anderson.

Steven Kwan: It was just dehydration, pretty bad dehydration. Jeremy (Ainsworth), our trainer, he was always jamming it down our throats "stay hydrated, stay hydrated. It's hot out here, it's sweaty." And for some reason, I thought that being hydrated meant chugging five, six water bottles and I'm fine. But as he explained it, obviously, you have to drink water constantly throughout the day and at a good pace. You can't just drink it all at once because you'll pee it right out, and that's exactly what I did. I drank five water bottles and two Gatorades, I remember because I was doing that in Zak Taylor's room, and there I go, I thought I was hydrated. I didn't drink any water the next day, wasn't even concerned about it.

On an overthrow from Rutsch, I'm backing up second. And (Chris Anderson), our strength coach, always talked about how I needed to work on my running form, so I'm conscious of that when I'm running down to first base or going after a fly ball. But on a backed-up ball, I was just making sure I got the ball, didn't let it snake on me, and I threw my running form out the window and I tweaked it. It was just a combination of dehydration and bad running form. I knew I felt it pull, it brought like a sizzle down my leg. I was kind of trying to be ignorant about it, but I told Trev "hey man, I think I just pulled my hammy. We'll see how it goes." And then I told Preston to get ready right when I got in the dugout. I think I was up third that inning, and I remember there was a runner on first and I hit a ball pretty good right to short. It was going to be a double-play ball so I was like "OK, I have to get out of the box." I took one hard step and it cramped up on me, and I was just like "I can't play. I'm going to be a liability to the team." I knew it instantly.

Pat Bailey: That was hard. And the hardest part for me is Kwany is such a great guy, and he was such a big part of our team until he got hurt. For him to not be in our lineup, I probably felt worse for him than I did for our team. We had plenty of capable guys to take his spot. They weren't Kwany, but they were plenty capable.

FINISH

Cadyn Grenier: Nobody wants to see anybody get hurt, especially when it's somebody like Kwan who is such a high-energy guy. Everybody loves him. When it's someone like that, you really don't want to see it happen because you know how much he means to the baseball team as a player, but also as a person. The kind of energy he brings to the team, you want it on the field, you want to see him do well because he can be so deadly, and he was all year. So, to see that happen, that was tough and you go "dang, man. Now we just lost our leadoff guy and one of our best players." It was tough, but everybody had to make it work, and we did.

Nick Madrigal: He was probably one of the best leadoff hitters in the country that year, and to lose him was a blow. Some guys battled with injuries throughout the year, losing some guys, and it was tough. We thought it would be hard to replace him, but we knew we had a strong enough team with the next guy up. You knew it was pretty serious when Kwan couldn't go because he's a tough guy. It had to be a serious injury, everyone knew that, he wouldn't pull himself for anything. So, it was tough. I hadn't hit leadoff for most of the year, but I was willing to do it.

Preston Jones, outfielder: That was definitely tough to see, especially since Kwan is one of my best friends and he did a lot for our team and contributed so much. He forewarned me when he came in after playing the outfield, that's when he pulled his hamstring, and told me "hey, this just happened. I'm going to continue to try and play, but be ready to go in." It was tough, but that's why you prepare and practice outside of practice just in case you get called.

Steven Kwan: (The hamstring) hurt. I think the adrenaline of that situation didn't allow me to understand the magnitude of it. Like I thought I would be good the next day, thought I would play, but obviously with hammys, it's a nagging thing. I think I dealt with it as good as I could've in the moment. It was "all right, next man up." And we had the next man up. We obviously saw Preston hit that (double) down the line after I got taken out, that's just how that year was. We had dogs on that team, we had guys ready to go.

After four lethargic innings on another warm and breezy Omaha afternoon, Oregon State finally showed signs of life in the fifth. Assistant coach Andy Jenkins gave a rousing speech in the dugout and the Beavers put together a two-out rally, getting consecutive singles from Kyle Nobach and Anderson. In just his seventh plate appearance of the postseason, pinch hitter Tyler Malone then ripped a first-pitch fastball up the middle to get OSU on the board. Next up was Jones, who'd booted a ball in center after taking over for Kwan. Jones hadn't taken an in-game swing in a month, but the sophomore from Vancouver, Washington, sliced a double down the right-field line that tied the game. Jones later scored on a passed ball to give OSU a 4-3 lead. Seemingly out of nowhere, the Beavers were back in business.

Andy Jenkins: We were kind of spooked and it was like "hey, this team from our own league is going to knock us out of the World Series?" I think it was the fifth inning when I rallied the guys in the dugout. What set me off was I was standing over there at third base and they had three players that were basically over the rail just having a party and chirping at me and saying stuff about our hitters that were coming up to the plate. They were really, really enjoying their (3-0) lead in the fifth, and it fired me up. I got the guys together and I just said "don't forget who you are and what you've done. If you think we can't come back from this deficit with this team and our will to win, then you've got to be fooling yourself." And I think it fired our guys a little bit. A lot of times Case inspires them, and I think when you can get a different voice, whether it's me or Yeskie or Bails or one of the other coaches, I felt it was my time to rally the troops a little bit.

Tyler Malone, infielder/outfielder: I just thought I was going to get my chance, eventually. I didn't know when that exactly was going to be, but I wanted to make sure I was locked in and ready for any moment Case called on me. So even though I wasn't playing, we all had a role and we all had to be invested in our role and be ready for anything basically. So, when Case called on me to pinch hit, it was pretty early in the game, but I knew I was ready and I knew I was going to be as locked in as I possibly could. I was able to hit that base hit up the middle and score a run … and we weren't done. It provided that spark and a lot of baseball is momentum, especially in that World Series. Gosh, we rode momentum like crazy. But yeah, I was just trying to get something going and luckily I was able to get that base hit up the middle and provide a little energy.

Preston Jones: (The two-RBI double) definitely felt good, especially because Case blew up on me going into that inning because of me booting that one ball. It was good to hit that double and tie the game for our team.

Kyle Nobach: I scored a run early in the UW game and Yeskie came up to me and said "Kyle, if you don't want this to be the end of your guys' season, you better do something about it and get these guys together."

Drew Rasmussen, pitcher: Then, the clutchest rain delay of all time happened.

Kevin Abel replaced Fehmel in the fifth and Washington benefitted from some early wildness

FINISH

to regain the lead at 5-4. Oregon State fought right back, loading the bases with two down in the home half as dark clouds approached. Play was suspended for 4 hours, 31 minutes, giving both teams plenty of time to rest, regroup and have some fun.

Joe Casey, outfielder: The North Carolina game was just sloppy. Didn't pitch well, played bad defense. And then the UW game we got down early, and I think in the rain delay we just gathered together as a team. We had a ton of fun in the locker room, we loosened up a lot and I think we got that feeling back, that 2017 feeling where we're not going to lose. We were so loose that no one was worried we were going to lose, no one was anxious. We had runners on, it was only a one-run game and it was UW, so we knew we were going to beat them.

Nick Madrigal: We were keeping it light in the clubhouse, playing games. It wasn't all about baseball at that moment. We just went back to having fun with each other, joking around. I don't know how it was on the Washington side, but we weren't even thinking about baseball for a while.

Zak Taylor: It was funny because we were all in the locker room just chilling and I had actually come out of that game by that time, so I knew I wasn't going to play. It was this funny dynamic because you've got certain personalities in your clubhouse where some guys really like to play cards or play games and be loose, other guys are really trying to focus in. Everyone let everyone else do their own thing.

Michael Gretler: The lockers are pretty spacious and there's a big pitching area, so guys were running around back there. I don't even remember how long that break was ... all I know is it was light when the game started and when we came back out it was getting dark. So, it was definitely a long, long game. The weather that year in Omaha was pretty crazy.

Jake Mulholland: My glove got soaked out in the bullpen, I couldn't even go out to get it.

Dylan Pearce: I took a nap and it had to have been like 55 degrees inside of our locker room, it was freezing cold. I went in there to take a nap, I fell asleep and I ended up waking up like three-and-a-half, four hours later, and everyone was still in there. And I'm like "what is going on?!"

Kevin Abel: We were playing a bunch of games. Hangman, Mafia, all that stuff. We were just having a good old time, same way we always do to kill time on a bus or in an airport.

Joe Casey: I love bubblegum, and I was shoving a bunch in my mouth and told everyone I was doing it for the win. Someone was like "you've got to throw 30 in!" So, we called it the bubblegum challenge and I had 30 pieces of Double Bubble in my mouth. I call it the rally gum. It was tough, but I did it for the guys.

Nate Yeskie: I took a nap; a couple other guys took naps and everyone was just doing their thing. I remember being like "all right, I'm going to see what's going on out here," just to get a pulse and a temperature of what the spirits were like. So, I go out there and our guys were in pretty good spirits, they were playing games and I'm like "oh, I think we're going to be OK." Because Adley had been going so good and I couldn't find Nick or Larnach or anybody else, I saw Adley there and I said "hey, when you go back out, try to bring those guys together if you can and tell them 'listen, we've got (four) innings left to make this work. Let's not worry about where we are or what we're doing, let's just find a way to pick up the energy levels and see how well we can play.'" And he says "OK, yeah, sure." Whether he did or not, I don't know. But the bottom line is we came out considerably different.

Jake Mulholland: We had a team meeting without the coaches and just talked about "hey guys, do you want this to be the end of our season? Because that's the way it's looking. We're going to go home in about an hour and we're going to get on a plane and head back home, and if that's what you guys want, we're going to continue doing what we're doing. But if not, we're going to fight until the very last out is made and we're just going to play the way that we play and play hard until the game is over and see what happens."

Luke Heimlich: When we got to the rain delay, I think everybody was able to take a breath and look at the situation and be like "we're playing Washington. We've played them three games every year we've been here in college. We know this team, we know the players, we know we can take care of business." So, in that rain delay, people relaxed. We were playing games in there; little Drew was in there hanging out with us. We just got back to being ourselves and knowing who we were, so the situation didn't really matter anymore.

"Little Drew," Drew Boedigheimer, always brought a smile to those within the Oregon State program. At age 2, Boedigheimer was diagnosed with restrictive cardiomyopathy and underwent a heart transplant. Boedigheimer, born in 2008, has battled other medical issues since the transplant, but his love for baseball never waned.

Despite living in Arizona, Boedigheimer grew up rooting for his parents' alma mater:

FINISH

OSU. He got to attend games when the Beavers played in Arizona and the family would make trips to Corvallis during the season. The College World Series was always a can't-miss event for the Boedigheimers, and the Beavers were thrilled to have their No. 1 fan in the house.

Pat Casey: It started when Darwin Barney went and saw him in the hospital in Chicago (in 2011). We were alerted to the fact that his father was an Oregon State guy and that Darwin was going to do that and it was a special deal. Therefore, we wanted to reach out to the Boedigheimers and make contact with them. And of course, from that, he started coming to the park, started meeting some of the guys and became something special to us. When you get into this world of athletics and you see guys running and throwing at high levels and you can get up and do whatever you want every day, it sure brings you back to earth when you see someone like Drew who loves the game of baseball. Our guys wanted to make him part of the club, and they did. He was there every chance he could get, through good times and tough times. He inspired us. You always think about guys like that, what you're doing for them, but that's not really the way it is. How it ends up is what they do for you. For me, it's special to think that we get to be around Drew.

Nate Yeskie: Drew is just the epitome of toughness. That young man has gone through more than anybody could ever imagine, and I think his parents knew that we needed him maybe as much as he needed us. Kudos to their insight of just trying to put everybody in a great environment where we could enjoy our time together. They wanted to see their son be a kid, too, and it's good for our guys because it allows them to be kids. I see (Ben) Wetzler talking to him about Pokemon and Andrew Moore having those same conversations. I know Trevor Larnach has become close with him as well. Getting to know his mom and dad was great. His dad knows my wife's uncle a little bit, they've got a history of being at Oregon State at the same time. Becoming close with them was easy, they are just wonderful people and anything we can do to help Drew is great.

I certainly think when you look at '17 and '18, his dad would say that he'd have some tough days, but knowing that maybe we had a game that day in Omaha, he was there and he was ready to rock and roll, he was going to go. There wasn't going to be anything that slowed him down, and when our guys see him trucking into the dugout, that gets them going. He was a big source of energy for us and a source of perspective in really what we're doing this thing for. It's not just for ourselves, we're doing it for everybody else. He's awesome, just a special kid and special family. I'm glad they were able to enjoy that part of the journey with us.

Trevor Larnach: I first met them my freshman year. They were there every year in Arizona, and just seeing the respect coach Casey and the staff had for Drew and his family really, really made a huge impact on me. Not just because Drew is a really strong individual, stronger than most of us, but because of how that family is and the relationships they have with the coaches put in perspective for me what's hard and what's not, and what's strong and what's not. To go up to them and talk to them and be with Drew as a young kid, to see how they interact with the players and the coaching staff is a really special thing. I'm beyond grateful to have that family in my life because they've helped me out, they've helped my family out, they've helped any other type of Beaver family out. It's not just the perspective that they bring, it's the energy and the love and the passion that they have for the school and the sport of baseball and that baseball family that we had, they would bring that to the field every single time. Every time they would come in, everyone would start yelling "DREW!" He would start clapping and be all hyped and ready to go, you'd see their family smile. It's just a special family.

Zak Taylor: Drew is one of those special kids. He is young and has basically been fighting since the day he was born. You can see commercials on TV and stuff like that about donating to a children's hospital and see pictures of sick kids, but until you really get the chance to actually know some of those kids in person ... for me, once Drew came into my life, it brought on this new perspective. I mean he's battling for his life, but at the same time this kid's always got a smile on his face, he's always excited when he's at the baseball field. And to think that our team hopefully had some sort of an impact on him, and the fact that he wanted to keep coming back to us, that absolutely meant the world to us. Because I think for a lot of us, we're doing baseball all the time and it can get to a point where baseball can define you sometimes if you're not too careful. With Drew, at least for me personally, I could take a step back and go "you know what, baseball isn't everything. There's a lot more to life than just baseball." I mean you've got kids fighting for their lives, and I'm over here pissed off because I went 0 for 4 in a game. Again, there are a lot bigger things than having a bad baseball game. It helped me shed that perspective and really opened up my eyes, that kind, sweet soul that kid has and just the tenacity of getting up every day and getting after it. I love it. I never heard him complain once, anything like that. That kid is a true, true warrior and I'm happy I can call him a friend.

Michael Gretler: That kid is an inspiration. You might think you have it hard, but you've just got to picture him and realize what he's going through on a daily basis. That kid's a warrior, he's overcome more than any of us and he's got to fight his battle every single day.

FINISH

Once we met Drew and his family, those are the kind of people you want to be around. They are warriors, they're courageous and they're inspirational.

Steven Kwan: We made sure he was always there with us. First of all, what a kid. That is one strong, brave kid. He's gone through a lot. And just to still have that attitude, he's awesome. Case always talks about how if we think we're having a tough day, no. Drew's having a tough day. He's going through surgeries, he's going through tough times and he still has a smile on his face and is grateful for so many things. He's a better human being than I am. He could've been negative about life and stuff, but no. He's a positive, warm energy. I was actually really lucky to get close to him because he's really into Pokemon and I played a lot of Pokemon when I was younger. It was awesome to just talk to him as a normal kid and we'd talk about a lot of stuff. He gave me a Pokemon stuffed animal that I always keep around and yeah, he kept our spirits up so very high and is just a brave kid.

Boedigheimer participated in some of the locker room fun as the Beavers waited for play to resume against Washington. Malone found himself in the most interesting position, awaiting a bases-loaded at-bat with two outs and Oregon State trailing 5-4 in the sixth.

Tyler Malone: It was wild. I remember I was on-deck and I was literally walking up to the plate, and then they called it. It was bases-loaded, two outs and I'm just like "dang!" So now we've got this rain delay, we all go back up to the locker room and I mean it was chill, there's not much you can do. We were playing Mafia which got a lot of hype, Joe Casey was throwing pieces of bubble gum in his mouth, we were snacking. But yeah, I really wasn't thinking about (my at-bat) too much. It was just like "OK, we've got to wait this through until this weather clears."

Nick Madrigal: It was probably the biggest moment of the season up to that point. In the locker room and everything, he seemed pretty confident and relaxed. It was the same old Malone, just hanging out.

Steve Kwan: I still don't know how he did it. He was in a bases-loaded situation, and then the game got suspended. So, for that (four-and-a-half) hours we were waiting, Malone knew he was up with two outs and he had to have a productive at-bat. I don't know how he stayed so calm, like he was in our waiting area so calm, bat in his hand, just looked so focused.

Jack Anderson: The biggest moment of our lives was coming up, and we just had to sit there and wait. That was nuts. I always thought about being in Malone's shoes and I couldn't have done what he did, just sitting there. He was loose, hanging out. Whether he was nervous or not, he wasn't thinking about it. He was in the zone that whole time where he just felt so good and confident in his hitting. I think he was the perfect guy to be up in that situation.

Tyler Malone: I knew how big of a moment that was, and I was able to battle through and get a walk. I still have this picture in my house of my reaction after that walk. I remember turning to the guys and they were all hyped because it tied the game, and we just knew we were back in it and we were ready to go.

Steven Kwan: That took some stones out of him, I can only commend him for that. That was one of the most amazing at-bats I've ever seen.

Nate Yeskie: Malone walks, there's excitement and enthusiasm. And then it was just an ultimate ambush. We hit them over the head with a lead pipe.

Malone fouled off the first pitch and then took four straight balls to tie the game. The Beavers left the bases loaded in the sixth, but an offensive onslaught was coming. Washington native Michael Gretler delivered the go-ahead hit one inning later with a two-out, RBI double. Nobach, another Washingtonian, followed with a three-run homer to make it a 9-5 game. Oregon State plated five more in the eighth against a dejected Huskies team that knew their magical College World Series run was about to end. Final score: OSU 14, Washington 5. The Beavers plated 10 unanswered runs following the rain delay.

Pat Casey: It was a long, long wait, then we had to come back and be ready to go. To put big numbers up on them, I enjoyed that.

Christian Chamberlain: I think everyone in our dugout and all of our coaches knew that once we came back out, we were going to play the typical Beaver baseball that we'd played all year.

Ryan Gorton: The rain delay saved us, maybe saved our season. Because we were down and playing with no energy, and when we came back from that rain delay every player was up on the top step, rooting for their guys. It just changed the energy in our dugout. We got a little pick-me-up and took that momentum into the last four or five innings we played. And Nobach came up with this huge oppo home run that sealed the game, put them away, which was pretty cool because he's from the Seattle area and had a history with some of those guys.

FINISH

Kyle Nobach: This is a story Nate Yeskie actually told me. I wasn't going to play that day, and Madrigal walked into Case's office and told him that he wanted me to play. Thinking back now, I ended up hitting a homer that day. I remember standing in the on-deck circle. Gretler hits a double and I came up with runners on second and third. It was a 2-2 count and I remember swinging at that (2-1) pitch that was up and out. I looked in the dugout and Case was fired up at me, yelling at me of course. Every time you look at that guy on the field, you just have this sense of like "all right, Pat. I'm going to do this one for you because I'm going to show you I can do this." He was telling me to stay through the ball, I got back in the frickin' box and I caught a fastball up and out and I hit it out. I remember running the bases and … it was just silence. I was in such a zone from hitting a ball out in the World Series to right-center. I can't even put the home run into words, it was one of the coolest pieces for me. I had rehabbed so much and had put a lot into what I did, it was definitely one of the coolest moments I personally had from the World Series because I had never hit a ball like that in my life before. I can't believe I hit that ball out to right-center, it's deep over there in that park.

I got lucky with how the wind was that day because it was usually blowing in, and it wasn't that day. It was at the right time, and I remember connecting with that ball and thinking "all right man, we've got this." We just busted it open.

Nate Yeskie: That was the final body blow. It's hard enough to hit a home run there to begin with, but the guy goes opposite-field. A buddy of mine actually took a video of when Nobach came up and just said "something good's going to happen here." He's an old baseball guy, he played at Oregon State and he just had a feeling.

Ryan Gorton: That was probably my favorite play from the whole World Series because I love Nobey. He's an unsung hero of that team, and that hit was just so big for him to knock Washington out and send us on our way into that next one.

Tyler Malone: When Nobach hit his home run, he got everybody hyped. Then I hit a home run, and that's when we just knew that we'd put the nail in the coffin for that game and we were able to pour it on. It propelled us through the rest of the week.

Michael Gretler: Our offense just went on a tear right after that delay. They gave us some smoothies back in the locker room. I don't know if there was something in them or what. But that was a big shift, from an offensive standpoint at least.

Trevor Larnach: It's almost like the rain came back and it gave us a little spike of energy, we had Goss Stadium and Oregon weather behind us. But we came out on fire, we came out ready to go, and I think that goes into our preparation and how we were during that rain delay and the mindset of what the coaching staff wanted. We also looked at it like we were going to use this against them because they were on fire. They were coming out hot ready to go, but we knew that rain was going to tear their momentum down. Obviously baseball is a game of momentum, and we used it to our advantage.

Cadyn Grenier: We were pretty familiar with them, they were familiar with us, and whenever that happens it's tougher to beat somebody because they know how to get you out and you know how to get them out. It just becomes a tighter game, and we were losing that battle. And for whatever reason, we get back out of that rain delay and it was like a whole different ballgame. I don't know if we handled it better than they did, but we went out like it was a brand-new game and ended up putting it to them.

Andy Jenkins: It was certainly a great year for UW, I respect a lot of their players and it was good for the Pac-12 for them to get there and boost our conference a little bit. But definitely during some of those years at Oregon State, there was a rivalry between UW and Oregon State that was sparked in a lot of different ways. It certainly felt good to knock them out.

Luke Heimlich: After the UW game, we figured things out and relaxed a little bit. I think before that, obviously you lose the first one and are then struggling in the second one, you have some nerves, you have some doubts creep in. But once you come away from that UW game, we were all like "we've got a second life, let's make the most of it."

By defeating Washington, the Beavers (50-11-1) earned a second shot at North Carolina (44-19). The Tar Heels found themselves in the losers' bracket after suffering a 12-2 loss to Mississippi State, and were light on starting pitching due to Dalatri's injury. Cooper Criswell got the start for North Carolina while the Beavers again turned to Heimlich, who only threw 63 pitches in the opener. Heimlich looked more comfortable in the rematch, but was victimized by a handful of soft hits and bad breaks, including a third-inning Brandon Riley two-RBI chopped double down the right-field line — a non-reviewable play — that appeared foul on replay. The two-time Pac-12 pitcher of the year was pulled after 2 2/3 innings, allowing three runs (two earned) on six hits with one strikeout and no walks or hit batters.

Luke Heimlich: I felt a little better in that game. Still missed some pitches, made some bad mistakes, but that's the game of baseball. There are a lot of uncontrollables, and once the ball leaves my hand I don't know what's going to happen. Baseball has a way of evening out. I mean, the year before I had a (0.76) ERA when I probably shouldn't have. Baseball gives and takes. That was one of those games where I felt all right with what I was doing, I didn't feel like I was on and there were a couple of unlucky bounces.

Adley Rutschman: There were a bunch of bloop hits, off-the-end little bloopers. He pitched well that game, it just felt like he got a little unlucky at certain times. Other than that, he was rolling.

Kyle Nobach: There was a ball down the line that was foul by about two feet, I think that's what Trev said. I remember standing out in the outfield talking with him about that, he said it was way foul. That was a big piece at the time. Everybody came together and we talked about how we weren't going to let the umpires dictate the things that are happening. We can't control those things, and if you let yourself go into those emotions of letting that take over your game … it goes back to having the mental fortitude to stay calm and not worry about things. You have to just compete and perform because the emotions are high.

Trevor Larnach: That pissed me off so much. Like I said, we were prepared going into that World Series because we knew what could happen from the last year. But that was a cherry on top of umpires in the World Series for us. Because first it was LSU that first year, then it was little missed calls here and there in that game specifically, which would've been a huge, huge turnaround if they could review that because there's no way that ball was fair. Just little things like that really piss me off, and I probably didn't handle it very well because I would talk to the umpires and I would be staying stuff. Nick would always tell me to chill the hell out, but I wouldn't listen because I didn't want the same thing that happened the year before to happen to us again. It really pissed me off, man. It is what it is and I probably didn't handle it the best way, but I know our team did.

Riley's controversial double made it a 3-3 tie, and North Carolina took the lead in the fifth on an Ike Freeman RBI single off Christian Chamberlain. One inning later, Kyle Datres sent a changeup from the freshman left-hander off the left-field foul pole for a two-run homer, putting the Tar Heels up 6-3.

Christian Chamberlain: I think I threw probably 10 changeups all year and I was in a spot I had to throw one because he was pretty balanced on both fastball and curveball. I threw it and it's my third-best pitch and I cut it; it's not supposed to cut. He stayed on it and it went right off the foul pole.

Trevor Larnach: Those guys were just bastards to deal with. Datres hit that two-run bomb down the line, and it felt like they were always on top of us.

Kevin Abel: We knew going into it that UNC was going to be trouble for us, just the way they were stacked up and the way they played was going to make things really, really hard for us. Their style of play, they are kind of that mix of SEC and Pac-12, with Pac-12 small ball and SEC (power). UNC will jump the yard if you give them the opportunity to, but they will fight for that one run every inning. And then they had a really good pitching staff, they played defense well, they were just a sound team and they were versatile.

Jake Mulholland: We were losing when I started throwing in the seventh. I threw three innings in that game and it was kind of a flashback to Fullerton my freshman year where I was like "we're losing, and I'm not going to make it worse." That was my only goal, get the offense back up and let them play, let them do their thing because they've got it in them. As we saw when we played UW, we were capable of coming back. I knew we had that in us, we just had to make sure we could go through some quick innings on defense and give them a chance.

Jack Anderson: We knew we were getting deep into their bullpen, and we felt that confidence coming and coming. And once the rain came from the heavens … it was like "all right, we played in the hot humidity the first game. Now we have our environment that they have to work in."

North Carolina held the 6-3 lead heading to the top of the eighth, when a Pacific Northwest drizzle began to spill from the sky at TD Ameritrade Park. Zak Taylor was set to lead off the inning against Caden O'Brien, who had thrown 4 1/3 innings of one-hit relief after taking over for Criswell in the third. O'Brien was in complete control, but the precipitation felt like a positive omen for the Beavers.

Tyler Malone: We called it the magical mist because it was Corvallis weather. I remember that when it started raining there, we would all look at each other like "oh, something is about to happen."

Adley Rutschman, to the Corvallis Gazette-Times: It felt a little bit like home back there in Corvallis. I think when the rain starts coming, we get that sense of

… weather can affect you in one way, and I think we have that opposite reaction. When it starts raining, I think we get a little bit more excited. It's kind of weird, but I think it happens.

Zak Taylor: I knew (O'Brien) was trying to get after me, especially being the nine-hole guy. I was probably one of the guys in the lineup they were like "OK, we've got to go right after this guy, we're trying to get outs." And at that time especially, I was a pretty good fastball hitter and I understood where I was at in the lineup and how teams were trying to approach me. Guys were trying to get ahead so they could finish me with a breaking ball or whatever it may be, so I knew if I could get into an advantage count, maybe work the count a little bit, or get something early in the zone that's firm, I could put a pretty good swing on the ball. I got (an 0-1 fastball) that was middle-in that I hooked a little bit, but it was enough to get through that six-hole. All I needed to do was get on base.

Jack Anderson, to the Corvallis Gazette-Times: The first thing that probably gets overlooked is Zak's hit. I think we didn't have a hit in three or four innings, and he got down 0-1 and was ready to hit and hit a ball really well. Just seeing somebody get a hit, it's definitely contagious. So once that got things going and the rain started coming down a little harder, it really sparked our team.

Zak Taylor: Then you get a knock here, a knock there, the bases are loaded and Rutsch is coming up in that situation.

Ryan Gorton: That's one I'll never forget. In the rain, we're down, it's not looking good for us and here comes Clutchman, what do you know? Perfect guy, perfect situation.

Madrigal followed Taylor's inning-opening single with a base hit of his own off new pitcher Joey Lancellotti. Next up was Cadyn Grenier, who fell behind 1-2 and battled his way to an 11-pitch walk that loaded the bases. North Carolina went back to the pen with Larnach due up, and Brett Daniels struck the slugger out on three pitches. Rutschman was coming to the plate with one down and the tying runs on base.

Daniels missed low with a first-pitch changeup to Rutschman, and the switch hitter was ready for another. Batting from the left side, Rutschman unloaded on a 1-0 changeup and sent a screaming line drive to straightaway center field. Riley wasn't playing deep enough, and the ball one-hopped off the wall for a game-tying, bases-clearing double.

Adley Rutschman: I remember I was locked in. I was focused on getting a good pitch to hit and driving it, seeing it. I remember I saw a changeup out of hand and he left it up, and I just tried to hit it as hard as I could. It's one of those things, it's amazing when you just let your body work, it knows what to do.

Trevor Larnach: If coach Casey thinks that Kyle's hit against Minnesota is one of the top ones, I'm going to say that's probably also one of the biggest (hits in program history).

Luke Heimlich: Adley was just unreal that whole season, the postseason, everything. I don't know, that game it seemed like he hit three balls to center in the gap. I feel like I can see that on repeat, I don't even know what game it is, the ball was always flying out there.

Kevin Abel: They took that lefty out that was absolutely crushing us, we loaded up the bases, Rutsch hit that double — and I don't know why their center fielder wasn't playing no doubles, but whatever. We got a lot of lucky breaks I guess; a lot of things went our way as opposed to not our way like in Game 1.

Bryce Fehmel: I couldn't believe that they weren't playing him on the warning track to stop the double. That hit by Adley was something special. It got our crowd into it and really sealed the deal for us.

Pat Casey: I just remember the ball going over the center fielder's head and me thinking "he wasn't deep enough for (one) out with the bases loaded and a three-run lead." Now the ball was smoked, but for me I was just excited to see the fact that it got over his head. Because when he first hit it, it was close enough for me to be thinking about (him catching it).

Zak Taylor: I think what's not talked about enough on that play is Cadyn's ability to run the bases, scoring from first on a ball that honestly got back in pretty quick from center. But he got such a good jump, got such a good read with no hesitation. Little things like that were so important, and I think that was one of those turning moments where "OK, we're ready to go. We expect things like this to happen."

Cadyn Grenier: I remember him hitting it and me going "oh my God, I'm scoring!" That's it. I was on first getting my secondary (lead), he hits it, I look out in the outfield and go "there's no way he's catching that." I just remember being super pumped while I was running around because I knew I was scoring and what that was going to do for us. I remember putting my head down and going, hitting home plate and being super stoked.

FINISH

Andy Jenkins: That was a tough decision for me looking back, just because of how hard (Rutschman) hit it and how it bounced off the wall. Sometimes it's easier to send them or hold them when they're as fast as they are, but sometimes it's harder. That was another thing that team had. They didn't just hit, pitch and play defense, they could really run around the bases and they were confident, we were aggressive. He did a great job motoring around.

Nick Madrigal: That was really the worst thing they could do, let Cadyn score from first base. That really doesn't happen, but he got a great jump.

Zak Taylor: I remember being in that dugout and thinking "yeah, we've got this. We've really got this." And I think even UNC had that "what just happened?" kind of thing.

Brandon Eisert: I wasn't going to pitch that day but I was down in the bullpen just trying to mix things up, trying to get some good mojo going. I was in the pen when Adley got the hit over the center fielder's head, and there were a couple other guys down there. We were just super excited, running all over. The excitement that came in that atmosphere and all the clutch things that happened in that game, the wave of emotions from losing the lead, taking the lead, all kinds of things. There were just a lot of emotions going on.

Andy Jenkins: One thing about those '17 and '18 teams, if you look at the guys that weren't playing in the dugout, they were just going nuts and feeding from the energy of everything we had going. That's another little thing, but it's a big part of championship teams: everybody is in it for everybody. We really enjoyed those moments.

Later that inning, Daniels issued three straight walks to a pinch-hitting Kwan (intentional), Gretler and Anderson to force in the go-ahead run. Oregon State plated four more in the ninth to put it away, getting RBI singles from Larnach and Anderson and a two-run Malone homer. Final score: OSU 11, North Carolina 6.

Trevor Larnach: I think we were more relieved about knocking North Carolina out than anybody else because they were always giving us a run for our money.

Jack Anderson: It was the same thing as it was with Washington. We came back, got the lead and it was just fireworks. We got right on them and didn't let go. Those two games are eerily similar in that aspect. We came back and blew the doors off of them, which was sweet. It was good to beat North Carolina, kind of the 2006 feeling. Lose the first one and we didn't get to play them twice more, but sending them home was pretty good. Joe Casey was always laughing and saying "they can't beat us! They'll beat us once, but they're never able to get Oregon State out of the tournament." That was a fun deal playing them again.

Michael Gretler: It was a special, special time those games. We weren't out of it until that last out. If we had one out left, three outs, five outs, we were going to battle our ass off at the plate and give ourselves a chance to win.

Dylan Pearce: The one thing that I had never really personally experienced before other than when I played for the (West Coast League's Medford Rogues), and you still couldn't even compare it to that, was how confident our guys were and how clutch they were. You could never, ever, ever count us out of a game. It could be the eighth inning and we could be down by eight runs and I would still say "guys, we're going to win this game, we're going to come back." And it seemed like we always would. It did not matter what the pressure was, who we were facing, the count, the outs, the runs, anything. We were so, so clutch, it was honestly funny to literally bet on it. We'd be sitting there in the dugout and nobody was stressing about it because we knew we were going to come back. Being able to see our lineup come back that well was unbelievable.

Michael Gretler: That's what a good team does. There were times throughout the year when the pitching picked us up, there were times throughout the year when the defense picked us up. So, I just think in that part of the year where hey, the defense and pitching hasn't been great, so the offense did its job and carried the team.

Pat Casey, after the game: Our club represented everything that I ask teams to be. They were resilient, they were tough, they fought, they scrapped, put up with my emotions.

I always tell guys there's a difference between activity and achievement. Activity is shadow boxing and achievement is knocking somebody out.

Nick Madrigal: It was just a great team win. That was a Beaver win right there.

Drew Rasmussen: The minute that momentum shifted, it was going to be tough to beat Oregon State, especially with that lineup. The pitching staff was going to be what the pitching staff was every year, so with how good that position corps was there, that's just a tough lineup to stop. Once everybody got things rolling, from then on there was no chance. Oregon State was definitely going to get to the final series.

FINISH

Jake Mulholland: I think it helped us that we didn't get to go through the winners' bracket and have all these days off. We didn't have a choice anymore; it was win or go home. Our backs were against the wall, so the only option we had was to play and to win. In a way, I think it helped us to stay locked in. Obviously we were going to be more tired and go through more pitching having to play an extra two or three games, but I think we embraced that. When you don't have a choice, the only thing you can do is fight.

Kyle Nobach: The fact that we were playing in the losers' bracket, everybody was just getting used to playing every single day at that field, at that stadium. We were playing more than everybody else and we were getting not necessarily more comfortable on the field, but we just played together and we knew we could play very good baseball.

Jack Anderson: There was a no-zoo policy that year, which just killed me. As a joke it was like "hey, the zoo is a curse; we're not going." It was funny because we saw Mississippi State there on their day off, so once we played them we were like "oh, they've got the curse on them. There's no way they're playing well against us!"

The College World Series typically has at least one underdog success story, and in 2018 it was Mississippi State. Ranked No. 12 in D1Baseball's preseason top 25, the Bulldogs were swept by Southern Miss on opening weekend. Head coach Andy Cannizaro resigned the day after the series ended, when details of an extramarital affair with an athletic department employee surfaced. Pitching coach Gary Henderson, a Eugene native and former assistant to Pat Casey from 1999-2003, was promoted to interim head coach following Cannizaro's resignation.

For the first few weeks under Henderson's leadership, Mississippi State appeared to be a team going nowhere. The Bulldogs entered the month of April 14-15 overall and 2-7 in SEC play, but a home series victory over rival Ole Miss helped the team get back on track. Mississippi State rallied to finish 15-15 in SEC play and earn a No. 2 seed in the Tallahassee Regional, but a 20-10 loss to Oklahoma left Henderson's club on the brink of elimination. Down to their final strike against Florida State, the Bulldogs got a spark of energy when Elijah MacNamee belted a three-run, walk-off home run to eliminate the host Seminoles. Mississippi State then won three games in two days to advance, and punched its ticket to Omaha by surviving a wild Nashville Super Regional against Vanderbilt. The first two super regional games were decided by walk-offs and the finale went 11 innings.

Playing with house money, the Bulldogs (39-27) started 2-0 in Omaha with victories over Washington and North Carolina. Next up was Oregon State (51-11-1), and the Beavers were ready to end the feel-good story. Eisert worked 5 1/3 one-hit, shutout innings in relief of Fehmel and OSU scored early and often. They got multi-hit games from Madrigal, Larnach, Nobach and Anderson, along with a big two-RBI Taylor triple. The end result was a runaway 12-2 Beavers victory, setting up a winner-take-all game for a spot in the CWS finals.

Michael Gretler: Mississippi State had a lot of fans there. They had a good team, and people were starting to think they were that fairy tale team of destiny. They had a great run to get there and I don't think at the beginning of the World Series people would've picked them to be in the driver's seat.

Andy Jenkins: They were a Cinderella team coming into the whole deal and had some great moments, and those types of teams are scary.

Trevor Larnach: We came out guns hot, man. We were ready to go. There was no elimination factor, right? Or was there? Oh yeah there was, just goes to show you that we didn't feel that way. There was no fear or anxiety about losing or going home, it was more like we were on the attack all the time and kept laying it on them, laying it on them. I don't remember the score of that game, but we were just on it.

Zak Taylor: I don't think I'd ever hit a triple, I'm pretty sure that was my only (career) triple. I was really sick that game, too. I was feeling terrible, not like the flu, but I was just beat up and achy. Before the game, I wasn't out there long for BP because it's 90-plus degrees out and it's humid. So, I'm feeling bad and I actually got hit (by pitches) twice that game.

It was an 0-2 count, the guy tried to extend a heater and missed his spot, he left it over the plate. I put a good swing on it and was able to get it in the gap, especially with their center fielder (Jake Mangum) shifted over. Thank goodness he laid out for it because I don't think I was going to be able to stretch a double into a triple. I was able to walk into third, and that was a cool moment.

Nate Yeskie: That first game against Mississippi State, I feel like we blinked and it was over with. It just never felt like there was much of a game. Fehmel again was just OK, but Eisert was really good behind him.

Bryce Fehmel: I don't think I threw my best, but I was able to hand it off to the bullpen and the bullpen did what they did, which was put up zero after zero and give our offense a chance. They did that all year long, particularly in the postseason. (Eisert) came in after me and absolutely shoved.

FINISH

Brandon Eisert: I remember coming out of the pen a little bit early and my job was to go as long as I could to save the rest of our arms. I was just doing what got me through the entire season: throw strikes, get ahead in counts and work from there. I think my off-speed was working pretty well against them, and just being able to locate fastballs was huge. I took it inning by inning and stretched it out as long as I could, and luckily I was able to save the rest of the arms for the following game.

No stranger to elimination games, the Bulldogs (39-28) didn't lack confidence entering their rematch with Oregon State (52-11-1). Mississippi State ace Ethan Small turned some heads with a quote after the 12-2 loss, saying "I think they can swing it as good as any team here. I don't think they are anything incredibly special. We put them on (base) 11 times free today. ... Fill the zone up, throw off-speed for strikes and just get them out."

Small, a left-hander, worked a 1-2-3 top of the first and wiggled out of a second-inning jam before running into trouble in the third. With two down and nobody on, Grenier ripped a double to left field. Larnach, Rutschman and Gretler followed with consecutive singles to put the Beavers up 2-0 as a red-hot Malone came to the plate.

Malone primarily pinch hit during his freshman season in 2017, going 11 for 43 (.256) with an eye-popping .441 on-base percentage. He worked his way into the designated hitter rotation as a sophomore but was batting a meager .255 entering the team's road trip to Missouri State. Around the same time, Malone began working with Tyler Graham to improve his mental game. He saw immediate results at Missouri State, homering in both games — the first two of his college career — to begin a streak of five straight games with a long ball. Malone cooled back down late in the regular season before catching fire in Omaha, launching homers in consecutive games against Washington and North Carolina. After going 1 for 2 with a pair of walks in the 12-2 win over Mississippi State, Malone was ready to do some more damage. He jumped all over a 3-1 fastball and connected, sending the ball over the fence in right-center for a three-run shot. The streaky Malone was boiling hot at the perfect time.

Tyler Malone: I remember that earlier in the game, I just missed a pitch and popped it up to right field. But I felt really good, I felt like I maybe pulled off it a bit. I remembered to maintain my direction toward center field basically to keep me working through the ball. I forget the count but he came with a fastball and it was middle, low and awayish. I was thinking about maintaining my direction to center so I was able to stay on the ball a little bit longer, and I took it out to right field. It's funny, because if you look at the video, I'm booking it to second base because MacNamee and Mangum ran into each other in the outfield. They were hopping around out there so I didn't think it got out at first, I thought they were trying to get the ball. Then I looked at Jenks at third base and he's clapping his hands so I'm like "oh dang, that ball got out!"

Dylan Pearce: It was so cool because he was a guy who kind of struggled for part of the year, and then he just went off when we were at Missouri State. It was insane. And then we got to the College World Series and he did the same thing, he started racking up balls.

Joe Casey: I lived with Malone for all three years (he was at Oregon State), so we'd always get on him. "Malone, what are you doing?! You were hitting like crap and then hit five straight bombs!" We always knew he was a great hitter, and I think part of the reason he was streaky was being a younger guy that year and not having a ton of at-bats the year before. But he got hot when we needed him.

Adley Rutschman: Me and Ty actually roomed together in Omaha. It was funny because we would talk after games and we would have these conversations about what we were feeling, and it was really in-depth and that was really where I feel like me and Ty got a lot closer. We're both very religious people, so we were just talking about it and it felt like we were both in very good headspaces during that time. It was cool to see that and I remember we would sit in the room and watch the highlights together after the game. After his home run that game, we played it probably 15 times in a row and were just smiling and laughing about it.

Kyle Nobach: He hit a lot of homers, man. In some really big games, too. He was another guy that got extra batting practice in, he was working on some type of development to make himself better. The mental game, the physical side, he trained hard in the weight room. He lifted weights, he pushed himself and he did a lot of extra hitting. He got in a groove … and he sure ran into some balls.

Bryce Fehmel: It was unbelievable to watch, and he couldn't believe it himself, either. He was like a robot up there, just hitting home run after home run and coming into the dugout saying "I have no idea what's going on, but here comes another one."

Trevor Larnach: He would go on tears like that, and then he'd have spells of dryness or whatever. But when you have him in the World Series doing that for us, it's like "all right, this is just another factor for a team to worry about pitching against us." Because when he's on fire like that, he's as good as anybody and is going to do damage, and that's exactly what he did. It was a huge help for us obviously and it was awesome for him, too.

FINISH

Pat Casey: I never lost any confidence in Malone. I think that he was never a guy that had a lot of failure. Maybe when he wasn't going good he was putting too much pressure on himself and thinking too much, and when he was going good he just let everything happen.

Tyler Malone: After (my regular-season home run streak), I remember I started getting pitched differently. I didn't see a lot of fastballs anymore and they were totally pitching me backwards, so I had to learn and get through that. I struggled for a couple weeks and I wasn't even playing the two weeks before the World Series. I can't explain where the streaks come from or whatever, but I was just super lucky to get hot during the World Series and help the team out and provide some extra run support when we needed it. But yeah, it was just a surreal experience. To have that success in those moments, I mean I'll remember it for the rest of my life.

Oregon State's two-out rally left Abel, who was making his first College World Series start, with a five-run lead to protect. The rested freshman proceeded to deliver the Beavers' first quality start of the CWS, surrendering a single run on three hits in seven superb innings. Closer Jake Mulholland took over in the eighth and retired the side in order on just 12 pitches. Protecting a 5-1 advantage, Mulholland recorded two easy outs in the ninth before things got interesting. MacNamee fell behind in the count 0-2, but the power hitter wound up working a walk to give the Bulldogs a modicum of life. Justin Foscue then walked on five pitches, and Luke Alexander followed with a bloop RBI single to make it a 5-2 game. Mulholland again jumped ahead 0-2 on Tanner Poole, but the next offering plunked the pinch hitter in the leg to load the bases. With a finals berth on the line, the typically calm and stoic Mulholland was feeling the pressure of the moment.

Jake Mulholland: Oh, man. Well, if you want to blame it on anything, I had an ear infection. I think I got it right when we were playing UNC. We had a day off before playing Mississippi State, so I went to the doctor and he gave me some antibiotics and I was just in my hotel room trying to take naps all the time. But that did not matter. I actually remember getting two outs very quickly and it was looking good. That's the thing about closing games though, there seems to be something about that 27th out. It's never given to you, you've got to earn it because teams do not like losing. When you get two outs quickly, it's really easy to lose focus and you immediately start looking at the next game, stuff like that. I just struggled for a couple batters there. I know I hit a guy, gave up a little base hit. But I knew "hey, calm down, settle down a little bit. You've got this, make your pitch."

Pat Casey: The thing about that particular situation, first of all, I don't find it difficult to coach in the World Series and I don't feel any pressure. I think there's pressure getting to the World Series, but I don't think coaching the World Series there is. I'm not suggesting that it's easy to manage in Omaha, I'm just saying that there's no pressure for me. The only time I ever felt real pressure in Omaha was when we had never won a game and were playing Georgia (in 2006) and we were going to be the first team in the history of the College World Series to lose six games in a row, and I wasn't even alive when we lost the first two. They lost two in '52, we'd lost two in '05 and then we lost the first one in '06, so we were going on number six if we lost, and I just knew we could win. After that, I felt like if we did our job for 56, 60 games to get them here, we've got to let them play.

But that situation right there, I could see his facial expression change. I could see him getting tight. I could see him starting to aim the ball, and that bothered me. Like I said, I think when you're in a World Series, if you're the head coach and you've got anxiety, then the players do, too. And I think there's a difference between having anxiety and being tight as opposed to yelling in the dugout and doing things that are exciting. But in that particular situation, I was certainly concerned with the fact that he was starting to tighten up a little bit, and that wasn't Mully. Mully was usually pretty cool on the mound, but he started to get a little tight and I could visibly see it. I talked to Nate and we were thinking "well, what are we going to do now?"

Nick Madrigal: I had never seen Mully like that before. It seemed like he was a little bit nervous, or something just didn't feel right to him. After one thing led to another, I remember trying to slow things down, go out there and try to talk to him, get his mind off it for a second. He'd pitched in some big games for us … but that one was obviously the biggest one of our season (to that point). But I knew he could get it done and I think everyone else on the team would agree that he was the right guy for that situation.

Trevor Larnach: Yeskie called a huddle, and everyone's coming in. This story is coming from Nick. Yeskie runs up to the huddle, and Jake's eyes looked like he'd seen a ghost. His eyes were wide open, his chest was breathing super tightly and he was panting, looking around the whole stadium and he couldn't even focus. Nick told me that after, and everyone started busting up laughing, because Mully's always a really chill Fehmel-esque type of pitcher, not really giving a shit and just getting it done. But that whole end of the game went haywire for him. And it was funny to hear it, because that's not how Mully usually goes about his business.

Nate Yeskie: I was getting ready to look at one of the infielders or Rutsch and figure out which one of them was going to give him CPR because I didn't think it was going to be me. Or were we going to have to get the trainer out? He was pasty white and breathing way too fast. Just caught up in the moment, the whole thing is snowballing and going and I tried to calm him down and tell him "hey man, this is just on your own. There's no big deal here, you've done this to yourself. They haven't done anything to you."

Adley Rutschman: Yeskie came out to the mound and basically said what we were going to do. He's like "send us to the championship right here, let's get after it. You've closed out how many games here at Oregon State? You're the guy for the job, I trust you out here and just get after it."

Yeskie, I think he was trying to light a fire a little bit. I think that's what the goal was, remind him that you're the dude, you're the man.

Christian Chamberlain: I remember Case yelling at me and Heimlich to go down to the pen because we hadn't played catch all day. We had to go down and warm up with two outs and two strikes in the ninth inning. That was kind of weird. I don't know who was going in, but they called down and said that if he let another run in, one of us was probably coming in.

Kevin Abel: There was never a doubt that he was going to get it done, he just made it a little harder than what it needed to be.

Jake Mulholland: It was bases loaded and we were up (5-2) at that point, so a grand slam would've won it for them. And (Jordan Westburg) was the guy who had just done that recently, and of course I had watched that and knew about that.

Four days prior, Jordan Westburg had a grand slam and three-RBI double in Mississippi State's victory over North Carolina. Westburg was also the inventor of the team's "rally banana," which made its first appearance during the Tallahassee Regional. While playing Oklahoma in an elimination game, a hungry Westburg grabbed a banana and put it on his head like a rally cap. The team proceeded to score eight runs that inning, and the rally banana stuck. Banana shirts, signs and balloons were commonplace at Mississippi State games moving forward, and a new banana sat in the dugout each game. What began as a joke morphed into something far greater, and Westburg had a chance to send Mississippi State to the College World Series finals.

Preston Jones: There were some thoughts going through our heads because Mississippi State was that team that year. They did some special things and had a few walk-offs and big hits throughout their playoff run.

Michael Gretler: Having won games the way they'd won late in the season with the rallies and walk-off home runs, it's in the back of your mind. They are loading the bases and it's like "uh oh. They've been here, they've found a way to win as well." You obviously aren't thinking about it a lot, but it's definitely a thought.

Brandon Eisert: It was a little nerve-wracking towards the end there. Maybe the bananas really did have some powers and they were going to come through?

Ryan Gorton: I was at the game when Westburg hit the grand slam and I'd watched most of those games. If I wasn't watching live, I watched them on TV. So, I was totally aware of it, I saw all of their fans with bananas and stuff and knew what that meant. In the bullpen, right when Mulholland hits the guy to make it 5-2 with the bases loaded, I'm charting out there and I'm like "oh my God, it's Westburg coming up." I think my heart sank and it was just like "well, I hope this guy doesn't hit another grand slam."

Pat Casey: I did not know that was the guy who had hit the grand slam, but I knew about the rally banana, I knew about how many comebacks they had. I saw them walk-off Vanderbilt (in the super regionals), I knew they were playing at an elite level. But no, at that particular time I wasn't thinking about the guy hitting a grand slam; I was thinking about trying to get his ass out.

Jake Mulholland: I knew that he was going to get a healthy dose of changeups low and away. I ended up throwing a pretty good changeup, he hit it right to Cadyn and we lived to see another day.

Ahead in the count 1-2, Mulholland got Westburg to hit a chopper right at Grenier. The Pac-12 defensive player of the year fielded the grounder cleanly but had a little trouble getting his right hand on the ball. Taking his time, Grenier flipped it to Madrigal at second for the game's final out. After opening the tournament with a ghastly loss, the Beavers were back in the College World Series finals for the first time since 2007.

Pat Casey: The funny thing is (Westburg) hit a ball firm right at Grenier, and he couldn't get the ball out of his glove. Fortunately for us, we were in the right place at the right time.

Nate Yeskie: Grenier, once he double-clutches it I'm going "ahh!" Then I see Nick catch the ball the way he does at second, his feet are backwards, but they call him out and the game is over.

FINISH

Jake Mulholland: I was like "Cadyn, I know you're good and you've got some time, but let's not make this too interesting here. Let's just get rid of it!" But he knew what he was doing and it all worked out.

Cadyn Grenier: I just lost it in the pocket a little bit, but I knew I had time and I knew that Nick was going to be there. I tell everybody this, if I would have panicked and tried to hurry up and do everything I probably would have (made a mistake). But in that moment I was able to stay calm and find that ball on the second grab and make a good throw to Nick, and I knew the guy would still be out. Obviously that was nerve-wracking, but when I thought about it after I was happy with myself. I felt like I did a really good job of staying calm in that moment and doing what we trained to do all year during practice when we'd have high-speed ground balls and stuff like that, going game speed. I just remembered to stay calm and keep it simple, and that's exactly what I did.

Nick Madrigal: I've seen the replay and it looks worse than it was. I knew when it got hit to Cadyn that it was a pretty for-sure out. It was one of those things where you kind of hold your breath for a second when he double-clutched, but it all worked out.

Tyler Malone: I just remember Mully, once we got that third out, he almost had a heart attack. Everybody was hugging him and his hat was all over the place. After we won, we were definitely laughing about that.

Preston Jones: (Mulholland's) facial expression after was just one big sigh of relief, which was funny to see. But it was special because we were headed to the finals.

Nate Yeskie: The game finishes with the bases loaded, a guy ... who'd hit a home run earlier in Omaha on I believe a changeup, and we got him to ground out to end the game on a changeup.

And who was on deck? Mangum, who'd foolishly got a base hit in the (fifth) and tried to press a single into a double. Grenier had a great relay to second, Nick put the tag down and the inning was over with, and Abel got to last (two) more innings.

Michael Gretler: That was our (fourth) elimination win in a row, so it was like "all right, now we're on to the finals and it's a two out of three series."

Joe Casey: We didn't play one game like it was an elimination game at all. No one was nervous or scared, I think we played every game the opposite way like we had nothing to lose. And honestly, maybe losing that first game helped. Because the year before, we went and lost those two to LSU and people had high expectations for us again. Then we lose, so I think we were all like "well, we've got nothing to lose now. Let's just win out, why not?"

FINISH

CHAPTER IX

FINISHING THE JOB

Oregon State eliminated Mississippi State the evening of Saturday, June 23, seven days after its opening loss to North Carolina in the College World Series. The long journey through the losers' bracket left no time for a breather, and the third-seeded Beavers (53-11-1) were back at TD Ameritrade Park Sunday afternoon for an on-field practice. Despite a looming best-of-three CWS championship matchup with rested No. 4 national seed Arkansas (47-19), OSU was as loose as ever during its final practice of the season. On another hot, sticky Midwest day, the team wrapped things up with a little buffoonery.

Pat Bailey, associate head coach: I thought it was awesome the day the water balloons came out at the end of practice when we were getting ready to play the championship. First of all, just for Case to allow it to happen because a lot of coaches would say "we're not doing that on the field," because we were at the ballpark where we would play for the national championship. I just thought it was great, there was a looseness about us, the guys were having fun. Kyle Nobach, who is such a great teammate and such a crazy man, he gets those eyes that look like a serial killer and he's got balloons in his hands. I just laughed watching Kyle and some of the guys run around because I remember somebody hit Kyle and Kyle was going after guys. That part was fun.

Kyle Nobach, outfielder: That was the best practice ever! It was awesome, man. We were out there having a water balloon fight on this beautiful field right before we're about to play for the national championship. It kind of loosened things up.

Christian Chamberlain, pitcher: Obviously it's a high-intensity tournament, we had been through hell and back through the season with injuries and everything else. It was a moment at the biggest stage in college baseball to realize that it is still a game, that we are just playing baseball. I think it put everything into perspective and it was a lot of fun to go out there and do something we all did as kids, whether it was after a Little League practice or something like that.

Brandon Eisert, pitcher: That was just the team that we were. We weren't going to think the moment was too big for us or anything like that, we weren't going to let anything get in our heads, get uptight and be super laser-focused. Just being loose, relaxed, we wanted to have fun as a team. Obviously we would be focused the next day at the game and we were still going to have a good practice, but staying relaxed and being in the moment and taking in everything and what we'd accomplished so far was something we definitely wanted to do.

Cadyn Grenier, infielder: I mean we had a water balloon fight, how much looser can you get? I think that was the coaches, man. We had a staff that really knew that our team was going to do the best we could if we were under those circumstances where we didn't feel like we had the weight of the world on us, where we didn't feel like we had to do something or we were a disappointment. The coaches and players and everyone together were just like "hey, we've got nothing to lose. We made it to where we are, the only thing we can do is keep playing the way we play. That's how we're going to play at our best." I think the coaches did a really good job of helping us stay calm and have some fun.

Pat Casey, head coach: Everybody thinks that you go in there … I'm not going to change things. I'm not going to tell guys "hey, we should do this or that." Guys told me one day they wanted to wear shorts, so we wore shorts. I think that you can't try to do something that you haven't done all year and make it something it's not. You have to win a baseball game, then you have to win another one, then you have to win another one.

Jake Rodriguez, assistant coordinator of camps: Every game in Omaha, I would sit with coach. He would do the lineup and hand it to me, then I would write the lineup card up and hand it in. I just remember every day, he would say the same thing: "this could be the last one, this could be the last one," always joking around. And coach Casey in the postseason, he seems to be a little bit less on edge all the time. I mean he's still as intense as it gets, but you can tell that he is excited and more relaxed because he knows how good the team is, so he was able to joke around a little bit.

FINISH

Kyle Nobach: At that point in time, I wouldn't say Pat had necessarily stepped back, but he knew that if we were going to win this thing, it was up to the players. He knew we were never going to stop fighting and never stop competing because that was the mindset we all had.

Andy Jenkins, assistant coach: There are a lot of times where it's a tough environment or Case can come at you in a hard way, but there's also a looseness, there's also a sense of fun in the program. Case doesn't dictate what the players are always doing. As long as they play hard, are good people, are good students, are good in the community, you can go out and have fun and joke around before or after practice, throw the football around, have a water balloon fight. He was really good about the balance of what we were doing, and our kids loved each other. Whether it was on the field or off the field, they had a true brotherhood, and that's what you need to win championships. That was really the theme that's been in the program since I played, and much before me, too. The bond of the players was always there.

Led by longtime head coach Dave Van Horn, Arkansas' recent history was similar to Oregon State's. The Razorbacks also missed the 2016 NCAA Tournament and were selected to host a regional the following year. Missouri State ended Arkansas' postseason run before the College World Series, but the Razorbacks returned loads of talent in 2018 and went on to share the SEC West Division title with Ole Miss. Arkansas made it to Omaha with ease and went 3-0 on its side of the bracket, taking down Texas, Texas Tech and defending CWS champion Florida.

Luck is required to win a national title, and the Beavers received a fortunate break before a pitch was even thrown in the championship series. Scheduled to begin play Monday, June 25, OSU and Arkansas arrived at TD Ameritrade Park a few hours before the game and took batting practice in perfect conditions, but the doppler radar showed incoming inclement weather. The start of Game 1 was delayed and eventually postponed until Tuesday, giving OSU an extra 24 hours to rest its pitching staff. The Razorbacks, who'd played two fewer games at the CWS, didn't need the additional time to get their regular starting rotation of Blaine Knight, Kacey Murphy and Isaiah Campbell ready to go. For OSU, it was a lifesaver.

Kevin Abel, pitcher: Arkansas had a pretty seamless run through their bracket, and we did not. Having that extra day of rest and just having that day to really take a breath and focus up for the next three games was big.

Luke Heimlich, pitcher: I was slated to start Game 1. It was going to be short rest, but I hadn't gone deep in either of my two starts and my pitch count was low. Then it rained, so it got delayed a day, and I was like "oh man, I get an extra day." So, I was feeling good, and I think everyone was feeling good going into it.

Steven Kwan, outfielder: I remember thinking that I was getting so lucky, so blessed, that I got another day to recover, but same with the whole team. We had been grinding through all our games, obviously the rest never hurts.

Nate Yeskie, pitching coach: Just think about the math in and of itself. You don't get Kevin Abel in Game 3 if we don't get rained out, not as a starter. You might get him in relief, but he ain't starting that game. And if he does, he's certainly not going more than two or three innings.

So that rain delay, I remember Pat (Casey) comes in and he goes "hey, what are you thinking? Do you want to try and get this in tonight? Do you have a reason for or against?" They hadn't made a decision, but he was trying to figure it out in his mind and he was just doing as you do as a head coach. He was taking in all the information that you can so you can make the best decision possible. And I said "boy, if we could get one more day, there's no telling how far that could go." Because we'd used Eisert long against Mississippi State as well, so that rest for him was every bit as significant.

Pat Casey: I think the day's rest helped, there was no question. And I think that the fact that we couldn't play, there was no question. I sat in a room with Dave (Van Horn) and everybody there, and they kept showing us the radar and said "we'll let you know in an hour, we'll let you know in an hour and a half." Dave and I had the same thought. We were OK either way, just don't make us start a game, stop it after four innings and say that we've got to come back and play tomorrow, that's all we asked. If we could play, let's play. If not, let's not. And they ultimately said we couldn't, and I do think it was more beneficial to us than it was to Arkansas.

The Beavers used the rainout to recuperate and get ready for Arkansas, a balanced squad that entered the finals batting .302 with 98 home runs and a sound pitching staff. Knight, a third-round pick of the Baltimore Orioles, had a perfect 13-0 record and nasty stuff from the right side. Oregon State knew Knight would present a challenge, but the team was caught off guard by Arkansas' boisterous army of supporters.

Michael Gretler, infielder: We didn't really know a whole lot about Arkansas. They had rolled through their whole year, the regional, super regional and World Series, and I honestly didn't know a lot about them. They obviously had a lot of talent on that team, but I didn't know a lot of their guys. I hadn't heard much about them, there weren't really any big names or whatnot. It wasn't like the year before when you're playing LSU and they've got a couple big names and a couple first-round picks and all that. It was definitely different from that standpoint.

Trevor Larnach, outfielder: I remember the scouting report on Knight was that he did well against every good team they played. I think we prepared the best way we could for him, but I don't think we could've prepared for the turnout that team had as far as support and fans go, because that was just nuts.

Tyler Malone, infielder/outfielder: It was crazy how many Arkansas fans were there. They would do their whole Woo Pig (Sooie) thing and we had no clue what they were saying.

Jack Anderson, outfielder: They had the freakin' Woo Pig Sooie chant, that's all they had in their repertoire and they used it every time they could.

Luke Heimlich: All those Woo Pig Sooie chants, I never want to hear that again.

Steven Kwan: It was so loud; I couldn't even hear myself think. I remember during BP before the games would start, they would open the gates and the Arkansas fans, it was almost a little scary. They ran from the gates all the way. You could see them sprawling all over the outfield bleachers, it was like a zombie movie. They were running straight to us to start talking smack, and it was an endless sea of people. And it was all Arkansas fans because Arkansas was the closest team. It was a (six-hour) drive from Fayetteville. Man, it was so loud. They would bang the metal gates in the outfield and that would just add to the noise, I couldn't even hear myself think. It was crazy. Like I remember in BP if there was a ball that went to the wall and I was trying to make a play at the wall, they would just start banging stuff, being so loud. It was definitely an advantage that they had.

Michael Gretler: I remember coming out of the tunnels for BP the first game and the whole outfield was a sea of red. You're just sitting there like "oh my God, this is unbelievable." It was so cool, but obviously at one point in that first game when they started scoring some runs and guys were sidling in, I remember that place just shaking. I remember standing at third base and their base coach was trying to talk to the runner at third, we were all standing by the base and the coach was screaming at the top of his lungs to talk to the guy, and he's right in his ear. That's how loud it was. It was a completely different environment than I think anyone on our team had ever played in.

Joe Casey, outfielder: Shagging before those Arkansas games, they've looked up stuff on your whole life history and they're talking smack. The funniest one for me is I was in center field just taking fly balls before the second game. And you know Arkansas, their fans are all confident because they won the first one and their fans like to ride the wave when they're winning, they were pretty quiet after the second game. But I'm out there and this section is chanting "daddy's boy!" And I think that stuff's funny, I don't take it personal, and I look back at them and point and they all start laughing because I acknowledged them. My brother went out there to take some fly balls and they are saying stuff to him and he can't take the joking around. He got all pissed off and was yelling at them, and I'm like "Jon, get off the field!" But all that stuff was fun, the fans who come and love you as well as the fans who like to talk smack.

Jack Anderson: It was just terrible. I remember the LSU fans (the previous year) were talking to you, trying to get on your nerves. When we played Mississippi State, I thought their fans were pretty chill, probably because we were winning most of those games so they didn't do too much. But Arkansas fans brought a whole 'nother level of just being mean, laying it all out there. Talking how much you suck, talking about anything they could find on social media, Facebook, whatever it was. Whoever was in any outfield position, they had a "sucks" chant. It was like "Jack," and then everyone else would yell "sucks!"

Kyle Nobach: Oh man, they were definitely over the line. There were a lot of points in time during those games when people were yelling at me and saying stuff where I was like "man, this is probably not OK." It would literally be somebody standing behind you for three hours and going "hey Kyle!" every two seconds. It would be things like "hey Kyle, your aunt left her phone charger in my room last night!" It was just a crazy environment, man.

Jack Anderson: Me and Nobey were coming in and out of those games and he'd be like "dude, how is it out there for you?" And I'm like "Nobey, they are ruthless!" He's like "yeah man, I can't even pay attention, they're just saying shit!" It was brutal stuff, but you expect it out of those people. I mean I'm sure that's just how they roll, that's how it is. We're not used to it, but that was the closest they'd been to a national championship in a long time and all they've got down there is their Arkansas Razorbacks. They were laying it all on the table against us out there in the outfield. You definitely didn't want to go out there after you made a mistake, that's for sure. They were going to let you know about it.

Christian Chamberlain: Troy (Claunch) had one of those shots you get from a gas station thrown off his helmet, someone tried pouring a beer on me. The security out there did a great job and shut it down pretty quickly and a lot of it was just words, but that wasn't an easy place to warm up and you have to tune it out the best you can.

Dylan Pearce, pitcher: Arkansas and North Carolina were bad. There were some things that I wouldn't really repeat. It would've been different if they were saying funny stuff, but it got to the point where they were saying some stuff that was pretty bad. I was just like "come on guys, it's a college baseball game." And look, I understand if you want to heckle, that's OK. And there was some funny stuff, we had some Arkansas fans that would find the names of our girlfriends and our sisters and stuff and would throw that at us. That part was funny, but the other half … it was to the point where we had to have an officer stay in our bullpen and there were a few people we had to have removed from the stadium because of what they were doing.

Christian Chamberlain: I remember me and Troy were out in the outfield, my number is 34 and his is 17. One of the Arkansas fans who obviously had a few drinks in him was like "17 times 2 is 34, we know math!" They had some funny comments, but some of the stuff went too far.

Trevor Larnach: I thought it was fun, man. A lot of those guys did their homework. They were chanting out some of my family members' names, they were chanting out my girlfriend's name. You don't expect to hear stuff like that and depending on the person you are, you can either take it really hard or you can just laugh it off, and that's how I am. I understand what they're trying to do, they're trying to get in my head or whatever it is, but it was funny to me because I wasn't expecting it at all. There was some shit they were saying that was messed up, but I'm sure it's pretty similar to what you would hear as an outfielder in Yankee Stadium or Boston. It's almost like you're getting prepared for the biggest stage possible, but you're also trying to finish off the goal we've had forever. Nothing was going to prevent us from doing that.

Tyler Malone: We were never too fond of the Arkansas fans, but the Mississippi State fans on the other hand were great. We saw a lot of them outside of the games because they were at our hotel, and they were super nice and super respectful. I actually met some Mississippi State fans at an ice cream parlor downtown and took a picture with their son, and we've stayed in contact ever since. That was a super cool experience and that's what baseball is all about. At the end of the day it is a game, and it gives you the opportunity to meet people and establish those connections and relationships you never thought you would have.

After a 24-hour delay, the College World Series championship series finally began on a pleasant Omaha evening. Knight was as good as advertised, limiting Oregon State to one run on seven hits in six innings. The Beavers were again imperfect in the field and had a couple more breaks go against them in a 4-1 loss. OSU was back in a familiar spot — facing elimination, with no margin for error.

Pat Bailey: We just didn't hit. We had some opportunities to score some runs with runners in scoring position and couldn't get a hit. And I have to tip my hat to (Blaine Knight), I thought he threw a great game against us.

Pat Casey: Their guy was good, man.

Ryan Gorton, undergraduate assistant coach: Blaine Knight threw really well against us. He was down in the zone, his stuff had good life. Sometimes that happens in baseball, you just get beat by a better pitcher. I don't think it was anything more than that. Baseball is a weird sport. It's tough to be perfect.

Cadyn Grenier: It was a really good game and Blaine Knight pitched really well against us. We're good buddies now, so we talk about that stuff literally all the time. But yeah, he pitched great and I felt like we played well. A couple things didn't go our way, they capitalized on a couple mistakes that we made, the ball just bounced in their direction and we couldn't really come back from it. They played a great game and they beat us in the end.

Nate Yeskie: (Knight) was tough. I thought we put together some decent at-bats early, and it was kind of like the LSU game the year before where we had (Alex) Lange in a position where we could've twisted him. When Rutschman's interference call happened, it was like "wait a minute, what are we talking about here? This makes no sense."

Oregon State held a 1-0 lead in the bottom of the fourth when Trevor Larnach led off with a sun-aided double. Adley Rutschman followed with a single to put runners on the corners for Tyler Malone, who hit a grounder to Jared Gates at first base. Gates was willing to trade a run for a double play and promptly fired it down to shortstop Jax Biggers covering at second. Biggers was forced to double-clutch on the return throw because Arkansas didn't have a defender covering first base. A hustling Malone slid in safely at first as Knight and second baseman Carson Shaddy, who secured the return throw, collided on top of the bag. Larnach scored on the bizarre play to put OSU up 2-0. They thought.

Rutschman was caught in an awkward spot on the sharp grounder. He was close enough to be in Biggers' direct vision but too far away to slide. He chose to duck as he approached the base, giving Biggers plenty of room to throw over him. Second base umpire Chris Coskey ruled it interference on Rutschman, which made Malone out at first and forced Larnach to return to third. Knight then fanned Michael Gretler to end the inning, and the Razorbacks suddenly had the momentum down just 1-0.

Adley Rutschman, catcher: Oh my gosh, I remember I was halfway to second base and it was one of those things where it felt like it was too early to slide, I wouldn't have made it to the base if I would've slid. So, I just tried to crouch, get out of the way, basically. Looking back, I don't think I interfered with the actual play itself. It didn't seem like … I mean knowing the rule now, yes, I should've slid, but it didn't seem like it interfered with the actual play. It's one of those things I get upset about if I think about too much because I thought (the call) was … bad.

Pat Casey: There is absolutely no question that interference should not have been called, no question.

Nate Yeskie: He did nothing to obstruct that thing. The guy panicked, double-clutched, couldn't get it out. That's one of those calls where somebody should be able to go back and review. They said "oh, it's not a reviewable call, it's a judgment call." Well, it was poor judgment. That would be like a guy throwing a ball four feet outside and having it called a strike. It's not a strike, it's four feet outside.

Tyler Malone: It made absolutely zero sense. It was just weird, and sometimes in baseball things won't go your way. Looking at the replay and everything after, people absolutely lost it because we were like "what else is he supposed to do?" But yeah, that was definitely a weird moment for sure and Case was losing it, rightfully so.

Trevor Larnach: I just remember thinking to myself "all right, here we go again. We're going to get screwed by an umpire, and it is what it is." I remember looking at the replay and seeing how pissed coach Casey was. If coach Casey was going to get pissed like that, it's probably for good reason because he's well aware of how the game works and everything. I watched the replay of it and the kid didn't throw the ball to first (immediately) because nobody was there!

He made it look like Adley was going to run him over or whatever it was, that wasn't the case. I think the umpire got fooled, but of course ESPN and the SEC Networks are going to cover their asses and say, "the rulebook says he has to slide" and whatever. But you know what, there were plenty of times I didn't slide on the base paths and nobody said shit to me, so I don't care who says what. I think however long we were there playing for Oregon State, there was always someone against us and multiple people against us, and that's just how we looked at it. Whether it was true or not, doesn't matter. It worked for us.

One inning later, Steven Kwan — playing through his nagging hamstring injury — got aboard via a two-out single, and then Cadyn Grenier sent a line drive down the right-field line that was ruled foul. It was a close call, but replay confirmed the ball did catch the line. Oregon State challenged the reviewable play and won, but Grenier was only awarded a single on what would've been a surefire double while a hobbled Kwan was placed at third base. Two pitches later, Nick Madrigal lined out to Shaddy and the inning came to an end. It was OSU's last true threat of the evening.

Pat Casey: Grenier hits a ball down the right-field line. They call it foul, it's fair, and they give him a single?! Like, how do you do that? It was just a lot of things.

Cadyn Grenier: I remember being really upset because I'm running down the line and I know for a fact it's a fair ball because I'm staring at it. So, I'm rounding first and they call it foul, I look over and am like "that was fair, that was definitely fair." I started walking back and Case was looking at me and I told him it was definitely fair. So, he challenges it, and then I just remember them going "hey, you're on first." I looked at the umpire and I was like "I'm what?" And he goes "yeah, you're on first (because you stopped running)," and I was like "you guys called it foul, what was I supposed to do!?" I remember everything about that because once again it gets brought up all the time between me and Blaine Knight.

Michael Gretler: We were never able to get anything going offensively. We were never able to string together any hits, and I remember they were getting bloop hits to fall in. It was one of those games where you're like "oh man, the ball is just not falling our way."

Case in point: Luke Heimlich. Through four innings, Heimlich appeared to be en route to one of his quintessential lights-out performances. He faced the minimum in three of the first four innings and entered the fifth with five strikeouts and only one hit surrendered. Dominic Fletcher popped up to open the fifth, and seemingly out of nowhere things fell apart. It started with a four-pitch walk, then Arkansas strung together consecutive singles to tie the game. Heimlich hit the next two batters to force in a run, then Madrigal committed a rare error to bring in another. In a matter of six batters, Heimlich went from domination to the dugout.

Luke Heimlich: I felt loose, but it was still kind of the same thing. I had a couple bad misses with the breaking ball, was just a little amped up. I was definitely better through the first few innings.

Pat Casey: He lost command; I think that was the deal. He threw a couple balls and thought "OK, I haven't been pitching well, I REALLY have to be good." Because those guys, you know, they are cognizant of the fact that they've been our leaders and they hadn't pitched well, so he probably pressed a little bit and went to too much effort.

Nate Yeskie: The previous two starts in Omaha he had something that just wiggled and went sideways, and those were the things that he dealt with his first two years in college where he could be really good for a while, and then all of a sudden he'd get the speed wobbles and things would go sideways. It just played itself over again in that sense. The weirdness of not having been there, maybe had he been there the year before, that might've played itself out differently just from a familiarity sake and things like that. Because he's a smart kid, I think he knew in the back of his mind it was the last time he was going to pitch in college. I do think, based on the draft having come and gone and his name not being called, I think he thought "as good as I've been and as hard as I've thrown and everything else, if I just do everything better, then somebody is going to give me a chance to keep playing." I think he tried to do too much at some point. I could be completely wrong, that's just my own two cents.

Steven Kwan: It was definitely interesting. Luke is one of the most strong-minded people I've ever met, and that crowd, that Arkansas crowd was so loud and so negative towards him. I just assumed that he was going to work through that one as well, but I think a lot of people have their breaking point. Luke still battled how Luke will, but I think that crowd was definitely a game-changer for him.

Luke Heimlich: I'd rather not go into that.

Zak Taylor, infielder: You should never have to worry about fans throwing beer on you or food on you or saying these slurs. Of course, they're going to have an effect on you because those things aren't just said normally. That was hard to see and I know it was tough for him and like I said, no player should have to go through that. It's already enough playing in that setting, playing in Omaha. You're trying to make a run at this thing and you don't know how many opportunities you're going to get. It was just unfortunate. I remember him going to warm up, and he had a security guard with him. It was hard for all of us, but he's a strong-willed human and I think he took it as best he could and handled the situation really well.

After Heimlich got the early hook, Oregon State turned to its bullpen, which had performed admirably throughout the postseason. Freshman Christian Chamberlain was thrown head-first into the fire, taking over for Heimlich with the bases loaded and one down. Chamberlain promptly walked Heston Kjerstad to force in another run, but the left-hander came back to strike out Luke Bonfield and Fletcher on curveballs to end the inning. Chamberlain settled in from there and finished the game, striking out 11 in 4 2/3 shutout innings while giving up two hits with five walks. He was a little wild at times, but Arkansas — similar to Mississippi State and LSU — didn't fare well against his off-speed offerings.

Christian Chamberlain: I felt really good against North Carolina Game 1, but I'd say the most nervous or excited I got was that Game 1 against Arkansas. I realized that was the finals and Luke had left me with a "ball eight" chant going on throughout the stadium. I couldn't really hear anything warming up, I had only thrown like four warmup pitches before coming in, and I came in to a (1-0) count with the bases loaded.

Kevin Abel: Luke obviously didn't pitch the way he wanted to, but Christian came out and saved a lot of arms for Game 2 and Game 3 by going (almost) five innings and not giving up any more runs. That was really big and showed to the rest of our pitching staff that they're not the greatest offense ever in the world, they're not a major-league team. We can still get them out.

Nate Yeskie: If Chamberlain doesn't give us the length in Game 1 that we lost against Arkansas, we probably would've had to use our pen a little bit differently, maybe it gives them a little more confidence because they scratched across a couple more runs. He's another unsung hero in the whole deal because he kept their bats, I want to say he kept them cold. He kept them suppressed.

Brandon Eisert: (Off-speed) was definitely part of the game plan. We do scouting, obviously, and see what our strengths can be against these teams, and we felt that our off-speed was definitely going to be a benefit to us. It seems like the SEC sees a lot of hard velo and we had some guys that threw hard, but not a ton of mid- to- upper-90s guys. So, we definitely thought off-speed was going to be a strength of ours, and we were able to use that to our advantage pretty well.

Kevin Abel: I think it's just a big equalizer, especially when you're in a fastball count where they're going to absolutely hack and want to get their pitch. A nice 2-0 changeup, you see them Tasmanian Devil-spin in the batter's box. It's kind of cheating I guess. Well, not cheating. It's just pitching.

FINISH

Christian Chamberlain: All the three- and- four-hitters on pretty much every team in the SEC are hitting 15 to 20 home runs, where in the Pac-12 there's probably three guys who do that in the whole conference. When guys take those big of swings at the plate, you've got more room to pitch to them. They were swinging at 45-foot curveballs or fastballs at the eyes. I know Kevin had the same success with it, and it was a lot different than Pac-12 where people just lay off.

I'd say I was effectively wild that game. Sometimes the hardest people to hit are when you can't zone in and know they're going to throw a strike 100% of the time.

Nate Yeskie: He stymied and neutralized those guys a little bit, and it gave me some ideas of things I could do the next night if we had to do some stuff. I felt like I had a pretty good game plan watching those guys and just getting a better sense of what their overall approach was and how we could do some things.

Another Game 1 storyline was Kwan's return to the lineup. After injuring his left hamstring against Washington, Kwan pinch hit in the North Carolina win and sat out the 12-2 Mississippi State victory. He was a late-game replacement the next day against the Bulldogs, talking his way into a ninth-inning pinch hit appearance and one inning of work in center. Kwan told Pat Casey he was healthy enough to start Game 1 of the finals, but his hamstring was not quite ready. He finished the game but made just one appearance the rest of the way, a pinch hit at-bat in Game 2.

Steven Kwan: I lied straight to Case's face, I told him I was good. It was good enough I would say, I could get like a good, brisk jog, almost to a sprint if I needed to. I knew I could play center pretty well, it was just the full-out sprints that really made me nervous, and that's exactly what happened.

Cadyn hit a ball down the line, and we were down, so I knew I had to bust it out, I had to sprint. I got around second, and when I got to third I felt it pull on me and it started hurting really bad. But I couldn't tell, I couldn't pull myself out of the game at that point. And yeah, I'll be honest, I was pretty selfish at the end. I probably couldn't have gone to catch a fly ball after that if something came to me. That was probably not the best on my part, but I just wanted it so bad that I tried to convince myself that it was fine.

Jeremy Ainsworth, trainer: He wanted to be on the field just as much as anybody, and to have that happen was disappointing for him. Part of his game was speed and his ability to cover ground and feel comfortable doing so, and that's something that just wasn't in the cards at the time. We were doing treatment multiple times during the day, trying to do everything we could to get back on the field. But in that short period of time, it's hard for some of those injuries to speed up the physiological healing process. Your body can only do so much so fast. And even if you have all the technology in the world, which we were blessed to have a lot of different resources, we still just weren't quite able to turn a corner in those last five or seven days.

Steven Kwan: It really hit me after the (second) North Carolina game like "yep, this isn't getting better." I was doing everything I could, I was seeing Jeremy every day. That's actually how I got really close to his family. I'd wake up at like seven and I'd do rehab stuff in their room while Jeremy's wife and kids were still sleeping. I knew I was doing everything I could, and it wasn't getting much better.

I finally told Case (before Game 2 of the finals), and T Graham came up to me, too. He knew I was hurting and said "I know you want to play, but think about the team. You can't be the reason why we lose this game." And I told him, "yeah, I totally understand." Then I went up to Case and I was like "Case, I can't do it. I can't help the team right now." And I think he knew that I was hurting. So, it was "Preston, get in there," and that was that.

Preston Jones and Jack Anderson got plenty of center-field action earlier in the tournament, and both were again called upon in the finals. Jones was the rangier defender, while Anderson, typically a corner outfielder, brought more to the table offensively.

Pat Bailey: Case and I together decided who to start each game in the World Series bases on matchups and other things. I think that's just another example of how tough-minded we were, the character of our guys, the never-quit attitude. No matter what happens, there would be a relentless pursuit of a national title.

Jack Anderson: That's the one thing I'll never forgive Bails and Case for. I'd been there for five years and I tried so hard to get reps in center during practice and during scrimmages, and they'd flat out tell me, "no, you're not going to play there. You're a corner guy, you're not going to play center for us." So, I was always like "all right, I'll just play the corners." Then Kwany goes down and I was doing the math in my head thinking I might go to center when I'd been told my whole career that I was never going to play there. I feel like I was ready for anything in Omaha, but I definitely wasn't ready to play center field. I hadn't gotten one rep out there at all and Case was just like "you ready?" And I said, "yep, sounds good."

Pat Casey: First of all, I trusted Jack being a guy that was real, real solid. We obviously felt like Jack was giving us more offensively when we had him in there. Preston had more speed, but we felt Jack was plenty good enough to cover what we were doing.

FINISH

I just think it maybe came down to if we wanted to be a little better offensively or better defensively. And then the matchups always come into play, and Jack's experience came into play and some things like that.

Pat Bailey: I told Case when Kwany got hurt, I said "Pat, I told you several times when we had a chance to start Joe we should've played him more so that when we did have an injury, Joe could've played center." And he goes "I know, you're right." Because I really thought when Kwany got hurt that Joe would be the next guy to play, but he had so many less at-bats than the other guys, plus the maturity of the other guys who had been in a lot of games in Jack and Preston. So, we did what we did.

Preston Jones, outfielder: I'd played center halfway through the Fullerton game the year before (in Omaha), so it was nothing new for me. I felt comfortable out there.

Jack Anderson: We didn't get to hit BP before playing North Carolina (the second time), so my first rep in center was in the game in Omaha. I was a nervous wreck out there. Case and Bails pretty much told me to play really far back and not let anything get behind me. I watch those games now and the announcers are like "Anderson is playing WAY far back there." And I'm like "yeah, that's my first time playing there you dickhead, get off of me! I'm just trying to survive out here." The North Carolina game I had a collision with Cadyn. Against Mississippi State, I think I dove for a ball and it went off my knee and shot out to Trevor, which has never happened in my life. It was kind of like Bad News Bears for me. So, it was a project, but I'd played there in high school and I didn't try to think about it too much. "Go get the ball, catch it, throw it in." It ain't that hard playing the outfield. In that big of a stadium, so many people wearing white always messed with your eyes, too. It was crazy out there for sure. Especially with the fans and stuff, ugh. It was a time and a half in center field.

Pat Bailey: (Jack Anderson) played center field in high school, and he did an adequate job. Jack's not fast enough to be an everyday center fielder, but any ball within his range he's going to catch, and that's what we expect.

Steven Kwan: I knew they would give their all. Like I said, we had dogs on that team, they were always ready to go. I made a joke of it, too, because every game that I would start, we'd lose. So, it was probably best if I just sat out. Because I started the first UNC game, we didn't win that one. Then I started the first game against Arkansas, and we lost that one. So, I told everybody "hey, I'll collect my ring from the bench. Just go win it."

With Jones getting the start in center, Oregon State handed the ball to Bryce Fehmel in Game 2 of the finals. The Beavers' two-headed monster of Heimlich and Fehmel had been reliable all season, but neither pitcher could find their footing at TD Ameritrade Park. One day after Heimlich's rough exit, Fehmel lasted just two-plus innings against Arkansas, allowing only one run on one hit but issuing three walks with a hit batter.

Heimlich and Fehmel started three games apiece in Omaha, working a combined 19 innings with an ERA of 8.53. With its staff leaders struggling, the bullpen saved the day by giving up nine total runs in 37 innings at the College World Series for a 1.95 ERA. It was a different formula, but OSU made it work.

Pat Casey: We just couldn't get our starters to go deep into games, and it was odd because they had been so good for us all year long.

It's absolutely unbelievable to think that Kwan's out and we're not going to get (five) innings out of Heimlich or Fehmel. I just, I don't know. It had nothing to do with effort, it had nothing to do with confidence. I don't think they ever got in sync and I think they were obviously really, really wanting to do well, and they just didn't pitch the way they had all year long.

Nate Yeskie: It's not easy, that's the best way I can put it. The other team over there, they're extremely talented no matter who you're playing. It's not easy. You look at some of those guys from the other teams — first, second, third-rounders, All-Americans, all-conference players, conference players of the year, conference pitchers of the year. It's just a different dynamic and guys scuffle, and it gets magnified because it's on national TV, it's for all the marbles. We certainly would never have been where we were without the effort of those guys. And I tell them all the time that I don't care if you pitch three innings or eight innings or whatever it is, just give me your best effort and we'll make do with what you've got on that day and we'll find a way to piece it together. We had enough pieces to cover our mistakes here and there.

Dylan Pearce: It was tough to watch because you had two starters that were so dominant the whole year, and then it completely switched. It was nice to see our bullpen and everybody start lighting it up, but our starting pitching just struggled and I don't know exactly why. It was kind of like the (Clayton) Kershaw and (Justin) Verlander curse, they go through the whole year destroying everybody and something happens when they get into the postseason and everyone is like "what is going on?" But those guys still battled for us.

Brandon Eisert: Obviously Fehm and Luke were what got us there throughout the entire season and they had their struggles in Omaha. But it was good to see the bullpen respond, to not necessarily being a weakness during the regular season, but not one of our biggest strengths as a team. Being part of that bullpen, obviously we wanted to show what we were capable of and pick them up just like any other teammate. We wouldn't have been where we were without them, so to be able to pick them up was definitely important for us.

Bryce Fehmel, pitcher: That's what a pitching staff is for, the bullpen to pick up the starters or the starters to pick up the bullpen on any given day. We were able to do that all year long, and the bullpen picked us up in Omaha big time. To be able to watch them go out and perform, no matter who it was, was special.

Luke Heimlich: Our bullpen was incredible all of Omaha. I was out early in basically every game and the relievers were coming in, going four or five innings and throwing really well. That's what kept us alive.

Steven Kwan: I knew the bullpen would come through. Yeskie is the best pitching coach ever; he would get the guys ready and they would step up when they needed to. That was always the MO of the year, somebody was going to step up if somebody else couldn't get the job done.

Nate Yeskie: Everybody had been knocking our bullpen as the Achilles' Heel of our team, and if you look back at it, we set the College World Series record for strikeouts by relievers. You look at the ERA of those guys and what they did in our time there, they carried us. Eisert was good, Chamberlain was good, Abel was good, (Mulholland and Pearce) held their own. For them to do what they did collectively as a group was really, at least for me, something special to take away from that. And I know Adley went bonkers and Larnach set the record for doubles and you had some other special moments, but everybody did something for us to accomplish what we did.

Oregon State trailed 1-0 after two innings, but plated runs in the fourth and fifth on a Rutschman solo home run and a Grenier RBI bunt single. Arkansas jumped back ahead 3-2 in the bottom of the fifth and wiggled out of jams over the next few innings. The Beavers were threatening but had nothing to show for it.

Kevin Abel: It was pretty normal for us I guess. We always knew that all it was going to take was one guy coming through. We were getting baserunners on, getting things going and just couldn't push all the way through. But we knew it was going to happen, we never felt like we were out of it.

Zach Clayton, outfielder: There might have been a little tension because obviously you're competitive, you don't want to lose. But I think that we trusted the guys that were in the lineup, we trusted the guys that were in the dugout that no matter who was going to be called on, we were going to get the job done. We'd had so many comeback victories the last two years that it was hard to believe we weren't going to pull it off in one of the biggest games that we had ever played in.

Joe Casey: Just as a culture, we are the only program to ever win six elimination games (at the CWS). I think we all knew that this is Oregon State baseball and if anybody can do it, it's us. And this team can do it.

Kyle Nobach: Early on in the game, Trev struck out on a couple at-bats. I remember going up to him and saying "it's all right, bro. You're going to have a big at-bat later. I believe in you, brother." Just giving him some love and encouragement.

Jack Anderson: In the sixth inning we had first and third, no outs. I tried to get a bunt down, popped it up and they got a double play off of it. I was just like "oh man, is this really going to be my last memory on a baseball field?" I was super down on it, and then I went back in the outfield and all those fans were sure to tell me about it.

We were kind of running out of gas. Every time something went right, we found a way to shoot ourselves in the foot and we couldn't put anything together. They had great pitchers and we just … in those bigger moments we were putting a lot of pressure on ourselves that we hadn't been the whole time we were there. It definitely showed. Those were some tough, tough innings for us to get through.

Steven Kwan: I'll be honest, at that point I was actually getting really worried. Like I mentioned before, a lot of things would go our way and I'd be like "of course they went our way. That's the kind of year we're having." I think baseball is a very momentum-based game, so when everything started going their way I was like "oh, gosh. This might be it." I definitely had some doubt that I'd never felt earlier that year.

Trevor Larnach: It didn't really seem like we were in sync with things. I felt like we weren't totally playing as one maybe. I don't know how to explain it. Maybe we weren't locked in, maybe we were worried about losing, I don't know what it was. I just think things weren't happening for us and things were going down for them. We were struggling with pitch locating and defense and were struggling with offense and whatever, but the main thing is we didn't let it affect us in the long run.

Cadyn Grenier: In all honestly, I don't remember it being that tense. I don't remember it being any different than it normally was. I don't feel like we had fake energy or fake motivation. Every inning we were going in there and guys were like "hey, we've got this. We've still got plenty of time, we can do this, we've been doing it all year, blah, blah, blah." But I don't feel like there was any panic. Nobody was goofing around like we normally did so it was a little bit tighter, a little bit more business-like in the dugout for sure. But there definitely wasn't any panic, at least none that I could sense.

Michael Gretler: There was a completely different feel than that (final) LSU game in 2017. And I think that's where you look back at the North Carolina game and the UW game and you're like "we literally did this a week ago. We were down late, we had five outs to work with, we can do this." And I don't know if it's because in that LSU game we might've felt like things were taken out of our control a little bit, but there was never that disengaged dugout. Everyone was into the game and had obviously seen what we did those first few days in Omaha.

Joe Casey: I went in to play in the eighth inning in left field, and I was more nervous watching the game than when I was in it. In the dugout I was just thinking to myself "we need to come back, we need to come back." Then I went in the game and when I came back to the dugout in the top of the ninth, I had a different kind of energy. I wasn't as stressed out. And I remember sitting next to Preston on the bench and I had a towel around my neck, relaxed and also confident that we were going to come back, but also thinking that if we didn't … we looked at each other and we said something like "we're going to come back and win this, but we've had such a good year." Not thinking we were going to lose, but it had been such an awesome year.

Andy Jenkins: Certainly, I knew there was a chance we'd get back in it. If you were on that team or watched that team or followed Oregon State baseball, you knew that something special was going to happen. There was just a relentless will to stick your chest out and make sure that you weren't the guy that was going to make the last out, you were going to get the next guy up. And next thing you know, one of the coolest moments in Oregon State and College World Series history.

Brandon Eisert stymied Arkansas in the sixth and seventh before handing it off to Kevin Abel, who struck out the side in the eighth. Abel was projected to be Oregon State's Game 3 starter, but the team needed to get there first. Pat Casey and Nate Yeskie felt Abel was the Beavers' best option for the eighth, and the freshman delivered to keep it a 3-2 game.

Zak Taylor was set to lead off the top of the ninth, followed by a pinch-hitting Andy Armstrong, and then Madrigal. They would be facing Arkansas closer Matt Cronin, a hard-throwing left-hander who saved the opener and got the final two outs of the eighth in Game 2. Cronin had an Arkansas single-season school-record 14 saves but was throwing on consecutive days for the first time all year.

Andy Armstrong, infielder: We were on defense and Case was like "you're hitting," so I grabbed my bat and got ready. I was in the little back room behind the dugout where you can hit off a tee, and my heart was racing. Like it was hard to really catch my breath because obviously the stakes were so high. I can vividly recall when I'm through that tunnel in the back room hitting off the tee. I saw the stadium staff bringing out the plywood and stuff to set up for the celebration because they figured Arkansas was going to win. So, they are wheeling down all that equipment and I'm sitting there about to go up to the plate and hit, and sure enough we come off the field and I'm the second one in the order scheduled to hit that inning. I remember Kyle Nobach looked at me, because he had also seen all the celebration equipment being brought down, and Nobach just looked at me with his crazy eyes and said "make them put that shit away!"

Tyler Graham, director of player development: It was right outside of our dugout, back there in the tunnel. I don't think a lot of kids liked that, but who knows if it had an effect on what happened.

I remember the moon came right above the hitter's eye in center field right before the inning started. I'll always remember that, that there was a full moon above the hitter's eye, and you could almost feel it before it happened. It's easy to say that now obviously, but I'll always remember thinking it was pretty cool that the moon happened to pop up above the center-field wall right before the inning started.

Zak Taylor: It seemed like I came up in a leadoff position quite a bit, especially that year. Kevin strikes out the side, and I was mentally prepared. Of course, I knew where we were at in the lineup, but again … that's where T Graham and Alan (Jaeger) really came into play because I was so bought-in to my process. I talk with Alan about this all the time, it was almost like you become your process. Yes, I have this ability to really slow the game down, not make things bigger than they are and just be in the present moment. So, for me, that was huge. I was so happy with how I prepared for that postseason, especially mentally. I was so locked into that at-bat that the game didn't get too much for me. I think anyone could tell if you watch that at-bat, if you look at my facial expressions, if you look at my body language, I tell people that was probably the most locked-in, most freeing at-bat I had that entire season.

I was just feeling so good and so clear in the box, and knowing in the back of my head that there was no other option, I'm going to get on base somehow. Whether it's a knock or I walk, I'm getting on base, there's no other option. I had that in my head and I believed it, 100%. I was all-in on that. I don't want to come across as cocky or anything like that, but I knew in my head that I was getting on base. Developing that mentality and having that going into that at-bat was huge for me.

Alan Jaeger, Jaeger Sports: Here's something that a lot of people don't know, and to me it's mind-blowing. Zak told me, and we all know based on the fans, so many Arkansas fans, and what was at stake, he was a (junior), that's maybe the last at-bat of his career, and he told me that it was the most relaxed he had been at the plate all year. And if you think about that, what makes it even more profound is that if you're not as relaxed as he was — and it's understandable with all that was going on that you could feel some stress — you could feel the pressures of the consequences of the moment.

The reason I'm saying all this is because as a hitter, when I talk about hitting I actually say the most important thing — until someone proves me wrong — and I've said this to a lot of hitting coaches, the most important thing a hitter needs to do is see the ball well. It's just the number one thing. Some other people might say being confident, but even if you're confident, if you're not seeing the ball well, it's hard to hit.

Zak had a few key takes and he had to foul off a few tough pitches, and if your mind is not clear and relaxed and present so to speak, it just would be so hard to have executed his plan. And we don't know, he could've flared a double down the line, but the point is for someone to say in that situation with everything that was on the line, to say it was the most relaxed he'd been all year, it made me feel good. It made me feel like it was a byproduct of the process because of how much he'd bought into the process. His process was so much his default because he was connected and familiar with it because it was something he'd practiced so much. The opportunity presented itself for him to stay with it and default to it as opposed to getting caught up with all of the distractions of the moment. I just found that to be very, very unique, for him to say that the time he was the most relaxed was that at-bat with so much on the line.

Brandon Eisert: One of the biggest things was Zak Taylor's at-bat. He kept battling, fouling things off, launched a couple foul balls that ended up pretty foul, but we got excited for those. Just getting a guy on base is always a big thing to be able to make things happen.

Taylor, one of the less-heralded members of the Beavers' dynamic 2015 recruiting class, began his showdown with Cronin by taking two balls. He fouled off three fastballs during the eight-pitch at-bat, eventually working a walk to give Oregon State the leadoff runner it desperately needed.

Michael Gretler: I think the most overlooked thing, the least sexy thing in that whole inning is the leadoff walk by Zak Taylor. None of the other stuff happens without that.

Kevin Abel: If you talk to Zak, he'll tell you that he was sitting fastball the entire time because he knew Cronin wasn't going to throw a curveball. He threw a curveball first pitch, bounced it, and from that point on Zak knew he wasn't getting another curveball because Cronin didn't trust it. And that's why you saw him absolutely turn on 94 on the inner half to hit it a mile foul because that's all he was sitting on. But man, he battled up there, did the Oregon State thing and saw some pitches and worked a walk.

Zak Taylor: We knew because of the scouting report that if he threw (a curveball) to me early and missed with it, I'd sit heater the entire time after that, so I knew that pitch was coming. That was another confidence boost for me. And I think another big thing was he wanted to see how the start of that at-bat would go if he flipped in a breaking ball. I knew he wanted to get ahead, especially in that moment, being up by one, so I knew I was going to get heaters. I turned on two of them a little bit, got the head out and pulled through them hard. That helped me, knowing that this was a firmer left-handed arm, turning that around real quick on him for me was like "you're not going to get in here. I'm going to be aggressive still. Yes, I'm the nine hitter and I'm trying to get on base, but I'm trying to do a job."

Ryan Gorton: Zak Taylor's at-bat was heroic. That was just a shot in the arm for the team. Zak … wasn't one of our best players. He was a great role player and a great teammate, but there was maybe a little bit of "well if he's doing this, then I'm doing this." I think that inspired other guys to have that confidence to be able to do it.

Pat Casey: It was one of the biggest at-bats of his career and he walked, just like Billy Rowe walked in 2006 for one of the biggest at-bats of his career. It was important, it was an important at-bat.

Bill Rowe, undergraduate assistant coach: It's just crazy. Zak's one of the most amazing players I've ever seen, I think he has so much potential. Sometimes your greatest at-bat is a walk, and that's something that I preached to these guys throughout the entire season because that was the case for me. It was the greatest at-bat I ever had, and that's because it led to a national championship. You don't think about that in the moment, but every pitch you've taken in your entire life leads you to that. If I didn't grind hard in all my fall ball games and all my practice ABs in the cage, if I wasn't focused during all those times, I wouldn't have been able to execute in that moment. As a coach, that's what I tried to instill in the players throughout the regular season. By the time Zak got to that moment, he knew that could be the biggest at-bat of his life. He treated it as such and was ready for it.

Andy Jenkins: Zak Taylor, before he even came in (to the program), we didn't know where he was going to play. Could he catch? Could he play first? Third? There was no way we were going to let a kid with that talent out of the Portland area go somewhere else, and we kind of called him a glue guy. He was a guy that was going to be able to do this and do that. He didn't play a ton his freshman and sophomore years, but that (walk) was a role play, that was Zak's personality, basically. Being selfless, taking his walk and understanding that it wasn't about him, it was about the team. Walks aren't glorified, but that one certainly was.

Zak Taylor: Being able to start that thing was awesome, something I'll always remember personally.

Bill Rowe: One of the things people would yell from the dugout was "this is where it starts!" Every time a guy would walk or get on base ever, they would yell that and the whole team would get this feeling that a rally was about to happen for us. Whether it did or it didn't, it didn't matter. We'd still have that feeling all the time, and a lot of the time it did happen.

To get a little more speed on the basepaths, seldom-used freshman Zach Clayton was called upon to pinch run for Taylor. Clayton hadn't seen the field since early April, but the Beavers were short on options due to Kwan's injury. The plan was to bunt Clayton over and have Madrigal or Grenier drive him in.

Zach Clayton: I wasn't really too worried about (playing), but I knew if they did call on me for whatever reason it was, that I would be ready. I did like to always stay loose towards the end of the game. They had some tees in the cages (behind) the Omaha dugouts, so I went in there to get a little loose, did some dynamic stretching. If they called my number, I was going to go out there and do the job they told me to do.

When Zak Taylor was at bat, they told me if he gets on that I was going to go pinch run for him. That was when I started doing some extra stuff to make sure I was extra loose. Any tension that I had before that, get that out there so when I was on the field, it was just natural.

Kevin Abel: Of course, Case is freaking out because Zach Clayton is out there and he's like "I swear if you get picked off man …"

Pat Casey: I told him "just don't get back picked, see the ball down. Look for the ball down." It was a guy that hadn't been out there, so it was something where we really probably refreshed what the baserunning rules are for a bunt situation.

Zak Taylor: It was funny to see Clayton out there running because he was at first kind of like a chicken with its head cut off, just making sure he touched every bag.

Zach Clayton: I was never a pinch runner during the regular season. We had some pretty fast guys on our team, and I like to think that I'm more of a bruiser. They told me to just be smart. We had guys at the plate that were going to be moving the runner over. I didn't have to do anything special; I wasn't stealing a base or anything. Andy Armstrong was going to come up and lay down a beautiful bunt.

Pinch hitting for Jones, Armstrong — an adept bunter — was tasked with moving Clayton over. Armstrong, who shined as Madrigal's replacement during the first half of the season, now had to star in a different way: sacrificing himself to put Clayton in scoring position.

Andy Armstrong: ZT gets up there and puts together an incredible at-bat. Obviously I knew that if he got on base, I was going to bunt, that's why they put me in there. At this point, all I could think to myself was "everything that you've done in your baseball career leading up to this has prepared you for this moment." I didn't think anything about having to get the bunt down, I didn't think about "if you don't get it down, this is going to happen." The only thing that was going through my mind honestly was me and my dad on the softball field right by our house at the middle school when he'd have me bunt baseballs over and over back when I thought it was stupid and I didn't want to do it. I just remember thinking back to that moment, which had helped me get to the point I was at, at that time. I was going to do this for the team, and I remember telling myself that if I had to wear it square in the face, I would wear it square in the face because that was going to give us the best opportunity to win.

Trevor Larnach: Armstrong comes in, and you couldn't find a bigger position to try and bunt. There couldn't be more pressure on yourself to get a bunt down. I remember he popped up the first one, and the whole staff was just like "oh gosh, this isn't good."

Pat Casey, to OSUBeavers.com in 2020: Well, it kind of makes me laugh now because I did say something to Andy and that was "Andy, don't bunt anything above your hands." Anytime you bunt anything above your hands against a guy with big velocity, it goes straight up in the air. First thing he does is bunt the ball up at his eyes, but it went out of play. Heat of the moment, that's pretty tough.

Andy Armstrong: I had seen (Cronin) the night before because I got in for a late AB. I remember that first bunt, I popped it up straight back. I told myself to not look in the dugout because Case is pissed, obviously. So I didn't look in the dugout. I figured he was going to go high again to get me to pop it up, and I just stuck my nose in there. It was up and in, I got on top of it and yeah, he was definitely a very difficult guy to bunt off of because of his velocity and also the situation.

I think the bunt I got down, if I wouldn't have bunted it, it may have hit me in the face because it was up and in. I just stuck my nose in there, and as soon as I saw that ball go into fair territory, it was an unbelievable feeling. We obviously hadn't won the game yet, but it felt like the world was lifted off my shoulders.

Pat Casey, to OSUBeavers.com in 2020: He got it down and made an unbelievable bunt. That ball he bunted down the first-base line was not an easy bunt; it was running in on him at probably 93 miles per hour. It was a huge bunt.

Trevor Larnach: He gets down a money bunt, and we're like "all right, there we go. Now we've got the top of the lineup coming." And from there, there wasn't really a worry because we've got the best players in the country at the top of our lineup.

Oregon State gave away one of its final three outs for good reason. The next three scheduled batters were first-round picks Madrigal, Grenier and Larnach, and extending the game would likely require nothing more than a single. Madrigal, who was hitless in his first eight plate appearances of the finals, received the first crack at bringing home Clayton.

Nick Madrigal, infielder: I fouled off a couple pitches that were right there that I probably could've gotten. I felt good in the box and I remember not even being nervous at all, I just wanted to come through for the team. We actually sat down and watched the game the other day just for fun, and I remember seeing my at-bat and seeing me foul back a ball and just wishing I connected on some of those. Then I eventually grounded out to first, and I came back to the dugout and was so hopeful that something would happen.

Michael Gretler: That was the one thing where it was like "all right, Nick's up. Nick's going to tie the game, right? That's our guy. There's no way Nick doesn't get a hit right here." And he gets jammed and hits a ground ball to the right side, but he moved Zach to third. That was the second out of the inning, everyone thought it was going to be Nick, but it's like "OK, it's not going to be Nick. It's going to be someone else who plays hero."

Cadyn Grenier: Zak draws that huge walk and Army, just a grinder, he does exactly what we need him to do, gets Clayton over to second. Then you've got the ground ball that Nick hits that gets Clayton over to third, and at that point you're kind of like "dang, we really thought Nick was going to do it here. He's been doing it all year, he's been doing it his whole career," so we thought he had this and was going to do this. And when he grounded out, everyone was like "oh dang, man. Well, here comes Cadyn."

Nate Yeskie: I had a hunch Cadyn would get a hit because the guy hit the game-winning home run in the state finals his senior year of high school, so he's got some clutch gene to him.

Cadyn Grenier: My senior year of high school, we were in the state championship game. We had gone two innings of extra innings, it was the ninth inning (high school games are seven innings), and I hit a walk-off home run to win the state title. It was my last high school at-bat. We were in the winners' bracket so the other team had to beat us twice, but we were losing that first game and our first baseman hits his first home run of the year to tie it up in the seventh. We go to the ninth, I lead off and I hit like a 1-1 or 2-1 fastball to right-center, it went over the fence and that was it. Yeah, that was incredible, my last at-bat and I walk off in the state championship game. That was pretty cool.

Nate Yeskie: But more than anything, Case hit him in the two-hole to start the year and I think a lot of us were wondering "is that maybe a little too high?" We thought maybe he'd be better-suited hitting sixth, but Pat just said "I've got a hunch" and put him in the two-hole.

With two down and Clayton standing 90 feet away on third base, Grenier settled in for his match-up with Cronin. The pro-Arkansas crowd sensed the end was near, but the 27th out is always the toughest to obtain.

Grenier, who was 2 for 4 on the day with singles in his previous two at-bats, took a first-pitch strike, followed by a ball. Cronin came right after the junior shortstop with a low fastball, and Grenier popped it up down the right-field line in foul territory. Gates (first base), Shaddy (second) and right fielder Eric Cole all converged on the ball a few feet from the stands. It seemed like the only question left was which of the three would catch the national championship-clinching final out.

Cadyn Grenier: I remember hitting it and knowing it was foul, but looking at the ball and the territory that it's in. It's hooking back, and I'm sitting there going "they're going to catch this." I had the worst feeling about everything at that moment, just standing there going "they're going to catch this, it's over. We just lost, I lost it for us." I slowly jog-walked down the line thinking this was it.

Joe Casey: I thought it was going to go out at first into the stands, and then I realized there was a lot of room.

Luke Heimlich: Pop fly goes up, I drop my head. I'm like "come on, get out of play, get out of play," but you can tell it's not. The wind always blew in from that right-field line, and it actually helped us earlier in the tournament. I think against UW, somebody hit one deep into the corner and it blew back in play.

Tyler Malone: It was like slow motion, honestly.

Trevor Larnach: Everyone stopped. I stopped swinging the bat on deck, everyone stopped what they were doing in the dugout. Not that I was looking into the dugout, but I could see in my peripherals that everyone was leaning up because that was the moment, a make-or-break moment whether we're done or get to keep on fighting. It didn't feel like the end to me, it wasn't an "oh fuck, this is it." It was more of a "what's going to happen?" I wasn't worried, I think some of the other guys can say they weren't worried.

Steven Kwan: I feel bad even saying this, but I remember when that ball went up I put my head down and I was like "that's it." The stadium got super loud, and I thought that was it.

Zak Taylor: Seeing that ball go up in the air, everyone just stopped for a minute. Because usually when something like that happens, the ball gets caught, especially with the level our teams were at. I would say like nine times out of 10 that ball is caught. But when you get into a situation like that when things are heightened and there's a lot of noise, of course miscommunication happens and things like that can happen.

Dylan Pearce: As soon as he hit the popup, everyone put their head down. We were like "that's it, it's over." We ended up looking up, seeing the ball drift back and nobody is communicating. Nobody says anything, and the ball hits the ground.

Far from a routine foul popup, the three Arkansas defenders sprinted over and formed a near-perfect triangle in no man's land. Shaddy, the Razorbacks' lone first-team all-SEC selection, went after it with the most gumption, but overran the ball as Gates and Cole looked on. The baseball landed harmlessly between the three, hitting the warning track dirt and bounding into the stands. It was a monumental gift for Grenier and the Beavers.

Kyle Nobach: I guess I can understand (what happened) because when I was playing out in left field, it was hard to read the ball in the air because the wind was so crazy. And also, it was loud in the stadium, so communicating and hearing was hard. That was a tough ball and a tough triangle play, and (Shaddy) overran it, too. So, it was a tough play, it wasn't like that was an easy play. That ball is working back on you.

Pat Casey: It's dark and there are three guys going at it at once. I'm not saying the play shouldn't have been made, I'd expect my second baseman to make the play. But in all actuality when you look at it, probably a better play for the right fielder. I don't know what their communication level was.

Pat Bailey: That's the right fielder's ball. I heard the ESPN guys say that the second baseman should've caught it, that's not his ball. The right fielder has the best angle out of anybody, he should've called everyone off. But there's so much noise in that stadium, I could see where something like that could happen.

Trevor Larnach: I remember watching the video, and (the right fielder) was standing there watching it. I think he could've been playing under it before the second baseman got there. And yeah it's a tough spot … and I know the second baseman called it for them, but I just know that right fielder has to call that ball because that's his ball. I think he had more than enough time to get there, which is the main thing. If it was me, I would've tackled Nick Madrigal and caught it before I would've let him call me off.

Zak Taylor: I honestly thought that should've been the right fielder's ball. Of course, I thought about if that was me, Nick and Trevor out there, and I just think we're coming down with that ball. It might be a collision or something, but we're going after that ball. Especially with it being in foul territory like that, you don't really have anything to lose. So yeah, we definitely talked about that and to this day, I think Nick would've caught that ball. I mean, of course easier said than done, especially in that moment.

FINISH

Nick Madrigal: It was definitely an in-between (ball), but I think someone has to go for it. I think the right fielder had a good chance at it if he just comes in and calls everyone off. That's his ball I would say, he has the priority over everyone. As an outfielder coming in, it's easier than going back and to the side. But yeah in that situation, it has to be someone's ball. Thankfully for us, it ended up being dropped.

Trevor Larnach: Not to knock them, but if they would've wanted it, they would've caught it. Because three of them had a chance to catch it, and they didn't.

Jack Anderson: We always say "want the ball." You've got to want the ball in those moments. It definitely was a far run for (the right fielder), but the first baseman is not getting it. That's a really hard ball for him to get back on. Usually, the second baseman has a good shot at it but I think the right fielder could've gotten it, and that's his ball for sure. It's just easier to see that spin when you're coming into it instead of going behind it.

I think if we were in that situation and I was in right and Nick Madrigal calls me off, I probably would've let him try to get it because I trusted Nick. But that's the kind of thing where I'm sure that second baseman's called that right fielder off so many times, and he's always been like "OK, that's his." But in reality, that's an easier ball for the right fielder and he has to make that play because it does that little vortex thing. It happens at Goss, too. It goes over there, almost goes foul and comes back from the stands into foul territory.

So yeah, I think the second baseman gets a bad rap for going 100% at it, which is just tough. I saw the right fielder stop and I was like "uh, that's not the way they teach it, for sure." As an outfielder, I think the right fielder needs to get that one.

Michael Gretler: It all happened so fast that I don't think anyone in the dugout had time to be like "oh my God, that's the game." There is so much more foul territory there than what people think. We play on this small field at Goss where there's no foul territory because of the brick walls. So, you see that ball go up and your first instinct is like "oh, that's a foul ball." But then you see the size of foul territory and are thinking "that might stay in play." Then you just see the three guys there and you're like "oh my God," and the next thing you know you see the ball bounce up. I can't even say it was a sigh of relief for me because it happened so fast, it was just "oh my God, they didn't catch it."

Preston Jones: That's just the game of baseball. Things weren't going our way, and then the ball took a good spin for us.

Bryce Fehmel: I remember pretty vividly the stadium going absolutely quiet when that popup fell. Right when that happened, I felt like the team felt the game was over and the series was over. We were going to win the game and win the series the following day.

Steven Kwan: When we saw that ball hit the ground, I remember the feeling in the dugout instantly changed. It was like "you can't do that. You can't give us that chance because now something is going to happen."

Nick Madrigal: I've watched so much baseball in my life and usually when you drop a ball like that, something crazy happens the very next play. And when that ball dropped, I remember thinking that immediately. Whenever you get another chance at a high level, something always ends up working out differently.

Cadyn Grenier: Everything changed after that. There was so much chatter coming from our dugout, guys yelling the same stuff like "hey, new life!" I'm hearing that all throughout the stands and the dugout. There was a buzz in the building because they just made that one mistake that our team could turn around and take advantage of all the time.

I tried (to refocus), but it was very tough to do. After that, it's back to two strikes, you're still the last out. I tried as hard as I could to try and block everything out and get back to hitting the ball and being in that at-bat, and it was so difficult to do, man. I was fully aware of the situation and what was going on, and honestly my legs were shaking in the box. I was so nervous, I was so … I wouldn't say uptight, but I was so stressed because of everything that had just happened and how I had gotten a new life and I wanted to make it count.

Zak Taylor: I actually remember a cool story that I don't think a ton of people know about. I was out of the game because I got pinch ran for, I'm not the fastest individual. I'm next to Nate Yeskie, and we're standing there bullshitting a little bit, he's kind of quiet and has his arms crossed in front of me on the front steps. He looked at me after that ball dropped and he was really chill. I was the one who was freaking out, looking, up against the fence. Yeskie goes "Cadyn's going to hit a ball through the six-hole right here, just watch."

Nate Yeskie: As that ninth inning unfolded, I was standing next to Zak Taylor. When Grenier's popup falls, I go "watch this, he's going to hook one through the six-hole." And Zak goes "no kidding, right?" Our dugout was so calm, there was no anxiety. You can watch the replays, everybody in the dugout was still just "hey, you haven't recorded 27 outs. We're in this."

FINISH

After receiving a second life, Grenier took a ball and fouled off another nasty offering from Cronin. Sitting fastball in a 2-2 count, Grenier got one he liked and shot it between the shortstop and third baseman. Clayton trotted home, Grenier celebrated with first base coach Ryan Ortiz and it was a new game with two outs in the top of the ninth.

Cadyn Grenier: I just remember getting that pitch and hitting it. As soon as I hit it, I knew exactly where it went, I knew exactly how hard I hit it and I knew that they weren't getting it. I still have a picture in my room of me a couple steps down the line. I don't remember anything except for hitting it, being halfway down the line, giving the biggest fist-punch of my life and rounding first. I don't remember what the crowd sounded like, I don't remember what my teammates sounded like, I don't remember anything other than what it felt like to give that fist pump down the line and turn around and give a huge high-five to Ortiz at first, then look into the dugout and start screaming. It was incredible, man.

Zak Taylor: I'm just looking at Yeskie and I'm bewildered, like "what?! How?!" And he remained calm the entire time and it was so awesome. I knew he was just dying inside, but he kept a straight face.

Zach Clayton: I saw him make contact and I knew it was roped and I was just hoping it was going to be enough to get through the six-hole, and it was. It was hard for me not to keep looking back while I was running home, and I was just making sure that I touched home so nothing could possibly go wrong. So, it was kind of a celebration while making sure I stayed in the moment to finish what I had to do for our team.

It was unreal, I had so much energy going through me and the whole team behind me was going absolutely insane. I was getting hit left and right. It almost felt like I was going through a football game again, just how much contact there was with everyone so excited.

Nate Yeskie: It's interesting to see how teams play certain guys differently. North Carolina played Grenier in the six-hole there the whole time. Arkansas didn't. The guy hits a base hit through there and it's just … baseball's a funny game.

Pat Casey: You've got to give Grenier so much credit for staying with it, staying focused and getting the big hit.

Kyle Nobach: It gives me chills just thinking about it. What clutch means is doing what you normally do when it matters most. That's what Cadyn did in that moment.

Michael Gretler: For him as a hitter to be able to stay in the moment, stay with his approach and really just battle until the very, very last pitch of that at-bat ... I think that whole inning, the Zak Taylor walk, the bunt, that inning really, really showcased what got us through the whole 2018 World Series, which was the offense isn't going to be done until the very final out is made.

Trevor Larnach: Another argument for best at-bat of that year goes to Cadyn. Because without him, we wouldn't have tied it and given us a chance to win it. But you could argue without Kyle (against Minnesota), we possibly wouldn't have had a chance to go to the World Series. And you could argue without Adley (against North Carolina), we wouldn't have had a chance to move on to the finals. There were just so many factors that go into it, and to think of all that now is pretty nuts. I'm glad I didn't think about it in the moment because it's pretty distracting.

Joe Casey: I just remember hopping over that railing, and I've never been more excited in my life than when that happened. But we're still tied, we're still tied.

As Larnach approached the batter's box in a 3-3 tie, Cronin was showing signs of fatigue. The sophomore closer threw 15 pitches in Game 1 and was tasked with getting a multi-inning save the following day, something Cronin hadn't done all season. Grenier singled off Cronin's 36th pitch of Game 2, 35 of which were fastballs. Larnach entered the at-bat expecting heaters and nothing else.

Andy Jenkins: It slipped away from a great pitcher. The thing that hurt him was he really had one pitch, and our guys were smart enough to know that he wasn't finding anything else.

Dylan Pearce: We knew he couldn't locate any off-speed at all, he was just living on his fastball.

Trevor Larnach: Curveball didn't have me worried one bit. I think he threw one or two of them and they weren't even close. When you give a hitter a chance to cross off a pitch like that, it gives them more of an advantage.

Kevin Abel: Trev gets up, Cronin is getting tired, velo is going down. We knew that he had never gone back-to-back days going into that, so we knew he wasn't going to have much in the tank. He wasn't prepared to do something like that and throw as many pitches as he did.

Brandon Eisert: Zak's at-bat also had a big part in that. He threw a lot more pitches, and you could tell he wasn't quite as sharp as he had been earlier in the game and the day before. You could feel that something was going to break our way finally.

Pat Casey: I wasn't thinking about how many pitches he'd thrown, I just thought about how good he was, how good Trevor was. I didn't have time to think. Next time I blinked …

Trevor Larnach: I remember that whole at-bat, that whole thing very vividly even though I told all the reporters after that I blacked out because I wanted to save it for myself, you know?

I got my mind focused on that moment when I was in the dugout, when I was praying for the team and getting ready for it and just hoping for one last chance. When I got on deck, it was like my mindset switched from "I hope this doesn't happen" to "this is what's going to happen," and I was solely focused on that.

Kevin Abel: Trev got ahead in the count, and that's not a good place for the pitcher.

Trevor Larnach: I saw the pitches that he was throwing pretty well. His misses weren't too far off to me, they were low and away but nothing near to what I would've wanted to swing at. I just remember telling myself on the 2-0 pitch "be early. Don't try and wait for the pitch you want to hit, just be early for it because here it comes and he has no idea where it's going."

Luke Heimlich: Everyone knew he was throwing fastballs. All the fans, Arkansas, all of us. Kyle comes over next to me and is like "don't be late."

Kyle Nobach: I remember sitting on the end of the dugout and I had my arm around Luke. I was out of the game at this point, and I'm just sitting there and it's 2-0 (to Larnach) with that kid throwing cheese balls and I'm going "don't be late, don't be late." That's all I was saying, and Trev was not late.

Andy Armstrong: Everyone knew he was going to do it. Yeskie was like "all right, here comes a Trevor Larnach home run."

Nick Madrigal: A couple pitches went by and I remember Yeskie on the bench, he yelled out "hit the ball out of here!"

Brandon Eisert: Yeskie does have a way of predicting things. We'll be sitting in the dugout, and he'll say "on this slider, he's going to roll over to second base" or something like that, and that exact thing happens. So, I wouldn't be too surprised if he actually called it, but I didn't hear anything myself.

Nate Yeskie: Larnach gets to 2-0 ... and I'm thinking in my head "come on big man, just one time, one time." So, I bellow out "hit it outta here!" And of course, we know what happens next.

Cronin's 39th pitch of the game was a 2-0 fastball to Larnach. The pitch caught too much plate, and Larnach unleashed a screaming line drive to straightaway right field. The ball sizzled over the fence into the bullpen — hitting a large portrait of former high school teammate and Washington ace Joe DeMers in the nether regions — for one of the most dramatic home runs in College World Series history. Oregon State was down to its final strike when Grenier lifted his foul popup. About four minutes later, the Beavers held a 5-3 lead.

Trevor Larnach: I knew I got it, but it was the trajectory that worried me. Because I knew it wasn't backspun and it was on a line, so my concern was whether it was going to hit the top of the fence or not. But once it went out man, I don't think there's a single moment in my life where I was more emotional than that.

Luke Heimlich: He top-spun it, so I was a little nervous that it was going to hook over and not get over the fence. To be able to top-spin one out there is just incredible. Obviously he crushed the ball, and we're all erupting. And at that point moving forward, we all knew this was our series.

Michael Gretler: I remember standing next to Yeskie and hearing him be like "come on, Trevor. Just put one into the right-field bullpen." And sure enough, the next pitch Trevor hits it hard and Yeskie turns to me and we're like "no he didn't!" We both jumped up to the railing, saw it go over the wall and gave each other a big hug. Right before the pitch, Yeskie called it. And obviously from there, it was just chaos.

Dylan Pearce: I don't know if you can see it on the (ESPN broadcast), but I had actually called it myself. When you call a home run, you take your hat off and you point the bill in the direction you think it will go. And I had taken my hat off and pointed it towards right, and I was like "OK, I'm calling a home run here." And you can actually hear Yeskie in the background go "hit it outta here!" Then you hear a ding, he sends it out and we all just lost it at that point.

FINISH

Nate Yeskie: You watch things long enough and you just know how guys' stuff plays. You know that if guys throw certain pitches in certain places, you're kind of taking a hunch at what the odds are. The fact that these kids remember these stories tells you how special these things were to be that clear of thought with regards to everything. In those moments where everybody else is losing their minds, how many thousands of people had their phones out ready to take a picture of Arkansas winning the whole thing?

We're in the dugout and I just remember telling Zak Taylor "watch this, he's going to get a base hit through the six-hole." The Larnach one … it's been a funny point of discussion between me and my buddies ever since because a handful of them have seen it and just laugh and are like "yeah, some things never change."

Ryan Gorton: No, I called it! No, no, no. But I was in the dugout, and I really don't remember the two pitches before because Zach had just scored, we'd tied it and everyone was going crazy in the dugout. I don't even remember the two pitches before, but I do remember looking up and seeing it was 2-0 and I was like "this guy has been losing velocity and he only throws fastballs." And gosh, then he hit it, our whole dugout just exploded, went crazy. I think everyone did in the state of Oregon, probably.

Jake Mulholland, pitcher: Obviously Trevor's hit was incredible, maybe the biggest hit ever at Oregon State. I don't know if I've ever seen a ball get out that quickly. That ball was shot into orbit and very quickly went into the bullpen. It disappeared into the night for a second.

Kevin Abel: I want to point out that I said after he hit his first one in Arizona that he was going to hit 20 home runs, and he finished with 19. Nobody believed me, they all thought I was crazy saying that he was going to hit 20 home runs, and he hit 19. I would say that was a big reason why we were so good that year.

Cadyn Grenier: It felt like Trevor hit a home run instantly. It felt like I got on base, blinked an eye and Trevor had hit a home run. In that moment, everything was fine. It wasn't tense anymore, at least for me, as I started to hone things back in and really be like "wow, we've got this. This just happened."

Trevor up 2-0 in the count, it felt like I was there for 10 seconds. Trevor hits the ball and I start busting butt to try and score because off his bat I'm like "that's a double, I have a chance here to score." So, I pick my head up rounding second base looking for coach Jenkins to send me, and he's in mid-air, hands up, feet up, celebrating. I looked back and the umpire was signaling home run. It was just the best feeling ever to be on a full dead sprint, look up and know that Trevor hit it out and we took a huge lead.

Andy Jenkins: One of my favorite pictures I have is Trevor rounding first, it's an up-close picture of him. The pitcher is looking down in sorrow and you see me in my orange jacket, it looked like I'm doing the air guitar in the air. I don't remember jumping, I don't remember any of that, but the picture shows I was about a foot up in the air. I was lucky to be a third-base coach during those times. As a third base coach, there aren't a lot of things you can do right, there are only things you can do wrong. I'll take all those long days when you're sitting out on an island for those moments just to give him a handshake and be a part of the on-field excitement.

It was a great moment for everybody and a true testament to the work our team had put in. Trevor Larnach, being one of the hardest workers on our team, was ready for that moment because of the time he put in throughout his career.

Bill Rowe: For me, the ultimate strangest moment was when Trevor Larnach hit that home run because it was nearly the same situation as when I hit my home run in the second game of the championship series against North Carolina. It was almost to the same spot in the stadium, a low line-drive. For him to have that happen ... I remember I was being so superstitious the whole time with Jake Rodriguez. We had this orange HydroFlask cup of Gatorade that had to have the exact right amount of ice in it and Dylan Pearce would throw a specific combination of candy into it before every game that was the right Juju to beat the other team. It was either color-based or flavor-based. Jake and I would be talking about the Gatorade and sipping on it throughout the game whenever we needed big moments to happen. So, between that and turning around and grabbing coach Yeskie by the shirt, he was screaming "he did it! He just did it!" The whole dugout was erupting, I'll never forget that moment. It was probably the greatest sports moment I've ever gotten to be a part of.

Trevor Larnach: That was just special. We went from damn near losing the season to tying it, to in front of them. For me it was like I hit it, it went over and I knew it put us up in the ninth inning and I knew that momentum was what we needed to finish these guys off that game.

It was all that into one big celebration when I'm rounding first, and it hit me even more when I saw our whole team jumping up and down at home plate. When you see your boys that you love doing that, that'll give you a sensation that you can't even describe or feel again, really. So yeah, there was a lot of emotion and I've heard from a lot of people that I usually don't show a whole lot. But when you care that deeply about those guys and that team, you're not not going to show emotion in that moment.

Joe Casey: Trevor hits the bomb, and that's another moment where I don't think I've ever been more excited in my life. I was slapping my towel on the ground and just looking at everyone, shaking everybody. Everyone is hugging each other, that was just awesome. Him rounding the bases and us mugging him at home, that's something I'll never forget. We're all mugging him, he spikes the helmet in the dugout.

Michael Gretler: Guys were just running around the field doing whatever we wanted to at that point. I remember seeing a video and Joe Casey is basically on the other side of the field jumping up and down. The umpire is trying to hold us all back, but it was just too special of a moment not to get that fired up. Having been through what we'd been through the last couple years, I think that was a huge, huge hit for all the guys on the team and program.

Christian Chamberlain: I've never seen more energy in a dugout. I remember me and Steven Kwan out in front of the dugout just shoving each other for no reason.

Steven Kwan: When Trevor's shooting star hit, I don't even remember how I got out of the dugout. I had to have been out of the dugout before the ball landed. I blacked out and next thing I know I'm in a mosh pit of guys just screaming. None of those reactions were my intent, those were as authentic as I could've been. I will admit though, that was the one time where I did feel my hamstring kind of pull. Because I got up there, I got a pretty high jump in. But gosh it was awesome.

Brandon Eisert: The fans were getting behind us, cheering us on. That's what you play for, that's what makes me love baseball so much is those kinds of moments that can happen. It was just crazy to be a part of.

Zak Taylor: It was like a paradigm shift, I mean it literally changed the entire momentum and I think changed the momentum leading into that next game.

Adley Rutschman: The combination from Cadyn to Trevor, that's probably going to be the best baseball memory I'll ever have, and I don't know if it'll be topped. Just the emotional high that you got seeing Cadyn hit the ball, and then to have Trevor do it the very next AB, I don't think that series of events is ever going to be topped for me. I hope it does, but that to me is one of the greatest memories I share with guys on that team.

Cronin retired Rutschman to escape further damage, and the Beavers still needed three outs to force a Game 3. Oregon State began the bottom of the ninth with Abel on the mound and an unusual defensive lineup that included Gretler at first, Armstrong at third, Clayton in left field and Joe Casey in center.

Nate Yeskie: When Grenier got the base hit in the ninth to tie it, my mind started going "OK, now what? When do we get Mulholland up? How long do we use him?" Obviously you're in an elimination game so you're going to use him as long as necessary, but when do you deploy him and how? Because there are different spots that are better for certain guys ... and I even thought "boy if we take the lead and Kevin finishes this thing, do we start Mulholland tomorrow?" Those are kind of the inner workings of what's going on in your head, how you're going to manage and navigate some of your arms. Those are all decisions that you've got to make throughout the game. Certainly, when Larnach ran his ball out of the house, that made it easier for us to leave Kevin in and go to Jake at any certain point.

Jake Mulholland: I was not even warming up because we were losing, I very rarely would throw if we were losing, only if it's tied or we were winning. So, I was in the dugout and Cadyn hits that popup, it drops, he ends up getting on first and Trevor had the big hit. I was there celebrating for a second and I look over at Yeskie, and he's pointing at the bullpen. So, I basically sprint down to the bullpen to get ready as fast as I can because we have a lead now. I didn't really see the rest of the inning because I had about three minutes to warm up.

Joe Casey: Everyone in the dugout is still freaking out about the bomb and I remember Bails and my dad looking like they're talking to each other. I'm right next to them, they're looking (really tense), and they go "Joe, you've got to go play center field!" Because (Armstrong) had pinch hit for (Jones) in the ninth. And I'm like "all right, sounds good." My dad looks at me and he says "just play it like you've played center your whole life," and I was like "true that!" I just thought it was funny because everyone in the dugout was still freaking out about Trevor's bomb, but the coaches were like "oh shit, Joe has to go play center!"

Pat Casey: My concern at that point in time was what we were going to do the next inning defensively because we had used (almost) all of our players, so that was on my mind. When Trevor hit the home run, obviously that changed the picture from a tie game to a lead, so that all came into play.

I'm looking at the roster and looking at who had played where and realizing that Joe and Zach hadn't been out there hardly at all. Joe was more equipped to play center field than Zach. Gretler had to go play first, Army had to go play third. I didn't get caught up in the whirlwind, it was more that right when we tied it there was something on my mind, and right when we went ahead there was something on my mind.

FINISH

Jack Anderson: I remember looking in the outfield after Trevor hit that home run and we went out there in the bottom of the ninth, and it was Joe in center, Zach in left and Trevor in right. I was like "well, there's not a lot of experience out there. Oh man, Joe, Zach, you guys have got it, man. I'm sure you did not think you'd be out there in this moment, but go get 'em!"

Trevor Larnach: Obviously those are two younger guys, but it doesn't make them any less capable of doing their job. At that point in time, I think we were so focused on our momentum and winning that game that there was no worry about who or what or anything that could happen or stuff like that. I was just hyped to be out there because one, I didn't hear a single word from the fans in right field, so that was refreshing. But also to know that those guys aren't getting bugged either, that was going to make our job easier.

After 17 innings of obnoxiousness, Larnach couldn't resist throwing a little playful shade back at the Arkansas faithful.

Trevor Larnach: You know the hand motion of basically telling someone that you can't hear them? I did that to them and then they all yelled "you still fucking suck!" Then I started laughing and turned around, I didn't really look back at them and I didn't hear anything from them. It was funny, but I had to get them back because it was non-stop, every inning, every pitch. I'm glad they tried their hardest with that, but it didn't work out for them at all, though.

Zach Clayton: Oh, I still had to wear some of it because they see a freshman coming out there that didn't play a lot that season playing in one of the biggest innings of the game, and one of the biggest games in that College World Series. They saw an opportunity to try and rip at me, but I was so focused on getting those last three outs that it didn't matter what they were saying.

They were the ones that were scared, we were the ones that were in good position to finish it off. I wasn't really too worried about (being in the field). I had played the field thousands of times throughout my life, so this was just one more time. If a ball came to me, I just had to do what I had done my whole life. I really trusted that.

Joe Casey: Being out there in center field against Arkansas and seeing everyone was just awesome. I wasn't even nervous, I just thought to myself that this was awesome and I wanted to take advantage of the opportunity.

This is another thing we joked around about. They hit a ground ball out there to center and I fielded it. We joked that I was the only center fielder that (CWS) that didn't let a ball go by me because Jack, Kwan and Preston all had one go by them. I was like "sorry, guys!"

Preston Jones: Our exchanges were always more funny and filled with laughter. I mean obviously the game is serious, but when you're with your teammates and your brothers it's moments like that where it's kind of funny and when you bring some humor to it, it causes you to relax. I think Joe might've made a comment about how it was the most bizarre outfield Oregon State has ever run out there.

Nate Yeskie: Zach Clayton scores the game-tying run and I'm just thinking "that goofy kid, thank goodness." I didn't realize until that night ... every night in Omaha I'd go back and watch our game, win or lose, just to see if I could look at the game differently from the center field camera, maybe somebody might say something in the commentary that forced you to look at something different, so I'd go back and watch games. I wouldn't go to bed until 3 or 3:30, just looking at charts and replaying the game.

Going through that again and watching that replay itself how that inning went, I had no idea that defensively in the ninth we had Zach Clayton in left field, Joe Casey in center field and Trevor Larnach in right. That was mind-boggling to me. Between Joe and Zach, I don't think either one of them had a multitude of at-bats or innings throughout the course of the season. Zach Clayton had (six) at-bats, Joe (14). Joe touched the ball because a guy singled in the ninth, he picked it up and threw it back in. There were no fly balls to left for those guys to panic and freak out on. It just ran like clockwork.

Andy Armstrong: It goes to show that everyone is going to help the team win. We used all of our guys minus one I believe. It was a collective effort and in the moment I was just focused on catching the ball and doing my job. It was pretty cool because I don't remember being nervous at all, and that's because Case has a way of putting the pressure on you every single day in practice in everything that you do. So, when you're in a situation like that, you're used to it.

Kyle Nobach: There were a lot of guys going in and getting it done at different times. Chamberlain, Izzy, Abel, it wasn't just one person. Adley was coming up with extremely big hits, Trev, Malone was hitting homers, Gretler was hitting a couple doubles, everybody contributed and we were playing together.

Pat Casey: This is what happens when your elite players make the guys who aren't playing every game feel like they're as important as they are. You have a situation like

FINISH

what happened to us in the World Series in '18 where we didn't have (Heimlich or Fehmel) get out of the fifth inning, we lose our center fielder for the championship series, and in Game 2 we have to play (nearly) every position player on the roster because we're behind, so we've got to pinch hit, bunt, move runners, and we've got two guys in the outfield who have played three innings together the entire year, in Ameritrade to win a national championship. And they felt like they belonged, and they felt like that because of the way the elite players made them feel. They practiced that way, we traveled that way, we talked that way, we treated each other that way. People want to know about the difference. Everybody comes out with these unique ways to practice. "Hey, I've got a new drill." Some of those things are important. "Hey, I've got a new way for training." Well, some of those things can be really good. But ultimately it comes down to the men in the uniform, that's what it comes down to. I don't care what anybody says, it doesn't matter. You'll never convince me that what's underneath the uniform isn't more important than what you see outside the uniform.

When you win, there are so many pieces to the puzzle that are important. Just like any puzzle, if one piece is missing, it's glaring. You can put together a puzzle of the United States and there is one little, tiny county missing, one little piece in the middle of the country, and that's all you see. You don't see the rest of the country, all you see is that little, open spot in your puzzle. It's the same way with winning. If you don't have all the pieces to the puzzle in the right place, it's glaring and it costs you all the time.

Arkansas opened the bottom of the ninth with a leadoff single from Biggers, prompting Oregon State to bring in closer Jake Mulholland to face the top of the lineup. Mulholland struck out Cole on four pitches and quickly got ahead on No. 2 batter Casey Martin, one of the speediest players in college baseball. Martin grounded an 0-1 pitch right back to Mulholland, who picked it cleanly and fired it to a covering Madrigal at second. Madrigal completed the 1-4-3 double play to finish off the comeback, setting up a winner-take-all Game 3 the following day.

Jake Mulholland: I just threw my glove at the ball and caught it. I heard that was the first time Martin had hit into a double play on the year, he was so fast. That was the quickest I've ever turned by far, and we beat him by a step. It was crazy, but that's just the kind of team Arkansas was. There were no freebies with them.

Nate Yeskie: It's bang-bang at first on a 1-4-3 double play that couldn't have been run any cleaner. We knew that guy could run, that guy was the fastest guy we'd seen all year.

Nick Madrigal: That ball was hit hard back at Mully. For him to grab it, spin and throw right on the money was impressive, especially in that big of a situation. If we don't turn that and they get another out to work with, who knows? But yeah, that guy was flying down the line. I remember watching him score from second on a ball that fell in between left field and center earlier in the game and he scored easily. So yeah, he had a ton of speed, and for us to turn that was huge.

Cadyn Grenier: When they got that guy on first and Mully was able to roll up that double play with Nick, I just remember being so pumped, so pumped that we were that much closer. That was the mentality, we were on defense and we knew we were going to shut it down. We had all the momentum, we had all the confidence and Mully went out and did what he needed to do. Him and Nick turned that huge double play that sealed it, and obviously it was pretty cool.

Michael Gretler: I remember catching that final out, handing Mully the ball and being like "all right guys, it all comes down to tomorrow."

Jack Anderson: I had every emotion you can have in about 10 minutes, from "this is it" when that popup happened to "all right, now we've got another day together." It was crazy to go through those wide range of emotions that whole time. I went from "my baseball career is over," to "I've got one more game to make the best ending I can." It was just crazy.

Drew Rasmussen, pitcher: We drop Game 1, and then to fight back in Game 2, that's just what Oregon State baseball is. It's scrappy, it's competitive, it's gritty. And then to put all the talent that was on that roster on top of it …

Luke Heimlich: I remember getting back into the locker room after the game, and I was across from Gretler. Everybody is walking through and we made eye contact and he looks at me and basically was just like "we can't lose, right?" And I was like "yeah! There's no way we lose after that." It was just impossible for us to lose at that point.

Nick Madrigal: Everyone was coming back into the clubhouse just joking and saying amongst each other "these guys are screwed tomorrow because we're on. Nobody is going to stop us tomorrow; we're going to show up and end it." That was everyone's thought, and we weren't shy to say it amongst each other.

Cadyn Grenier: We were sure, we knew it. I don't think it was us being arrogant because we weren't an arrogant bunch, we weren't an overconfident bunch. But when we were in the locker room after and all the way up until game time the next day, we were 100% sure that we were going to win. We just had the feeling that we had taken everything that they had, and we smashed it. We took all the life from that game and we were holding onto that win, and it was ours to lose at that point, it wasn't theirs to win.

Kevin Abel: We knew momentum was on our side. We knew they were deflated, defeated after basically giving the game to us. ESPN (accidentally) posting online that they were the national champions was even better. That really lit a fire under us. It was typical I guess for the entire season, that was how things went. People just wanted to doubt us at every single chance and knock us down anytime. I mean we had to bust our ass to get to number one (in the polls). It took Florida losing a couple times for them to finally say "all right Oregon State, you can finally be number one." But that didn't matter to us, all we needed was to believe in ourselves, and that's exactly what we did.

Pat Bailey: When Trevor hit that ball out of the ballpark, honestly I knew we were going to win the next day. And I especially knew we were going to win when I heard their coach talk about it in his postgame interview. They just seemed really deflated, so I knew we were going to win the next day. To me he seemed deflated, shell-shocked, devastated.

It goes back to my thing, you can't do anything about the past. How you respond to what happened is way more important than what happened. And the response I saw on television, I went "wow, I don't think that's a very good response." And I'm not taking anything away from coach Van Horn because he's done amazing things at Arkansas and he's a great coach, but based on his response and how it came out, I just felt like we were going to win that game the next day.

Steven Kwan: It's a game of momentum, and that's the most momentum we could've ever gotten. A couple of us were watching some of Arkansas' postgame interviews. One of the guys said something like "yeah, you know, it's another baseball game. We're not worried about it; we still have a great pitcher going tomorrow." It was the fakest confidence I'd ever heard. Those guys were done.

Trevor Larnach: It really hit me when I was watching their team's press conference and it looked like they'd gotten their souls taken out of them. I literally told coach Casey "they're done, that's it, we've won. They're not going to come back and battle back tomorrow. Their momentum is crushed."

Joe Casey: We could obviously tell they were pretty down, but after I saw the highlights of Trev's home run and seeing the pitcher put his hand on his face and everyone in their dugout was in awe, that's when I more saw it. We know that feeling of not having it, too, from the year before. That made it even more exciting knowing that we don't have that feeling this time, it's someone else and someone we're trying to beat. Once Game 2 ended, there was no doubt in anyone's mind that we were going to win Game 3. We knew, I think they knew. Their fans knew, they all left. Well, they didn't all leave, but it wasn't nearly as full for that third game.

Christian Chamberlain: I think Arkansas lost the (final) game before it even started. If you walked through the hotels, there are fans leaving the night before because they thought they would beat us, two-and-done. I think even the players, like you watch that fly ball drop and it looked like they gave up.

Jack Anderson: That's a tough thing to come back from, and then knowing the Arkansas Razorback history of doing this kind of stuff ... I didn't know that until before the third game that this is typical Arkansas. Someone said it's like the Washington State mindset of "couging it," that's what Arkansas is known for in the SEC. I think losing that game brought up a lot of bad memories for a lot of people, and once we saw that there weren't as many fans in the stands, it switched the roles where we were in control of the stadium at that point. I think that wore on them too, going from a packed house to nobody there.

Pat Casey: Every guy says "I KNEW (when Grenier's popup fell) that you guys were going to win." I can't say that I felt like that, but I can tell you that after we did win the game, I told the guys that they were going to be a national champion tomorrow night. And I really believed that. I thought once we won the game that we were going to be real good the next night.

After winning Game 2 in dramatic fashion, Oregon State needed to pick a starting pitcher for the finale. Pat Casey and Yeskie settled on Abel, who had turned the corner following an up-and-down first half of the season.

Abel didn't pitch in the super regionals and was fresh coming into the College World Series having only thrown 60 1/3 innings on the year. He pitched four innings against Washington — throwing before and after the rain delay — and lasted seven innings during his start against Mississippi State. Four days later, he picked up his third CWS win with another solid relief appearance. Starting Game 3 of the finals would mean a fourth appearance in 11 days, but Abel was prepared to take the ball and go as long as possible.

FINISH

Jack Anderson: We thought Kevin was going to maybe pitch. I mean he pitched the day before but he was like "why not?" He was just a warrior at that point.

Kevin Abel: Nick came up to me and said that they wanted me to start Game 3. I was told that him and Cadyn went up to Case and said that they wanted me to start, whether I could go two innings, three innings, they just wanted me to start. When I walked into Case's office after Game 2, I said, "I want the ball Game 3."

Pat Casey: After (Game 2), Nate asked me "what are you thinking?" And I said "well, we'll talk about it tomorrow." We talked the next day and we were both thinking the same thing.

Nate Yeskie: Case just said "hey, I think we start Abel and we'll get as far as we can with him." And at that point he was pretty definitive with it and how he wanted to get that point across, so I just said "yeah, I'm fine with it. We'll see how far he can get us."

Kevin Abel: About an hour before we left the hotel, Yeskie called me and I went over to his hotel room. He said "hey, you're going to start. We don't need much from you, just give us what you've got. We want you to set the tone." And so it was just another day; my job was to go as long as I could.

Nate Yeskie: I remember talking with (ESPN announcer) Kyle Peterson before the game, he said, "what are you thinking today?" I said, "I don't know, he's going to get us as far as he can. I certainly don't anticipate any Brett Laxton-type performance." See when I was a senior in high school, Brett Laxton punched out (16) and LSU beat Wichita State that day to win the (1993) College World Series.

With all the momentum and Abel slated to start, it was positive vibes only for the Beavers entering Game 3. The previous night's ending made it seem like Arkansas had missed its shot and the national title was Oregon State's to lose.

Bill Rowe: I remember having the exact same feeling waking up that morning and going to bed that night as I did as a player. That feeling where one team is going home empty and another is winning the whole thing. That's just an incredible perspective and I was so appreciative and grateful for getting to have that experience, and I definitely tried to make the most of it.

Since I wasn't a player, I could walk around and talk to a bunch of people and talk to as many of the fans and stadium employees as I possibly could. I took full advantage of that and tried to meet everyone and talk to as many of the fans and the parents as I could, talk to them about their kids and enjoy it with them because that was the part I thought would've been so fun. My brother turned 21 at the College World Series when I was a player there. Just thinking about him and all the other brothers and sisters, moms and dads who got to hang out at the stadium and in town that whole week, I think it's so special for them, and that's one of the big reasons we do it.

There's so much pride for players in providing that type of experience for their loved ones and the people who support them throughout the year. I know that every player and coach on that team, we felt that love from Beaver Nation. So, getting to give that back to them is really special, and I think we just wanted to take advantage of that and be able to hang up another championship banner for everybody.

Andy Jenkins: I love the old-school logo, the O-S-U that I played under and all the guys before with Jack Riley. I had a couple of the old stickers in my desk and I told my buddy Brian Pecor, who worked in fundraising at the time, that Ortiz and I were going to put them on our helmets. The idea of that was just to represent all of the alumni and all the people who had come through the program. If we got any TV time, which the first base coach gets a ton, we'd be wearing that old-school logo and making Beaver Nation proud. It was just something Ryan and I did to respect the program and honor one of the best logos ever, one that was drawn up by Jack Riley's daughter (Pam Arey).

Kyle Nobach: We rolled in on that bus, and I remember just walking down that tunnel and into the locker room thinking "here we go man, this is for all the marbles. We're playing for a national championship." I'll never forget the speech Pat gave.

Jake Mulholland: We knew that was going to be the last game of the season, Case gave us a really good pregame speech and motivated the heck out of us. He reminded us all what we had been through, all the good times, the bad times and just the opportunity that we have right here, how few people ever get the chance to do stuff like this. That helped put into perspective the opportunity that we had. He can say anything and it gets me ready to run through a brick wall. He's a very good motivational guy, even when he's not trying to be. Just the way that he talks, he can silence a room quickly with anything he has to say. I don't remember the specifics of what he said, I just remember being ready to go through fire for him after that. We wanted to win for Case, win for Corvallis, Oregon State, Beaver Nation.

Andy Jenkins: From the moment we got to the field the next day, there was no doubt in my mind that we were going to win. There was really nothing Arkansas did to us that day and I felt like we were at ease. There was this calmness about everything that we did and a confidence that we were going to win this game. And you get on the back of Kevin Abel, and that certainly made those feelings feel even more real.

Trevor Larnach: I know that our team had this attitude that there was no way you could stop us from winning, and I know that Kevin couldn't have been more locked in that game because of how easy it was to him. He was making them look like he was untouchable, and in that game he was. It was special.

Abel was dialed in from the start, working through the top of the first on 16 pitches. The offense provided some early support with two runs in the home half, and Abel put up a comeback zero with a 1-2-3 second. Arkansas loaded the bases in third, but Abel got out of dodge with a strikeout and popup. The freshman right-hander was on, it was just a matter of how long he could last.

Jack Anderson: It was like "hey, we're going to get three innings out of Kevin and he's going to rock it, and we're going to figure it out from there." But obviously it went a little longer than that, which was just incredible.

It's so funny going from having no confidence in Kevin to having all the confidence in the world in him before that game. It's something that can really only happen in sports.

Pat Bailey: He's a freshman, 19 going on about 35. I go back to when we lost that game in Arizona when Kevin was on the mound and we were up 5-2. We ended up losing 6-5, and I think about that Kevin Abel back then and I think that was the turning point for him. It was time to grow up and man up, and I think he responded great after that. And he could've gone the other way, too. He could've been terrible the rest of the year, so I have to give him a ton of credit. He did a great job of responding to a situation that was pretty negative. That was a turning point for Kevin and he was lights-out after that, especially in the World Series.

Kevin Abel: The offense was just unreal with instant run support.

Nick Madrigal: From the very beginning, we were rolling. Adley had a big hit through the six-hole, Gretler, it seemed like everyone had a hit. It was nice to score first and get the pressure off of us, show up and do what we'd done all year.

Ryan Gorton: Rutsch came up clutch again in the first inning. It was just like "wow, this guy hits choppers and they're freaking base hits. I wish I could do that."

Adley Rutschman: The mentality going in for me was "if we score early, it's over." That's how I felt everyone was thinking. We got runs up on the board early, and it felt like the winds were out of their sail.

Michael Gretler: It felt like we had all the momentum, especially scoring runs the first inning like we did. I think that was a direct, direct correlation from the way the game ended the night before. And after that second game, I don't think any of us really even acknowledged that we had momentum. It was just like "good win, we've got one more game." But after we scored a couple runs early in that last game and Kevin turned in a couple quick innings, it felt like we were on the right side of the previous year's LSU game. The air had just been sucked out of their dugout, and that was the feeling we had. We sensed blood in the water.

There was never a big hit. Adley hit that single through the six-hole, I hit that chopper that their third baseman threw away that scored a run. It was different because in the other games there were doubles and home runs and whatnot, and in that game it was seeing-eyes singles, flares and hitting behind guys. I think that was probably a little more frustrating for them because we weren't just banging the ball around. Choppers were getting through, ground balls were getting through, flares were falling. That was when the air really got sucked out of their dugout.

Joe Casey: We got a few runs early and were like "OK, cool." They had bases loaded in the third, we were up 2-0, and we knew Kevin had pitched a lot so us guys on the bench were like "oh, we've got to get someone hot." Because he had thrown a lot, and if he gave up some runs we would probably need to bring someone in. I just remember the coaches getting someone loose and him getting out of that jam ... and it was after the fourth or fifth that someone was hot in the bullpen. We told him to sit down and see how Kevin does.

Dylan Pearce: They called me down to the pen in the third inning and were like "hey, you need to get moving around." And then they called down and said "make sure you're hot. We're going to try and get (Abel) through the fourth inning, we'll see how he does, and then you're it, you're going in." And he got out of it, and we were able to just rock-and-roll from there.

Adley Rutschman: He only had one inning where he was scuffling, and I remember based on the fact that he had thrown the previous day, I think it was like 20-something pitches, we didn't know how long he was going to go and I thought that might've been it during that inning and we were going to have to smorgasbord this thing all the way to the finish. After that inning, I remember the coaches were like "are you good to go another one or should we get another guy going?" And he was just locked. The whole game, it didn't matter, he was not coming out, that was the bottom line. Guys kind of let him go, let him run free. Just to be behind the plate and see what he was doing, it was video game. He was doing it. He was living it and I was just along for the ride. After Kevin got out of (the third), it seemed like he was untouchable.

Kevin Abel: Having the run support early was a big relief, but my goal was to go five innings. I wanted to at least get us into the fifth and then we could hand the ball off to anyone and everyone in our bullpen. That's why you can see I was like 88 to 90 (miles per hour) the first five innings, I'm kind of cruising. It was all about making pitches and getting guys out. And after that inning, Yeskie came over and said "you did what we needed you to do. Anything you can give now is just icing on the cake." And I said, "all right, I'm going to give you everything I've got." And you can see my velo jumped, I was probably 90 to 93 the rest of the game. I just left everything out there, what am I waiting for? There's no game tomorrow. It was just making pitches, that was it.

Jake Mulholland: I remember we had a pitchers' meeting before the game with Yeskie, and he had said that Kevin was going to try to get us through four, maybe five, and that's going to be it for him. He had thrown a lot, but Kevin basically took it upon himself to say "nope, that's not going to happen." He gave no reason to be pulled whatsoever, went through quick innings and just dominated. I've never seen a performance like that in Omaha. He competed every single pitch, and it showed.

Jack Anderson: I got taken out in the sixth inning, it was (4-0) at that point and Bails was like "hey, we're going to put Preston in to have a little more speed out there." And then that inning, Preston made a great play that I probably couldn't have made. So, I went up to Bails and was like "good call there." But once I got taken out, I knew it was over. I couldn't go back in the game, that was my career.

From there, I turned into fifth- and- sixth-grade Jack that was watching the World Series at that point, and now I was in the dugout. It was just super surreal, I was almost teary-eyed the whole time watching the game and thinking "get this out, get this out!" We were so close, we just had to keep it going. Because we saw the night before what can happen in baseball, so I was trying not to get too ahead of myself.

Brandon Eisert: Being in the dugout, I knew I wasn't going to be able to pitch at all that day, so I was able to sit back and almost be a fan watching the game. It was definitely a lot of fun seeing us get out to the early lead, and it was honestly relaxing because Kevin was so dominant. For me, it was a chill game. Not boring, but it was like "all right, here we go." He was just cruising through the innings. For me, it almost felt like a regular-season game with how dominant he was throughout the game. It definitely didn't feel like it was Game 3 of the College World Series finals.

It is weird to look back at all the games that we went through to get to that point, and the final game that it took was the most anticlimactic almost. But it was definitely still a joy to see how he was able to do so well and dominate that game.

Trevor Larnach: It was a really relieving feeling to be like that after that whole World Series of having our backs against the fence.

Cadyn Grenier: The whole time we were sitting in the dugout and nothing was going on, but that's the way we wanted it. It felt like that was perfect. After the night before, all we needed was that steady game where we did what we did. Draw walks, get hits, bunted, just whatever we had to do, and that's the way we wanted it to be. I feel like throughout the game, there wasn't a worry in the world because we knew we had them right where we wanted them and they weren't going to be able to come back from what happened the previous night and the start we got in Game 3.

Nate Yeskie: It was very storybook-like in the way that it ended because we'd overcome so much adversity and then you get that, I don't know what you'd call it in the movies, but it was like "here's the wrap at the end," and it's not as good as the previous 10 or 15 minutes of the movie you were watching.

The Beavers methodically added to their lead, getting a third-inning Rutschman RBI single and a Gretler sacrifice fly two innings later. By the time Abel took the mound in the top of the sixth with a four-run lead, there was visible irritation emanating from the Razorbacks dugout. Abel had done his job and then some, but he wasn't ready to give up the ball.

Kevin Abel: There was nothing to worry about. All I had to do was make my pitches, stay ahead in the count. I was able to use my weapons and really mix (curveball and changeup) in. I kept them off-balanced, and I could just see the frustration that they had. That was something Yeskie and I would always talk about, after you strike out a guy or something like that, watch them go back to the dugout and see how they're doing. And sometimes you'll see guys slamming their helmets or guys asking them like "hey, what are you doing?" When you see that going on, you know you're two steps ahead of them.

Pat Casey: In about the sixth inning, you could see that their hitters came to the plate completely defensive. Like "man, I don't know what he's throwing. I don't know where it is. I just can't see it." There was frustration, you name it. Once we got ahead, we were going to suffocate them with pitching and defense.

Michael Gretler: He obviously had tons of talent and three extremely good pitches, but he wasn't just getting guys out; he was making them look silly with the changeup and the curveball. I remember guys were ducking out of the way of the curveball and it was right down the middle, guys were swinging at the changeup that was dropping off the table. He was so locked in that game with all of his pitches that he was just making guys look silly out there.

Ryan Gorton: Nate's pitch calling was so good. I think he knew just exactly what to throw to those guys. He knew what they were looking for, and he'd call the other thing.

Nate Yeskie: We had guys up, we had guys ready to go, just trying to be cautious of where he was at and how he was going. The kid kept telling us throughout, and it's not a deal where he was running the ship because he certainly wasn't, but there wasn't any anxiety, there wasn't any tension, there was nothing. It was just "hey, I'm good." He even had some good insight at times, he'd say "the breaking ball is feeling pretty good, I think I'm about ready for it." So, I'd say "OK, let's jump it back in here. Here's how we'll try to use it," and we did. He took ownership and he just grew up a lot, and that's what you want. You want your players to get to that point where they can take ownership and do those things.

Luke Heimlich: I went down to the pen in like the sixth inning to start warming up, me and Mulholland were down there. Yeskie would call down every half-inning or so and be like "all right, if he gets in trouble we're going to need one of you hot." But Abel just kept rolling.

Bryce Fehmel: I remember Kevin coming into the dugout after the seventh or eighth inning and looking absolutely beat, but there was no way he was coming out of the game. Yeskie had all the trust in the world in him, and so did the team. It was fun to watch a freshman go out there and compete on that stage.

Nick Madrigal: I remember inning by inning, getting closer and closer to the ninth. We were getting more of a comfortable lead and Kevin on the mound was just, it felt like he was flying through innings. It was so easy being behind him on defense and gosh, everyone was so excited in the dugout. We stayed focused, but knew we were coming closer and closer to the goal that we'd had the whole year. Kevin on the mound was as locked in as you could get. Every pitch he threw it seemed like was right where he wanted it to be. It was really cool to witness something like that.

Steven Kwan: He just kept getting guys out, kept getting guys out, and it didn't stop. Next thing you know it's the ninth inning and I'm looking at Trevor while we're hitting and I'm like "dude, is this real?"

Abel was in such control that the innings began to run together. Many of Oregon State's College World Series games were lengthy, disjointed affairs with minimal flow. Game 3 of the finals was the exact opposite, as the Beavers grabbed the early lead and put up zero after zero on defense. Abel received a little more insurance in the eighth when Gretler drew a leadoff walk and was singled home by Taylor, putting OSU up 5-0 heading to the ninth. Abel, sitting on 114 pitches for the day, trotted back to the mound to try and finish off a performance for the ages.

Kyle Nobach: I remember my last at-bat a lot, running down the line and rolling my ankle really bad on the bag, then running back to the dugout I told ZT "pick my ass up, get a hit."

Zak Taylor: My last at-bat, I ended up singling through the right side to score Gret from third with two outs. I remember in my head being like "that's the dagger." Just being able to get that last run in, I feel like that was kind of that last gut-punch.

Kyle Nobach: That was the fifth run. Then we went out to the field for that last inning, Abel is still in the game, it's the top of the order and Abel just goes bam, bam, bam, bam.

Jake Mulholland: I was in the bullpen in the ninth because I was going to start the ninth, (Yeskie) told me that in the seventh. And then Kevin's eighth inning was (12) pitches, so Yeskie was like "Kevin's going to go back out. If a runner gets on, you're in." And he had been saying that for like four innings almost but nobody got on, so how are you going to pull him? You're not. He took the ball and ran with it.

Kevin Abel: There was only one guy I was going to hand it off to, and that was Luke, that's for sure. I wasn't going to hand it to anyone else. He was the main reason why we were there. If it wasn't for him being consistent all year long, being the role model for our staff, really being the benchmark for everyone to work towards including myself, none of that would've happened. He deserved it.

FINISH

Luke Heimlich: I just wanted to win. Whether that was me, Mully, Abel, it didn't really matter. I just wanted to win.

Zak Taylor: We go into that last inning, Kev got two quick outs. I look back at Trev and I remember getting these butterflies in my stomach. I had never felt that on the field like that, knowing you're so close to your ultimate goal. I look back at Trev, he's shaking and bobbing his head like "we got this!" I looked over at Nick and he's just locked in, so I was like "all right, I'm not going to look at Nick again." But Trev was pumped and some of the guys were excited on the field, and I'm just telling myself to stay with my fielding process.

Trevor Larnach: I remember the last inning when there were two outs and me and Zak Taylor kept looking at each other, and we kept nodding to each other because we were ready. It almost took away the excitement of my own experience of dogpiling because I already knew it was going to happen. I'd already psyched myself out at that point.

Steven Kwan: I have a really fond memory of right before that last out. I had my arms around Fehm and Luke, and the last strike came, and then it was another blackout. I don't remember what happened.

Nate Yeskie: Again, unsung heroes. Sam Tweedt didn't throw a pitch the whole College World Series, but he sat beside me from Game 2 on and he would tell guys "hey man, no, I'm doing the chart," because he felt that would help us win. I remember going into the ninth inning, he's sitting there and I go "well, we've come this far, right?" He looked at me and said "let's go win it."

You have ideas in your head of what it's going to look like, what it's going to sound like, smell like, feel like, the whole thing because you sit and dream about moments like this, at least I know I do, and I'm sure there are others who do as well. But as the ninth is unfolding, I looked at Pat (Casey) and said, "if he doesn't walk or hit anybody, this thing's over with. It's over." After the first out, I'm kind of looking around like "wow, this is going down." The second out, I'm just watching the kid on the mound go about his business and do what he needs to do. The last at-bat, Kevin throws him a 3-2 curveball which he must've shook to — I really don't believe we sent that pitch in — and the guy fouls it off. The next pitch we send in, it's a fastball. Sam puts the clipboard down and he's standing right in front of me, I can't even see the field. I look at him and I go "what the hell are you doing?" And he goes "getting ready to go dogpile." I wanted to tell him "sit down, dummy. You're goofing this whole thing up," just because of the baseball superstitions we all have to some degree. After that, pretty sure I blacked out for a couple seconds.

Abel retired the inning's first two batters on eight pitches and got ahead 1-2 on Luke Bonfield. The eighth pitch of the at-bat was a fastball just below Bonfield's knees that Rutschman framed to perfection for home plate umpire Joe Burleson. Burleson raised his arms to signal strike three, and pandemonium ensued. Oregon State had won its third national championship behind a two-hit shutout from Abel, who struck out 10 and retired the final 20 Razorbacks in order to end the game. Abel became the first pitcher to win four games in a single College World Series.

Kevin Abel: It got called a strike, too close to take. It wasn't as bad as some people made it seem. I throw with a lot more tilt, so if you look at where it crossed the plate, it's not as low. Rutsch made it look good. If you look at the pitches the guy swung at and fouled off that were way worse, there's really no excuse to not swing at that one.

Nate Yeskie: Seeing Kyle (Peterson) afterwards, he goes "really, no Brett Laxton, huh?" And I just shrugged my shoulders and was like "hey, he didn't strike out (16)."

Cadyn Grenier: Game 3 was dumb, I'll tell you that right now. It was stupid. I just stood there. Some of the pitches he was throwing, the spots with him and Adley together, it was just … he made the second-best team in college baseball look like they didn't belong there. He threw that good of a game, and we were solid behind him. I don't really know how else to describe it. Obviously he was dominant, but just watching what he was able to do consistently from his playoff start, it was awesome. And for him to do that after throwing the night before and really needing to come through for the team because we were low on arms. You definitely can't take anything away from what Kevin did.

Pat Casey: I saw a guy named Jonah Nickerson do almost the same thing. But no, as far as being a freshman … Jonah did that his junior year (in 2006), but a freshman going on the mound in that game and doing it as easily as he did, it was phenomenal. He could throw any pitch, just about. And for a while there he didn't have his breaking ball. He just threw fastball-changeup, but he could throw them anytime he wanted and anywhere he wanted.

Bill Rowe: Oh man, Jonah Nickerson never had anything on Kevin Abel! That was just unreal. I charted pitches the whole season from the dugout. I'm looking at the side view of these pitches, so a lot of times you can tell the difference between a changeup and curveball just based on vertical break and how sharp it is. But with Kevin, you couldn't tell. I mean he had a hammer curveball but the changeup literally dropped off a table just as sharp, so you could only tell by the way the catcher was leaning.

Max Engelbrekt, pitcher: If you're watching games from Omaha, you have more or less a similar camera angle to how you would watch major leaguers pitch and just the aesthetics of the game. You can see just how much movement he has on his curveball and changeup (better than) Oregon State's camera shot. It's always funny when ESPN would do the K-Zone tracker in college and you get like a foot outside because the zone is so much bigger. But with Abel, he was just unhittable. He'll be a legend at Oregon State forever.

Andy Jenkins: Wherever Kevin threw it, they swung. They were a very aggressive team; they didn't apply a lot of pressure with the bunting game. That was their style, who they were, and we did apply pressure. We shrank the defense and did do stuff like that, and when you don't do a lot of that stuff, a pitcher can get real comfortable. And Kevin obviously got really comfortable, Nate had a great plan and Rutsch caught the ball really well. What a moment for everybody, and especially for a freshman that really had to grow up midseason. And he did.

Mitchell Verburg, pitcher: Kevin's always had the stuff. His talent has never been questioned. It was a matter of his brain, what he believed, his mental side. He was the most confident pitcher I have ever seen on that day. It just shows what he can do as a player and how talented he is and how much he grew that season. Watching him throw from the beginning as a freshman, he was inconsistent and showing spurts of success. Then he became an absolute lethal killer at the end of the season once he realized how good he was. It's not that he didn't think he was good, he just didn't 100% fully believe it. Kevin's an amazingly hard worker and he's grown a lot from that first pitch that he threw.

Luke Heimlich: For him to relieve the night before and then show up and be like "yeah, I'm good to go. Just let me go until I can't," it shows his attitude toward the team. He didn't expect to go that deep into the game, but he was going to give what he had left and then pass it on over. And he just kept chugging along.

Kevin Abel: It was a lot easier for me being Game 3 than it was for Luke or Bryce. Because by then we had gotten to see them for two games and understand what their hitters were trying to do. So, I guess having all that confidence and that preparation was big, and the night before, striking out the side, that gave me a lot of confidence.

Pat Casey: People don't realize that he had 15 days off. He threw against LSU and didn't throw in the supers due to the fact that we won in two. So, he was fresh, he was good and in that Game 3, he did it as easily as I've ever seen a guy do it. Now, did we think he was going to go nine? No. I thought if we got five we would be in good shape because we had Heimlich in the bullpen, we had everybody, basically. So, if he could get us five, we were in great shape. He was phenomenal. He could've pitched to the moon that day, or in the big leagues. If he pitches for anybody in the big leagues that day, he gets lots of people out.

FINISH

CHAPTER X

THE AFTERMATH

When Kevin Abel recorded the final out of the College World Series, it didn't take long for the Beavers to shift into celebration mode. Adley Rutschman sprinted to meet Abel in front of the mound and showed off his football background with a near-perfect form tackle. The dogpile quickly grew, with Abel and Rutschman at the bottom. The national championship trophy appeared moments later. The Beavers didn't make the NCAA Tournament in 2016, and had a dream season spoiled the following year. At long last, they were on top of the college baseball universe.

Kevin Abel, pitcher: The Nationals pitcher (Daniel Hudson) took one out of my playbook throwing his glove off to the side, which I took from (Kevin Gunderson) I guess. I remember doing that, turning around and seeing Rutsch right there and I was like "all right, I guess we're doing this." And he just wanted to get me off the mound and get me down because he knew everyone was coming. And I remember everything going black and feeling a lot of pressure on my stomach and on my rib cage.

Adley Rutschman, catcher: I was just trying to get him down to the ground before everyone came and ran into him and he fell awkwardly. I was trying to secure him safely on the ground and allow for a somewhat safe dogpile for him.

Kyle Nobach, outfielder: I threw my glove in the air, ran toward Nick and Gretler and those guys. We were giving each other really big hugs and I remember just running toward that dogpile and I jumped as high as I could, I really did.

Kevin Abel: If you look at our dogpile compared to others, it's very tall and narrow. Other teams spread the weight, but no, everyone was just on top of me. I couldn't breathe, and it was really dark.

Bryce Fehmel, pitcher: I think I somehow ended up on the bottom. That was painful, but it was definitely worth it.

Steven Kwan, outfielder: I remember I wanted to get on top but I couldn't jump up very high, so I tried to snake my way into the middle and fell out of the dogpile. Then I just laid on the ground, I couldn't believe it.

Jack Anderson, outfielder: Going from watching it on TV as a kid to being in that dogpile, I think that's every kid's dream from the Northwest who plays baseball. They want to be in that program and get that moment, and not a lot of people get it. It was super special to share it with the Beaver family and also my family that was there.

Michael Gretler, infielder: We had been through so much together, and for it all to come together with a storybook ending was pretty special. The year before, we dogpiled for going to Omaha. And in 2018, we said there was only one dogpile. So that was the only dogpile we had, and it was just pure excitement. That was obviously something you'll remember for the rest of your life, throwing your glove up in the air. I remember running over to Nick and Cadyn, seeing (Jordan Britton) and running into the middle of the pile, and obviously Kyle sprinting in from wherever he was coming from.

Cadyn Grenier, infielder: When he struck that last batter out, I remember dropping to a knee and being like "there's no way we just did this." Then I look over and Nick is halfway to me, so I get up, we threw our gloves up and I had this big jumping embrace with Nick. Some of the other guys got over to us and we were late to the dogpile party, but I remember getting in there and jumping on top and everybody being right there, screaming and yelling. Then everyone was getting up and hugging each other and all that, all the parents started filing on the field and you were just finding people to hug, it didn't matter who it was. Everybody was embracing and really in disbelief that we did it.

Brandon Eisert, pitcher: Throughout the game, you're feeling like "all right, we're going to win." But it doesn't really hit you until a little bit after the final out is recorded. Running out to the dogpile and really just seeing each player that got you there, seeing everyone face-to-face. Giving everyone a hug, giving the coaches a hug,

FINISH

I finally realized "we did it!" We had finally reached the goal, this is what we had come to Oregon State for and what we had worked so hard for. We finally did it, and being able to share that with all my teammates and coaches was definitely incredible, then all the families got to come onto the field. Just seeing them and everyone, it was something I'll never forget. And it's why I came to Oregon State, why everyone came to Oregon State.

Tyler Malone, infielder/outfielder: We dumped the Gatorade jug on Case, and that's probably the most happy and excited we've ever seen Case in our lives. He's got a huge smile on his face and is like "dang boys, look what we did."

Morgan Pearson, assistant to Pat Casey: I think the coolest memory I have from Omaha was immediately getting out of the dogpile, I see Pat Casey running straight towards me to give me this big bearhug. The joy in his face and knowing we completed something really special, I'll never forget that.

Cadyn Grenier: As intense as Case is and how standoffish he can seem to some people, after we won I'll never forget the absolute bearhug that Case and I had. I mean it was … you just felt the care, you felt how much work everyone had put in and you felt how much he cared about all of us. There was a happiness in his eyes about us winning and seeing us succeed that was just amazing for him. That's the kind of guy Case is.

Nate Yeskie, pitching coach: I told Jack and Michael before the thing, I said "hey guys, I had a weird dream. I had a dream that we took a selfie on the field after we won the national title together." This was picture day before the tournament started, so we took one out in front of the stadium with the statue in the back, and I've got another one with them at the end that I have framed. It gives me goosebumps every time I think about it.

Jack Anderson: We were taking our pictures before the World Series in 2018 and it was me, Yeskie and Gretler next to each other. Nate had his phone out and he was like "hey guys, let's take a selfie. We'll take another one when we win it." At the moment I was just thinking "oh, that's a cool gesture. We'll see if that actually happens." Once we won it, I remember, it was me and Gretler and Yeskie ran over to us. I still have that picture on my phone. It's Yeskie in the middle, then me and Gret and a bunch of guys behind us. That's one of those cool moments that even I forgot about and then I just scroll through my phone and am like "oh man, those two photos are right next to each other." It's special for Nate and special for me and Gret because we'd had that relationship for four years. Even though we were position guys, we still really appreciated the way Nate supported us as position players. That was really cool and I know he always sends it to me and Gret in a little group text, he'll just throw it to us every now again when he's going through old photos on his phone. That's a sweet one for sure.

Michael Gretler: We just enjoyed it. At that point, we knew we had limited time left together. Having everyone there and having the family members come down from the stands and being able to see all of them … we obviously had gotten close to each others' family, so it wasn't just us giving our parents hugs, it was giving Jack's parents hugs, it was giving Luke's parents hugs. Everyone was together. And obviously the parents make huge sacrifices, coming out there and they supported us through all of our childhoods growing up, taking us to practice. It was just a real, real special moment to finish the job, but at the same time be able to share such an exciting moment in our lives with the people you care about the most.

Luke Heimlich, pitcher: There's that video that always circulates where I'm crying and hugging Kyle, not a great look. Because Kyle and I were the two guys that didn't get to go the year before, so for us to be there and get to do it … just those guys like Kyle, Gretler, Sam, Jack, all those guys I'd been there with for four years. Same classes, in the weight room every morning, eat meals, I lived with half the guys. Just to be able to finish off four years together with that moment was really special.

Steven Kwan: I was trying to find my parents, just freaking out, hugging all my buddies, hugging all the guys. Then I see Fehm's dad, Fehm's mom, all these random parents and I immediately go "where's my mom and dad?" I ran over to the side and made sure they got on the field. Security was trying to make sure people went one-by-one, but I was like "dude, we just won the natty. Chill out." Everybody got on the field and it was just awesome.

Nick Madrigal, infielder: I had my family, my brothers, my girlfriend, everyone was there for me. It was awesome being able to share it with them, and also the guys on the team. I'd always watched celebrations from championships and things like that and sometimes people would get emotional, and I would never understand that. But I was emotional in that moment, I was so happy just because we worked so hard for that. I remember seeing guys hug each other and being so happy, it was a lot of fun. We took a ton of pictures and I remember just trying to take it all in. It seemed like it happened fast, but it was such a special moment.

FINISH

Nate Yeskie: My family was there, and being able to enjoy all of those experiences with them, it's incredible. My grandfather was 91, 92 at the time. In '17 he was there, in '18 he was there. I had family driving back and forth from Wisconsin to come down and watch. I had friends that flew out from California and different parts of the country. Being able to slow it down and enjoy it with those people, I caught myself doing the same thing, looking at the reaction on the kids' faces and looking at their families and feeling like you made good on a promise when you're recruiting some of those people. It was like "hey, this is what we told you. We told you we were going to give it a run at this. We didn't guarantee you were going to win anything, but we told you we'd put you in a position to have a chance to do it." It was just very unique and very special.

Drew Rasmussen, pitcher: For that group of guys, the senior class and the juniors who were lucky enough to be drafted, it was a picture-perfect ending. It was an incredible feeling just knowing the guys that you had strapped it up with and gone to work with every single day, they were able to see the finished product of their college careers and accomplish what every team's goal is at the beginning of the season. It was amazing.

Nick Madrigal: The way it worked out was not how we'd planned, but in the end that's what we were going for the whole year. It's just kind of funny the road we took in Omaha to get there.

Pat Bailey, associate head coach: It was really interesting in 2018 because when you look at our overall pitching staff, we didn't throw that well in the World Series. And we had 10 errors, which is a lot, and we had a lot of defensive mistakes that we don't normally make. If you just look at what we did pitching-wise and defensively, you'd go "there's no way Oregon State won the World Series." At all levels, you normally win with unbelievable pitching and defense when games are close. It's very unusual to win a World Series with offense.

Trevor Larnach, outfielder: It's just amazing what our team overcame and what they did, and the teamwork that went into it to accomplish that mission and that goal was pretty substantial. It was a thing of beauty, man. It's some of the reasons why you play the game, for that adrenaline of coming back and never backing down and fighting to the end. It puts our whole team's perspective and mentality into one year, almost. Because we went through adversity, we fought through, had our backs against the wall and came out on top because we believed and loved each other.

Andy Armstrong, infielder: Everyone was looking at Oregon State because they knew we had unfinished business and they knew that we felt the same thing. A lot of people didn't think we would be able to do it after that first loss, but you know what, the only other team to win the World Series after losing (two games) was Oregon State in 2006, and then it was us in 2018 again. That's pretty special because it's the Beaver way, we're never out of it. We'll claw back, we're never out of a fight. Until that last out is recorded, we're never out of it. And that's exactly what happened. We got down to that last strike and we ended up finding a way to get the job done and we finished. It made it even sweeter.

Bill Rowe, undergraduate assistant coach: There were obviously just so many similarities between the way that the 2018 team won their championship and the way that the 2006 team won their championship, coming back through the losers' bracket. I'm not really a superstitious guy, but when you get to that sort of stage and so many intangible things are going on, you have to somehow go with what's happening and make it work, and that's what we did. There were just so many individual moments where things happened that went our way. And that comes from multiple seasons of guys banding together, working on their crafts and being dedicated to getting back to that stage and getting it done.

Tyler Graham, director of player development: It goes back to family. We all loved each other, we all rooted for each other, and I think it comes down to that. The teams that love each other and are a family, those are the teams you see win national championships and world championships. I don't think there are too many teams in the history of sports that have won it with talent alone. Talent will only get you so far. I always say that chemistry doesn't guarantee you a win, but it's essential to a championship team. Culture and chemistry are absolutely essential, and we had both. We had an unbelievable family culture and unbelievable team chemistry. I think both teams (2006 and 2018) had that exact same thing, and it's a huge tribute to what Case did to build that type of culture, just a hard-nosed family culture of a bunch of guys that loved each other.

2018 was like the 2006 season when we went to the World Series in '05 and didn't win it, and we talked about that a lot. We talked about what we had to do to get back and win it because I don't think either team would've been happy to just get back to the World Series once they got a taste of it in '05 and 2017. It was a very similar situation, and I think they did everything they could, just like we did, and had that ultimate confidence that they could not only get back to the World Series, but win the World Series.

To have that belief before you get there, it's huge. I think that's also an essential part of championship teams, that they believe they can do it before they actually do it. In '05 and 2017, maybe some people were just happy to be there because it's a pretty cool place to be and quite an accomplishment in itself to reach the College World Series. I think you're more content the first time, but the second go-around you're definitely not content just to get there.

Nate Yeskie: I had the same thoughts after winning Game 3 as I did during Game 2: how can we stop time? How can we stop this whole thing right now? I didn't want to leave the field. If they would've given us a choice to camp out and stay at the field and told us they'd pick us up on the way to the airport and you can come home in your uniform, I would've said "sure! Leave the lights on, I'll flip them off tomorrow morning." Because you just don't ever look at those things and think "well, that was easy. We'll just show up and do it again next year." It doesn't work that way, and you just try to hold onto those special moments as much as possible.

It's really neat to think about being able to accomplish those things, and that was our ultimate goal. But the real victory for me was being able to enjoy that with those guys and watch them grow and evolve as men, and watch them accomplish things that they set out to do and overcome some adversity to get there, so it meant a little bit more. It wasn't just something easy that was handed to them.

Drew Rasmussen: It's different to be able to take a step back and take in the full picture. Because I knew I wasn't going to be able to play, I knew I wasn't going to travel with the team, so it was awesome to see the younger guys grow and have success, but also the success of the older guys and just see the leadership. Especially being able to see the freshman class of 2016 and my class as well, just what we were able to accomplish in those three and four years for those classes, respectively, was absolutely incredible. I mean, we saw the lowest of lows. Oregon State doesn't miss the postseason, that's just how it goes. The expectation is you're going to make the postseason, you're going to play well in the postseason and hopefully you'll get an opportunity to play in Omaha. In 2016 we hit the lowest of lows the program could imagine, and then to see us in '17 bounce back and win ... I mean, we won (111) games those two years.

Doing it all together as the young group we were in 2016, I think that was the reason we were able to bond really well together and become closer as a team. Because at 18, 19, 20 years old, none of us had ever experienced failure on a baseball field to that extent. For us to miss the postseason, it was heartbreaking. We had to come together and we had to grow together, so we were able to become more tight-knit and ultimately I think that led to the success we had in '17 and '18.

Steven Kwan: The love the whole team had for each other was off the charts. I don't think any team had first of all the talent we had, but also the love for each other was just different. We would do anything for each other, and I think that's something that gets overlooked. Because not only were we a really good team, but we were the best of friends. I'm very grateful that I can call literally any of those guys on there my best friend.

Ryan Gorton, undergraduate assistant coach: We were mentally tough, we were for sure mentally tough, but we were just so good. We had great, great players at third base, shortstop, second base, catcher, pitcher, centerfield, right field. Like we had really, really good players. We wouldn't have won it if we had the same talent but guys weren't as mentally tough or not as together as a team, we certainly did a great job of building that team chemistry and team atmosphere, but at the end of the day we were just really good. We had great players. Like, I don't know if a college team will be assembled that's that good ever again.

Pat Bailey: After things calmed down when we won it and we finally got everybody out of there, the reporters and everybody, Case said, "we won this thing because of character." Then he said a few other things, but when he said that, I was like "oh my gosh, that's the most important thing we talk about all the time, and this team bought into that, he's right. This team won this because of character." And there are a lot of things that go into the character of a team, but the character traits of that team — their work habits, how great of students they were, how good of citizens they were in the community here in Corvallis, the way they respected and honored each other — it was just really fun. I've only been a part of two teams in college that were like that, and that was '04 at George Fox, which was the same type of team in terms of how close and tight they were and how much they cared for each other, and then us in '18.

Pat Casey, head coach: It was a team that just had tremendous will, a team that wanted to … they felt like they let themselves down by not winning the '17 championship. They really felt like they could've and should've played better. I think baseball is a very unforgiving sport. A two-day momentum swing this way or that way, that was the only time we lost two games in a row that year. I thought they played fabulous and played their fannies off the entire year, and it was a tough way to end it. It was a team that was just relentless in their will to finish, and relentless in their will to get back and show everybody that they were the best program in the country, not only in '18, but in '17.

I think about what they did to LSU in a two-game series in the regional, we played them twice knowing that's the team that knocked us out. Our guys never blinked, that team never blinked. They never backed down, they never doubted, they never panicked. Just an immense amount of swag, an immense amount of

FINISH

confidence. You blend that with guys that had huge work ethic and huge character, and man they loved one another. It was a real, real family, there's no doubt about that. If you took a photo of that group, that's the blueprint of what a team should be.

Oregon State's postgame celebration continued in the locker room and back at the team hotel. The party lasted through the night until it was time to head for the airport early in the morning.

Andy Armstrong: In the locker room we were blasting music, everyone was happy and hugging each other, taking turns holding the trophy. We got back on the bus and they handed out our national championship watches from the NCAA, which were pretty cool. We got back to the hotel, the lobby was filled with temporary bars and stuff where parents and fans and everyone were just hanging out.

Jack Anderson: The hotel right after was so cool. All the Beavers fans were there, we'd been there for so long. I think the 2007 team was at that hotel, too, so there were good vibes that whole time we were there. Me and Kyle were a couple of the seniors that were done, everyone was coming up to us and saying how much they loved watching us play and stuff, that was super cool. People were buying you beer, buying you drinks and it was a pretty good way to go out on your last night in Omaha.

Kyle Nobach: The hotel was wild. I'll tell you what, I don't know what time I went to bed. I mean it was very late.

Bryce Fehmel: It was a great night. I don't remember getting home, but it was a great night.

Steven Kwan: I got to wear the Benny the Beaver head, there are a lot of pictures of that. I was super excited about that. Gosh, what a blur.

Kevin Abel: It was just fun being at the hotel and getting to celebrate with my family. I had a lot of people that flew out after Game 2, got on a plane early the next morning and it was great to see them. We had finished what we set out to do. I didn't like the fact that our flight was so early, I couldn't go to sleep that night. I was really tired, but it was really great. We were just living the life.

Nick Madrigal: There wasn't a whole lot of sleep that night because we all kind of celebrated together. The hotel was swarmed with Beaver fans and there was a bunch of people around, families. Yeah, there was not a whole lot of sleep that night, but that was OK.

Pat Bailey: I didn't see anybody get out of hand. I think part of that is we had a pretty mature group of guys. There were a couple guys in 2017 that got on the plane that next day after we lost and looked like they had pretty rough nights, but I really didn't notice that in 2018.

Tyler Malone: I remember that I got back to my room at like seven because we had to leave for the airport at eight. I packed up all my stuff and we hopped on the bus.

Nate Yeskie: I got 20 minutes of sleep that night. I got back upstairs, my wife had pretty much everything packed up and I said, "I'm just going to take a nap for a second." She said "take a nap? We're leaving in like 30 minutes!" But I just needed to sleep for 20 minutes. Then I got up, changed, went downstairs, we got on the bus and I fell asleep on the plane.

Cadyn Grenier: Obviously we were all pretty exhausted. It was a long, long couple of days. We got up early for that flight and everyone was still pretty juiced that we'd just won it.

Kyle Nobach: When we caught that bus in the morning, I was not feeling very good. I didn't sleep much, it was hot, we were dehydrated and we had just drunk a bunch of alcohol, so I think we were all feeling the same way.

Jack Anderson: In 2006, I went to the deal in Portland and was in the front row watching. I saw all the guys come out in sunglasses and I just thought they were being cool, but now I know it was because they were hungover. I remember thinking "oh, that's why those guys did it like that."

Steven Kwan: The trip back, I don't remember any of that. I was in a different state, I would say. It was just funny because all of us were kind of like that. I remember during the season, if somebody did that, they would walk by Case very gingerly to make sure Case didn't recognize him. They'd brush their teeth really well, make sure nothing looked like they had gone out or anything. But I remember that next morning, we were all like "what's up, Case?!" We all just looked like crap and were laughing at each other. It was really funny. But yeah, that trip back was a well-needed nap, I can tell you that much.

The four-hour flight from Omaha to Portland provided an opportunity to rest up for a long day of festivities. Instead of buses, the team was greeted at the airport by Stretch

FINISH

Hummer limousines for their journey home. Celebrations were scheduled in downtown Portland's Pioneer Courthouse Square and Goss Stadium.

Nate Yeskie: We land in Portland, I hear some scuttlebutt and all of a sudden they've got limos and this big old luxury van, and I'm thinking "OK!"

Michael Gretler: You don't really know what's coming, but you hear "oh, we're getting picked up in limos, we're going to downtown Portland," and all that. So it was a pretty quiet plane ride, everyone got their rest because we didn't sleep much the night before. Getting to the airport, they had another set of shirts and hats for us. We go into Pioneer Square and seeing the amount of people there, it was just like "wow!" We literally won the game the day before, and here are all these people piled into Pioneer Square to come celebrate and enjoy it with us. That just shows how special of a place Oregon State is. You have people who probably wanted to be in Omaha, but they took time out of their days to come celebrate with us.

Zak Taylor, infielder: That was so cool to see the amount of people that were so excited for us. To think that we didn't only win this for our team, this was for Oregon State, this was for all of our fans, people of Oregon, the state of Oregon, the West Coast in general. It was such a bigger impact than just winning a national championship for the university. I've had so many people tell me where they watched the game, what they were doing, how they felt, and to think you played a part in having an impact on their life, things people will never forget, that was special to me.

Andy Jenkins, assistant coach: I don't think our guys really understood what that day was going to look like. I knew they thought a crowd of people was going to be around, I knew they thought people would be celebrating. But to see all of Portland and what our administration put together for us on the chance we'd win, because there was a chance we didn't, for them to put that all together was truly remarkable. Kudos to all those people who didn't go to Omaha that put on the party.

Tyler Malone: That stretch from I-5 to Corvallis, cars were parked on the side honking at us, it was super cool. Me and a couple of the other guys were up through the sunroof. People were honking at us and there were banners up on the overpasses.

Luke Heimlich: The school or the team wanted to put us in those Hummer limousines, make it a big deal and spoil us. And that was the worst possible thing ever because we all had headaches, we were all stuffed in there. They only got three of them for like 30 guys, and they're not supposed to seat that many people. So we're crammed in there, we don't have any leg space, the air conditioning wasn't working and there's no bathroom in the limos, whereas we have bathrooms on the bus and there's plenty of space. So we're all crammed in these limos, trying to roll the windows down, we've all got to use the bathroom and everyone is kind of laughing. It was like "great, we're in limos, but we're all struggling!" But then once we got closer to Corvallis, all the overpasses that we'd drive by there would be people holding Beaver flags. And pulling into town, there were fans everywhere, all the fans would honk at us.

Adley Rutschman: We had a little bit of a breather from the Portland parade to the Corvallis parade and there were signs along the bridges as we were going on I-5 saying "congrats on the national championship," which was awesome to see. But I remember once we got off the exit to go to Corvallis off of I-5, all of the traffic was stopped on the other side of the highway as we were going through. We were cruising on Highway 34, it took us like 30 minutes to get to the field from there because we were moving slowly and all the cars were honking and people were out of their cars clapping, and we were playing music and vibing with everyone. That was awesome.

Nate Yeskie: It was a hero's welcome. It was like a bunch of rockstars' final stop on their tour. The state, the city, everybody, it was just great. It was a really neat moment for the kids, the fans that supported us, just the whole dynamic for it to come full circle. And I didn't know, I'd fallen asleep again trying to catch up on the ride down, I looked at my watch at some point and went "how are we not in Corvallis? We've been on the road for like three and a half hours. What's the deal here?" I come to find out that traffic was just a standstill the whole way, they were dropping banners at every overpass as we were driving back, and Kwan and some of these guys had their heads out the roof of the limos and were waiving at people all the way down. People knew who it was and what it was all about. Pulling into Goss was pretty incredible. Just seeing all those people that were there who had supported us, and a lot of the people there really had grown up with those kids. Because some of (the players) were local, some of them came in there as unknowns and turned themselves into somebody, and others were embraced and made to feel welcome. So it was just a cool moment to watch everybody kind of get their curtain call and relieve some of those moments.

Luke Heimlich: Pulling up to Goss, that was a crazy moment. There were so many people there ready to celebrate. We went straight from the airport to the Portland town square and did a gathering there, and got right back in the Hummers and went straight to Corvallis and that gathering. I think we got done with that one at like 5 p.m. or something and I hadn't eaten all day, but it was a great time.

FINISH

Andy Jenkins: We weren't planning on pulling a limo onto the field, but I think Case said, "hey, let's pull this thing on there!" We adjusted, and Mike Parker, what better way to finish off a celebration than with him being the presenter.

Bryce Fehmel: I think the coolest part was pulling into the stadium in the limos, and that place was packed. Mike Parker was reading off the roster, everyone was getting a standing ovation, and listening to Case speak to the entire crowd was pretty awesome.

Every player in the program received tribute, including those who didn't travel with the team to the College World Series. One of them was freshman Kyler McMahan, who started a pair of games at second base while Nick Madrigal was sidelined. In mid-May, McMahan appeared in both of Oregon State's non-conference wins over San Diego before a road trip to USC. A freak accident during pregame batting practice in Los Angeles ended his season early.

Kyler McMahan, infielder: It was the Sunday game. We did all our stretching and stuff in the morning out in left field. We had just gotten out there to play catch and some coaches were out there watching to make sure no balls would come into our throwing lines while they were taking BP. I mean there was no one to blame here, everyone was just getting out there. Sure enough, a line drive comes from whoever was hitting BP and I was unfortunately standing in the wrong area at the wrong time and it hit my jaw in the bottom-left corner. I had to go over and get an X-ray and it was broken into two pieces. Then they had to determine if I was able to fly home or not, when I could get surgery and all that. So I spent the entire game just talking to people at USC with Jeremy (Ainsworth), our trainer, trying to figure out what the next step was.

Pat Bailey: Oh my goodness, I don't think ever in my life I've seen that much blood. It was just unbelievable. We went and grabbed a garbage can so he could keep spitting in it. It was just so sad and such a weird thing. I've been coaching for a long time, and I've never seen a guy get hit like that warming up while the other team was taking BP. It was one of those unfortunate things that happened, and I think worse than the blood part was watching the doctor with all of his different array of shots come in and shoot his mouth up so he could fly home with us before he had to have surgery. He unfortunately missed the World Series because of that, and I feel terrible that happened to him because he's just a great young man.

Pat Casey: That was out of nowhere, just standing around playing catch. I'm surprised that doesn't happen more often with as small as some of the fields are and you've got to play catch. The ball hit him in the wrong place and here he is going to the dentist and getting wired up.

That was the year Nick (six) games into the season breaks his hand. The next day, Rutsch is playing first, has a collision and they thought he had broken his leg. Just, things happen, man. They happen, and that deal with Kyler was just odd. I'd never seen anything like that, I mean I'd seen guys get hit and things like that but never anything where it was that tough.

Kyler McMahan: I flew back home and went to the ER right away just to make sure the pain and everything was OK, which it was. And then we already had surgery planned out for the next day around four o'clock in the afternoon. So I just slept in, the pain was OK and I got surgery the next day and was wired shut for eight or nine weeks.

The UCLA series I was in the dugout, and when it came to regionals and super regionals I wasn't able to be in the dugout. I think it was because you had to be on the 27-man roster, and because I was hurt they threw me on the 35-man. My family came down for the games, so I was up in the stands cheering them on. I was there before the games saying hi to everyone and all that, but they were tight with their rules about who was in the dugout. So unfortunately I wasn't there, and then come World Series, it was a decision of would I be able to go there and when the team goes out to eat, I'd have to blend up food in a blender and try to suck it through a straw. It was going to be a lot more of a hassle for me to try and get the food and nutrition I needed and get my weight back and all that stuff because when I was wired shut I lost 20 pounds.

I decided to go up to Seattle to my parents' house and watch the World Series with them, and man we had TVs on in both rooms and were hooting and hollering. Everyone was so great to me and making sure I was feeling OK. Case texted me while they were over there to check in and see how I was doing, which was really nice just knowing the coaches cared to give me a shoutout even in the most crucial time at the World Series. That really made me feel like I was a part of the team.

Pat Bailey: Case was great with stuff like that, I mean really good about making sure guys felt like they were a part of things even if they got hurt or were injured, any of that kind of stuff. Coach Casey was just really, really good with stuff like that and Kyler, he was part of our team. I mean he was part of it. He would've went to the World Series with us had he been healthy.

Pat Casey: The hard thing for coaches is when you have to make roster decisions. You've got 35 guys and when you get to conference, you can only take 27. You go to

FINISH

the World Series, you can only (take 27). Those things are tough because everybody is important, everybody works and everybody is a part of it. To see some guys not in uniform, that's tough. And then when you see a guy that's not only not in uniform but can't be in uniform and is going through what he went through, you've got to make sure that they know that you're thinking about them. Like I've said, it's all about the things that happen along the way and how you handle them.

Kyler McMahan: Bails called me and he said that they had a ceremony planned in Portland. They got off the plane, took a limo and had a little celebration there. Then they headed down to Corvallis, but the traffic was so bad. I was waiting over at the field and I think they were delayed like almost two hours, so I was just sitting in the locker room waiting eagerly for them to come down. And sure enough, Bails gives me a call and says they're coming into town. I meet up, hop on top of the limo and ride into the stadium. That was really cool to see everyone and celebrate with everyone and have a celebration at Goss with all the great fans. It was really cool because even though I wasn't able to be there in Omaha, they brought Omaha back to me.

The over-capacity crowd at Goss Stadium soaked up every moment of the championship celebration. For some, the accomplishments finally began to register: a two-year overall record of 111-18-1, back-to-back College World Series appearances and the program's third national title in 13 seasons.

Oregon State outscored the opposition 59-30 over the course of eight games at the 2018 CWS. The Beavers plated 35 of those runs with two outs and 28 in the seventh inning or later. Pitching and defense were largely inconsistent in Omaha, but OSU committed just two errors in the championship series and held offensive juggernaut Arkansas to a .147 batting average (14 for 95). The Razorbacks collected a measly four extra-base hits (all doubles) and struck out 38 times against Beavers pitching. It truly was a team effort, and OSU became the first three-time champion since NCAA Tournament expansion in 1999.

Kyle Nobach: By the time we got to Goss, it had been 24 hours since (we'd won). It was a long travel back and I remember standing on top of those limos as we rolled into Goss. There were thousands of people in Goss, it was packed. There were people all over the field and everything. It was crazy. I remember Mike Parker just giving all these speeches about all these different guys and thinking about how this is something that not only impacted myself and my family and everybody around me, but it's affected so many other people. I don't think any of us really realized how special it was until we got back there. For me at least, that's when it hit me that we had just won the national championship.

Tyler Graham: I think the kids really, really took it all in and enjoyed it, getting to ride the stretch limos into Portland, getting to go to downtown Portland and get in front of the fans. And then, obviously, when they got back to Corvallis, getting to come onto the field in front of the home fans was a pretty special moment for everybody. I know all the kids and all the players will never, ever forget that.

Trevor Larnach: I personally just wish that it didn't go by so fast. We were on the plane, we touched down, we started parading. Then that was done and two days later everyone was gone. It was just like there was all that buildup for that moment, and then everyone was gone. That's how it is sometimes, but it doesn't take away how special all of that was and those guys are.

Steven Kwan: The Goss Stadium rally actually makes me really sad. Because obviously we go through all the talks, Mike Parker is introducing all of us, asking us some questions, but that was the last time our whole team was together. We went into the locker room, maybe we were together for five minutes, and that was the last time the whole team was together.

I actually have sad memories of that to this day because that whole team will probably never be together again. That was the last moment. A lot of the guys took off for pro ball, the younger guys went off to summer ball. We didn't really savor that time, which makes me really sad. I have a teammate now who played at Florida when they won it and he said they went on like a week-long bender. He said guys who had to go to summer ball just didn't report, they would get calls and didn't answer them. Guys who had to report to pro ball didn't go, they told them they were just hanging out. And nobody could tell them otherwise because they had just won a natty. I was envisioning maybe not something to that degree, but something close to it. And yeah, guys started leaving, and it was really sad.

Jack Anderson: That night we were like "all right, should we go out?," but we were all so exhausted. We went to (Clodfelter's), had one drink and after that it was just like "I want to go to bed. Bed sounds better than anything at this point." That was the last time we saw some of the guys, that last day we had together in Corvallis.

Kyle Nobach: Jack and I were two older guys that weren't going to go on and play (professional baseball). We came back with that trophy and all those other guys basically got to leave, it was really Jack and I that were hanging out for the next couple of weeks. I was down at his place for a little bit, we went down to a rodeo and did some things. That was really fun, we were literally going on a tour. We went to the St. Paul Rodeo, we went to a news station, we went to Baseballism, we went to a Hillsboro

Hops game. We were just going places and getting things for free. We weren't in the NCAA anymore; we were graduating and out of it.

NCAA rules also no longer applied to Cadyn Grenier, Michael Gretler, Steven Kwan, Trevor Larnach, Madrigal and Drew Rasmussen, who all jumped right to professional baseball. Luke Heimlich got his chance a few months later, signing with the Mexican League's Tecolotes de los Dos Laredos. The rest of Oregon State's players geared up for another season of college baseball.

The 2018 Beavers did reconvene a few months later in November to receive their championship rings at a football game. The team also got back together in November 2019 for a visit to the White House. Both celebrations provided ample time for relieving past glory and swapping stories from their time at OSU.

Nick Madrigal: Everything happened so fast that I don't think I had a chance to really understand what we accomplished. Looking back on it, it was just such a great feeling. And it's funny, so many things happen over the years. Things had to bounce our way, we had to come up with big hits, and I think what the best part was is it took every single guy on the team. There wasn't just one guy that carried us, it seemed like every single guy had a moment that year, whether it was in the playoffs or whenever we needed it. I think that's the most special part.

Kyle Nobach: When I opened up our rings for the national championship, there was a letter from coach Case with the quote "the strength of the wolf is the pack, the strength of the pack is the wolf." Each guy on that team upheld that quote. That's how we went about our culture. Each guy prepared themselves to the best of their ability, and if each guy was doing that it would collectively make the entire unit one. And if the entire unit was one, then that entire unit can make each individual player on that team better.

Pat Bailey: I can't tell you how many times I came to the ballpark early, 12, 12:30 when we had a one o'clock practice, and I'd see Nick Madrigal in the batting cage hitting off a tee by himself. It's what separates people who are good from people who are great, just that focus. I truly believe people who are great at anything live really narrow lives. They have three or four things that are really important to them, and that's what they spend their time doing. That's the difference between somebody who is really great versus somebody who is just average or good. And we had a lot of guys on that team that were not just great students and people, but were also very focused on the task at hand that needed to be accomplished.

Andy Armstrong: We were relentless and fearless, never out of a fight. It's a next-guy-up mentality, it's not one guy that's going to do it, it's the whole team. We did what we had to do in the offseason, we took care of business off the field and it was just a collective effort from everyone in order to achieve a common goal. That was pounded in through Case and we lived it, we lived it before it even came true. We lived and breathed national champions before we ever were crowned because there was an unwavering belief that it was going to be us.

Luke Heimlich: For it to all fully settle in, I think people handle that differently. Someone like Kyle is much more appreciative of the things that we did and the journey, and people look at things differently. Me personally, I'm just not very good at reminiscing and appreciating the things that we've done or personal accomplishments, so I don't think it's fully set in for me yet. I think going to the White House and seeing everybody a year later, that was amazing. A lot of the guys I hadn't seen in about a year, and getting back together and being able to celebrate again … things like that are going to happen years down the road, and I think it's slowly going to come to me that our team those two years was a pretty historic team.

Kyle Nobach: It was a long time coming for me personally, just being able to be a part of it. When I have a bad day, I just think "dude, you won a national championship. You can do anything you want." It showed me that there are no limits, you can actually achieve goals and do things you never thought you could do. I'm not saying I never thought I could do it, but I was a kid who came from a small town, I didn't go to a lot of (camps), I walked on to the team. It was awesome, it was incredible.

Jack Anderson: Every time we get back together, it sinks in a little bit more. When we got our rings, that definitely sunk in. When we went to the White House, we were like "wow, we're all back together again. How cool is this?"

Whenever a new season starts and that text group shoots back up again, we start talking about the team, talking about the players, talking about stories that just pop up in our heads from when we were playing. I think it will always hit me once the season starts, and when regionals and Omaha start it will consistently pop up. Case told us "it's really cool right now, in five years it's going to be amazing and 10 years from now you're going to be like 'those were some of the best moments of my life.'" He's been around it, he knows it, and I'm sure each year it gets a little bit more special. As we go our separate ways in baseball and start having families, it'll be pretty cool to share those moments with all the guys again.

Bill Rowe: I tell these guys to cherish those moments where we're back together.

They're going to happen forever, luckily, because they're a national champion now. There's always going to be events and things where there's a reason for everyone to get back together, and that doesn't happen for a lot of programs, it's really difficult to try and make that work. But because of the really special bond these guys have, they're going to be getting together forever. Until they're 75 years old and there's only a handful of them left, they're going to be inviting them out to football games, and that's something that's never going to go away for them. As they move along in life, they're going to realize it's way more special than they thought it was at the time. The impact of that championship is going to ripple through every area of their life, it's always something they're going to have with each other and it's a bond not many athletes get to share, especially at the college level.

Andy Jenkins: I just think about some of the big moments that certain individuals had. I think about Kyle's big hit (against Minnesota) after having his surgery and not being able to play the year before, maybe thinking his career was over. I think about Luke's hardships and being able to overcome and pitch in Omaha. Maybe he wasn't as sharp as he would've liked, but he logged innings and when you play that many games you need to log innings and give your staff a chance. Obviously, Larnach and Grenier, and just the big moments that all those players had. You have Nick Madrigal who wasn't very good offensively in the World Series (finals), who was our catalyst, our best player. To know that your best player cannot produce like he had in the past and we still come forward is amazing. Adley, his coming out party continued and the hype he had going on. Kevin Abel making that adjustment. There are so many great stories and it's not like one person went out there and won it for us, it was a true team effort, a fan base effort. Everyone who was involved in that run knows how it felt.

Cadyn Grenier: I think of it just in the sense of I've had a couple moments in my baseball career now that have been really, really clutch. And I couldn't be more grateful to my teams and my coaches that ended up putting me in those situations. However it's happened, in both college and high school now, I've been put into situations where I needed to come through, and looking back I'm so glad I got the opportunity to. Well mainly because I succeeded in them, but nobody gets those opportunities. Nobody gets the opportunity to walk off their high school state championship game, then turn around and play in the College World Series twice and get the chance to do what I did my junior year.

I'm super grateful that happened and I'll never forget any of it. About 99% of (questions I get) are about my hit. And it's funny because I'd say about 90% of the people who ask don't realize that I was also the one who hit the foul ball — which is funny to me because it was the same at-bat. Even Blaine Knight's wife, who we hang out with all the time during the season and stuff, she didn't know that I'd hit the fly ball. How that happened, I don't know, but it's just hilarious because everybody always asks "dude, what was your hit like that tied it? And Trevor's home run, what was that like?" And I'm like "yeah, after I hit that foul ball," and they're always like "wait, YOU hit the foul ball?!" And I'm like "yeah, what do you mean?" I would say that is about 99% of the questions I get asked. And then the other 1% is usually "dude, what was it like winning?" And I say, "it was frickin' amazing."

Trevor Larnach: Generally people just ask "how was it?" Because some of those guys in pro ball, they're not college guys. And a lot of the guys I've met that are college guys didn't enjoy their experience even remotely close to how much we enjoyed our experience. So I almost feel bad telling these guys that I had the best time of my life because some of them don't feel like that, and a lot of high school guys will just never understand that bond that you make. But I obviously give them my straight-up answer and tell them how awesome it was, but I try to keep it nice and short because there's no amount of words or any type of expression that would be able to define that experience of being here, playing for coach Casey, playing for those guys and wearing that uniform, winning those rings and all that stuff.

It'll always bring a smile to my face, but it definitely won't help me relive every single moment of being back in school with those guys. Because that's definitely what I miss the most, being with those guys every single day and living that college lifestyle and all that. I think I've told my girlfriend countless times how much I miss college, and it's true. The impact that it had on myself and those guys is something that I think will last a lot longer than a single home run in a World Series. So yeah, it's special as hell and it'll always bring a smile to me and my family's face, but the memories of being with those guys are what's most special to me.

Adley Rutschman: Honestly, I think it took until I was out of college for it to sink in, just on how crazy of a ride it all was. When you take off the uniform for the last time, you're like "wow, this has been a special ride." That's the sad part about it, you're never going to play with those guys again. I think every year when you have a new set of guys that graduate or get drafted, you realize, and I realize now playing in pro ball, just how special college is and the college experience is. It's sad every time you think about it, but you're just thankful for the memories and the people you've been fortunate enough to be around. It's crazy, you always have to keep looking forward to the next thing, because if I get caught up too much thinking about college, it's sad. Because it was just such a good time.

FINISH

Pat Casey: When we went to the College World Series in 2017, guys thought "how in the world are you guys 54-4?" In the sport of baseball it's just really, really crazy to think you can get to the World Series and only lose four games. To maintain that and sustain that over a two-year period, those guys, to me, man they had something underneath that uniform that was way more important than ability. It was "you're not going to stop us." The '16 thing fueled the '17 deal, the '17 not winning it fueled the '18 deal. It would be hard for me to imagine there was a better team in the modern era over a two-year period at any time than the Oregon State baseball team in 2017 and '18.

Despite significant losses to the MLB Draft and graduation, the Beavers had enough pieces in place to remain a contender in 2019. Rutschman, who earned College World Series most outstanding player honors, was back to receive for a pitching staff that returned 10 of its top 11 arms from the previous season. Other notable returnees included Andy Armstrong, Joe Casey, backup catcher Troy Claunch, Preston Jones, Tyler Malone and Zak Taylor, and the full-time coaching staff of Casey, Yeskie, Pat Bailey and Andy Jenkins was set to enter its seventh season together. Many talented players were departing, but things appeared to be stable at the top. Or were they?

Pat Casey retirement rumors were a regular offseason occurrence dating all the way back to the late oughts. Casey had been courted by other schools over the years — notably turning down Notre Dame in 2006 and Texas in 2016 — but always stuck with the program he built. Beginning in 2008, Casey would conduct a self-evaluation following each season to assess if it was time to step away. The answer was always no, until 2018. About a week after Oregon State returned from the CWS, Kerry Eggers of the Portland Tribune reported that Casey, then 59 years old, was considering retirement. The news generated plenty of hullabaloo, but many assumed it was the same old story and Casey would be back to lead the title defense. July and August came and went with no update, but OSU announced a press conference on Sept. 6 without a stated purpose. After 31 seasons in coaching, Casey was stepping away from the field to be the senior associate athletic director and special assistant to the vice president and director of athletics, Scott Barnes. Bailey was promoted to interim head coach with Yeskie and Jenkins remaining on staff. The monumental announcement was equally predictable and shocking.

Pat Casey: I think you think about retirement every year in about the eighth inning when you're pissing away a lead. I'm not sure, that's just a hard thing. Because there are things about it that make you never want to leave, and then there are things about it ... and none of those things really have anything to do with coaching, it's all the other responsibilities and all the other things you have to do, which is part of it. That's what you have to do. To run a program, you have to fundraise. You have to recruit. You have to do administrative stuff. Lots of things come into play for that.

I don't know if there was ever any one second where I said (that's it, I'm retiring), but I just know there's a level at which I always expect myself to coach at, and that's always at the same level that I expect the players to practice at. On the way back, that thing was so mind-blowing to me and it almost seemed like the season never ended after we lost in '17. It was almost like we were immediately on the quest to show that we were going to win this thing in '18, and it was a long thing. I never could bring myself, by the time they came back to school, to feeling like "OK, I'm going to do this at the level I've been doing it." And I didn't think that was fair, I didn't think that would be the right thing to do and I think guys would recognize that, they would see through that and I didn't want to do that. It'd be easy at that point in time to just go out and coach and have everybody do the things you didn't want to do, but I didn't want to do that. It would be hard to find a better year, a better group of guys, and I've had some great ones. But when you win it all and you've got guys who are as team-oriented as that team was, it was pretty gratifying to say "OK, right now, if this is the time that I have to step down, it's a pretty good time."

Andy Jenkins: I played for Case, I've been around Corvallis and I really knew him not just as a boss. I knew his family and you know, it's a tight-knit community. I remember maybe in 2009, I was back from a professional season training and I got a phone call from him when I was up in Portland. He didn't need anything, he didn't have a question, I could tell he just wanted to talk. My sense was that he was reaching out to people because he was soul-searching on whether he wanted to coach or not. This is after the media and a lot of people had speculated on whether he was going to come back or not, I'm not sure exactly what year it was. But I think ever since then, after a couple championships, anybody that's been close to the program has already heard rumblings about his intensity and his health, his competitiveness, and wanting to get out of it. One year led to another and he never left, so I think we all knew it might happen.

Ron Northcutt, director of operations: Case made a statement, I want to say in '11 or '12, when he was talking to a reporter to the effect of "I'm not going to be around forever." That ended up on OregonLive, and I remember the day, I was sitting at my desk and at that time coach Bailey and coach Yeskie shared an office, and Marty Lees was in there. Something came up on the TV and they yelled at me to get in there. And I said "what's up, what's this about Case? What do you guys mean, he's been saying this for years!" So we had a meeting that day and finally I said to him "Case, you're like the president. Whatever you say, people take it at 100%. They think it's going to happen, like right now." And he goes "ah, no." And of course our assistants were concerned about recruiting, and he made the comment to the coaches "you guys are the guys that do the recruiting. You have the relationships with those players." And of course they go "Case, they want to play for you. They know about you, they've seen what you've done."

My wife and I, his wife and I, we cornered him one night back in probably '11 or '12 and he kept saying "I need to quit, I need to get out of here." So finally we got on him and of course we said "Pat, we're concerned about your health. If this is tearing you up that much, I support you, I support you 100% because I'd rather have you as my friend around for a long time than you not being here." The next day, I think we went to Oregon and he said to me "boy, you and the wife got on me pretty good last night." And I said "Case, we care about you. Baseball's a game, you can do anything else." I mean, he was a real estate agent when he was coaching at George Fox and I was a real estate appraiser, we didn't make any money coaching.

Nate Yeskie: I never really gave it much thought to be honest with you because he'd been talking about it for a couple years. We'd heard it, he was always back and I never gave it much thought. You get used to seeing somebody for 10 years in the office every day, there's never any thought to "all right, I won't see you in here tomorrow." Recruiting was going on, too, so we got moving and we had to hit the road and get going. Because when you're in Omaha, there are events going on that you can't get to. Everyone else is out at those events, and now you've got to go play catch-up.

Pat Bailey: Case and I never really talked about it. I remember the day we got back from the CWS, Case said to me when we were driving down "why don't you just relax and take a couple days off before you get on the road." And I said "Case, I've already missed a ton of stuff. I need to get on the road immediately." We got back on Friday, we had been gone 15 days, that Saturday I did some yard work, I think I paid our bills and Sunday morning I got up at five o'clock, headed to the airport and went to Arizona for a tournament and was gone the rest of the summer recruiting. I didn't really have an indication (that he was pondering retirement) until we talked in August. It was probably the first week in August and I told him "Case, until you are 100% sure, don't do it," because he was thinking about doing it at the beginning of August. So he waited, and I just think he felt like it was time.

Andy Jenkins: I specifically remember sitting in the war room, the meeting room, the recruiting room, whatever you want to call it. It was me, Jake Rodriguez, Ron Northcutt, Yeskie and Bails. He kind of stood up and told us and got emotional. Whatever his decision was, you knew it was something he really felt deep down inside was the right thing to do. Next thing you know, it's business as usual. I think he might've told Bails that he was going to take the reins and he wanted us to go out and win, and it kind of went from there.

I know that was around August, mid-August. Because we always had a trip down to where I live now in Anaheim and we'd go to Disneyland. I remember thinking that he was going to come back after wanting to retire, and I think when I got back he shifted back into that he was going to give it up.

Tyler Graham: You thought it could be a possibility, but I didn't know. You think he might, you think he might not. At the same time, you know he's had a good run, he's obviously going to go down as one of the best coaches in the history of NCAA baseball and one of the best baseball coaches there is. So deep down, you don't ever want to see a guy like that go because he's made such a big impact on not only my life and all the guys I played with … you never want to see a guy go that can make that big of an impact on not only an individual player, but on a team, an entire city. You just don't ever want to believe it.

Brandon Eisert: I didn't really have any thoughts that he would retire. I was hoping to have him as a coach throughout my college career, I never really thought anything of the possibility. There were never really any signs of it happening or anything.

Nick Madrigal: I knew he was thinking about it. We were close and he made some comments throughout the last couple of years, but honestly I could never have pictured him not coaching just because it seemed like that was his life.

Jack Anderson: I think my parents knew before I did, honestly, because they were hanging around (Pat Casey's wife) Susan and stuff. I never got that inclination; I was never looking for that at all. But I knew, just from what my parents had said and how relieved (Casey's) family was, that tipped them off like "whoa, is Case thinking about retiring?"

It kind of blindsided me, but it made sense once I looked at it. I was like "hey, if he wants to leave with me, that's all good! We can ride out into the sunset together." It was something I didn't really see coming at first, but once it did happen and the shock got over, I could see where it was time for him to take some time off.

Bryce Fehmel: He had spoken to some of us before and let us know what was on his mind and what he might do. It wasn't a big surprise to me, and Case deserves it. He's one of the greatest of all time, so to see him finish his career out on top was something he deserves and is definitely special.

FINISH

Cadyn Grenier: After the parades, I had about 24 hours to pack my house up as much as I could and get on a plane to Baltimore to sign and all that. So the night before I left, I went over to Case's house and Yeskie's house just to say goodbye and have a chat with them for a minute. When I talked to Case, he didn't know. He realized he had to step back and go "can I still do it 100%? And if I can't, I'm not going to." When I walked out of that house, I realized that there couldn't be a better time. The guy had coached for (31) years, he's one of the most successful coaches in the history of college baseball, why not go out on top? He's got grandkids now, stuff like that. So when I walked out of that house, I was kind of thinking "man, this would be a great time." I just had a feeling that it was going to happen, so when a few weeks later it came out, I was like "dude, I don't blame him."

Ron Northcutt: College athletics is getting harder on the coaches' side. You've got academics and kids who want to be paid, you've got to feed them and this, that and the other. It's just hard, and I could see it kind of draw on him, it took the air out of him at times. He'd get frustrated and I'd say "Pat, don't worry about it, we'll take care of it." But you know, like anything else, if a kid did something he wasn't supposed to do or had an issue in the weight room, he's the guy that heard about it. I'm happy for him, I'm honored to have him as my friend.

Years ago when we were in high school (Northcutt and Pat Casey both attended Newberg High School), he didn't say anything. I remember one time we went to a party — Pat and I both played football, basketball and baseball — and some of our ex-schoolmates came up and went "what are you guys doing here?" I was just like "we like to drink beer," and at one point a guy says to me "Pat's here?!" And I said "yeah, get to know him." The roles changed. He was somewhat introverted and I was outgoing in high school, and later when we started coaching together it flip-flopped. He had to do all the speaking engagements, he took care of what was needed to defend his team and defend his players and all that stuff, and I sat back and said "you know what, I don't want any praise. I'm just going to do what I'm supposed to do, and I don't care about any honors or any praise." And that's how we worked together so well. For the years we coached together, my wife said it was a good cop, bad cop. I was the good cop, Case would get on somebody's act and I'd come over and pat him on the ass and say "OK, let's go," and it worked great.

Joe Casey, outfielder: I couldn't tell (if he was tired) as much during the season because I was around him all the time, but afterward I'd see highlights and pictures or people would tell me "I could see that your dad looked really worn down and stressed during the World Series." I think other coaches who do it for so long, I'm not saying they're not competitive, but they can do it for a long time because the stress doesn't get to them. My dad is the most competitive guy I've ever met, the most competitive guy ever. He says he takes a Tuesday game against Portland as seriously as he takes a World Series game. He just wants to win so bad and he wants us to play to the best of our abilities and he loves the players so much, I think that took a lot out of him, not in a bad way, and I think that's why he was such a good coach because he treated it that way. But I just think sometimes you need a break.

He talked to me about it, but I wasn't sure until about two days before it happened. A couple years before, the Texas job was offered to him, and he obviously didn't take it. And I didn't know if he would have that many years after that, and he had been talking about it for a few years, but he finally pulled the trigger. Some people think we won it so it was a good one to end on, but I think it was more his feeling. It obviously helps that we won and had a great year to end on. That summer I was playing summer ball and when I came back, that's when I think he really started considering it. He talked to me, talked to my family, but he wasn't completely sure. We went up and hit a few times and talked one-on-one about it, talked about the positives behind it and what he thought it would help. I told him that I wanted to play for him.

Obviously, I don't think he did it because of me, I think he was tired and you could tell how much stress it put on him during the World Series. I do think I was part of the reason because he enjoys being able to coach me now one-on-one. I don't know if that was part of his decision, but now that he is retired I think he's realized that's good to do and it's great for me too because I get a different perspective of him. I'm older now, more mature and he treats me like I'm older. I think he enjoys being able to coach me, but not be my coach. It's fun for him to go throw me batting practice, but not have to be on the field and experience that.

Before Pat Casey could address the team, news of his retirement leaked on social media. He gave a heartfelt goodbye and headed over to Valley Football Center for a press conference. Flanked by Barnes and Oregon State President Ed Ray, an emotional Casey announced his decision to step away. "I have no oceans to sail, no mountains to climb. I have no hobbies. I don't know what the hell I'm going to do," Casey said during his opening statement. "But I am ever grateful. I am a blessed man." Casey, a five-time Pac-10/12 coach of the year, walked away with a career coaching record of 1,071–572–7 (900–458–6 in 24 seasons at OSU) with six College World Series appearances and three national titles.

Dylan Pearce, pitcher: That was hard. I think it was even harder because we were convinced that he wasn't going to (retire). There were a lot of people that had interviewed him and there was nothing that told us he was going to retire. We had no feel that he was going to retire at all. It actually kind of sucked because they were like "hey, we've got a quick team meeting and then we're going to practice." We show up for the team meeting, we were there like a half-hour early or something just eating lunch. All of our phones go off, we check our phones and it was like "ESPN breaking news: College World Series champion coach Pat Casey retires from Oregon State baseball," and we were like "what?" We were freaking out and he walked in just a couple minutes after that and was like "guys, I guess the cat's out of the bag. I'm so sorry, this meeting was for me to tell you guys that I was retiring. I have no idea who opened their mouth or who published that, but I'm sorry you had to find out before I was able to come and tell you guys." That was hard, that was hard to hear.

Tyler Malone: I had no clue, I had absolutely no idea. I found out on Twitter and then we got a text that said we had a team meeting. I was getting lunch or something and was looking on Twitter. I forget which came first, if I saw we were having a team meeting or if I saw it on Twitter. But yeah, I found out 40 minutes before our team meeting. I'm pretty sure I was picking up a sandwich at Jersey Mike's.

It's kind of a weird comparison, but it's the most similar thing I can think of. I know Case didn't pass away, but it was almost like when I found out Kobe Bryant passed away and you get this weird feeling like "what the heck is going on, did it really happen?" That type of thing, and that's how we felt when Case talked to us. It was just weird because you could tell he was sad, and it was super short, it was like five minutes, and it was basically like he had to walk out to compose himself. We could see that he was sad and was fighting back tears, and then he leaves and we're all sitting in there like "dang, this is tough. This has been our guy, and he's the one who's been motivating us and pushing us to be better players and human beings." It was definitely a "what's next?" type of thing.

Ryan Gorton: It was pretty wild because we didn't know anything. I mean everybody had heard rumors that he was going to retire before I got to Oregon State, all the way back in 2008 we were hearing that. So everybody was just like "yeah, what's Case going to do without baseball? Yeah, right." And then when it came time to practice next year, I think it was that first practice in the fall where we went over before practice and he had that press conference to announce his retirement. I don't know, it was a sad time, honestly.

Everyone loved Case and they wanted him to keep coaching, and it was just like "why?" And I understand his side of things and totally respect that, but I think a lot of us just didn't want it to end. I mean he's awesome, he's a great coach and for me, coaching under him, every time he brought the team up or anytime we had a team meeting, I was not going to miss that. Because I learned just as much when I was coaching under him as I did as a player. I didn't want that to end, but I suppose all good things come to an end at some point.

Bill Rowe: I'm still a little bit confused about the whole situation. I think there's been a lot of respect for Case and his privacy and the whole team understanding that he's given enough to the program to be able to do whatever he feels comfortable with at this point.

I do think it was tough on a lot of the players not knowing and hearing about it right before it happened. We just tried to respect his privacy and everyone dealt with it in their own way, but I know it was really hard on everyone knowing we weren't going to get to be around Case all year.

Nate Yeskie: There's a finality to everything. At some point, we're all going to be gone, so you kind of keep a spot reserved in the back of your mind for when those things do eventually happen. And you knew that Case wasn't going to coach forever, at some point it was going to go. When you heard that it was happening and things like that, it's different. It forces you to look at things differently than you may have otherwise, but I don't think it changes the perspective of what you have to do because my job was still the same: try to find good players, try to help them get better on the field, try to help them get better off the field, try to help them get a degree and make good decisions that are going to impact the rest of their lives and the people that are around them.

It's just how I've always maintained my perspective; I don't really get caught up in the moments of some of those things. It might just be a side effect of being a pitching coach because it's not like softball where you send your pitcher out there and they pitch every inning of every game. You're constantly having to make changes, so maybe I'm just used to it more than some others and I'm not thrown off when the time happens.

Adley Rutschman: Obviously I love him as a coach and as a person, but I remember hearing that and it was sad to think that he was no longer going to be the coach, but the whole Oregon State staff is full of good people. I've always been impressed with how the staff handles themselves, so I was confident in the people that we had coming back and that we were going to have a good year and continue to have the same culture and the same traditions.

Kyle Nobach: I mean I wouldn't say I knew it was coming just because deep down inside I know who Case is as a person and how much drive he has to want to be great and be a part of something that's great, but I get it, I absolutely get it. It's not easy to do what he did, and what I mean by doing what he did is to be a leader. He's a leader, and leadership is a hard thing to do. With the burden of leadership, you've got a lot of things on your shoulders. I think when we won that national championship, he knew it was special ... and if anything, it made it special for all of us because we put it all on the line for coach. Without question, I know every single guy on that team, when we stepped on the field, we were playing for coach Casey. Every guy had that attitude and he loved all of us, and that's why we were great to begin with. Everything starts with a leader. I think it just got to a point where he was probably a little tired and wanted to step away from the game and pursue some different things in life, and can you blame the guy? Competition is draining, it's tough. The chances of winning a national championship are very (low), the chances of winning three? That's impressive, man. You know what you're doing then.

Nick Madrigal: For him to go out the way he did was only right. He's a winner and he's a great person to look up to. I know myself and a lot of guys in that locker room looked up to him and I'm very thankful for him to be in my life. We still talk every couple weeks and he still reaches out to a lot of those guys on the team. He was a special person not only on the baseball side of it, but off the field as well. He was someone you don't come across every day ... and he's one of the greatest leaders I've ever been around and played for.

Tyler Graham: I look at Case as like a second father. He's been absolutely amazing to me and has given me every opportunity to get to impact these kids, I don't think any of us will ever get to impact kids like he did. Playing for him, you don't really know what it's all about until you're done. And when you're a little bit older, you look back and see what he's trying to do, and it's absolutely genius the way he goes about it, how he challenges your mentality and never lets a kid think that he's reached his full potential. There's always more in everyone, and he stressed that on a daily basis to not only all of us when we played for him, but all the kids that I've been around as a staff member. He holds the bar very high as the leader, and everyone buys into that. It's one of the most special things that I've ever been a part of and it will always be a part of me.

Josh Therrien, trainer: There are times where coaches and individuals within college sports are promoting themselves and talk about themselves a lot. Coach Casey, he was not just talk. ... He was always first to say that it was about the players, it was about the guys that put the jersey on and wear Beavers across their chest. He was in no way motivated by propping himself up. He was the driving force behind the program with the players out in front, getting the credit and getting their due on the hard work they'd put in.

Jake Rodriguez, assistant coordinator of baseball camps: His message never changed from when I was a player until his last game in 2018, where he talked about the importance of playing for one another, playing for the brothers that we have beside us, playing for the guys that wore that uniform before us and the guys that are going to wear it after you. That's always been his message. He's always put us as student-athletes first, and I think that's why everybody loves him so much and why he just wants the best for us.

When you have moments like that where you see it all come together and you're the last team standing in Omaha, you know why he's so hard on guys on a Tuesday after a three-game sweep and he's just as intense there as he is in the third game of the championship series in Omaha. He never loses that edge, and he expects the most of you every day whether you're a manager, a player, an athletic trainer or a coach. He demands you to be at your best every single day, and I think that's why he had so much success over his time as a player and a coach, and why Oregon State's where it is now as a baseball program.

Pat Bailey: Case and I didn't do a lot off the field, him and I together, but I can tell you right now that I love that guy. I have so much respect for him, we both have a very similar philosophy in what life is all about, and Case is a big family guy, too. I really enjoyed coaching with him, I really respect just how great of a motivator he was.

Jack Anderson: It's funny, I always laugh at his presser when he was like "I don't know what I'm going to do." Just so honest, he was like "I don't fish, I don't golf, I don't really do anything but coach." So I always text Joe and ask "what's Pat doing today, man? How's he doing? Is he finding someone to coach or mentor?" Luckily he's got two little grandkids to play around with and keep him busy.

Joe Casey: It was really sad for a while, but I think it's helped him. He's put some weight back on, he has much less stress and he's got grandkids now. I think he's enjoying the fact that he gets to watch me play. He didn't go to any home games (in 2019), he just watched me on TV, but he got to go to all the away games where people didn't bug him as much. And it's good for him because he's done it for such a long time.

People don't understand sometimes how he's feeling, he just needs a break. I think it was a good time for him to want to go, for many reasons. I really think it's helped him. I think he does really enjoy being able to watch me play. I think it would be stressful for him to watch me play while coaching. He told me, too, he said something like "I think I should've played you a little more the year we won it." Some coaches play their kids more than other people, he's the opposite. He said maybe he played me less than he should've and things like that.

He's got other stuff he's doing now, retired stuff. So he's doing really good and the retirement thing was hard on a lot of people, but I think it's been good for him.

Pat Casey: You miss everything you'd think you'd miss. You miss the players; you miss the competition and you miss the uniform. And then I think you don't miss the things you don't think you'd miss. You don't miss the requirements to recruit and run camps and fundraise and build stadiums. I was a head coach for 31 years and I thought that if I couldn't do it at the energy level and the pace that I wanted to do it and they expected me to do it, then I wasn't going to do it. Because they'd look right at me and they'd do "that ain't Case." That's all there is to it.

(Being a spectator in 2019) was just odd. You wanted to talk to guys, you wanted to be in the dugout. You're being a parent; you're being a coach. It's odd, it was very difficult. I watched every pitch. If I wasn't at the game, I had everything streamed so I watched every pitch. I was very proud of the club and how they handled themselves, but it wasn't as easy as I thought it would be, and I didn't think it would be easy. It was difficult and that's the way it should be. If somebody does something for 31 years and they don't miss it, they should've never done it. Without question I missed it, without question I missed things that are directly related to coaching the game of baseball. I did not miss facets of the administrative stuff, of NCAA regulations, time restraints and everything else. Those things are things, whether they're good for the game or not, is not the point. The point is I think if a coach could just coach in practice and in games, he would be a lot better suited to continue to do that. But there are a lot of things in being an NCAA Division I coach that you have to deal with and you should deal with, and I did deal with. There are times where you just say "at this point in time, that's not really something I'm interested in dealing with anymore." I think if you could drive somebody up in their uniform, drop them off at practice and games, you could do that for a long, long time, but that's not how it works.

I was very blessed to be able to coach, I'm very thankful for the players that made this program what it is. I'm very thankful for the coaches that I got to coach with. Strength coaches, trainers, doctors, academic people, you name it. I felt like we always had good people around us, and you need that. The more good people you get around you, the better you are. We feel like from about 2005 through 2018, I would tell you that it would be hard to find a program that had as much success as we did. We won three national championships during that time and had a lot of draft picks, a lot of wins, a lot of kids that went on and had a lot of success, a lot of academic success. There were just a lot of great things, and I think they'll continue to do that.

Much like the retirement rumors that persisted for years, it didn't take long for speculation of a potential Pat Casey return to emerge. Casey was openly conflicted during the press conference, stating that he would try to get back into coaching if he later felt walking away was a mistake.

Adding fuel to the rumor fire was Bailey's appointment to interim coach and Barnes' declaration that a national search for Casey's replacement would not begin until the conclusion of the 2019 season (Barnes said it was too late in the year for a search to pay off). A week or so after the press conference, details of Casey's new contract surfaced. A clause was included that allowed Casey to be reassigned as head baseball coach by June 1, 2019, or earlier. Naturally, many assumed that Casey's retirement was actually a one-year sabbatical and the legendary coach would be back in the dugout for the 2020 season.

Despite Casey's departure, little appeared to change as Oregon State went through its fall practice schedule. Bailey, previously a successful head coach at George Fox University, took over for Casey with Yeskie remaining in his role as pitching coach. Jenkins was elevated from volunteer assistant to paid (Division I college baseball only allows three paid coaches and one unpaid assistant), while the vacant volunteer spot was filled by Ryan Gipson, a player on OSU's 2006 national championship team who was then the head coach at Linn-Benton Community College.

Expectations remained sky-high in Corvallis even with the loss of three first-round picks, a two-time Pac-12 pitcher of the year and the winningest head coach in program history. The Beavers were picked to finish third in the preseason Pac-12 coaches poll and opened the season ranked eighth in D1Baseball's top 25. Yeskie repeatedly told the team that they were about to get in a fight after school that their big brother had picked. "Some of the guys understood what that meant, others had a hard time grasping it," Yeskie said. Oregon State got off to a blistering 13-1-1 start and sat at 31-10-1 (17-4 Pac-12) following a home sweep of Washington State. Rutschman was the lone offensive star but a deep bullpen and lights-out starting rotation of Brandon Eisert, Bryce Fehmel and reclamation project Grant Gambrell kept the Beavers in nearly every game. The formula was working, and OSU appeared to be on track for another College World Series berth.

Injuries are a fact of life in sports, and the Beavers suffered their fair share in 2017 and 2018. The 2019 season was a whole different story. Veteran arm Jordan Britton never threw a pitch and was forced to redshirt due to an elbow issue. CWS hero Kevin Abel, who entered the season as the team's ace after earning national freshman of the year honors from Baseball America and D1Baseball, made three starts before he was shut down. Abel underwent Tommy John surgery, sparking speculation that he was overused in Omaha. Abel has defended the coaching staff, telling OregonLive "Case took a lot of heat for that and it was very wrong to do that to him. I know what my body is capable of and he and Yeskie have my best interest at heart. I felt I was doing exactly what I had prepared to do." Abel made a full recovery and returned to the mound in 2021 as a redshirt junior.

Oregon State's injury issues didn't end there. Hard-throwing reliever Mitchell Verburg, who clinched the Arizona State series by striking out 2020 No. 1 overall pick Spencer Torkelson, suffered an elbow injury against Washington State and underwent season-ending surgery. Beau Philip, Cadyn Grenier's replacement at shortstop, missed 13 games in the middle of the year with a hamstring injury. Gambrell took two weeks off in May with a tender arm while Eisert, who transformed himself into one of the Pac-12's top starters, didn't throw again after a stellar May 3 outing against Oklahoma State due to an elbow issue.

As the injuries mounted, the losses did, too. Oregon State went just 5-8 overall to close the regular season but was still awarded a home regional and the No. 16 national seed. Cincinnati upset the Beavers to open the regional and the reigning national champions were knocked out of the tournament the following day by Creighton. Michigan, the regional's No. 3 seed, went on to make the CWS finals, falling to Vanderbilt. OSU finished 36-20-1 overall and 21-8 in Pac-12 play.

With the season ending early, many Beavers turned their attention to the MLB Draft. Rutschman, considered the likely No. 1 pick for months, was taken first overall by the Baltimore Orioles after setting numerous school records. The unanimous 2019 national player of the year, Rutschman became the first Oregon State player to win the Golden Spikes Award, Dick Howser Trophy and Buster Posey Award. One round later, Philip was selected 60th overall by the Atlanta Braves. Five other Beavers heard their names called during the draft: Gambrell (third round, Kansas City Royals), Eisert (18th round, Toronto Blue Jays), Fehmel (21st round, San Francisco Giants), Malone (27th round, San Diego Padres) and Dylan Pearce (31st round, St. Louis Cardinals). The seven drafted players were the most for OSU since 2014, surpassing the program's 2017 (five) and 2018 (six) totals.

While the three-day draft was unfolding, Barnes released a bombshell letter to the public: Pat Casey would not be returning to the dugout. In the letter, Barnes wrote "when Pat announced that he would be stepping down as head coach last September, I wanted to give him time to think about his decision and leave open a path where he could return as head coach. Over those nine months, I had numerous conversations with Pat to gauge his interest in returning to the leadership role. My hope was that he would return as head coach after taking a break to refresh. Unfortunately, we know now that will not be the case. Moving forward, we will conduct a national search and consider the very best candidates in the nation. We already have tremendous interest from individuals who aspire to lead this storied program, including from interim head coach Pat Bailey."

Nine days later, Mitch Canham was chosen to lead the program moving forward. Canham, the starting catcher on the Beavers' 2005-07 CWS teams, had been a manager in the Seattle Mariners' organization since 2016. During his introductory press conference, Canham, then 34 years old, said "this is the only job I've ever dreamt of." Bailey and Yeskie also interviewed for the position, but Canham's vision for the program won out. Canham planned to retain Bailey and Yeskie with Gipson staying on as the volunteer assistant. Yeskie changed his mind when he received a lucrative offer from Arizona, leaving in July to become the Wildcats' associate head coach and pitching coach. To replace Yeskie, Canham hired Grand Canyon University pitching coach Rich Dorman, a North Medford High School graduate who worked with Canham in the Mariners' organization. Jenkins, the odd man out in the coaching shakeup, landed at Cal State Fullerton.

With a young team and a new head coach, the Beavers were unranked in the 2020 D1Baseball preseason top 25. The team got off to a 5-9 start while playing a brutal non-conference schedule that included a trip to Mississippi State.

Canham was then thrown the ultimate curveball as the COVID-19 pandemic wiped out the rest of the season, ending the first-year coach's maiden voyage after just 14 games. Another consequence of the pandemic was the cancellation of all summer baseball camps, the primary source of income for volunteer college coaches. That left Gipson, a 35-year-old with two young children, in a tough spot. Canham made the uncomfortable call to promote Gipson to a paid assistant position and let the 64-year-old Bailey go. To fill the vacant volunteer assistant spot, Canham turned to another former Oregon State teammate: Darwin Barney. Barney also starred for the Beavers from 2005-07 and played eight seasons in Major League Baseball, winning the 2012 National League Gold Glove Award at second base. The youthful staff is light on experience, but so was Pat Casey back in the mid-90s.

Casey has yet to return to coaching, but that could change at a moment's notice. The program he built appears to be in capable hands, and Casey's legacy at Oregon State is unassailable. Upgrades have continued at Goss Stadium, including a large deck down the right-field line appropriately named Casey Corner. Goss' outfield walls are covered with reminders of Casey's five conference titles, six College World Series appearances and three national titles. There is plenty of space for more tributes, but the memory of Casey's 24 seasons in charge will live on forever in the state of Oregon and beyond. It's only fitting that the greatest coach in OSU athletics history went out on top with a dogpile under the lights at TD Ameritrade Park.

FINISH

ACKNOWLEDGMENTS

To be honest, I used to gloss over or outright skip the acknowledgments section after finishing a book. Unsurprisingly, taking on this project made me rethink my indifference towards acknowledgments. Writing a book is harder than I expected (I know, shocker), and the amount of help and cooperation I received along the way made the arduous task possible. For that, I'm forever grateful.

To Pat Casey, all I can say is, "Thank You." Thank you for reliving the past with me over multiple hours. And thank you for dealing with my seemingly never-ending list of follow-up questions. In the three seasons I covered your team, you always treated me with respect and allowed the media in during a time when access has largely been restricted. This book couldn't have happened without your participation, and I'm beyond grateful for the memories you shared. It's not hard to see why you've had so much success in life.

I have similar admiration for other coaches and staff members I got to know over the years. At the ballpark, Nate Yeskie loved to throw a playful jab or two my way, but he was always willing to share his immense baseball wisdom. Pat Bailey was a true professional, and a person who genuinely practiced what he preached. Andy Jenkins, the youngest of the full-time staff, knew what it meant to be a Beaver and play for Pat Casey on the biggest stage. And a special thank you to Tyler Graham, another Oregon State legend who was an open book on many topics.

But Pat Casey's program was always about the players, and this book is no exception. The story would've been one-sided without the contributions of the players, many of whom took time away from their busy lives in professional baseball to talk about their college days. The players were consistently a joy to be around in my time covering the team from 2016 to 2019. Their bond on and off the field was readily apparent. Getting to know several of the guys over multiple seasons was a special experience.

I'd be remiss not to acknowledge my editors, coworkers and colleagues over the years who helped me become a better reporter and thinker. There are too many to name, but thanks to each of you. I must thank Corvallis Gazette-Times sports editor

Steve Gress in particular for giving me the keys to the Oregon State baseball beat prior to the 2016 season. I arrived at the same time as the vaunted 2015 signing class and watched Cadyn Grenier, Trevor Larnach, Nick Madrigal and others go through the college experience. It was a remarkable group to work with and the highlight of my young career to date.

One name not featured in the book who deserves special recognition is Hank Hager, a man who seemingly wears many hats at Oregon State. Hager, better known as OmaHank, is the baseball sports information director. He went out of his way on numerous occasions to assist me, and never complained about it. Thanks for making life easy, OmaHank.

Lastly and most importantly, thank you to my wife, Amanda, for supporting me through this journey. My better half had to read the early rough draft of chapters and worked hard at her job during a global pandemic while I toiled away on this book for months. Your understanding meant the world to me. Love you, babe.

FINISH

Made in the USA
Middletown, DE
08 February 2022